Reflections on Resemblance, Ritual, and Religion

Reflections on Resemblance, Ritual, and Religion

BRIAN K. SMITH

New York   Oxford
OXFORD UNIVERSITY PRESS
1989

Oxford University Press

Oxford New York Toronto
Delhi Bombay Calcutta Madras Karachi
Petaling Jaya Singapore Hong Kong Tokyo
Nairobi Dar es Salaam Cape Town
Melbourne Auckland
and associated companies in
Berlin Ibadan

Published by Oxford University Press, Inc.,
200 Madison Avenue, New York, New York 10016

Library of Congress Cataloging-in-Publication Data

Smith, Brian K., 1953–
Reflections on resemblance, ritual, and religion / Brian K. Smith.
p. cm. Bibliography: p. Includes indexes.
ISBN 0-19-505545-4
1. Hinduism—Rituals. 2. Hinduism—Doctrines. I. Title.
BL1226.12.S65 1989
294.5′38—dc19 88-4009 CIP

Printing (last digit): 9 8 7 6 5 4 3 2 1

Printed in the United States of America
on acid-free paper

To the memory of Dr. V. V. Bhide, who rectified the names: teacher, scholar, pandit, friend, host, Brahmin, father, and man. I miss him terribly.

And for Wendy, who made it all more-ish.

Preface

Scholars of the discipline alternately labeled Comparative Religion or the History of Religions are notoriously, and sometimes dangerously, schizophrenic. I speak here not of the more ordinary academic malaise that splits the individual into two personae—teacher of the uninitiated and hair-splitting author of learned works for other specialists, friends, and fellow conventioneers. The particular bifurcation I am referring to is peculiar to a discipline that requires its adherents to address, simultaneously, two different audiences in their research reports.

On the one hand, in order to be taken seriously at all in a highly territorial academic world, one must engage one or more of the established bureaus of academic knowledge, such as sociology, anthropology, history (and all its branches), area studies, Sinology, Buddhology, Indology, and ancient studies. On the other hand, one is expected as a comparativist to uncover something of comparative consequence to those in the field of religion in all its diversity. It is often a difficult tightrope to walk.

I have attempted to address two audiences in this work, and I hope that by doing so I have not lost both. Straight comparativists (if I might be forgiven the oxymoron) and those simply interested in the problems and methods of an approach to religion which is neither theological nor "scientific" might find much of the Indological detail of the work tough going. Philologically oriented Indologists and other specialists in Things Indian may very well become exasperated with the introductory and concluding chapters, as well as certain portions interspersed throughout the book, in which I attempt to move out of the specifics of Vedism into the larger realm of theoretical and methodological issues pertaining to the study of religion as a whole. I will only say here that the author's intention was to write a book whose parts cohered, and whose data and approach to them were in a relation of mutual resemblance. But then the author's intention these days is far from being the only criterion of either meaning or value.

Although this book is meant primarily as a contribution to Indian studies, it is simultaneously an attempt to exercise one kind of interpretation of culturally and historically specific material from the vantage point of the discipline of Comparative Religion or the History of Religions. This is not simply because issues of comparative interest—the definition of religion, the nature and purpose of ritual, the dynamics of sacrifice and substitution, change and continuity in religious traditions—are directly addressed at various junctures. More critically, I have tried to present the specifics of Vedism and Hinduism in such a way as to exemplify theoretical and methodological issues of general import within the larger study of religion.

I have not always been explicit in my intention to make Vedism and Hinduism say something of interest to those whose professional or intellectual attention is not usually focused on Indian culture and religion; and I have not always spared the reader the particularistic details of often very technical Sanskritic texts. I have, for all that, tried to represent ancient Indian religion in such a way that it might usefully serve as an "e.g." for comparative and theoretical problems within the academic study of religion. In this I follow the programmatic trail blazed by recent thinkers who are attempting to reconstitute a field whose past excesses and errors still cling to it.

Parts of this book have been published before in other forms and in other places. Chapter 1 previously appeared as part of "Exorcising the Transcendent: Strategies for Defining Hinduism and Religion" in *History of Religions*. Portions of Chapter 2 were published as "Vedic Fieldwork" in *Religious Studies Review*. Other sections of Chapters 2 and 8 appeared in "Ideals and Realities in Indian Religions," also in *Religious Studies Review*. Some of Chapters 3 and 4 were incorporated in "Gods and Men in Vedic Ritualism: Toward a Hierarchy of Resemblance" in *History of Religions*, "Sacrifice and Being: Prajāpati's Cosmic Emission and Its Consequences" in *Numen*, and "Ritual, Knowledge, and Being: Initiation and Veda Study in Ancient India," also in *Numen*. Portions of Chapters 6 and 7 comprise "The Unity of Ritual: The Place of the Domestic Sacrifice in Vedic Ritualism" in *Indo-Indian Journal*, and "Sacrifice and Substitution: Ritual Mystification and Mythical Demystification," in *Numen*.

I would like to thank Barnard College and the American Institute of Indian Studies for timely grants that helped considerably in bringing this work to its conclusion. Special thanks are due to Wendy Doniger for preparing the index.

I also take this opportunity to acknowledge gratefully the debt I owe to those who, in one way or another, have taught me: Wendy Doniger, V. V. Bhide, Holland Hendrix, Wayne Proudfoot, Bruce Lincoln, Ron Inden, Frank Reynolds, Arthur Droge, Alan Segal, Marilyn Harran, G. U. Thite, Wade Wheelock, James Fitzgerald, Barbara Stoler Miller, John Stratton Hawley, Ainslie Embree, William Harman, David Carpenter, Frederick Smith, Karen Guberman, Craig, John, Tim, Chris, Madhav, Celia, Ann, Judy and Steve, Gene (wherever you are), Mom and Dad, Angela, Justin, Karen, and all my students. Sine qua non.

New York and Chicago
June 1988

B. K. S.

Contents

Abbreviations

ĀgGS	Āgniveśya Gṛhya Sūtra
AitĀ	Aitareya Āraṇyaka
AitB	Aitareya Brāhmaṇa
AitU	Aitareya Upaniṣad
ĀpDhS	Āpastamba Dharma Sūtra
ĀpGS	Āpastamba Gṛhya Sūtra
ĀpŚS	Āpastamba Śrauta Sūtra
ĀśvGS	Āśvalāyana Gṛhya Sūtra
ĀśvŚS	Āśvalāyana Śrauta Sūtra
AV	Atharva Veda Saṃhitā
BĀU	Bṛhadāraṇyaka Upaniṣad
BDhS	Baudhāyana Dharma Sūtra
BGS	Baudhāyana Gṛhya Sūtra
BGParis	Baudhāyana Gṛhya Paribhāṣā Sūtra
BhGS	Bhāradvāja Gṛhya Sūtra
BhŚS	Bhāradvāja Śrauta Sūtra
BPS	Baudhāyana Pitṛmedha Sūtra
BŚS	Baudhāyana Śrauta Sūtra
ChU	Chandogya Upaniṣad
GautDhS	Gautama Dharma Sūtra
GB	Gopatha Brāhmaṇa
GGS	Gobhila Gṛhya Sūtra
HGS	Hiraṇyakeśin Gṛhya Sūtra
HŚS	Hiraṇyakeśin Śrauta Sūtra

JB	Jaiminīya Brāhmaṇa
JGS	Jaiminīya Gṛhya Sūtra
JŚS	Jaiminīya Śrauta Sūtra
JUB	Jaiminīya Upaniṣad Brāhmaṇa
KB	Kauṣītaki Brāhmaṇa
KGS	Kāṭhaka Gṛhya Sūtra
KS	Kāṭhaka Saṃhitā
KhGS	Khādira Gṛhya Sūtra
KSS	Kātyāyana Śrauta Sūtra
LŚS	Lāṭyāyana Śrauta Sūtra
Manu	Manu Smṛti
Mbh	Mahābhārata
MGS	Mānava Gṛhya Sūtra
MS	Maitrāyaṇī Saṃhitā
MSS	Mānava Śrauta Sūtra
PB	Pañcaviṃśa Brāhmaṇa
PGS	Pāraskāra Gṛhya Sūtra
PMS	Pūrva Mīmāṃsā Sūtra of Jaimini
ṚV	Ṛg Veda Saṃhitā
ṢaḍB	Ṣaḍviṃśa Brāhmaṇa
ŚānĀ	Śānkhāyana Āraṇyaka
ŚB	Śatapatha Brāhmaṇa
ŚGS	Śānkhāyana Gṛhya Sūtra
ŚŚS	Śānkhāyana Śrauta Sūtra
TĀ	Taittirīya Āraṇyaka
TB	Taittirīya Brāhmaṇa
TS	Taittirīya Saṃhitā
TU	Taittirīya Upaniṣad
VaikhGS	Vaikhānasa Gṛhya Sūtra
VaikhSS	Vaikhānasa Śrauta Sūtra
VāsDhS	Vāsiṣṭha Dharma Sūtra
VGS	Vārāha Gṛhya Sūtra
VŚS	Vārāha Śrauta Sūtra
Yāj	Yājñavalkya Smṛti

Reflections on Resemblance, Ritual, and Religion

What was the prototype, what was the counterpart, and what was the connection between them?

Ṛig Veda 10.130.3

What is called a sincere work is one that is endowed with enough strength to give reality to an illusion.

MAX JACOB, *Art poétique*

1

Making Connections: Hinduism and Vedism

Working Definitions

There is considerable confusion about the nature of and need for definitions in humanistic studies in general and in religious studies particularly. Many seem to think that to offer a definition of an object is an enormous—and audacious—act. To propose a definition is at best something to be deferred to the indefinite future; more often it is delegated to others who have more accumulated intellectual resources than we.[1] Defining is too often imagined as finalizing—a statement of ultimate truth about the object of study, a sacred moment in which the whole of the knowledge of the subject has coalesced and is encapsulated.

Others regard those who presume to offer definitions not with awe but with suspicion. For these leery scholars of the humanities, definition is what lab-coated analysts in the "hard" sciences do, and the objects of humanistic studies are held to be too precious to be subjected to the same fate that natural objects have suffered. Rather, they are jealously guarded from the tyranny of the defining will; the endangered objects

1. Even such an authoritative personage as Max Weber hesitated before the definitional challenge, deferring it to the end of the study (and never delivering it): "To define 'religion,' to say what it *is,* is not possible at the start of a presentation such as this. Definition can be attempted, if at all, only at the conclusion of the study." *The Sociology of Religion,* trans. by Ephraim Fischoff (Boston: Beacon Press, 1953), p. 1.

are regarded as exempt from the shackles of defining strictures.[2] Here, too, defining is imagined as finalizing—an imprisonment of a once free object, a cruel pinning of an elusive butterfly.

Let us rethink the concept of definition in the humanities. To define need not be imagined as to finalize. To define is not to finish, but to start. To define is not to confine but to create something to refine—and eventually redefine. To define, finally, is not to destroy but to construct for the purpose of useful reflection.

It is somewhat delusory to imagine that we do not carry around all sorts of definitions in our heads. In fact, we have definitions, hazy and inarticulate as they might be, for every object about which we know something. It is not defining that is so problematic for so many but, rather, *explicitly* defining.[3] On the other hand, those who do make the effort to define objects of study in the humanities too often appear to regard it as an end in itself: they work *at* definition instead of working *with* definitions.

It seems to me that it is less than completely forthright not to define the object in question; it is less than realistic to regard such definitions as final explanations or canonical codifications; and it is less than maxi-

2. In the field of the study of religion, this protective attitude is sometimes manifested through the argument that religion is irreducible and sui generis, i.e., undefinable. See, e.g., Rudolph Otto, *The Idea of the Holy,* trans. by John W. Harvey (New York: Oxford University Press, 1957). esp. p. 4. For the philosophical poverty of such stances toward definition in the study of religion, see Hans Penner and Edward Yonan, "Is a Science of Religion Possible?" *Journal of Religion* 52 (1972): 107–33; Wayne Proudfoot, "Religion and Reduction," *Union Seminary Quarterly Review* 37 (Fall–Winter 1981–82): 13–25; and esp. Proudfoot's extended critique in his *Religious Experience* (Berkeley and Los Angeles: University of California Press, 1986).

3. See, e.g., Clifford Geertz, *Islam Observed: Religious Development in Morocco and Indonesia* (Chicago: University of Chicago Press, 1971). Although Geertz correctly notes that "the comparative study of religion has always been plagued by this peculiar embarrassment: the elusiveness of its subject matter," he attributes this confusion not to a poorly defined category but, rather, to the lack of sufficient empiricism: "The problem is not one of constructing definitions of religion. We have had quite enough of those; their very number is a symptom of our malaise. It is a matter of discovering just what sorts of beliefs and practices support what sorts of faith under what sorts of conditions. Our problem, and it grows worse by the day, is not to define religion but to find it" (p. 1). Categories such as religion, however, are a sine qua non and initially make possible "religious" facts, not vice versa. Furthermore, Geertz is disingenuous when he claims here and elsewhere (see pp. 96–97) that he will eschew (explicit) definitions of religion when, in fact, he proceeds to offer one. My thanks to Holland Hendrix for calling Geertz's statements to my attention.

mally productive to envision definitions as the exclusive aim of one's scholarship. Let us, then, define our concept of definition as a tentative classification of a phenomenon which allows us to begin an analysis of the phenomenon so defined. Let us regard the tentative classification as a "working definition"—one which permits us to begin work on our conception of that which is thus defined, and one which therefore also assumes the continual reworking of the working definition.

To that end, I propose to begin my study of an ancient Indian religion, Vedism, with a working definition of the whole of which it is usually regarded as a part: Hinduism. As we will see, defining Hinduism (at least in the way I will suggest) does not place Vedism as one tradition within this religion; it shifts the defining center from Hinduism to Vedism itself. And because, among other reasons, historical and contemporary Hinduism defines itself in relation to its archaic (and, in many respects, superseded) ancestor, our subsequent investigation of Vedic religion cannot be simply an antiquarian exercise. The bulk of the present work, which delves into the details of Vedic religion and ritualism, is thus more than a study of an ancient religion per se: it is equally an attempt to squeeze from the Veda the historically constitutive principles of Hinduism. First, however, we must establish that Hinduism, as we intend to define it, is best conceived as "Vedic."

Creating Hinduism

Like most (and perhaps all) particular religions, "Hinduism" as a unitary entity did not exist before it was created by outsiders. Hinduism is, one might say, an illusion. It is an imaginary category emerging from the minds of observers who felt an epistemological (and often political) need to unify a diversity. " 'Hinduism,' " notes Wilfred Cantwell Smith, "is a concept certainly [Hindus] did not have."[4]

Just who invented "Hinduism" first is a matter of scholarly debate.

4. Smith, *The Meaning and End of Religion: A Revolutionary Approach to the Great Traditions* (San Francisco: Harper and Row, 1962), p. 63. Whether Hindus had a concept and word homologous to our "religion" is also dubious according to Smith. See also Louis Renou, *Hinduism* (New York: George Braziller, 1961), p. 18: "In fact, there is no Hindu term corresponding to what we call 'religion.' " It is my view that this point deserves further investigation. Smith's arguments against *dharma* as such a correlate are not entirely persuasive, and other terms may also be possible true analogies to *religion* in Hinduism (e.g., *mārga.*).

Almost everyone agrees that it was not the Hindus.[5] Derived from the name of one of the principal rivers of the South Asian subcontinent (the Indus), the label was used first by the ancient Persians, and somewhat later by Central Asians, for the people and territory of Northwest India. As a term designating a religion, still inclusive of what were later to be differentiated as Hinduism, Buddhism, and Jainism, it may have been first deployed by the Muslim invaders of the early part of the second millennium.[6] As a discrete Indic religion among others, however, "Hinduism" was probably first imagined by the British in the early part of the nineteenth century to describe (and create and control) an enormously complex configuration of people and their traditions found in the South Asian subcontinent.[7] "Hinduism" made it possible for the British, and for us all (including Hindus), to speak of *a* religion when before there was none or, at best, many.

Although some have expressed their dissatisfaction with the fact that "Hinduism" is a product of the imagination of foreigners, it is nevertheless the case that Hinduism has come to take on a certain reality—for non-Hindus and for Hindus—and it is now beside the point to attempt to deconstruct it. It is more relevant to note what an odd religion it is, at least as it has been explicitly defined by some. Take, for example, J. A. B. van Buitenen's description published in that popular organ of knowledge, the *Encyclopedia Britannica:*

> As a religion, Hinduism is an utterly diverse conglomerate of doctrines, cults, and ways of life. . . . In principle, Hinduism incorporates all forms of belief and worship without necessitating the selection or elimination of any. The Hindu is inclined to revere the divine in every manifestation, whatever it may be, and is doctrinally tolerant, leaving others—including both Hindus and non-Hindus—whatever creed and worship practices suit them best. A Hindu may embrace a non-Hindu religion without ceasing to

5. See, however, J. Laine, "The Notion of 'Scripture' in Modern Indian Thought," *Annals of the Bhandarkar Oriental Research Institute* 64 (1983): 165–79. Laine argues with some persuasiveness that "Perhaps, then, 'Hinduism' *qua* 'religion' was the *creation* of nineteenth century Indians"; that is, the formation of "Hinduism" was a native response inspired by the confrontation with an already self-defined religion, namely the Christianity of the British colonizers and rulers.

6. Smith, *The Meaning and End of Religion,* p. 64.

7. See J. A. B. van Buitenen's article "Hinduism" in *Encyclopedia Britannica,* 11th ed., p. 888, in which the author claims the term was "introduced c. 1830 by English writers." Smith, ibid., p. 61, concurs, finding the earliest mention of Hinduism in the modern sense of the word in an English work published in 1829. See also P. J. Marshall, ed., *The British Discovery of Hinduism in the Eighteenth Century* (Cambridge: Cambridge University Press, 1970).

be a Hindu. . . . Few religious ideas are considered to be finally irreconcilable. The core of religion does not even depend on the existence or nonexistence of God or on whether there is one god or many. Since religious truth is said to transcend all verbal definition, it is not conceived in dogmatic terms.[8]

I have quoted van Buitenen at length in order to present a representative type of definition, put forward by one of this century's most eminent Indologists, which one can only call inchoate. In the best possible light, van Buitenen seems to want to indicate the artificiality and inadequacy of the general category of Hinduism (this, let us remember, in an encyclopedia article entitled "Hinduism"). This religion, the author implies, is exceedingly diverse (what tradition of three thousand years' duration is not?), and to speak naively of a monolithic "Hinduism" is to gloss over its manifold variability and complexity.

Still, van Buitenen also wants to provide the reader with a set of general characteristics of the religion about which he is writing. As part of its syncretistic essence ("an utterly diverse conglomerate of doctrines, cults, and ways of life"), Hinduism is presented as so "tolerant" (a key word in many such definitions) that virtually everything counts as "Hindu."[9] One can, apparently, believe and practice anything and still

8. Van Buitenen, "Hinduism," pp. 888–89.

9. Arvind Sharma investigates the basis of Hindu tolerance in his "Some Misunderstandings of the Hindu Approach to Religious Plurality," *Religion* 8 (Autumn 1978): 133–54, concluding that it is neither Vedāntic monism nor caste pluralism that provides the source of tolerance; it is rather, according to the author, the very essence of Hinduism as a whole: "To try to be crystal-clear—the Hindu tolerance of plurality is not an iridescence arising from the interplay of some of its facets; it is not an aspect but an ingredient of the 'substance' itself." See also Kaisa Puhakka, "The Roots of Religious Tolerance in Hinduism and Buddhism," *Temenos* 12 (1976): 50–61, whose similar thesis is that "Religious tolerance as practised in the Eastern traditions is neither a deliberately cultivated moral virtue nor something forced upon them by socio-political conditions; rather, it is firmly rooted in and hence arises spontaneously from the religious beliefs and practices themselves" (pp. 51–52). It is remarkable that such a stereotype can exist even in the face of enormous historical evidence (compounded almost daily) to the contrary. Among the few who seem to find it problematic to regard Hinduism as by definition tolerant in light of past and continuing events is Nirad C. Chaudhuri, *The Continent of Circe* (Bombay: Jaico Publishing House, 1965), esp. p. 33: "If the familiar words about tolerance and capacity for synthesis of the Hindus were true, one would be hard put to explain why there are such deep suspicions and enmities among the human groups of India, why there are endemic outbursts of murderous ferocity." Hindu tolerance, it would seem, is an idea that had and has ideological and definitional functions—both for Western observers and Hindus themselves—that override concrete realities, a scholarly examination of which remains a desideratum.

be classified a Hindu under this definition, and, remarkably, "a Hindu may embrace a non-Hindu religion without ceasing to be a Hindu."[10] According to another well-known authority,

> Hinduism has been linked to a vast sponge, which absorbs all that enters it without ceasing to be itself. The simile is not quite exact, because Hinduism has shown a remarkable power of assimilating as well as absorbing; the water becomes part of the sponge. Like a sponge it has no very clear outline on its borders and no apparent core at its centre.

And, the author concludes, "An approach to Hinduism provides a first lesson to the 'otherness' of Hindu ideas from those of Europe."[11]

This kind of inchoate definition, and there are many others like it, is far too inclusive to be meaningful, let alone useful.[12] To argue that there is no Hindu "orthodoxy" is also to deny that Hindus can have "heresy," which ignores abundant evidence to the contrary.[13] To define adequately (if tentatively) an object, in the humanities as elsewhere, is not only to say what it *is* but also to indicate what it is *not.*[14]

Among more coherent definitions scholars have offered of Hinduism in the past, one school focuses on religious or philosophical themes that seem to unite the religion—or, indeed, to constitute it as a religion in the scholar's mind. We might therefore label this the thematic type of

10. See J. D. M. Derrett, *Religion, Law and the State in India* (London: Faber and Faber, 1958), p. 49. Derrett cites legal rulings whereby a Hindu might convert to Christianity "without ceasing to be a Hindu in both social and spiritual terms."

11. Percival Spear, *India, Pakistan, and the West* (London: Oxford University Press, 1949), p. 57.

12. Virtually all definitions of Hinduism include some reference to the extraordinary social, doctrinal, historical, and practical "tolerance" of the religion. For another example of the extremes to which one can take this nearly universal notion of Hindu catholicism, witness the position of Govinda Das, who writes that Hinduism "rejects nothing. It is all-comprehensive, all-compliant." A Hindu is one who "does not repudiate that designation, or better still, because more positive, . . . says he is a Hindu, and accepts any of the many beliefs and follows any of the many practices that are anywhere regarded as Hindu." Quoted in Hervey DeWitt Griswold, *Insights into Modern Hinduism* (New York: Henry Holt, 1934), p. 15. "Hinduism," concludes Spear, "rests essentially on public opinion. Not to be a Hindu means simply not being thought to be a Hindu." *India, Pakistan, and the West,* p. 58.

13. See Wendy Doniger O'Flaherty, "The Origins of Heresy in Hindu Mythology," *History of Religions* 10 (May 1971): 271–333.

14. Nor is it adequate for the scholar of Hinduism to throw up his or her hands and declare, with Nehru, that the beast, by definition, defies definition: "Hinduism as a faith is vague, amorphous, many-sided, all things to all men. It is hardly possible to define it, or indeed to say precisely whether it is a religion or not, in the usual sense of the word." Jawaharlal Nehru, *The Discovery of India* (London: Meridian Books, 1960), p. 63.

definition. One principal form of this type of definition of Hinduism identifies the concepts of transmigration (*saṃsāra*), *karma,* and liberation from transmigration and *karma* (*mokṣa, mukti,* etc.) as definitive of the religion.[15] It is not clear, however, how this approach differentiates Hinduism from other Indic religions one usually does not regard as Hindu (Buddhism and Jainism, for example) which also are preoccupied with these themes.[16] It would seem that this kind of formulation is also too inclusive to serve as an adequate working definition of the object under scrutiny.[17]

In addition to the inchoate sort of definition (Hinduism as a vast and unorganized warehouse of possibilities) and the usually more coherent but still overly inclusive thematic definition (Hinduism defined by "key concepts" that other Indic religions share), there is a third possibility in the history of scholarship on Hinduism.[18] A definition of Hinduism

15. See, e.g., L. D. Barnett's presentation of Hinduism identified by three conceptual headings under which characteristically Hindu "ideas" cluster: "works" (*karma*), "wandering" (*saṃsāra*), and "release" (*mokṣa*). *Hinduism* (London: Constable, 1913), pp. 2–3. The best recent versions of the thematic approach to defining Hinduism may be found in R. C. Zaehner, *Hinduism* (New York: Oxford University Press, 1966), in which he explores *brahman, dharma, mokṣa, saṃsāra,* and *karma,* "the key concepts of classical Hinduism"; Jan Gonda, *Change and Continuity in Indian Religion* (The Hague: Mouton, 1965), a sprawling and unfocused work on themes common to all Indian religions; and W. Norman Brown, *Man in the Universe: Some Cultural Continuities in Indian Thought* (Berkeley and Los Angeles: University of California Press, 1970), which is also less concerned with Hinduism per se and more with what is typically and transhistorically Indic religion. For an extraordinarily eccentric version of this thematic approach to defining Hinduism, see Griswold, *Insights into Modern Hinduism,* pp. 17 ff.

16. See Brown, *Man in the Universe,* and David R. Kinsley, *Hinduism: A Cultural Perspective,* ed. by Robert S. Ellwood, Jr. (Englewood Cliffs, N.J.: Prentice-Hall, 1982), p. 53: "In many essential respects Buddhism and Jainism are very much like Hinduism. Both movements presuppose *karma* and *saṃsāra* and define man's ultimate spiritual goal in terms very similar to Hinduism."

17. Another form this type of definition takes is the identification of three "paths" (*mārgas*) or possibilities for the religious life that collectively constitute the Hindu religion: the path of works (*karma*), the path of gnosis (*jñāna*), and the path of faith (*bhakti*). See Charles Eliot, *Hinduism and Buddhism: An Historical Sketch,* 3 vols. (New York: Barnes & Noble, 1954), I: xvi–xvii. On first sight this definition might appear to be more adequate (although overemphasizing syncretistic formulations such as that in the Bhagavad Gītā), but upon reflection it is not clear that here, too, Indian Buddhism, e.g., could not fit within the definition.

18. One should note, as Penner and Yonan point out in "Is a Science of Religion Possible?" that recounting the history of definitions offered for the object does not in itself constitute a definition of the object. At the same time, because it is, in fact, the Western scholars of Hinduism who constituted that object in the first place, one cannot ignore or bypass the semantic possibilities Hinduism has had for them.

that one might call the social and/or canonical identifies either or both of two criteria as constitutive of Hinduism: (1) recognition of the authority of the Brahmin class and (2) recognition of the authority of the Veda. According to this position, those who accept either or both the authority of the Brahmins and the authority of the Veda are Hindus; those who do not accept one or both are not.

The authority of the Brahmin class as a definitional criterion of Hinduism is often linked to the caste system (in which the Brahmins, of course, have made for themselves a privileged position), and Hinduism is regarded as either identical with the institution of caste or essentially defined by it. In some works, Hinduism and the particular social system of India are thoroughly conflated. From this point of view, as R. C. Zaehner puts it, Hinduism is

> as much a social system as a religion. . . . Its social framework has from very early times been the caste system, and this has, until very recently, become increasingly rigid, increasingly complicated, and increasingly identified with Hinduism as such. Indeed until a century or so ago the acceptance of the caste system was considered by the orthodox to be the sole effective criterion of whether one was or was not a Hindu.[19]

A variant of this position has both Hinduism and the caste system pivoting on the place of the Brahmin in Indian religious and social life. Hinduism is not quite equated with caste, but both Hinduism and caste are defined by the authoritative position of the Brahmins. The Brahmins, writes Eliot,

> are an interesting social phenomenon, without exact parallel elsewhere. They are not, like the Catholic or Moslem clergy, a priesthood pledged to support certain doctrines but an intellectual, hereditary aristocracy who claim to direct the thought of India whatever forms it may take. All who admit this claim and accord a nominal recognition to the authority of the Veda are within the spacious fold or menagerie. . . . [Hinduism's] unity

19. Zaehner, *Hinduism,* p. 8. See also Eliot, *Hinduism and Buddhism,* I: xxxvii–xxxiii: Hinduism is "a mode of life as much as a faith. To be a Hindu it is not sufficient to hold the doctrine of the Upanishads or any other scriptures: it is necessary to be a member of a Hindu caste and observe its regulations." For Hinduism as a national culture, identified in large part by the caste system, see Sridhar V. Ketkar's statement: "There is no 'Hindu religion.' Hinduism, which means Hindu society and its traditions, is not a religion, but is akin to tribal or national culture." Quoted in Griswold, *Insights into Modern Hinduism,* p. 14. For more sophisticated arguments that Hinduism is a "way of life" of a particular culture, and thus similar to Hellenism and Judaism, consult Zaehner, p. 1; A. C. Bouquet, *Hinduism* (London: Hutchinson's University Library, 1948), p. 11; and esp. S. Radhakrishnan, *The Hindu View of Life* (New York: Macmillan, 1973).

and vitality are clear and depend chiefly on its association with the Brahman class.[20]

Hinduism, according to the logic of this position, may also be labeled "Brahminism," for it is "the spiritual prerogative of the Brahman caste which is the cornerstone on which the whole Hindu social edifice was built."[21]

Standing alone, however, the authoritative position of the Brahmins within the caste structure cannot adequately function as a criterion for a working definition of Hinduism. First, the definition becomes less one of the Hindu religion and more one of the Indic social system, and from within the discipline of the academic and humanistic study of religion there *is* a difference between religion and the social structure it legitimizes.[22] The caste system is certainly grounded in and legitimized by Hindu religious ideas and practices, but Hinduism clearly entails far more than caste. Furthermore, it is well known in the West (and better known in India) that the caste system harbors different religions within it; there are and have been Buddhist, Jaina, Muslim, Sikh, Parsi, Christian, Jewish, tribal, and secular Anglo-Indian castes in addition to Hindu castes in India.

Second, there have been major movements and entire traditions normally regarded as Hindu that have rejected, at least at the level of cultic belief and practice, both the authority of the Brahmins and the legitimacy of caste hierarchy. Many of the tantric traditions (with their reversals of bourgeois Hinduism) and the *bhakti* movements (emphasizing personalized and unmediated faith in and devotion to a gracious deity) have been characterized doctrinally by a more or less radical denial of the inherent religious prerogative of the Brahmin caste.[23]

20. Eliot, *Hinduism and Buddhism,* I: xvii, 34.

21. Zaehner, *Hinduism,* p. 5. Hinduism, as "Brahminism," is thus also regarded as inextricably linked to a national culture. See Bouquet, *Hinduism,* p. 70: "Hinduism, dependent as it is upon the accepted dominance of the Brahmin caste as a hereditary spiritual aristocracy, is tied to the country of its origin."

22. Were there no difference posited between religion and social structure, the study of religion would be entirely encompassed within the study of society. This is indeed the position of many sociologists and social anthropologists, from Durkheim to the present. It is not mine, and those who argue so from within the academic rubric of "religion" or "religious studies" appear to me to have something of a death wish for the discipline. I hope to deal with the many and complex issues of the relationship between religion and society, in general, and Indian religion and the caste system, specifically, in another work.

23. For a "Hindu" tantric tradition and their attitudes toward caste, see Edward Dimock, *The Place of the Hidden Moon* (Chicago: University of Chicago Press, 1966). For one set of examples of anticaste, anti-Brahmin rhetoric from within an otherwise quite

Recognition of the authority of the Brahmins, then, is not a sufficient criterion in itself to determine what counts as Hindu. It might, however, begin to differentiate Hinduism from other Indic religions in ways that alternative types of definitions do not (Buddhist, Jains, and others might be excluded on the basis of this criterion)[24] and thus avoids the problem of overinclusiveness: too much that would appear to common sense as Hindu, such as many of the *bhakti* traditions, is ruled out. Further, a large question is left hanging: on what is the authority of the Brahmins established and legitimized?

To address this query, scholars call up the second criterion mentioned above. Brahmins are recognized as religious authorities because of their intimate, special relationship to the Vedas, the authoritative (and in this sense canonical) texts of Hinduism.[25] The Brahmins are the tradi-

---

orthodox Hindu devotionalistic text, see Thomas Hopkins, "The Social Teachings of the Bhāgavata Purāṇa," in *Krishna: Myths, Rites, and Attitudes,* ed. by Milton Singer (Chicago: University of Chicago Press, 1966), pp. 3–22. See also A. K. Ramanujan's *Speaking of Śiva* (Baltimore: Penguin Books, 1973) for similar sentiments among the Vīraśaivas; and David N. Lorenzen's paper on the followers of Kabir, "Traditions of Non-caste Hinduism: The Kabir Panth," an unpublished manuscript. I do not wish to overemphasize the anti-Brahmin streak in these movements, however. It seems to me that what was often at issue was not the concept of Brahminical authority but on what grounds that authority was based. In other words, the critical point was usually not *whether* the Brahmins had religious authority but *how* and *why*. There was as much discussion of who was the "true Brahmin" in these movements as there was anti-Brahmin rhetoric.

24. "Another guideline for orthodoxy in Hinduism is reverence for the Brahmins and the implicit acceptance of the social hierarchy known as the caste system. Here again the Buddhist and Jains represent a dissenting view, declaring that Brahmins have no special religious status." Kinsley, *Hinduism: A Cultural Perspective,* p. 53. Again, one must be careful here. As J. C. Heesterman has pointed out, the apparently anti-Brahminical discourse of the "heterodox" religions was often not directed at the authority of the Brahmins per se but at the sources on which they had claimed it. The issue was not Brahmins versus others but on what basis one was a Brahmin: "The question that occupies religious thought does not appear to . . . turn on brahmin superiority or its rejection, but on the point of who is the true brahmin. On these points, both orthodox and heterodox thinkers seem to agree to a great extent." "Brahmin, Ritual, and Renouncer," *Wiener Zeitschrift für die Kunde Süd- und Ostasiens* 8 (1964): 1–31, reprinted in a slightly different form (from which this and all subsequent citations are taken) in *The Inner Conflict of Tradition: Essays in Indian Ritual, Kingship, and Society* (Chicago: University of Chicago Press), p. 42.

25. Not *all* Brahmins have had such a relationship with the Veda, of course, and those who have not are ranked hierarchically lower. The point is that a certain knowledge of the Veda is expected of the Brahmin whether or not individual Brahmins fulfill that expectation. See Brian K. Smith, "Ritual, Knowledge, and Being: Initiation and Veda Study in Ancient India," *Numen* 33 (1986): 65–89.

tional bearers, purveyors, interpreters, and protectors of the Veda;[26] the authority of the Brahmin is dependent on the authority of the Veda, and the Veda exists only because of the traditional function the Brahmin has assumed for its preservation. Thus, Hinduism has also been defined by appealing to both of these interdependent criteria: "The only essential tenets of Hinduism are recognition of the Brahman caste and the divine authority of the Vedas. Those who publicly deny these doctrines as the Buddhists, Jains and Sikhs have done, put themselves outside the pale."[27]

Vedic Hinduism

Having reviewed the analytically separable (but in actuality usually conflated) types of definitions Indologists have constructed for the construct called Hinduism—the inchoate, the thematic, and the social and/or canonical—I now wish to offer my own working definition, locating myself firmly within the camp of the canonical authority as constitutive of the religion:[28] *Hinduism is the religion of those humans who create,*

26. They were also, from the point of view of the humanistic study of religion, in all probability the creators or "authors" of the Veda, although Brahmins past and present would deny that the Veda had human authors at all.

27. Eliot, *Hinduism and Buddhism,* I: 40. See also Barnett, *Hinduism,* p. 2, for the religion as partly defined by "the conception of a social order, or caste-system, at the head of which stand the Brahmans as completest [*sic*] incarnation of the Godhead and authoritative exponents of Its revelation"; and Zaehner, *Hinduism,* pp. 8–12, who wants to say that although Hinduism traditionally was defined by these two criteria, it has undergone many changes in the past century or so. "Thus while it was once possible to define a Hindu as one who performs his caste duties and accepts the Veda as revealed truth, this simple formula can no longer satisfy, for Hinduism is today, more than any other religion, in the melting-pot: what were once considered to be essentials are in the process of being discarded, but the hard core remains" (p. 9). This "hard core" is, according to Zaehner, a thematic configuration. See above, footnote 15.

28. A discussion of the canon in Hinduism, with varying degrees of comparative awareness, may be found in the following works, some of which I use extensively below: Thomas B. Coburn, " 'Scripture' in India: Towards a Typology of the Word in Hindu Life," *Journal of the American Academy of Religion* 52 (September 1984): 435–59, and "The Study of the Purāṇas and the Study of Religion," *Religious Studies* 16 (1980): 341–52; J. F. Staal, "The Concept of Scripture in the Indian Tradition," in Mark Juergensmeyer and N. Gerald Barrier, eds., *Sikh Studies: Comparative Perspectives on a Changing Tradition,* (Berkeley: Graduate Theological Union, 1979), pp. 121–24; J. C. Heesterman, "Veda and Dharma," in Wendy Doniger O'Flaherty and J. Duncan M. Derrett, eds., *The Concept of Duty in South Asia* (Columbia, Mo.: South Asia Books, 1978), pp. 80–95, and "Die Autorität des Veda," in G. Oberhammer, ed., *Offenbarung* (Vienna: Indologisches Institut der Universität Wien, 1974), pp. 29–40; Laine, "The

perpetuate, and transform traditions with legitimizing reference to the authority of the Veda.

I do not claim that this definition (or any other presently available, for that matter) is perfect. A perfect definition, fully explanatory and logically unassailable, would finish the scholarly labor on Hinduism. My definition allows for an interesting point of departure for further reflection along lines not fully explored in past scholarship. I would here like to unpack its components and implications in order to argue for its basic worth as a starting place.

First, the definition is fully consonant with a humanistic orientation for the study of religion. Hinduism, like all other religions from this point of view, centers on *human beings* who create, perpetuate, and transform their traditions. Hinduism was created by human imagination;[29] it was and is perpetuated by humans who regard their ancestors' creation as valuable and worth preserving; and it is transformed by humans who over time adapt and revise their ancestors' religion. The Hindus who create, perpetuate, and transform their traditions include Brahmins, of course, but not to the exclusion of other classes and castes of human creators, perpetuators, and transformers of traditions. The Brahmins, insofar as they have for millennia monopolized the functions of preserving and perpetuating the Veda, the authority of which all Hindus call upon to legitimize their doctrines and practices, are critical to Hindu orthodoxy but not definitive of it.

From this point of view, Indic religions might be classified into four types: (1) those that accept the authority of both the Veda and the Brahmin class (the mainline Hindu traditions); (2) those that accept the authority of the Veda but reject the notion of inborn prerogatives for the Brahmins (some of the more radically devotionalistic *bhakti* sects and some strains of what is called Tantricism); (3) those that, although sharing many important concepts with the other two (e.g., *karma, saṃsāra, dharma,* liberation), reject both the absolute authority of the Veda and the Brahmins (Buddhism, Jainism, Sikhism, and other "heterodox" movements); and (4) those religions imported to the Indian subconti-

Notion of 'Scripture' in Modern Indian Thought"; and Robert C. Lester, "Hinduism: Veda and Sacred Texts," in Frederick M. Denny and Rodney L. Taylor, eds., *The Holy Book in Comparative Perspective* (Columbia, S.C.: University of South Carolina Press, 1985), pp. 126–47.

29. Here I agree with Wilfred Cantwell Smith's oft-repeated thesis that there is no (e.g.) Hinduism apart from Hindus. I have noted above the fact that there was no Hinduism before scholars (also human) so constituted it as a religion.

nent that reject *both* the authority of the Veda and the Brahmin *and* the aforementioned concepts (Islam, Christianity, Judaism, et al.). The first two listed in this scheme, by virtue of their adherence to the authority of the Veda, are, under the definition here set forth, equally "Hindu"; the third and the fourth are not.[30]

A second strength of such a definition of Hinduism might be that by making the definition of Hinduism pivot on the legitimizing reference to the Veda, the canon, Hinduism ceases to be utterly different from the Western religions created, perpetuated, and transformed by "peoples of the book."[31] Indeed, it is arguable that all religions, by definition, must have a fixed canon (although not necessarily a written one) and a ruled set of exegetical strategies for its interpretation.[32] Although there are critical distinctions between the concept of the Veda on the one hand and those of (for instance) the Torah, the Bible, and the Qur'an on the other, the points of similarity have too often been elided in academic discourse—perhaps as part of the general Orientalist project to encode Asian religions and cultures as exotically strange and foreign to the rest of humankind.[33]

30. My thanks to Bruce Lincoln for his help in organizing my thinking on this matter.

31. For Hinduism as wholly other than Western religions, see the quotation of Percival Spear cited above, p. 8, and Paul Younger's statement in *Introduction to Indian Religious Thought* (Philadelphia: Westminster Press, 1972): "Even a superficial acquaintance leaves one with the impression that the religious life of India is fascinating, complex, and mysterious, but, above all, *different* from the religious traditions of the West" (p. 9; emphasis added). For a general discussion of the constitution of the Oriental "other," consult Edward Said, *Orientalism* (New York: Pantheon Books, 1978).

32. This is an extremely important topic for the study of religion which has not received sufficient theoretical and comparative treatment. For now, the best study (suggestive rather than definitive, however) is Jonathan Z. Smith's "Sacred Persistence: Toward a Redescription of Canon," in *Imagining Religion: From Babylon to Jonestown* (Chicago: University of Chicago Press, 1982), pp. 36–52. See also the essays collected in Wendy Doniger O'Flaherty, ed., *The Critical Study of Sacred Texts* (Berkeley: Graduate Theological Union, 1979); and the surveys for particular traditions in Denny and Taylor, *The Holy Book in Comparative Perspective.*

33. This is not to overrule the possibility that a unitary and fixed conception of "the Veda" as a scripture on a par with the Torah, the Christian Bible, and the Qur'an was a rather recent notion in India. Laine has argued just this: "Because 'Hinduism' is no one 'religion,' it has no one 'scripture.' The British were not so disposed to see this, however, and consequently neither were a number of the Hindu intelligentsia with whom they were in contact. Confronted by two religions of the book, Islam and (primarily Protestant) Christianity, Hindu intellectuals sought to establish the 'true' scripture of 'Hinduism.' " "The Notion of 'Scripture' in Modern Indian Thought," p. 167. See also the interesting

Third, this definition of Hinduism is neither too inclusive nor too exclusive. It is not too inclusive, as some we have considered are, for it clearly and unequivocally factors out Buddhism, Jainism, Sikhism, and other Indic religions that do *not* create, perpetuate, and transform their traditions with legitimizing reference to the authority of the Veda. They have other canonical sources to whose authority they refer for legitimization and certainly do not feel compelled to revert to the Veda, which they do not regard as authoritative. It is on this very point, as we will see, that Hindus themselves have regarded Buddhists, Jains, and others as heretics.

The definition is also not too exclusive. The point deserves further attention, but it does seem, for example, that even those *bhakti* traditions that have expressed cultic resistance to the authority of the Brahmin caste privilege have not institutionalized resistance to the authority of the Veda.[34] Some *bhakti* texts insist that the personalized Hindu deity to which their devotion is directed is to be known through knowledge of the Veda.[35] Indeed, both the Tantric and devotionalistic movements seem to have taken great pains to emphasize not only their allegiance to the Veda but also, as we will see, their reproduction of the Veda in their own sectarian texts.[36]

Finally, although our working definitions in the academic and humanistic study of religion need not fully correspond to the definitional criteria used within religions themselves,[37] it is problematic if the two do

texts collected and analyzed in Richard Fox Young's *Resistance Hinduism: Sanskrit Sources on Anti-Christian Apologetics in Early Nineteenth-Century India* (Vienna: Institut für Indologie der Universität Wien, 1981).

34. This is not to say that within *bhakti* discourse there cannot be found disparaging remarks about the value of the Veda, even within a very Hindu text such as the Bhagavad Gītā (e.g., 2.41–46). Indeed, the tendency to minimize the value of the Vedic textual learning can be traced to the Veda itself: the much debated hymn at Ṛg Veda 7.103 may be a satirization of Brahmin recitation of Vedic hymns, and one encounters many instances of deprecating remarks on the worth of the "lower" Vedic knowledge in the Upanishads (e.g., Muṇḍaka Upanishad 1.1.4–5). In all cases, however, it does not appear that the authority of the Veda is being challenged as much as built upon.

35. See, e.g., Varāha Purāṇa 70.40.44 and Kūrma Purāṇa 1.50.21–24.

36. For a general discussion of the Vedic allegiance of the Tantric and South Indian *bhakti* movements, see Louis Renou, *The Destiny of the Veda in India,* trans. by Dev Raj Chanana (Delhi: Motilal Banarsidass, 1965), pp. 5–6, esp. the notes. For particulars, see N. Subbu Reddiar, *Religion and Philosophy of the Nālāyiram* (Tirupati: Sri Venkateswara University, 1977), esp. pp. 680–93 ("The Nālāyiram as Dravida Veda"). I am grateful to Francis X. Clooney for bringing this latter work to my attention.

37. I here disagree with one of the premises of Jonathan Z. Smith's otherwise admirable attempt at a "polythetic" definition of Judaism, "Fences and Neighbors: Some

not at least converge at certain points. Defining the Hindu religion in the manner I am suggesting here certainly does not completely and slavishly reproduce what seems to be the full array of criteria used by Hindus themselves to speak of their religion (and these, of course, vary from Hindu to Hindu). It does, however, pick up and highlight many of the critical features of what appears to be the dominant native point of view.

That Hindus do indeed see themselves as defined, in part or in whole, by their relationship to the Veda (a relationship usually mediated by the Brahmin class) seems certain. The Veda, a massive collection of ancient "texts" or "scripture" composed and orally preserved in Sanskrit,[38] has been regarded by many Indic people (those we call Hindus) for several millennia as sacred—or to use the terminology of the religion itself, the Veda was "revealed" to or "heard" (*śruti*) by the foundational ancestors (the *ṛṣi*s).

Acceptance of the absolute authority of the Veda has been the criterion of orthodoxy among Hindus from at least the time of the early Dharma Sūtras and Smṛtis (ca. third or second century B.C.E.). Manu,[39] for example, declares (rather intolerantly, one might add): "All traditions (*smṛti*s) and misperceived philosophies (*kudṛṣṭi*s) which are outside of [the authority of] the Veda produce no reward after death, for they are founded on darkness, it is said."[40] Elsewhere in the text we read that the *śruti* (i.e., the Veda) is *amīmāṃsā* ("unquestionable"), and those who persist in challenging its dictates are to be scorned and avoided; their doctrines are *anṛta* ("untrue" and "disordered").[41]

Contours of Early Judaism," in *Imagining Religion,* pp. 1–18. For an example of such a polythetic definition in the hands of Indianists, one might again cite Spear, *India, Pakistan, and the West,* pp. 59–60: "We have, then, a body of ideas, beliefs and values, which together make up the mysterious amorphous entity which is called Hinduism. Each is present in some one part of Hinduism and few in every part. Any one can be dispensed with in any one section without forfeiting the title of Hinduism, and no item is absolutely essential. But some of each class must always be there."

38. It has often been noted that the use of the categories "text" and "scripture" for the orally transmitted Veda is somewhat misleading and inappropriate. See, e.g., Staal, "The Concept of Scripture." The Veda is a collective term for four different Vedas (Ṛg, Sāma, Yajur, and Atharva), each comprised of four types of "text": Saṃhitā, Brāhmaṇa, Āraṇyaka, and Upaniṣad. For a survey of the components, dates, and contexts of the Veda, see Jan Gonda, *Vedic Literature (Saṃhitās and Brāhmaṇas),* Vol. 1, fasc. 1 of Jan Gonda, ed., *A History of Indian Literature* (Wiesbaden: Otto Harrassowitz, 1975).

39. For the full names of texts abbreviated in this work, see the list at the front of this volume, and for full bibliographical citations, consult the Bibliography. All translations, unless otherwise noted, are my own.

40. Manu 12.95.

41. Manu 2.10–11, 12.96.

Hindu scholastics for the past several millennia have consistently maintained that orthodoxy turned on acceptance of the foundational authority of the Vedas. Kumārila, the teacher of Mīmāṃsā ("orthodoxy par excellence," according to Renou), ranked all religions and philosophies on the basis of their stated adherence to the Veda. Buddhists, Jains, and others are heretical, "for they do not accept the fact that the Vedas are the source [of their teachings], just as an evil son who hates his parents is ashamed to admit his descent from them."[42] Śankara, the great teacher of Advaita Vedānta, determined heresy on the basis of *veda-virodha* ("contradicting the Veda").[43] Indeed, acceptance of the authority of the Veda marks orthodoxy even in modern Hindu reformational movements,[44] and most scholars have not wholly disregarded the fact that "tolerant" Hinduism in general has its limits: those Indians who did not and do not accept the sacrality of the Veda have been and are regarded as non-Hindus by those who did and do.[45]

42. *Tantravārttika of Kumārila Bhaṭṭa,* ed. and trans. by G. Jha (Calcutta: Bibliotheca Indica, 1924), p. 165. Kumārila's statement, implying that Buddhist and Jaina doctrines are not new at all but are already found, in essence at least, in the Veda, is reminiscent of the claim in the Mahābhārata that whatever is can be found there, and what is not there does not exist.

43. Commenting on Taittirīya Upanishad. For this and other similar citations, consult O'Flaherty, "The Origins of Heresy," pp. 272–73, 275.

44. For the place of the Veda in modern Hindu revival movements, see D. S. Sharma, *The Renaissance of Hinduism* (Varanasi: Benares Hindu University, 1944); and A. Bharati, "The Hindu Renaissance and Its Apologetic Patterns," *Journal of Asian Studies* 29 (February 1970): 267–88, esp. p. 276: "A radical statement of the tenets of the Renaissance would be: *In nuce*—India has forgotten her marvelous past; this past contained not only material and cultural wealth, it also offered a complete solution of all problems of the individual and of society. . . . It is all contained in the Vedas and the Gītā." Gandhi's Hindu credentials may also be gauged by statements such as the following: "I claim myself to be sanatanist. . . . For me, Sanatana Dharma is the vital faith handed down from the generations belonging even to the prehistoric times and based upon the Vedas and the writings that followed them." Quoted in D. G. Tendulkar, *Mahātma,* 8 vols. (New Delhi: Publications Divisions, Ministry of Information and Broadcasting, Govt. of India, 1961–69), III: 180. See also the citations from the writings of Rammohun Roy, Debendranath Tagore, Vivekananda, and others in Laine, "The Notion of 'Scripture' in Modern Indian Thought."

45. "Traditionally, Hinduism divides all philosophies into orthodox and nonorthodox. Of the latter, all of which deny the sacredness of the *Vedas,* the most famous are the Buddhists and the Jains. . . . [B]oth religions are considered nonorthodox by Hindus primarily because they deny the authority of the *Vedas,* considering them mere human products." Kinsley, *Hinduism,* p. 53. See also Lester, "Hinduism," p. 126: "Hinduism holds much in common with other religions having their roots in India: Buddhism, Jainism and Sikhism; its distingusihing mark is reverence for Veda"; Heesterman, "Veda and

So it is that a definition such as the one proposed here that centers on the relationship of people to the Veda does not radically depart from similar discussions within the religion itself. At the same time, it does not accept some of the assumptions about the Veda that Hindus appear to think are crucial to their self-definition.

The orthodox claim that the Veda is a body of transcendent and super- or extra-human knowledge[46] is not included within *our* definitional statement. From the standpoint of the academic and humanistic study of religion, the Veda, like all other canonical literatures, was entirely composed of human beings. This very statement, from the native point of view, defines *us* as *not* Hindu—and when we seriously play the role of humanistic scholars of religion we are excluded from being Hindu, or Christian, or Jewish, and so forth, so long as we are playing the role. Refusal to follow Hindus on this point of authorship does not, however, close off the possibility of following native definitional statements in other regards.[47] The definition proposed here *resembles,* but does not reduplicate, statements of what constitutes a Hindu issuing forth from Hindus themselves.

Another juncture at which the definition we are considering here and the self-definitions put forth by Hindus both converge and diverge concerns the historical use of the Veda. Hindus by definition, we have claimed, are those humans who create, perpetuate, and transform tradi-

---

Dharma," p. 80: "The respect for the Vedas and the acknowledgment of its ultimate authority are therefore quite logically given as the decisive criteria for Hindu orthodoxy"; Renou, *The Destiny of the Veda in India,* p. 2: "We have just spoken of orthodoxy: the Veda is precisely the sign, perhaps the only one, of Indian orthodoxy"; O'Flaherty, "The Origin of Heresy," p. 272: "The contradiction of the Vedas remains the basis of heresy in the Hindu viewpoint"; and Gonda, *Change and Continuity,* p. 7; Hinduism "is defined as a complex of socio-religious phenomena which are based on the authority of the ancient corpora, called Veda."

46. *Veda* derives from the Sanskrit root *vid,* "to know," and means "true knowledge" in the sense of timeless, absolute Truth. Transcendence is also implied in the concept of *śruti,* for it is said to be eternal and *apauruṣeya,* i.e., not created by human beings, for which claims see, e.g., PMS 1.1.27–32. For the even more extravagant position that the Veda is the creative source of all beings, see the Vedānta Sūtras 1.3.27–29.

47. A suggestive possibility for rapprochement of the divergence on the question of the authorship of the Veda is found in a Feuerbachian reading of Coburn's " 'Scripture' in India." In a discussion of Hindu concepts of revelation turning on the metaphors of hearing and seeing, Coburn writes: "This identification of two senses of the *ṛṣi*'s experience is no mixing of metaphor but an effort to convey the holistic and supremely compelling nature of that experience. It engages one through, and yet transcends, the senses. It seizes one with a unique and irresistible immediacy. It is in such experiences that *the human becomes contiguous, even identical, with the divine*" (p. 442; emphasis added).

tions with legitimizing reference to the authority of the Veda. Hinduism is thus, for non-Hindus, not timeless, static, or changeless (it is a series of creations and transformations), although—and here is the point of divergence—it is usually presented as such by its adherents (it is simply a perpetuation).[48] This disjuncture between Hinduism perceived and defined by non-Hindus and Hinduism perceived and defined by Hindus brings us to the heart of what it means to define Hinduism as suggested here.

The Veda and Strategies for Orthodoxy

The great paradox of Hinduism, defined in this manner, is that although the religion is inextricably tied to the legitimizing authority of the Veda, in post-Vedic times the subject matter of the Veda was and is largely unknown by those who define themselves in relation to it. Its contents (almost entirely concerning the meaning and performance of sacrificial rituals that Hindus do not perform) are at best reworked (being, for example, reconstituted into ritual formulas or mantras for use in Hindu ceremonies), and many cases appear to be totally irrelevant for Hindu doctrine and practice. The paradox is stated succinctly by Paul Younger, who notes, "In spite of the acknowledgment of its authority, the content of the Veda does not seem to be used very directly in guiding the later development of the Religious Tradition."[49] Or, as Heesterman puts it, when post-Vedic Hinduism "appeals to the authority of the Vedas, it more often than not refers to an unknown entity."[50] Although it appears to be the case that Hindus do acknowledge the absolute authority of the Veda for legitimizing post-Vedic Hindu beliefs and practices, the relationship to the Veda often seems to be, as Renou writes, like "a simple 'raising of the hat' in passing to an idol by which one no longer intends to be encumbered later on."[51] The Hindus, it would seem, use only the "outside" of the Veda, oblivious to its "inside."[52]

48. For an overview, and overgeneralization, of the Hindu devaluation of historical change, see Louis Dumont, *La Civilisation indienne et nous* (Paris: Armand Colin, 1975), chap. 2: "La Problème de l'histoire"; and Madeleine Biardeau, "L'Inde et l'histoire," *Revue historique* 234 (1965): 47–58.

49. Younger, *Introduction to Indian Religious Thought p. 71.*

50. Heesterman, "Veda and Dharma," p. 80.

51. Renou, *The Destiny of the Veda in India,* p. 2.

52. See Wendy Doniger O'Flaherty, *Other Peoples' Myths* (New York: Macmillan, 1988), for an exploration of this distinction.

If, then, the content of the Veda is by and large irrelevant to post-Vedic Hindus, in what possible sense can Hinduism depend on Vedic authority for its legitimacy and integrity as a religion? And how do Hindus, from our point of view, transform their traditions over time without, from their point of view, diverging from the simple repetition of the eternal truth of the Veda?

One answer to this conundrum of a "Vedic Hinduism"—which appears in doctrine and practice to be mostly non-Vedic—is that the Veda is not always treated as a closed canon. A clear example of the suppleness of the Veda qua canon is the fact that new Upanishads (one of the components of the Veda or *śruti* according to traditional classification) have been composed throughout the history of Hinduism. New texts are in this purely nominal way given the authority of the Veda, indicating also that the Veda, as Hindus use it, is something of an "open book."

Furthermore, religious literature in Hinduism is not confined to the Veda or *śruti;* it is also comprised of what is classed as *smṛti,* "remembered" or traditional wisdom. The *smṛti,* in opposition to the *śruti,* is regarded by Hindus themselves as wholly composed by human beings and passed on from generation to generation. The relation of *smṛti* to *śruti* is complex, but two points are relevant for our purposes here. On the one hand, virtually all the literature in which the actual doctrines and practices of Hindu sects are codified is technically regarded as *smṛti* and therefore *not* the Veda. At the same time, these same admittedly noncanonical texts are often said to be entirely in conformity with—if not a mere restatement of—the (largely unknown and unexplored) canonical Veda and therefore are regarded as authoritative and, indeed, canonical. Robert Lingat observes:

> If one takes *smṛti* in its etymological sense of human tradition founded on memory, its authority cannot but be inferior to that of *śruti,* which is direct revelation of the rule. But in course of time its authority grew to the point of equalling that of *śruti.*[53]

How does the non-Vedic, noncanonical, purely human *smṛti* take on all the authority of the canonical, transcendent, and eternal Veda? How is transformation and change, embodied in *smṛti,* made to appear as perpetuation and continuity of the *śruti?* Several different kinds of strategies for investing *smṛti* texts with all the authority and timelessness of the Veda might be enumerated.

One method is to assert that the *smṛti is the Veda,* the *śruti.* In

53. Robert Lingat, *The Classical Law of India,* trans. by J. Duncan M. Derrett (Berkeley: University of California Press, 1973), p. 13.

addition to texts called Upanishads, some post-Vedic texts designate themselves, with some pointedness, "Saṃhitās." Other texts created in the post-Vedic age that represent actual (and usually non-Vedic) Hindu doctrine and practice sometimes call themselves the "fifth Veda," also to claim "Vedic" status.[54] Still others, as Thomas Coburn has pointed out for the principal scripture of Hindu goddess worship (the Devī-Māhātmya)[55] and others have noted for the Rāmāyaṇa,[56] are treated exactly as if they were Veda—that is, they are chanted according to schema of Vedic recitation. In this way, innovations are legitimized (and denied as innovations) by simply expanding what counts as, or is treated as, the eternal Veda.

Many other Hindu texts explicitly claim to be *vedasaṃmita* ("equivalent to the Veda") or *vedārthasaṃmita* ("equivalent in meaning to the Veda"). The line between transcendent *śruti* and man-made *smṛti* seems here to evaporate as both become "Veda." A most dramatic instance of this rather common stratagem is the case of compositions of Nammāḷvār, a South Indian Śūdra, devotee, and poet whose four principal works were equated in various ways to the four Vedas—and became known as the "Dravidian" or "Tamil Veda."[57]

Another approach is the apparently more modest argument that the *smṛti* is *based on the Veda* and has, as D. S. Sarma points out, only derivative authority:

> [T]he Śruti forms the supreme authority for Hinduism. All the other scriptures which form the Smriti, are secondary, deriving their authority

54. Both of the great epics of Hinduism, the Rāmāyana and the Mahābhārata, have made this claim, and so, too, have many of the Purāṇas that represent the doctrines and practices of certain forms of sectarian Hinduism in the first and early second millennia C.E. (e.g., Skanda Purāṇa 5.3.1.18; see also Chandogya Upanishad 7.1.2, providing a Vedic charter for the "fifth Veda" phenomenon: *itihāsapurāṇāṃ pañcamaṃ vedānāṃ vedaṃ*). A closely connected notion is that the great Purāṇas were emitted from the fifth mouth of the god Brahmā (Bhaviṣya Purāṇa 1.2.56–57).

55. Thomas Coburn, *Devī-Māhātmya: The Crystallization of the Goddess Tradition* (Columbia, Mo.: South Asia Books, 1985), pp. 63–67, concluding that "Considerations of content indicate that the DM is clearly *smṛti.* Considerations of function suggest an analogy with the function of *śruti.*"

56. Milton Singer, "The Cultural Pattern of Indian Civilization: A Preliminary Report of a Methodological Field Study," *Far Eastern Quarterly* 15 (November 1955): 33; and esp. Philip Lutgendorf, *The Life of a Text: Tulsidas's Rāmcāritamānasa in Performance,* Ph.D. dissertation, University of Chicago, 1986.

57. See N. Subbu Reddiar, "The Nālāyiram as Dravida Veda," pp. 680–93 of his *Religion and Philosophy of the Nālāyiram.* Reddiar also notes that the same status was conferred on the works of others of the Āḷvārs as well.

from the Vedas, and are accepted as authoritative only in so far as they follow the teachings of the primary scriptures.[58]

This is the position, worked out in great detail, of the *mīmāṃsaka* Śabara, who argues that the authority of the *smṛti* is vouchsafed only by demonstrating its ties to particular *śruti* passsages. This is not often difficult to do, given a certain flexibility of interpretation.

But the basis in the Veda of the *smṛti* teachings can be inferred by other means. The original (human) teacher and "author" of the *smṛti* text can be regarded as omniscient, that is, the master of the Veda, of Truth: "Whatever duty has been ordained for anyone by Manu has already been fully declared in the Veda; for [Manu was] omniscient (*sarvajñānamaya*)."[59] Failure to find distinct precedents for *smṛti* teachings is thus a result of incomplete knowledge of the interpreter, and not due to a discrepancy in the text; the *smṛti* can be regarded as, inevitably, *yathāśrutam* ("in accord with the Veda").

The Veda is here treated not so much as a set of texts but as a body of knowledge that is incorporated in certain individuals who have memorized and mastered it. Human teachers and exemplars, then, can serve as the guarantors of the Vedic authority of post-Vedic Hinduism, just as the *ṛṣi*s did for the ancestors *in illo tempore.*[60] In delineating the sources of Hindu *dharma,* many texts[61] list three such founts: the Veda itself; the *smṛti* (which is regarded as at least based on the Veda, if not a complete replication of it); and "custom," more fully descried as *sadācāra* ("good custom") or *śiṣṭācāra* ("the custom of learned men"). The *śiṣṭa*s are those Brahmins "who are properly trained in the Veda and its supplements and who know how to make discerning inferences from the *śruti.*"[62]

As noted above, the Brahmin class is, by virtue of its traditional rights to knowledge and perpetuation of the Veda, critically important for determining orthodoxy, for determining what is "Vedic." Their authority, however, is clearly derivative. The third source of *dharma* (the

58. D. S. Sarma, "The Nature and History of Hinduism," in Kenneth W. Morgan, ed., *The Religion of the Hindus* (New York: Ronald Press, 1953), p. 7. Sarma's article, which explicates Hinduism's "underlying unity" as consisting of common scriptures, common deities, common ideals, common beliefs, and common practices, is among the best short but comprehensive definitional statements of the religion currently available.

59. Manu 2.7.

60. The *ṛṣis,* according to Nirukta 1.20, had "direct intuitive insight into *dharma.*"

61. These include ĀpDhS 1.1.1.1–2; GautDhS 1.1–2; VāsDhS 1.4–7; Yāj 1.7; Manu 1.6.

62. BDhS 1.1.1.6.

customs of learned Brahmins), then, no less than the second, is wholly borrowed from and based on the Veda, as Lingat notes:

> *Sadācāra* is a religious life, exclusively orientated towards the acquisition of spiritual merit. It amounts to the practices observed from generation to generation by *śiṣṭas,* or those who are at once *instructed* and virtuous. They have not only plumbed the depths of the Veda and its related texts, but they can deduce from them all the consequences which are implied, and, what is more, they conform to these teachings in their conduct.[63]

Such a personalized conception of Vedic authority continues in recent Hinduism. The modern saint Ramakrishna was said to be a living embodiment of the "nectar" of the Vedas:

> That nectar which has been obtained by churning the infinite ocean of the Vedas, into which Brahmā, Vishnu, Shiva, and the other gods have poured their strength, which is charged with the life essence of the Avatāras—Gods Incarnate on earth—Shri Ramakrishna holds that nectar in his person, in its fullest measure.[64]

Another way Hindus guarantee the Vedic authority of their post-Vedic texts is to contend that in cases where the Vedic precedent is not found, the *smṛti* is *based on a lost Veda.* Already in the ritualistic Sūtras (ca. seventh through third centuries B.C.E.) *smṛti* texts were claiming *śruti* basis: the ĀpGS (1.4.12.10) states that the rules for domestic rituals were once given in Brāhmaṇas but that these *śruti* texts have been lost. This is also the argument of last resort of Kumārila, the *mīmāṃsaka* who went even farther than his colleague Śabara in claiming that the *smṛti* was invariably based on Vedic authority. Lingat summarizes his position: "When a rule of *dharma* has no source, we must conclude that it rests upon a part of the Veda which is lost or somehow hidden from view."[65] Similarly, in the Purāṇas, one finds the claim that those texts were composed when parts or the whole of the Veda vanished from the earth.[66]

This argument is tied in certain ways to the Hindu doctrine of the degenerating nature of time, the present age, need it be said, envisioned as the most degenerate of all.[67] One result of this decline from better

63. Lingat, *The Classical Law of India,* pp. 14–15; see also pp. 178–80.

64. Vivekananda, quoted in Laine, "The Notion of 'Scripture' in Modern Indian Thought," p. 172.

65. Lingat, *The Classical Law of India,* p. 8.

66. See, e.g., Śiva Purāṇa 7.1.1.35.

67. For the theory of declining *yugas*, resulting in degeneration of human capabilities and necessitating changes in the *dharma* appropriate to each age, see Lingat, *The Classical Law of India,* pp. 183–89, and his "Time and the Dharma," *Contributions to Indian Sociology* 6 (1962): 7–16.

times is that the Veda, once one hundred thousand verses in length, has been reduced to its present, smaller size, with the lost portions only incompletely known by untraceable *smṛti* passages. Making a virtue out of a potentially embarrassing necessity, Hindu texts with no visible Vedic precedents can thus claim to be retrieving for Hindus parts of their canon otherwise unavailable.

Closely related is the notion that Hindu texts are *simplified forms of the Veda.* In these corrupt times, people are unable to understand the Veda, and therefore simplified, "digest" versions have been created for simple minds: "Those who have lost [the sense of] *śruti* must run back to the Tantra to rediscover the path to the Vedas,"[68] and South Indian *bhakti* texts written in the vernacular were also said to contain the "cream," "purport," or "essential teachings" of the Veda.[69] Many Sanskrit Purāṇas also present themselves as streamlined renditions of Vedic wisdom now made available to women, Śūdras, and others previously excluded from learning the Veda.[70] With claims like this, the *smṛti* texts become "means of access to the Veda" and function as "intermediaries, if not intercessors."[71] Indeed, some texts warn, without the *smṛti* acting as a buffer the Veda is useless or dangerous.[72]

The *smṛti* is also regarded as *enlarging the Veda* in ways that complement rather than contradict the claim of simplification. As we have just observed, many of the Purāṇas see their role as both the amplification and clarification of the Veda.[73] The *smṛti* in general is thought to serve a popularizing function, bringing the message of the Veda (often in the form of epic tales and mythological stories) to the masses.[74] In addition to the myth of the shrinking Veda, one finds also the myth of the Veda divided and multiplied into, finally, all the *smṛti* texts of Hinduism.

Combining the themes of simplicity and enlargement (in the sense

68. Vīramitrodaya, cited by R. C. Hazra, *Studies in the Upapurāṇas* (Calcutta: Sanskrit College, 1963), p. 93.

69. Reddiar, *Religion and Philosophy of the Nālāyiram,* pp. 682–85.

70. E.g., Bhāgavata Purāṇa 1.4.25; Devi Bhāgavata Purāṇa 1.3.21.

71. Renou, *The Destiny of the Veda in India,* p. 8.

72. E.g., Mbh 1.1.204: "With both Epic and Purāṇa one should support the Veda—the Veda is afraid of one of little knowledge." J. A. B. van Buitenen, trans., *The Mahābhārata,* p. 31.

73. See Nāradīya Purāṇa 2.24.15 ff.

74. See Sarma, "The Nature and History of Hinduism," p. 8: "What the Vedas are for the learned, the Rāmāyaṇa, the Mahābhārata, and the Bhāgavad Purāṇa are for the common man. They are accepted as sacred books by all Hindus." See also J. A. B. van Buitenen, "Hindu Sacred Literature," *Encyclopedia Britannica,* 15th ed., VIII: 933; and C. Mackenzie Brown, "Purāṇa as Scripture: From Sound to Image of the Holy Word in the Hindu Tradition," *History of Religions* 26 (August 1986): 68–86, esp. p. 76.

of explication) is the notion that Hindu religious texts *condense the essence of the Veda.* The Purāṇas often state that they are *sarvavedasāra* or *akhilaśrutisāra* ("the quintessence of the whole Veda")[75] or "the essence of the meaning of the whole Veda" (*sarvavedārthasāra*),[76] or the "soul" (*ātman*) of the Vedas.[77] This strategy is also deployed in texts of the South Indian *bhakti* movement which claim to be the essence of the Ṛg Veda or, indeed, of all four Vedas.[78]

Finally, we come full circle when we read that the *smṛti* is not based on the Veda but, rather, that *the Veda is based on the smṛti.* According to the Matsya Purāṇa,[79] God thought of the Purāṇas before he spoke the Vedas, and other texts[80] clearly state that the Vedas are "established" (*pratiṣṭhā*) on the Purāṇas.

These are some of the ways (and there are undoubtedly more) in which post-Vedic Hindus create new traditions and transform older ones (i.e., change them, from the outsider's perspective) while they are perpetuating "the Vedic tradition" (i.e., do not change them, from the orthodox Hindu view). By representing, through deployment of these strategies for orthodoxy, new texts, doctrines, and practices as *connected* in some fashion or another to the Veda, change is both legitimized and denied, and continuity is both affirmed and stretched.

The working definition of Hinduism proposed here pivots on the notion that the Veda functions as a touchstone for Hindu orthodoxy. It functions, that is, as a kind of canon, a point of reference that is regarded as absolutely authoritative. It would seem, however, that the Veda is a rather peculiar canon—at once irrelevant and never ignored, open and unquestionable, endlessly reenvisioned and eternally unchanged. Some, seizing upon the first terms in these pairs of opposites,

75. Bhāgavata Purāṇa 1.2.3, 1.3.42, 12.13.15; Nāradīya Purāṇa 1.1.36.

76. Nāradīya Purāṇa 1.9.97.

77. Skanda Purāṇa 5.3.1.22.

78. See V. Rangacharya, "Śri Vaiṣṇavism in South India," in H. Bhattacharya, ed., *The Cultural Heritage of India,* 4 vols. (Calcutta: Ramakrishna Mission, 1953), IV:167; and Reddiar, *Religion and Philosophy of the Nālāyiram,* p. 683: "The first twenty-one verses of the *Tiruvāymoli* [of Nammāḷvār] convey clearly the purport of the Vedānta system. They represent the twenty-one recensions of the *Ṛg Veda.* The thousand verses which are set to music represent the *Sāma-veda* teachings in a thousand recensions. The hundred decads represent the *Yajur-veda* which has one hundred recensions. This composition abounds in the delineation of the eight sentiments and so represents the *Atharva-veda* which has eight recensions. Hence the *Tiruvāymoli* shall be taken to represent all the *Vedas*" (citing the *Drāmidopaniṣat-tātparyaratnāvali* 5).

79. Matsya Purāṇa 53.3.20.

80. Skanda Purāṇa 5.3.1.20; Nāradīya Purāṇa 2.24.16.

have suggested that Hindus indulge in a pious but transparent fiction with their claims of continuity with the Veda. The strategies for orthodoxy outlined above are dismissed as cynical rationalizations or downright deceptions.[81] Others, perplexed by the apparent use only of the "outside" of the Veda by Hindus (and the neglect of its "inside," its doctrines and practices), have attempted to uncover the "symbolic meaning" of the canonical Veda for post-Vedic Hindus.[82]

The Veda is thought by some to signify merely a Hindu notion of absolute knowledge or truth in a general sense. Lingat concludes that "in reality, it seems that when a Hindu affirms that *dharma* rests entirely upon the Veda, the word Veda does not mean in that connection the Vedic texts, but rather the totality of knowledge, the sum of all understanding, of all religious and moral truths."[83] Paul Younger takes an even more mystical view of the real meaning Veda has for Hindu orthodoxy. The Veda, Younger claims,

> cannot be defined in terms of boundaries in the way Western concepts are defined. There are no limits to where the Vedic ends and the non-Vedic begins. *Veda* is like a center of light from which concentric circles of truthfulness radiate outward.[84]

Recently, Jan Heesterman has suggested that the defining attachment Hindus have to the Veda is indicative of "the inescapable need for ultimate authority."[85] The Veda is preserved and sanctified in all its doctrinal and practical irrelevance for post-Vedic Hinduism because its irrelevance serves a purpose.[86] The canon can obtain its utter transcendence and authority precisely because of its utter irrelevance, because "it is unconcerned with and untouched by the vagaries of human life and

81. Vivekananda, e.g., pointedly complained that "in India . . . if I take certain passages of the Vedas, and if I juggle with the text and give it the most impossible meaning . . . all the imbeciles will follow me in a crowd." Quoted by Renou, *The Destiny of the Veda in India,* p. 61.

82. See Renou, *The Destiny of the Veda in India.* "One always believes oneself to be in the wake of the Veda, while one turns one's back on it. The term tends to serve as a symbol" (p. 1); and Lingat, *The Classical Law of India:* "It is this hypothetical or symbolic code, rather than the surviving Vedic texts, which the most ancient authors . . . have in mind when they proclaim that the Veda is the primary source of *dharma*" (p. 8).

83. Lingat, *The Classical Law of India,* p. 8.

84. Younger, *Introduction to Indian Religious Thought,* p. 70.

85. Heesterman, "Veda and Dharma," p. 84; see also "Die Autorität des Veda."

86. It is on this point that Heesterman's argument can be distinguished from an otherwise comparable theory put forward by Frits Staal on the "meaninglessness" (defined as purposelessness) of Vedic ritual. See Chapter 2 herein.

society."[87] The Veda, then, symbolizes nothing short of transcendence itself and maintains its authority by being intentionally divorced from human reality. Rather than solving the paradox, Heesterman ends up repositioning it as a conclusion: "The crux of the matter is that the Vedas hold the key to ultimate legitimation. Therefore, even if the Vedas are in no way related to the ways of human life and society, one is still forced to come to terms with them."[88]

It is, indeed, entirely because Hindus are "forced to come to terms" with the Veda that I have suggested my definition of Hinduism. A reimagining of Hinduism along these lines, however, can remain content neither with dismissing Hindu strategies for orthodoxy (connecting to the Veda) as contrived fictions nor with the conclusion that the Veda is a mere "symbol" for Hindus of more or less mystical notions of "Truth" or "transcendence." The first reduces Hindu orthodoxy to meaningless form; the second depends on restating Hindu orthodoxy's claims for the superhuman essence of the (now "symbolic") Veda.

Hinduism, I would argue, is to be defined as a process, not an essence. It is not the essential nature of the Veda (or what it "symbolizes") that is of defining import as much as it is the particular relationships Hindus establish and maintain with it. And these relationships, which we have called strategies for orthodoxy, might be regarded with less skepticism and with more historical depth. It is possible that it is here, with the connections themselves, that one will make and find the connections, so to speak, between the ancient and seemingly "irrelevant" Veda and post-Vedic Hinduism.

Let us take our cue from Giorgio Bonazzoli and his remarks on the nature of "canon" within religion:

> A canon can be either a mere list of works that are accepted as normative and therefore considered as authentic or it can be a *complex of rules through which one can establish whether a work should be accepted as authentic and normative or not.*[89]

Compare Jonathan Z. Smith's argument that a "canon cannot exist without a tradition and an interpreter. . . . The process of arbitrary limitation and of overcoming limitation through ingenuity recurs."[90]

It is clear from the foregoing that the principal rule for determining

87. Heesterman, "Veda and Dharma," p. 84.

88. Ibid., p. 93.

89. Giorgio Bonazzoli, "The Dynamic Canon of the Purāṇas," *Purāṇa* 26 (July 1979): 127–28; emphasis added.

90. Smith, "Sacred Persistence," pp. 49, 50.

"canon" (i.e., orthodox religious authority) in Hinduism is whether or not it is "Vedic." We have also observed the variety of strategies ("subrules" for "overcoming limitation through ingenuity") available for constituting post-Vedic texts, doctrines, and practices as "Vedic": reflection (this *is* the Veda); restatement (this is *based on* the Veda); reduction (this is the *simplified* Veda); reproduction (this *enlarges* the Veda); recapitulation (this is the *condensed essence* of the Veda); and even reversal (the Veda is *based on this*).

The common thread linking all these strategies is not only the necessity to *return* to the Veda in order to progress within the boundaries of Hinduism;[91] it is also the notion that the particular post-Vedic text, doctrine, or practice *resembles,* in one way or another, the Vedic prototype. The Veda is the prototypical canon that can lend its authority to resembling counterparts. It is here, as we will see, that some interesting possibilities open up for rethinking Hinduism as a set of "Vedic" traditions.

I have said that my intention in formulating a working definition of Hinduism was not to finish but to start. The proposed definition—Hinduism as the religion of those humans who create, perpetuate, and transform traditions with legitimizing reference to the authority of the Veda—has led to an investigation of the kinds of relationships post-Vedic traditions establish with the Veda. It has also led to the ponderous question of the relationship (or lack thereof) of Vedism, the religion of the Veda from the "inside" and Hindu traditions which, it is said, use only the "outside" of the Veda for their legitimization. Is it possible that the Veda has bequeathed more than just its covers to its Hindu offspring? Put more pointedly, is it possible that the strategies of orthodoxy themselves, connecting counterparts to prototype, are Vedic?

To answer these questions, we must begin another project, one which will preoccupy us through most of the remainder of this book: the attempt to delineate and demonstrate the underlying (which is not to say unconscious or hidden) principles of the religion represented in the Veda. We will then be in a better position to return to the definitional question of what we think Hinduism is, and why.

91. This process recalls Mircea Eliade's frequently stated notion that the "return to origins" is a central feature of religion in general. See, e.g., *The Myth of the Eternal Return,* trans. by Willard Trask (Princeton, N.J.: Princeton University Press, 1954); and *Myth and Reality,* trans. by Willlard Trask (New York: Harper Colophon, 1963).

2

Constructing Vedism

Mistaken Identities

Vedism, like Hinduism, does not come to us in an unmediated purity, untouched by the concerns of later ages. It too is the product of centuries of definitional choices and strategies which have prefabricated what we think we know about the oldest religion of the subcontinent. Although no individual or era can entirely think themselves out of such preconditions, it is worthwhile to attempt an understanding of how Vedism has been imagined in the past in order to imagine it in ways that might be more appropriate for the present.

As the history of scholarship on Vedism amply attests, the predominant feature of that religion[1] is an apparent preoccupation with the "discovery" or constitution of linkages between what others regard as wholly discrete objects, acts, or entities. Making connections has served as the defining feature of Vedism as a whole. The fact that one sees in all the multitude of ancient Vedic texts, produced by different authors at different times and to some degree for different purposes, a common concern to link together apparently unconnected things has itself made possible a certain generalization on the part of the scholar of these texts.

1. In the study of Vedism, as elsewhere, there has recently been a trend to deconstruct the object into historically, socially, geographically, and culturally discrete elements; that is, there has been an increased recognition that what we call Vedism is a general category comprised of originally differentiated strands. For the atomistic approach to Vedic religion, see, e.g., Asko Parpola, "The Pre-Vedic Indian Background of the Śrauta Rituals," in Frits Staal, ed., *Agni: The Vedic Ritual of the Fire Altar,* 2 vols. (Berkeley, Calif.: Asian Humanities Press, 1983) II: 41–75.

We can speak of *a* Vedic tradition, making and finding connections between texts from various sources and times, because all these texts are characterized by their tendency to make and find connections.

"Vedic thought," writes Renou, "as one catches glimpses of it in its ritual form in the Brāhmaṇas and in its speculative form in the Upaniṣads, defines itself as a system of equations."[2] The quintessentially Vedic system of "equations," "equivalences," "homologies," or "connections"—all possible translations of the Sanskrit word *bandhu*[3]—unites the ritual texts (Saṃhitās, Brāhmaṇas, and Sūtras)[4] with the more explicitly mystical, speculative texts (Āraṇyakas and Upaniṣads). There is an epistemological affinity between typically Brāhmaṇical and ritualistic declaration such as "The sacrifice/sacrificer is the year" and typically Upaniṣadic and mystical statements such as "The true self (*ātman*) is the universal principle (*brahman*)."[5]

An analysis of the very names by which Vedic texts are known seems to indicate a common theme underlying differences in genre. *Brāhmaṇa,* for example, designates texts "where the function is precisely to establish connections," as Lilian Silburn writes.[6] And, as Renou observes, "The word *upaniṣad* itself, as it is first used in the Śatapatha Brāhmaṇa, means only 'equivalence,' " and "the aim of the whole of

2. Louis Renou, " 'Connection' en védique, 'cause' en bouddhique," in *Dr. C. Kunhan Raja Presentation Volume* (Madras: Adyar Library, 1946), p. 55.

3. A partial bibliography on *bandhu*s in the Vedic texts would include Jan Gonda, "Bandhus in the Brāhmaṇas," *Adyar Library Bulletin* 29 (1965): 1–25; Armand Minard, *Trois enigmes sur les cent chemins: Recherches sur le Śatapatha Brāmaṇa,* 2 vols. (Paris: Société d'edition les belles lettres, 1949), 1:50–51; Boris Oguibenine, "*Bandhu* et *dakṣiṇā*. Deux termes védique illustrant le rapport entre le signifiant et le signifié," *Journal asiatigue* 276 (1983): 263–75; Hermann Oldenberg, *Vorwissenschaftliche Wissenschaft: Die Weltanschauung der Brāhmaṇa-texte* (Göttingen: Vandenhoeck and Ruprecht, 1919); Asko Parpola, "On the Symbol Concept of the Vedic Ritualists" in *Religious Symbols and Their Functions,* ed. by H. Biezais (Stockholm: Almquist and Wiksell, 1979), pp. 139–53; Louis Renou, " 'Connexion' en védique, 'cause' en bouddhique," pp. 55–60; Stanislov Schayer, "Die Struktur der magischen Weltanschauung nach dem Atharva-Veda und den Brāhmaṇa-Texten," *Zeitschrift für Buddhismus* 6 (1925): 259–99; and Michael Witzel, "On Magical Thought in the Veda," (Leiden: Universitaire Pers Leiden, 1979).

4. For the relationship between the Sūtras, technically classified as outside the canonical Veda, and the Vedic texts per se, see Chapter 5 herein.

5. I will return to the question of the continuity or discontinuity between the ritualistic texts and the Upanishads later in this work. For now, it is enough to point out that many scholars view these two types of ancient texts as linked on the grounds of their programmatic linkages.

6. Lilian Silburn, *Instant et cause: Le Discontinu dans la pensée philosophique de l'Inde* (Paris: Libraire philosophique J. Vrin, 1955), p. 64.

Vedic thought may be expressed as the attempt to formulate *upaniṣads*."[7] From Sylvain Lévi, who in 1898 argued that the priestly scholastics who produced the ritualistic Brāhmaṇas were the fathers of Indian philosophy,[8] to Jan Heesterman, who claims that Upaniṣadic doctrines of world renunciation and monism were "already implied in classical ritual thinking,"[9] a large segment of scholars of Vedism have concluded that the unity of the tradition derives from this fundamental, recurring imperative to make connections.

At the same time, it is a remarkable fact about the Western reconstruction of the Vedic religion that whereas the great identities of the Vedāntic Upaniṣads (linking the microcosmic true self to the macrocosmic One in an expression of mystical unity) have always seemed to inspire admiration, statements of equivalence in the ritualistic Brāhmaṇas are often scorned and disdained as so much mumbo jumbo from the imagination of the priests.[10]

F. Max Müller, the doyen of nineteenth-century Indology and the "editor" of the Ṛg Veda, despised the Brāhmaṇas as examples of the tragic corruption of the pure religiosity expressed in the earliest Vedic compositions, the Saṃhitās. He denounced the later works as

> a literature which for pedantry and downright absurdity can hardly be matched anywhere. . . . The general character of these works is marked by shallow and insipid grandiloquence, by priestly conceit, and antiquarian pedantry. . . . These works deserve to be studied as the physician studies the twaddle of idiots, and the raving of madmen.[11]

Müller later repeated his opinion that the Brāhaṇas were "twaddle, and what is worse, theological twaddle,"[12] and this view was shared by many others.

7. Louis Renou, *Religions of Ancient India* (New York: Schocken Books, 1968), p. 18. See also Harry Falk, "Vedisch *upaniṣad*," *Zeitschrift der Deutschen Morgenländischen Gesellschaft* 136 (1986): 80–97; and the older study by S. Schayer, "Über die Bedeutung des Wortes upaniṣad," *Rocznik Orientalistyczny* 3 (1925): 57–67.

8. Sylvain Lévi, *La Doctrine du sacrifice dans les Brāhmaṇas* (Paris: Ernest Leroux, 1898), esp. pp. 10–11.

9. Jan Heesterman, "Brahmin, Ritual and Renouncer," p. 41.

10. For a discussion of the history of Brāhmaṇa-bashing in the West, see Wendy Doniger O'Flaherty, *Tales of Sex and Violence: Folklore, Sacrifice, and Danger in the Jaiminīya Brāhmaṇa* (Chicago: University of Chicago Press, 1985), pp. 3–6.

11. F. Max Müller, *A History of Ancient Sanskrit Literature,* 2d ed. (London: Williams and Norgate, 1860), p. 389.

12. F. Max Müller, *Chips from a German Workshop,* 2 vols. (New York: Scribner, Armstrong and Co., 1871), I: 113.

Why were these works so regarded? As Arthur Macdonell would write, they are "full of sacerdotal conceits, and fanciful, or even absurd, identifications, such as is doubtless unparalleled anywhere else";[13] or, as Julius Eggeling, the translator of the Śatapatha Brāhmaṇa, reiterates, "For wearisome prolixity of exposition, characterised by dogmatic assertion and a flimsy symbolism rather than by serious reasoning, these works are perhaps not equalled anywhere."[14]

The system of equations, held to be characteristic—if not wholly definitive—of Vedism, when viewed in the Brāhmaṇas at least, was anything but systematic. Regardless of how the philosophical identifications in the Upaniṣads were received, for much of Indology the equivalences drawn in the Brāhmaṇas were "fanciful," "absurd," and "flimsy." And although it was not apparently perceived, such conclusions on the part of nineteenth- and early-twentieth-century scholars of ancient Indian religion reduplicated the conclusions drawn by those at work on "primitive" religion. The latter, no less than the former, found in such identifications proof positive of the utter difference, and usually the utter inferiority, of non-Western, nonmodern religions and "modes of thought."[15]

In the case of Vedism, the scorn generated by those who studied and represented it was (and largely still is) not only because Vedic Indians seemed to confound two or more distinct entities (a confusion of modern and western categories) but also because they did so, it appeared, randomly. "According to the Brāhmaṇa-texts," G. U. Thite could assert in 1975, "anything can be connected with anything else; anything can result from anything; everything is all."[16] Even more re-

13. Arthur Macdonell, *A History of Sanskrit Literature* (New York: D. Appleton and Co., 1900), p. 32.

14. Julius Eggleing, trans., *The Śatapatha Brāhmaṇa, according to the Text of the Mādhyandina School,* 5 vols. (Oxford: Clarendon Press, 1882–1900; reprint ed. Delhi: Motilal Banarsidass, 1963), I: ix.

15. The similarities between the Vedic system of connections and those definitive of what once what called the primitive mentality are striking. It remains somewhat strange that those who were concerned with identifications within primitive religions—from Taylor, Frazer, and Lévy-Bruhl to Evans-Pritchard and Lévi-Strauss—were oblivious to parallel (at least) instances in Vedic religion, and vice versa. For recent discussions of the problem in "primitive" religion, see Raymond Firth, "Twins, Birds and Vegetables: Problems of Identification in Primitive Religious Thought," *Man* (new series) 1 (1966): 1–17; Audrey Hayley, "Symbolic Equations: The Ox and the Cucumber," *Man* (new series) 3 (1968): 262–72; Robin Horton and Ruth Finnegan, eds., *Modes of Thought: Essays on Thinking in Western and Non-Western Societies* (London: Faber and Faber, 1973); and Bryan Wilson, ed., *Rationality* (Oxford: Basil Blackwell, 1977).

16. G. U. Thite, *Sacrifice in the Brāhmaṇa-Texts* (Poona: University of Poona, 1975), p. 5. Thite claims that the Brāhmaṇas can be understood as being guided by a

cently, Frits Staal carries on the Indological tradition of denigrating the Brāhmaṇas by contending that the explanatory connections drawn in those texts are inconsistent, contradictory, arbitrary, and, again, "fanciful."[17] One simply throws up one's hands in despair in the face of this kind of prelogical (and postlogical?) thinking.

Thus, in our first foray into the nature of Vedism we have discovered that, by general scholarly consensus, the religion is characterized (or, it could equally be said, created) in large part by its recurring concern with making connections. We have also learned, again on expert authority, that such connections are unintelligible; they are, at best, mistaken identities and, at worst, the random whims of flimsy minds. It is hard to imagine how texts whose subject matter is in this way represented could also be imagined as the definitional key to a world religion such as Hinduism—unless, of course, Hindus are imagined in a manner that makes such a connection possible, albeit neither respectable nor respectful. Is it not more valuable (to say nothing of its plausibility) to imagine that the mistake in the identities lies not with the Vedic Indians but with those who have represented them in this way?

The Overactive Imagination

The distinctively Vedic proclivity for making connections is intricately connected to another feature or characteristic of the religion. Vedism also appears to be preoccupied with the theory and practice of ritual. As a configuration of cosmogonies and cosmologies, of metaphysics and epistemology, of social structure and sociology, of ethics and values, of psychologies and anthropologies, wholly originating in and depending on ritual activity, what we call Vedism can equally be labeled Vedic ritualism.

The sacrifice, or *yajña,* was, in one way or another, the subject matter of an enormous corpus of texts (the Veda and its ancillaries, the

---

principle he calls "henoism," which considers "not only any deity . . . to be supreme successively, but anything which is the subject matter at a particular moment becomes the omnipotent, the highest, the only one identical with all etc., for the time being." This is, of course, an attempt to resurrect and rework what Max Müller labeled "henotheism" and is as obfuscating and bizarre in its new form as it was in the original.

17. Frits Staal, "The Meaninglessness of Ritual," *Numen* 26 (1979): 4; idem, *The Science of Ritual* (Poona: Bhandarkar Oriental Research Institute, 1982), pp. 11–12, 36; idem, *Agni,* I:3, 27–28, 67–68.

Vedāṅga), a literature that "consists almost entirely of sacred texts that were in use at, or centered around, the specific Vedic religion of sacrifice and ritual."[18] Although comparativists have largely ignored it, no body of materials is better suited for the study of ritual than the Vedic. As Staal argues, the Vedic ritual is not only distinctive of Vedism but is crucial for general ritual studies because it is "the richest, most elaborate and most complete among the rituals of mankind."[19]

But if the preoccupation with ritual provides us with a second principal component for describing Vedism as a religion, it also provides another occasion for many to denigrate it as a religion. The supposedly absurd and random nature of the equivalences in the Brāhmaṇas is only one reason why they (and those who proposed them) were, and are, so demeaned by those who, in most cases, spent large portions of their scholarly lives studying them. A second reason seems to be that these equations were invariably produced within a ritual context.

Whereas the religion of the Ṛg Veda (ca. 1200 B.C.E.) was coded by Indologists as one of guileless and creative poesy, later and more paradigmatic Vedism was said to be thoroughly enmeshed in priestly machinations. Hermann Oldenberg depicted this ritualistic Vedism as a "vorwissenschaftliche Wissenschaft," and Staal has recently spoken of a Vedic "science of ritual." And whereas the early Upaniṣads, from the usual point of view, reflect a certain healthy realism (by which is meant an antiritualism) and work out their magnificent philosophical monism in the purely metaphysical realm, the Brāhmaṇas are frankly, explicitly, and hopelessly concerned with "equations" only insofar as they help to explicate the hidden significances of the ritual.

The Upaniṣads breathe the air of the real world, or at least the real world of metaphysicians; the Brāhmaṇas operate in what Oldenberg called "a sphere of strangest activity and the playground of a subtle empty mummery":

> It has been fatal for all thought and poetry in India that a second world, filled with strangely fantastic shapes, was established at an early day beside the real world. This was the place of the sacrifice with its three sacred fires and the schools in which the virtuosos of the sacrificial art were

18. J. A. B. van Buitenen, "A Brief History of the Literatures of South Asia," in Edward C. Dimock et al., eds., *The Literatures of India: An Introduction* (Chicago: University of Chicago Press, 1974), p. 15. See also Renou's statement that "Vedic religion is first and foremost a liturgy." *Religions of Ancient India,* p. 29.

19. Fritz Staal, "Ritual Syntax," in M. Nagatomi et al., eds., *Sanskrit and Indian Studies in Honor of Ingalls* (Dordrecht, Neth.: D. Reidel, 1979), p. 122.

educated—a sphere of strangest activity and the playground of a subtle empty mummery, whose enervating power over the spirit of an entire nation we can scarcely comprehend in its full extent.[20]

Not only, then, were homologies said to have been mistakenly postulated and haphazardly formulated; what is worse is that the equations served as the basis of action. The identities were *manipulated* in order to effect a change on the entities, actions, or objects that had been put into such a relation. The bizarre imagination of the Vedic priests was quite overactive, and the rituals in which such a "strange activity" occurred are thus sometimes called magical.

Caught in a paradox equal to any we claim to see in "prelogical" peoples, scholars can thus simultaneously argue that the equivalences drawn in the Brāhmaṇas were both random and ruled. For inasmuch as *magic* means anything as a classificatory term, it generally creates a class of rituals performed out of the supposed belief that action within the ritual has an effect on the world because of certain "laws"—for example the "law of similarity" whereby like produces or acts on like, or the "law of contiguity" whereby action on the part produces an effect on the whole.[21] "Magic gives every outward appearance of being a gigantic variation on the theme of the principle of causality," wrote Marcel Mauss; its "exclusive aim, apparently, is to produce results."[22] Magic, then, is a type of ritual that presumes to cause an effect on y through the ruled actions performed on x, under the basic assumption that x and y are or can be essentially related because of certain universal "natural laws." For this reason, Vedic ritual can be called alternately magic or a kind of science.

Rather than seriously address the intricacies of Vedic "magic," however, most scholars have been content to envision it as the other side of the coin of the absurdity of Vedic connections. *Magic,* as a label, has rarely been applied to systems of belief and practice other than pejoratively, and this is at least in part because here, as with the Vedic identifications, the scholars is faced with what seems to be a confusion between the symbol (x) and what is symbolized (y). As John Skorupski observes,

20. Hermann Oldenberg, *Ancient India: Its Language and Religions,* 2d ed., (Calcutta: Punthi Pustak, 1962), pp. 21–22.

21. See Marcel Mauss, *A General Theory of Magic,* trans. by Robert Brain (New York: W. W. Norton, 1972), esp. pp. 63–74. For another classical analysis of the logic and coherence of magic, see E. E. Evans-Pritchard, *Witchcraft, Oracles and Magic among the Azande* (Oxford: Clarendon Press, 1937).

22. Mauss, *A General Theory of Magic,* p. 63.

> What is for *us* in the end most striking about magical practices is that they require assumptions which in one way or another run counter to the categorical framework within which we (at least officially) interpret the world: as with the notion of a real identity between symbol and thing symbolized. . . . In this lies their interest, and the strangeness which is from our point of view their common characteristic.[23]

To speak, then, of magical equations in Vedic ritual and philosophy, is at the very least to indicate their utter foreignness and *difference*. Even recent, sophisticated, and sympathetic treatments of Vedic ritualism are mitigated in their value when they resort to these assumptions and nomenclature. Thus, when Asko Parpola speaks of "magical equations, which are the most characteristic feature of the Brāhmaṇa texts" and which are "exploited" or "manipulated" within the ritual to give priests "control" over phenomena,[24] or when Michael Witzel asserts that "magical identifications" are meant as "a full equation of both entities and not to a mere similarity of both,"[25] it is the *problematic* nature of Vedic "magic" that is being emphasized.

Magic—as a categorical term—has also functioned in Indological discourse to imply that one should distinguish Vedism from proper religion. Sylvain Lévi, whose book *La Doctrine du sacrifice dans les Brāhmaṇas* has remained the standard for nearly a century, referred to the Vedic sacrifice as "a magical operation" complemented by a "brutal" and "material" theology. "Morality," wrote Lévi, "had no place in the system: the sacrifice which ruled the relations between men and gods is a mechanic operation which acts by its own energy."[26] By presenting Vedic ritualism as without morality, without real theology, indepen-

23. John Skorupski, *Symbol and Theory: A Philosophical Study of Theories of Religion in Social Anthropology* (Cambridge: Cambridge University Press, 1976), p. 159.

24. Also Parpola, "On the Symbol Concept of the Vedic Ritualists," in H. Biezais, ed., *Religious Symbols and Their Functions* (Stockholm: Almquist and Widsell, 1979), esp. p. 140.

25. Michael Witzel, "On Magical Thought in the Veda," lecture published by Universitaire Pers Leiden, 1979, esp. pp. 5, 10, 12. Witzel's article, valuable as it is as an analysis of Vedic connections, is at its best when it addresses the comparative questions, e.g., p. 12: "This way of thinking, strange as it may seem, is by no means foreign to present day Western man."

26. Lévi, *La Doctrine du sacrifice dans les Brāhmaṇas,* p. 9. See also p. 129: "The sacrifice has thus all the characteristics of a magical operation. It is independent of deities, effective through its own energy and susceptible to producing evil as well as good. It can be only slightly distinguished from magic proper by its regular and obligatory character; it is easy to direct it toward diverse goals, but it exists and imposes itself independently of circumstances."

dently or automatically operating apart from either gods or humans, Lévi succeeded in persuading many of his heirs that Vedism was magical: both strange and not deserving of the name *religion*.

One way, then, that Vedic ritualism (as a kind of definitional rubric) has been simultaneously depicted and (intentionally or not) deprecated was to use *magic* as a synonym for *ritual*—to highlight either its epistemological eccentricity or its spiritual insolvency. Recently, a new version (albeit with innovative twists) of this same project has been envisioned or, rather, *devised*.

The Meaningless Theory

Over the past several years—in a series of articles and published lectures, culminating in the mammoth *Agni: The Vedic Ritual of the Fire Altar*[27]—Frits Staal has put forth a representation of Vedic ritualism which functions as the cornerstone of his new general theory of ritual. Dismissing all previous and competing theories, Staal argues that ritual "has no meaning, goal, or aim" and is best described as "pure activity."[28] Ritual is neither symbolic nor meaningful activity but rather is purposeless and meaningless: "To say that ritual is done for its own sake is to say that it is meaningless, without function, aim or goal, or also that it constitutes its own aim or goal."[29]

This remarkable thesis is supported solely by the Vedic exemplum; here, apparently, Staal finds all the evidence he needs to reconstitute the "meaning" of the general category of ritual, for no other examples are anywhere given. He cannot make even the Vedic ritual "meaningless," however, without considerable methodological acrobatics.

At some points in his work, Staal asks us to imagine that meaningless (purposeless, useless) ritual is the historical result of the obsolescence of once meaningful activities.[30] In the case of Vedism, formerly purposeful activities such as battles, cattle raids, and their supporting

27. My review of this work and an extended version of the critique that follows here may be found in "Vedic Fieldwork," *Religious Studies Review* 11 (April 1985): 136–45.

28. Staal, "The Meaninglessness of Ritual," pp. 8–9.

29. Ibid., p. 9.

30. "Typically human forms of ritualization seem in general to dissolve meaning, not replace it." Ibid., p. 13. For Staal's speculations on the origin of rituals connected to the maintenance of fire ("The carrying around of fire became a ritual activity as soon as it was no longer necessary, viz., as soon as methods for kindling fire had been discovered"), see Staal, *Agni,* I: 84, 102.

acts (songs, recitations, and rituals) became meaningless as the ancient Vedic militaristic adventurers parked their chariots and made themselves at home in India:

> When the nomads began to settle in the subcontinent and established lasting relationships with the indigenous inhabitants, the expeditions receded to the background and the accompanying activities lost their accompanying functions. . . . Thus ritual was the sole survivor and all other activities were ritualized. . . . Rituals tend to absorb everything that has gone before and has lost its original function.[31]

Staal does not allow for the possibility that "obsolete" activities acquire *new* meanings over time by being ritualized, but he concludes that by losing their original meanings the activities must carry *no* meaning for those who have ritualized them.[32]

In the Vedic instance, however, there is a major obstacle to such an explication: the Brāhmaṇas, texts (late in Staal's scheme of things) that have as their very purpose the explanation of the meanings of the "purposeless" activities of the ritual. Faced with these texts, Staal reverses his quasi-historical argument. Instead of claiming that a meaningless ritual arose from formerly meaningful activity, the theorist now (or in addition) wants to say that originally pure and meaningless activity is over time encrusted with meaning:

> Much later, when ritual was contrasted with ordinary, everyday activity, its meaninglessness became patent and various rationalizations and explanations were constructed. Ritual became deeply involved with religion, which always stands in need of the mysterious and unexplained. . . . In the course of time rituals, instead of remaining useless and pure, became useful and meritorious.[33]

Further, the "rationalizations" one finds in abundance in the Brāhmaṇas are explained away, in time-honored Indological terms, as arbitrary, contradictory, and, once again, "fanciful."[34] These subsequently canonical Vedic texts mostly provide "piecemeal interpretations," and when they attempt "large-scale interpretations of ritual . . . these can often be shown to be failures."[35] Although the route taken is different, the end is

31. Staal, *Agni,* I: 102–3.
32. For further remarks on this methodological error, see Chapter 8 herein.
33. Staal, "The Meaninglessness of Ritual," p. 14.
34. Ibid., p. 4; Staal, *Agni,* I: 27–28, 67–68; idem, *The Science of Ritual,* pp. 11–12, 36.
35. Staal, *Agni,* I: 63; Idem, *The Science of Ritual,* p. 33.

the same: the Brāhmaṇas are castigated and the Vedic ritual shown to be, by normal standards, absurd.

Another version of the "meaninglessness of ritual" school of Vedic studies has been somewhat more persuasively propounded by J. C. Heesterman.[36] Heesterman posits a period before the Veda received its final redaction; behind the received texts, in the shadows of classical Vedism, is a "preclassical" age. The pattern of life established by the earliest Indo-European invaders of Northwest India was one of alternation between settled agriculturalist existence and raids on the fields and property of the peoples to the east in the lean season when the home crops lay dormant. The preclassical Vedic Indians in this way ricocheted between their settlements (the *grāma*) and the eastern wilds (the *araṇya*), and between the roles of householder (*śālīna*) and wanderer (*yāyāvara*), the domesticated man-in-society and the raiding warrior.

This cycle, Heesterman argues, also describes the structure of the preclassical sacrifice, as the munificent sacrificial patron—the *yajamāna* who gives gifts to his guests and sacrificial oblations to the gods—alternatively becomes a consecrated warrior—the *dīkṣita* who recoups his wealth in raids, contests, and battles. The sacrifice, the pivot of the cycle, climaxes with the slaughter of an animal, a communal banquet, and a distribution of gifts and prizes—an event equated with the rebirth of the sacrificer as he sheds onto his guests and rivals the impurity accrued by his engagement in violence and his responsibility for killing. The sacrificer, however, is then left emptied of material goods, which must be reacquired through violent confrontations and attendance at sacrificial contests sponsored by others. The cycle of stifling and dangerous interdependence and alternation repeats itself endlessly.

The "inner conflict" of the preclassical system is finally reducible to the problematics of killing and violence. There was, on the one hand, the necessary nastiness of the warrior's life—raiding and battling in the wilds because, in a "world of scarcity," the home-grown yield had to be supplemented. On the other hand, there was the violence and killing connected with the other half of the cycle, the offering of the sacrifice by the engorged patron. The sacrifice was the site of contests for the "goods of life"; Heesterman goes so far as to say that the place of sacrifice was originally a battleground where one fought for fire, food, and cattle: "Such fights may have been prearranged,

36. See esp. the essays collected in J. C. Heesterman, *The Inner Conflict of Tradition*. For a more developed description and critique of what follows, see my "Ideals and Realities in Indian Religion."

ceremonial, and conventional, but they were none the less violent because of it."[37] Furthermore, the preclassical sacrifice culminated in the violent death of the sacrificial victim. Thus, together with the uncertainties and dangers of reciprocity, cyclical exchanges, and violent encounters and contestations, the preclassical sacrifice held within it an insoluble paradox: "The life-giving ritual is intimately connected with life's opposite, with death and destruction."[38]

Having in this way reconstructed both the socioeconomic conditions and the religious practices of a preclassical age, Heesterman then presumes a radical reformation, an "axial breakthrough." The author occasionally hints that the revolution may have been stimulated by changing patterns of population distribution and economic advancement,[39] but his more fundamental assumption is that the transformation of the tradition was "orthogenetic," propelled by the tensions inherent in the preclassical pattern outlined above. In any event, Heesterman maintains that the transformation was sudden and studied; it was not "a gradual and cumulative process of erosion but a conscious reform."[40]

The reformation of the preclassical sacrifice was achieved by cutting up the cyclical paradigm and reorganizing the ritual in a linear fashion. In place of endlessly alternating phases, the ritual was made to have a clearly delineated beginning and end. This simultaneously eliminated the dependence on the participation of the rival/guest and the necessity for exchange and reciprocity. The place of the rival/guest was taken over by a fixed priesthood which was assimilated to the sacrificer in an overall attempt to unify the ritual, and the system of exchange was replaced by the belief in the automatic efficacy of the ritual itself.

The secret means the ritualistics developed to effect this revolution was the system of connections (*bandhu*s) which brought to an end the dependence on the other, the uncertainties of the sacrifice, and the violence and death that were at its center. What was once a sacrificial battleground "has been turned into a serene and perfectly ordered ritual emplacement."[41] Violence and death, the paradoxical centerpieces of the preclassical sacrifice, were exorcised, and the problematics of killing gave way to an obsessive concern for ritual exactitude and the fear of

37. J. C. Heesterman, "Other Folks' Fire," in Staal, *Agni,* II: 85. See also idem, "The Ritualist's Problem," in S. D. Joshi, ed., *Amṛtadhārā: Professor R. N. Dandekar Felicitation Volume* (Delhi: Ajanta Books, 1984), p. 172.

38. Heesterman, *The Inner Conflict of Tradition,* p. 68.

39. See ibid., pp. 106, 124–25.

40. Ibid., p. 91.

41. Ibid., p. 101.

error: "Uncertainty and catastrophe were replaced by the fail-safe certainty of ritualism."[42]

But competition, conflict, violence, and the strains of mutual dependence—that is, the realities of living in society—could not be eradicated, and indeed the reformation did not aim at doing so. They could, however, be stripped of religious meaning and legitimacy. The axial breakthrough "denied conflict its ultimate legitimacy. Instead it posited the ideal of an absolute transcendent order that is, as a matter of principle, incapable of worldly realization."[43] A transcendent ritual of the Brahmin was created out of the deconstructed elements of the warrior's sacrifice.

This historical narrative of the transition from preclassical to classical India implies a general theory of sacrifice and ritual. And there is,' Heesterman claims, a critical difference between the two. *Sacrifice* refers to rites in which offerings and exchanges are accompanied by violent death in an atmosphere of uncertainty, risk, and "controlled catastrophe." *Ritual* is, in many ways, the opposite of sacrifice.

The destruction of part or all of the oblation to the gods sets sacrifice apart from gift-giving transactions. Sacrifice is defined by Heesterman by its violent center, by its concern with the harsh realities of life and death: "Its primary material is what sustains life, that is: food. But food—its acquisition, preparation and consumption—equally involves death. Part of the food, therefore, even if it is only an infinitely small part, has to be destroyed."[44] As an exercise in "controlled catastrophe" with uncertain results—"It ends either in success or in failure, in triumphantly enriched life or in loss and death"[45]—sacrifice is not orderly and ritualistic. Because sacrifice "turns on destructive violence" it "overthrows order."[46]

With this emphasis on the violence of sacrifice, Heesterman joins recent theorists such as Walter Burkert and René Girard, who have also pinpointed the act of killing as the meaningful core of the sacrificial ritual.[47] Heesterman stands apart from both these other theorists, how-

42. Ibid., p. 91.

43. Ibid., p. 157.

44. J. C. Heesterman, "Veda and Society: Some Remarks apropos of the Film 'Altar of Fire,' " in Asko Parpola, ed., *Proceedings of the Nordic South Asia Conference, June 10–12, 1980* (Helsinki: Studia Orientalia, 1981), p. 55.

45. Heesterman, *The Inner Conflict of Tradition,* pp. 84–85.

46. Heesterman, "The Ritualist's Problem," p. 168.

47. Walter Burkert, *Homo Necans: The Anthropology of Ancient Greek Sacrificial Ritual and Myth,* trans. by Peter Bing (Berkeley: University of California Press, 1983);

ever, in his refusal to burden the act of sacrificial killing with either symbolic or emotional meaning. It is purely the actual and actualized logical conundrum and social problem of the necessity of death for the continuation of life that Heesterman posits as the mysterious heart of sacrificial darkness.

The systematized, individualized, sanitized, and idealized ritual codified in the ancient Vedic texts is radically different from *sacrifice* defined in such a way. Whereas sacrifice is depicted as "popular or organicist," ritual is described as "systematized or mechanistic." The ritualism exemplified in the Vedic texts, in Heesterman's opinion, is characterized by its lack of risk and uncertainty—that is, by its intentional and complete divergence from reality. Whereas sacrifice is "tied up with the life of the community in a comprehensive, many-stranded web of meaning," the Vedic ritual "is simply separate, unrelated to anything outside itself."[48] Ritual is an ersatz world of perfection, free from contingencies, closed and controllable.

The invention of a transcendent ritual was intended to carve out a place where human beings could become emancipated from the human condition, from reality and its insoluble paradoxes. The price paid, however, for the perfection of the ritual order was its complete divorce from the world. Perfection could "only be realized outside society and for the limited duration of the ritual."[49] The movement from sacrifice to ritual is, in sum, a movement from problematic reality to imaginary ideals. But by virtue of its transcendence of reality—that is, by virtue of its irrelevance to the world—the ritual has also been rendered meaningless: "It is a closed system that has meaning only in itself, in its own inner order—an order that is as strict as it is artificial. In this sense one may agree with Professor Staal's thesis of the meaninglessness of ritual."[50]

It is quite clear that, for all of Heesterman's argumentation and marshalling of evidence, the preclassical age of Indian history is the

René Girard, *Violence and the Sacred* (Baltimore: Johns Hopkins University Press, 1977). Briefly and oversimply, Girard argues that violence endemic to human society is displaced finally onto the sacrificial victim through a complicated series of substitutions (see Chapter 7 herein). Burkert sees sacrificial killing as a dramatization of the hunt and, eventually, of social survival in general. Consult also the recently published transcription of a symposium on the subject of sacrifice and violence, Robert G. Hamerton-Kelly, ed., *Violent Origins: Walter Burkert, René Girard, and Jonathan Z. Smith on Ritual Killing and Cultural Formation* (Stanford: Stanford University Press, 1987).

48. Heesterman, "Veda and Society," p. 54.

49. Heesterman, *The Inner Conflict of Tradition,* p. 101.

50. Heesterman, "The Ritualist's Problem," p. 175.

scholar's imaginative construct, as is the axial breakthrough on which Heesterman pins so much. Why the ritualists who so carefully put together a "classical" Vedic ritual would "be concerned with the preservation of obsolete diverging traditions . . . even at the price of contradicting the laboriously developed system"[51] is not at all obvious and in fact runs counter to the author's assumption that the ritualists consciously and systematically obliterated the preclassical pattern in the process of reinventing the sacrifice. Positing a preclassical age and an axial breakthrough serves primarily to establish an absolute distinction between a romanticized sacrifice and a meaningless ritual.

Sacrifice for Heesterman appears to be simultaneously realistic and chaotic. Sacrifice simply enacts a real struggle for incompatible goals: the goods of life, won by violence which entails impurity and evil; and religious purity which is gained at the expense of disastrous material dissipation. On the other hand, the success of the sacrifice is entirely unpredictable and wholly dependent on the cooperation of others, especially on their willingness to reciprocate—just like action in the real world. This vision of sacrifice, like that of the preclassical age as a whole, is an idealized scenario of primordial reality before the invention and implementation of ideals, before culture and its symbols (including symbolic actions such as rituals) were overlaid upon—or set next to—raw human life.

On the other side of the divide, Heesterman's ritual—meaningless, transcendent, ideal, and perfect—is also a creation beyond discussion, beyond disputation, and beyond interpretation. Indeed, discussion, disputation, and interpretation, according to Heesterman, are precisely what the Vedic ritual seeks to eliminate. This may or may not be true for the Vedic ritualists (and the point is arguable), but it is disingenuous for historians of religion to reposition such notions as scholarly conclusions. Moreover, Heesterman is not in fact simply transcribing native assumptions. It may not be too arcane to suggest that any thesis for the meaninglessness of any human creation is a meaningful interpretation of what is regarded as a previously improperly understood phenomenon—and thus is itself a paradox that cries for a solution.[52]

Heesterman does avoid some of the problems of more doctrinaire versions of the "meaninglessness of ritual" theory. Heesterman notes, as others of the school do not, that the Vedic ritualists—with their "science" of rules and controlled actions—could not succeed in their quest for per-

51. J. C. Heesterman, "Vrātya and Sacrifice," *Indo-Iranian Journal* 6 (1962): 3.
52. I return to this point in more detail in Chapter 8.

fection and exactitude.[53] Ritual, no less than human life outside its confines, is a product of fallible beings who cannot escape their nature, who cannot transcend the human condition, who cannot realize their ideals: "We find that Vedic ritual in fact undermines its own claim to be the absolute universal order. In the first place, one can, of course, never be completely sure that one has not unwittingly committed an error in the ritual proceedings, which, if unrepaired, will irretrievably impair the ritual order. Thus there is always an element of uncertainty."[54]

Indeed there is, and contemporary theorists of ritual sometimes ignore what the ritualists knew all too well. Ritual cannot be an idealized zone in which perfection is possible, for this sphere of activity, like all others, cannot be totally regulated and controlled—as we shall have occasion to observe in Chapter 4. The history of Vedic ritualism—a history too often left untraced by those with other axes to grind—is partly impelled by the fact that, even in ritual, perfection is impossible in this life. Ritual manuals or *prayoga*s, which attempt with ever increasing specificity to account for all eventualities, for all the minute detail of performing the ritual, were continuously produced through the millennia right up to the present. The enterprise is doomed to failure—there are too many possible contingencies to address, too many details to bring under control—but the tragically heroic attempt is one underexposed aspect of the destiny of the Vedic sacrifice in Indian history.

The second major criterion for constituting *a* Vedism, then—and really one that is complementary to the first—is its distinctive overriding concern with its particular system of ritual practice and ideology. But, again, as with the closely related first criterion (epistemological homologies), ritualism is made a definitional feature of Vedism in order to evaluate it and, most often, to devaluate it. It is represented in Indological discourse as the magical practices of different minds, the coercive spells of those without true religion, the pure activity of those who can do things without thought, or the realm of an artificial perfection created by those who have left reality altogether. The overactive Vedic imagina-

53. One might contrast this observation with Jonathan Z. Smith's notion that "ritual represents the creation of a controlled environment where the variables (i.e., the accidents) of ordinary life may be displaced precisely because they are felt to be so overwhelmingly present and powerful. Ritual is a means of performing the way things ought to be in conscious tension to the way things are in such a way that this ritualized perfection is recollected in the ordinary, uncontrolled, course of things." "The Bare Facts of Ritual" in *Imagining Religion,* p. 63.

54. Heesterman, *The Inner Conflict of Tradition,* p. 88.

tion engenders, as Oldenberg wrote, "a second world" in which occurs "a subtle empty mummery"; or, as Lévi insisted, an amoral machine; or, as Staal and Heesterman would have it, a world of meaningless activity, occasionally overlaid with "fanciful" native exegesis. Again, we must ask, Whose imagination is it that is really overactive? Whose ritual—and theory of ritual—is really meaningless to whom?

Rethinking Vedism

Any attempt to reimagine Vedism more valuably—and more realistically in light of the importance of the Vedas to the Hindu religion—must begin with the reexamination of these two definitional data: epistemological connections and ritualism. The two are interlinked. Problematic representations of Vedic ritualism often appear to be caused in large part by assumptions or conclusions about Vedic homological thinking, and vice versa.

In following chapters, I will show that Vedic "equations" are neither absurd nor random but are rather systematic expressions made possible (and logical) by fundamental Vedic principles of metaphysics and epistemology—of how the world is and how humans know and represent their knowledge. I will also reevaluate the place of ritualism in Vedic religion. I will argue that ritual action was presented in Vedic texts not as symbolic or dramatic playacting, magical hocus-pocus, or "pure," transcendent, or meaningless activity. Rather, the sacrifice was displayed as a *constructive* activity, creating the human being (ontology), the afterlife (soteriology), and the cosmos as a whole (cosmology). It was also, of course, a social instrument—constructing individuals as part of a class and defining both the classified individual and the classes themselves from within the universe of the ritual. In sum, I will maintain that Vedism was a coherent and comprehensive system of doctrine and practice.

Vedic philosophy turns on the assumption that it is possible to correlate corresponding elements lying on three discrete planes of reality: the macrocosmos (whose contents and forces are collectively called *adhidevatā,* "relating to the godly") the ritual sphere (*adhiyajña,* "relating to the sacrifice"), and the microcosmos (*adhyātman,* "relating to the self"). And, as Jean Filliozat, among others, has observed, connections made and found among the cosmos, ritual, and self were not designed solely to reduce these levels to any one, nor were they simple metaphors. Such homologies were to express metaphysical truth and to make all three levels mutually explicative.[55]

Furthermore, the credibility of the Indological notion that these connections were random and whimsical has recently received a blow in the form of a detailed study of one text by Klaus Mylius. Limiting himself to a thorough analysis of the Kauṣītakī Brāhmaṇa, Mylius has shown the homologies posed in that text to be consistent, principled, and interlocking.[56]

What remains largely undone is the full articulation of principles that guided Vedic connections; the revelation of the scope, variety, and nuances and practice that were made possible assuming those principles; and the drawing out of the implications for our knowledge of both Vedism and the later Indic religions that regard themselves as perpetuating it.

I would suggest here, and will be at pains to prove throughout the remainder of this study, that there is a philosophical center around which all Vedic thought resolves. That center I will call resemblance. Although Vedic writers do not utilize a Sanskrit word that adequately translates as "resemblance" until the time of the composition of the ritual Sūtras (*sāmānya;* see Chapters 5 and 7 herein), the *concept,* I believe, underlies Vedic religious and philosophical discourse in its entirety. Vedic resemblance is, in sum, not unlike what Michel Foucault has called an "episteme," a central principle or rule that generates and governs knowledge of all sorts.

Universal resemblance, whereby entities, things, forces, activities, cosmic planes—indeed, all the components of the universe as a whole—have essential affinities to related others, helps us to reform our understanding of the Vedic preoccupation with making and finding connections. I will maintain that to call these connections or *bandhu*s equations or equivalences is to mistake the relation of *resemblance* for a relation of *identity* (which Vedic thought, no less than modern scholarly thought, usually found abhorrent, although perhaps for somewhat different reasons).

Further, Vedic resemblance, as an epistemological, metaphysical,

55. Jean Filliozat, "La Force organique et la force cosmique dans la philosophie médicale de l'Inde et dans le Véda," *Revue philosophique* 116 (1933): 410–29.

56. Klaus Mylius, "Die vedischen Identifikationen am Beispiel des *Kauṣītakī-Brāhmaṇa,*" *Klio* 58 (1976): 145–66; and idem, "Die Identifikationen im *Kauṣītakī-Brāhmaṇa,*" *Altorientalische Forschungen* 5 (1977): 237–44.

and ontological principle, itself resembles "epistemes" well known in the history of Western thought.[57] Although the Vedic version of resemblance is distinctive in ways to be discussed shortly, it is not a bizarre, incomprehensible bit of exotica; it is, rather, an ancient Indian example of a well-known phenomenon in the history of forms of knowing, saying, and acting.

This Vedic principle, again not unlike comparable systems centering on resemblance elsewhere, operates within and is modified by hierarchy. The hierarchical nature of Vedism is only recently becoming clearly visible and articulated in Indological discourse—one of the many wakes created by Louis Dumont's already classic work, *Homo Hierarchicus*.[58] Dumont argues that the Hindu caste system is made possible by a body of assumed ideas and values, an ideology of holism, interdependence, and hierarchy. Furthermore, Dumont claims, a single principle governs the hierarchically ordered caste structure and ideology: the principle of relative purity based on the opposition between the pure (represented by the Brahmins) and the impure (represented by the Untouchables). Castes are ranked according to their relative purity and impurity—that is, how closely they *resemble* the Brahmins on the one hand and the Untouchables on the other. Finally, in this hierarchical system, the higher castes are said to "encompass" those lower. Although Dumont does not fully work this out, what seems to be implied here is an ontology of "relative completeness," the Brahmin being the "more complete" instance of the human being while others, relative to the Brahmin, are "less complete."

Dumont did not apply his insights into the hierarchical nature of Hindu caste—and Hinduism as a whole—to the pre-Hindu Vedic religion. It is clear that Dumont's formulation must be adjusted to the rather different circumstances of Vedism ("purity" and "impurity," for example, are certainly present but far less central), but it is also increasingly obvious that Vedism, no less than Hinduism, is organized hierarchically.

One step toward reenvisioning Vedism as systematically ordered on

57. A partial bibliography of resemblance in Western epistemology would include Michel Foucault, *The Order of Things: An Archeology of the Human Sciences,* trans. of *Les Mots et les choses,* (New York: Vintage Books, 1973); Arthur Lovejoy, *The Great Chain of Being: A Study of the History of an Idea* (Cambridge, Mass.: Harvard University Press, 1936) Ralph Withington Church, *An Analysis of Resemblance* (London: George Allen and Unwin, 1952); and Panayot Butchvarov, *Resemblance and Identity: An Examination of the Problem of Universals* (Bloomington: Indiana University Press, 1966).

58. Louis Dumont, *Homo Hierarchicus: The Caste System and Its Implications,* trans. by Mark Sainsbury et al. (Chicago: University of Chicago Press, 1980).

a hierarchical basis has been taken by Frits Staal, who has demonstrated the hierarchical nature of the Vedic repertoire of rituals. Concentrating on the "syntax" and denying any "semantics" (rituals, it will be recalled, are for him meaningless), Staal rightly insists that "We must start with the observation that the *śrauta* rituals constitute a hierarchy."[59] The ritual system forms a continuum or sequence, beginning with the most simple and ending with the most complex. And, Staal hints (but does not further explicate), there is a correlated hierarchical order of ritualists based on relative competency and experience:

> This sequence [of the ritual order] is not arbitrary. There is increasing complexity. A person is in general only eligible to perform a later ritual in the sequence, if he has already performed the earlier ones. Each later ritual presupposes the former and incorporates one or more occurrences of one or more of the former rituals. Sometimes these embedded rituals are abbreviated. In general, they undergo modifications.[60]

Staal argues here, in ways highly reminiscent of some of Dumont's points regarding the caste hierarchy, that the ritual system is ordered on the basis of relative complexity of form and relative inclusivity of structure—that is, on the basis of what I have called relative completion. Hierarchically superior rituals are those that incorporate within themselves a number of inferior rituals, recapitulated in the ritual in representative, albeit abbreviated and condensed, forms. The Vedic ritual hierarchy, as in the caste hierarchy as explained by Dumont, operates on the basis of the encompassment of the inferior (the "embedded" rituals) by the superior and more complete on a scale of mutually *resembling* elements.

This is an important beginning, but it is only a beginning. Hierarchical resemblance is a principle with far more hermeneutical possibilities for the study of Vedism—and, I might add, for the study of Hinduism as well—than have yet been realized. Furthermore, the importance of ritual practice has not yet been integrated into this developing picture of Vedism. The questions that will guide us in our rethinking of Vedism are: how might the concept of hierarchical resemblance help us to reimagine the religion in its entirety, and why did ritual activity so preoccupy the authors of the Vedic texts?

59. Staal, "The Meaninglessness of Ritual," p. 15.
60. Staal, "Ritual Syntax," p. 125.

3

Ritual and Reality

Natural Chaos and Ritual Order

Reality, according to the Vedic savants, is not given but made. These early philosophers of the sacrifice were ritualists through and through. Their texts convey the sensibilities of those who endowed their intricate ceremonial with enormous importance. Sacrifice, for them, was not primarily on honorific gift-giving exchange between gods and humans. Neither was it regarded as a symbolic representation of an already concretized reality. The Brahmin ritualists themselves certainly did not understand the sacrifice to be meaningless activity done for its own sake or as a ritualized realm of antireality. Rather, the ritual was the workshop in which all reality was forged.

This study of Vedic ritualism and the principle of resemblance that guides its operation and organization is premised on the recognition of a fundamental Vedic assumption: what is natural is inherently defective; or, as Lilian Silburn has put it in her invaluable study, what is "immédiatement donné est discontinu et qu'il n'est d'autre continu que du structuré."[1] From this perspective, the natural is the chaotic, the disorganized, the unformed. In cosmological terms, what is merely procreated by the creator god is not a cosmos or a universal whole made up of ordered parts. The origins of true cosmos are found not in this primary generative act but rather in a secondary operation—a ritual act that lends structure and order to a chaotic creation.

Mircea Eliade tirelessly argued that "every creation has a paradig-

1. Silburn, *Instant et cause,* p. 1.

matic model—the creation of the universe by the gods."[2] but the Vedic instance seems to elude the archetypical by posing a radical disjuncture between divine creation and sacred cosmos. In the beginning, the creative act of "emission" by the Lord of Creatures, Prajāpati, is not a cosmogonic paradigm of sacred order but rather what Silburn rightly calls a "profane act."[3] Put otherwise, cosmic procreation, in the imaginations of the Brahmins, does not engender a ready-made universal order but results in a problematic metaphysical excess. Similarly (as will be detailed in the next chapter), at the level of individual human beginnings, birth and anthropogony are distinct and separate moments, the first being only the necessary precondition for the second. As cosmic creation is not cosmogony, biological reproduction is not the production of a true human being.

It is characteristic—and perhaps also close to definitive—of Vedism that between mere procreation one the one hand and true cosmogony and anthropogony on the other is inserted a set of constructive rituals. Between Prajāpati's creation and the origin of the cosmos are sacrificial acts of the gods, giving form to formless nature. And between the procreation of every person and the origin of true being are also rituals, making a human out of the human in potens only. Cosmogony and anthropogony in Vedic ritualism are *actualized* only within the sacrifice and *realized* only by ritual labor or *karman*.

For the Vedic priests and metaphysicians, ritual activity does not "symbolize" or "dramatize" reality; it constructs, integrates, and constitutes the real. Ritual forms the naturally formless, it connects the inherently disconnected, and it heals the ontological disease of unreconstructed nature, the state toward which all created things and beings perpetually tend.

All viable forms, all properly structured beings, are found only in the ontological space between what Jean-Marie Verpoorten has called "two symmetrical excesses."[4] The first is denoted in Vedic texts with the word *jāmi*, describing the unproductive condition of homogeneity or redundancy—an excess of resemblance.[5] The term is applied to

2. Mircea Eliade, *The Sacred and Profane*, trans. by Willard Trask (New York: Harcourt, Brace and World, 1959), p. 31.

3. Silburn, *Instant et cause*, p. 54.

4. Jean-Marie Verpoorten, "Unité et distinction dans les spéculations rituelles védique," *Archiv für Begriffsgeschichte* 21 (1977): 59–85.

5. For a study of a similar, but not identical, Vedic concept—*atirikta* ("superfluous" or "redundant")—see Jan Gonda, "The Redundant and the Deficient in Vedic Ritual." *Vishveshvaranand Indological Journal* 21 (June–December 1983): 1–34.

various but comparable situations. In the ritual vocabulary, *jāmi* designates rites that are fruitlessly reduplicative within a ritual sequence: "There is *jāmi* in the sacrifice when on the same day he employs the same verses as offering verses. Even if there are many wives, as it were, one husband is [necessary for forming] a proper pair with them."[6] The word also appears in Vedic kinship terminology to describe those who are closely related to oneself to marry. A. C. Banerjea concludes a study of the term by noting that *jāmi* "in all probability is a common designation for the members of a non-marriageable group, and as such non-approachable by those who abided by the exogamous system."[7] Here again, *jāmi* connotes the excess resemblance or lack of sufficient differentiation between two or more entities and the attending unproductive nature of the relation. Yet another application of the term is found in the Jaiminīya Brāhmaṇa, in which the undifferentiated and sterile quality of *jāmi* is likened to homosexual union, the barren joining of those too alike:

> An improper pairing and unproductive is *jāmi,* as is the fruitless coupling of two men or two women. . . . That, on the other hand, which is not *jāmi* is a productive and proper pairing. . . . What is uniform [*ekarūpa*] is incapable of copulation and is unproductive.[8]

If fecundity requires a mitigation of excessive resemblance or uniformity, it is also possible only if separate elements are capable of joining with others. Complementary to, and the inverse of, the nonontological state of *jāmi* is that of total distinction, isolation, and utter separation—the excess of differentiation known as *pṛthak.* This and similar terms, such as *bahutva* ("fragmented multiplicity") and *nānātva* ("unrelated variety"), refer to a condition of overdiversification, unconnected dispersion, and atomism which is as inimical to true being as are homogeneity, reduplication, and redundancy. Things and entities must be differentiated in order to avoid the quality of *jāmi,* but they must also be connected to escape the equally dangerous, and ultimately lifeless, condition of *pṛthak.*

6. AitB 3.47, 3.48. For other examples of the ritual employment of the term and concept of *jāmi,* see KB 3.6, 8.8, 13.9, 28.5, 30.11; PB 7.2.5, 8.8.10, 10.4.7, 14.3.17, 16.5.1; ŚB 1.3.2.8, 1.8.1.25, 2.2.3.11, 2.2.3.27, 4.2.2.9, 4.2.3.18, 12.9.3.5; TB 1.8.2.1, 3.3.4.6, 3.4.19.9, 3.7.5.13; and Verpoorten, "Unité et distinction," p. 68. At LŚS 9.11.15, it is called a "fault" (*jāmidoṣa*).

7. A. C. Banerjea, *Studies in the Brāhmaṇas* (Delhi: Motilal Barnarsidass, 1963), p. 31.

8. JB 1.300, 1.330.

In Vedic ritualism, as Silburn observes, "nonbeing is that which is devoid of connection," whereas "being appears to be precisely that which is welded together. . . ."[9] Both *jāmi* and *pṛthak* depict conditions off the ontological scale—symmetrical and opposing states of nonbeing—because they describe situations in which this ontology of composition and connection is impossible. That which is *jāmi* precludes production of true being because there are no sufficiently distinct components to join together; that which is *pṛthak* precludes production because no connections are possible between overly individualized components. All true being locates itself (or, rather, is made and placed) between these twin excesses of identity and isolation. Ontological formation is the result neither of the reduplication of the same nor of the radical differentiation of the dispersed many but is the consequence of the construction of an integrated unity out of distinct but interrelated parts.

This brief overview of the groundwork of Vedic metaphysics and ontology already points to the real logic of the "homological" thinking and the rationale behind the "obsession" with ritual activity so characteristic of the religion. Vedic connections could not have been posed as simple and confused identifications (for here would be the excessive resemblance the Brahmins called *jāmi*), and I have intimated why connections between otherwise unrelated elements must be made (to avoid the excessive differentiation termed *pṛthak*). Further, the critical importance of ritual activity is inexorably bound up with both of these considerations, for it is the ritual labor that effects both separation and unification of parts into wholes.

These points will be further illustrated in the following pages, first in an exposition of the Vedic cosmogonic myths which provide a paradigmatic blueprint of the origins of present metaphysical conditions and the raison d'être for sacrificial action. Next, I will go into some detail on the question of Vedic connections and the forces at work in the universe that counteract disintegration and chaos and make possible linkages between resembling forms and counterforms, prototypes and counterparts. The metaphysics of resemblance, in turn, is the condition of possibility for the efficacy of ritual work. Cosmic prototypes were thought to be manipulated by ritual operations performed on accessible counterparts. Vedic ritualism was directed toward activating the connections that bind the ritual world to the world(s) at large; the ritual order lends its form to a cosmic order, a universal structure emanating from the structured se-

9. Silburn, *Instant et cause,* p. 44.

quence of rites. Such grand results, however, depend on the perfect performance of the ceremonial. In the construction of a ritual production, each detail must be attended to and properly executed. The sacrificial solution to the problem of chaos creates its own set of new problems, turning on the impossible demand the ritualists made of themselves for perfection in their sacrificial creations. For, as we will see in the next chapter, the enterprise which the Vedic ritualists set out on is depicted in their texts as a "dangerous ascension."

Creation Is Not Cosmos

In the post-Ṛgvedic texts, the locus classicus of the developed ritualism typifying Vedism, the function and pride of place of creator gods in the Ṛg Veda Saṃhitā (and, most especially, the god Puruṣa, the sacrificial hero of RV 10.90)[10] is usurped by the deity Prajāpati, Lord of Creatures. Or, rather, the imagery, philosophical speculations, and implications of the mythology of Puruṣa are extended to and developed in the mythology of Prajāpati. There can be no doubt that in the minds of the writers of the later texts the two deities are the same; they are explicitly identified in several places,[11] and the characteristics and functions of Prajāpati are obviously of a piece with those of Puruṣa as he appears in the famous Ṛgvedic hymn.

In the later Saṃhitās and the Brāhmaṇas, Prajāpati is clearly the overarching deity.[12] Vedism traditionally counts thirty-three gods in its

10. For the cosmogonic myths of the ṚV in general, consult W. Norman Brown, "Theories of Creation in the Ṛg Veda," *Journal of the American Oriental Society* 85 (1965): 23–34; idem, "The Creation Myth of the Ṛg Veda," *Journal of the American Oriental Society* 62 (1942): 85–98; and F. B. J. Kuiper, *Ancient Indian Cosmogony* (New Delhi: Vikas, 1983). For a sampling of the vast literature on ṚV 10.90, the primordial and cosmogonic sacrificial dismemberment of Puruṣa, see Paul Mus, "Du Nouveau sur Ṛg Veda 10.90?" in Ernest Bender, ed., *Indological Studies in Honor of W. Norman Brown* (New Haven, Conn.: American Oriental Society, 1962), pp. 165–85; idem, "Ou finit Puruṣa?" in *Mélanges d'Indianisme à la mémoire de Louis Renou* (Paris: E. de Boccard, 1968), pp. 539–63; and W. Norman Brown, "The Sources and Nature of Puruṣa in the Puruṣa Sūkta," *Journal of the American Oriental Society* 51 (1931): 108–18.

11. That same Puruṣa became Prajāpati." ŚB 6.1.1.5. See also ŚB 6.1.1.8, 7.4.1.15, 11.1.6.2; TB 2.2.5.3; and JB 2.47.

12. Recent works on Prajāpati include Jan Gonda, "In the Beginning," *Annals of the Bhandarkar Oriental Research Institute* 63 (1982): 43–62; idem, "The Popular Prajāpati," *History of Religions* 22 (November 1982): 129–49; idem, "Prajāpati and Prāyaścitta," *Journal of the Royal Asiatic Society* (1983): 32–54; idem, "The Creator and His Spirit (Manas and

cosmos; in these texts, Prajāpati is said to be the thirty-fourth and the summation of all the gods.[13] Like Puruṣa, who is "this all," Prajāpati is also described as "all" or *idam sarvam,* the universal whole and totality.[14] He is the Cosmic One, the principle of unity and uniformity (*ekarūpatva*) who is, again like Puruṣa, all-encompassing.[15]

Prajāpati is both space and time in their entirety, in their whole forms. He is "these worlds," and the worlds and the spatial directions (the "quarters") are, in turn, "this all."[16] This deity's completeness and totality are also expressed by identifying him with the year,[17] for the year is also said to be "all" or "this all"[18] and contains within it both the past and the future[19]—which is to say that the "year" is time itself. Or Prajāpati may be equated with the sum of the year's parts: the six seasons, the twelve months, the twenty-four new and full moon half-months, the three hundred sixty days, or the seven hundred twenty days

---

Prajāpati)," *Wiener Zeitschrift für die Kunde Südasiens* 27 (1983): 5–42; idem, *Prajāpati's Rise to Higher Rank* (Leiden: E. J. Brill, 1986); idem, *Prajāpati and the Year* (Amsterdam: North Holland, 1984); J. R. Joshi, "Prajāpati in Vedic Mythology and Ritual," *Annals of the Bhandarkar Oriental Research Institute* 53 (1972): 101–25; R. T. Vyas, "The Concept of Prajāpati in Vedic Literature," *Bhāratīya Vidyā* 38 (1978): 95–101; Santi Banerjee, "Prajāpati in the Brāhmaṇas," *Vishveshvaranand Indological Journal* 19 (June–December 1981): 14–19; and S. Bhattacharji, "Rise of Prajāpati in the Brāhmaṇas," *Annals of the Bhandarkar Oriental Research Institute* 64 (1983): 205–13. See also the somewhat older work by A. W. Macdonald, "A propos de Prajāpati," *Journal asiatique* 240 (1952): 323–38.

13. For Prajāpati as the thirty-fourth god, see ŚB 4.5.7.2, 5.1.2.13; 5.3.4.23; PB 17.11.3, 22.7.5. For the deity as "all the gods," see TB 3.3.7.3, 3.5.9.1; JB 1.342.

14. For Prajāpati as "all" or "this all," ŚB 1.3.5.10, 5.1.1.6, 5.1.3.11, 13.6.1.6; KB 6.15, 25.12; JUB 1.46.2. See also Jan Gonda, "Reflections on *Sarva-* in Vedic Texts," *Indian Linguistics* 16 (November 1955): 53–71; and idem, "All, Universe and Totality in the Śatapatha Brāhmaṇa," *Journal of the Oriental Institute* (*Baroda*) 32, (September–December 1982): 1–7.

15. "O Prajāpati, no one but you encompasses all these creatures." ṚV 10.121.10. See also ŚB 10.4.2.2, 10.4.2.27, 10.4.2.31).

16. ŚB 6.3.1.11, 7.5.1.27, 13.6.1.3. See also ŚB 5.1.3.11.

17. E.g., ŚB 1.6.3.35, 3.2.2.4, 11.1.1.1; PB 16.4.12; JB 1.167. See also Gonda, *Prajāpati and the Year.*

18. ŚB 1.6.1.19, 2.6.3.1, 5.4.5.14, 6.6.4.3, 10.2.5.16, etc. See also the etymological explanation for the year as "all" at ŚB 11.1.6.12: "Prajāpati reflected, 'All (*sarva*) I have obtained by stealth, I who have emitted these deities.' This became *sarvatsara,* for *sarvatsara* is the same name as the year (*saṃvatsara*)." See also 11.1.6.13, where the connection is explained in terms of the fact that Prajāpati and *saṃvatsara* both have four syllables.

19. PB 18.9.7.

and nights.[20] The frequent connection between Prajāpati and the number seventeen[21] is sometimes explained by adding the number of seasons (here reckoned at five; see ŚB 3.9.4.11) and months: "There are twelve months in a year and five seasons. This is the seventeen-fold Prajāpati. Truly Prajāpati is all [*sarva*]."[22]

And if Prajāpati is both the spatial and temporal wholes, these two may also be connected to each other in the logic of resemblance: the year and "these worlds" are images of each other, for either may be regarded as the "all."[23] Space and time are both seventeen-fold, and thus "the year is indeed space" and "everything here, whatever is, is the year."[24] Prajāpati may then also be regarded as twenty-one-fold, encompassing within him the twelve months, five seasons, three worlds, and the sun.[25]

But just as Puruṣa was not restricted to his pantheistic immanence (he is said to be one-quarter here, three-quarters beyond), so too is Prajāpati said to be yet more than the manifest. He is, as we have seen, the thirty-fourth of the thirty-three gods; he is also said to be a fourth "world" over and above the three worlds of heaven, middle space, and earth.[26] He is further imagined as "exorbitant" (*atirikta*),[27] "inexhaustible" (*ayātayāma*),[28] and, by analogy, the seventeen syllables of a certain ritual formula are said to be the inexhaustible portion of the sacrifice.[29] Elsewhere, the deity's transcendence is indicated by describing him as "unlimited" (*aparimita*)[30] or the "unexpressed" or

20. Prajāpati as the six seasons: ŚB 2.2.2.3, 5.2.1.3–4. Twelve months: ŚB 2.2.2.4, 4.6.1.11, 5.2.1.2, 5.4.5.20; JB 1.135. Twenty-four fortnights: ŚB 2.2.2.5, 4.6.1.12, 5.4.5.21; see also KB 6.15. Three hundred sixty days and seven hundred twenty days and nights: ŚB 10.4.2.2.

21. E.g., ŚB 5.2.1.5; 5.3.4.22, 5.4.5.19; PB 2.10.5, 18.6.5, 19.7.6, 20.4.2

22. ŚB 1.3.5.10; see also ŚB 8.4.1.11.

23. ŚB 8.2.1.17, 13.6.1.11.

24. ŚB 8.4.1.11, 12.8.2.36.

25. ŚB 6.2.2.3.

26. ŚB 4.6.1.4.

27. ŚB 11.1.2.5ff; KS 28.9; JB 2.192. See also Gonda, "The Redundant and the Deficient in Vedic Ritual."

28. TS 2.6.3.1.

29. ŚB 12.3.3.1. The formula is the series said by the *adhvaryu* priest at the time of offering: "*o śrāvaya, astu śrauṣaṭ, yaja, ye yajāmahe, vauṣaṭ.*" The text claims, "This is the seventeen-fold Prajāpati."

30. E.g., TS 1.7.3.2, 5.1.8.4; AitB 2.17; KB 11.7. See also ŚB 1.3.5.10, where the "all" is also unlimited.

"undefined" (*anirukta*),[31] and these two qualities are not essentially different ("*aparimitaṃ vai anirutktaṃ*").[32] Prajāpati, then, like his elder alter ego Puruṣa, is both immanent and transcendent, the one underlying the universe and extending beyond it, simultaneously finite and infinite. He is both the gods and men, the divine and the human, the mortal and the immortal;[33] he is both the defined and the undefined (*nirukta/anirukta*), the limited and the unlimited (*parimita/aparimita*).[34]

As his name suggests, the Lord of Creatures is chiefly charged with the role of creation and as such is identified in the ritual texts not only with Puruṣa but also with Viśvakarman, the "All-Maker."[35] Prajāpati, alone and stricken with desire for offspring[36] or for company,[37] "emits" (*sṛj-*) or emanates from himself the creatures.[38] This cosmic emission (*sṛṣṭi*) is, or becomes, the manifest universe, the three worlds and four quarters[39] and all things within them.[40]

> Prajāpati had a desire. "May I be propagated; may I be multiplied." He heated up ascetic heat, and when he had done so, emitted these worlds—earth, middle space, and heaven. He warmed up these worlds, and when he had done so the luminaries [i.e., gods] were born. . . . He warmed up the luminaries, and when he had done so the three Vedas were born.[41]

31. E.g., PB 7.8.3, 18.6.8; ŚB 6.4.1.6, 14.2.2.21, 14.3.2.15. See also ŚB 1.4.1.21, 2.2.1.3, "*sarvaṃ vai aniruktaṃ.*" Consult also Louis Renou and Lilian Silburn, "Nirukta and Anirukta in Vedic," in J. N. Agrawal and B. D. Shastri, eds., *Sarūpa-Bhāratī or the Homage of Indology: The Dr. Lakshaman Sarup Memorial Volume* (Hoshiarpur: Vishveshvaranand Institute Publications, 1954), pp. 68–79. For the related ritual phenomenon of offering to Prajāpati silently, without *mantra* (*upāṃśu* or *tūṣṇīm*), because he is *anirukta* and "all," see, e.g., ŚB 7.2.2.14 and 12.4.2.1.

32. ŚB 5.4.4.13. Prajāpati, in his guise as the year, is also described as *akṣayya* ("imperishable"). See ŚB 1.6.1.19 and 2.6.3.1; see also 11.1.2.12 and 12.3.4.11.

33. ŚB 6.8.1.4, 4.5.7.2. See also ŚB 10.4.2.2.

34. ŚB 14.1.2.18.

35. See ŚB 7.4.2.5, 8.2.1.10, 8.2.3.13, 9.4.1.12, etc.

36. E.g., KB 6.1; TS 3.1.1.1

37. "May I be more, may I be reproduced." PB 6.5.1, 7.5.1; JUB 1.46.1.

38. For Prajāpati's creation, see Lévi, *La Doctrine du sacrifice,* pp. 18–21; and Gonda, "The Creator and His Spirit." For an analysis of the verbal root *sṛj-* and the relationship between universal creation and the private "projection" of human dreamers, see Wendy Doniger O'Flaherty, *Dreams, Illusion and Other Realities* (Chicago: University of Chicago Press, 1983), pp. 16–17.

39. ŚB 6.3.1.11.

40. "Whatever there is." ŚB 6.1.2.11.

41. AitB 5.32.

The creator and his creation are in the Veda ultimately the same being, made of the same stuff.[42] The universe, in Vedic speculation, is (or should be) theomorphic. Prajāpati is the vital life force (the "breath," *prāṇa*) of his creation[43] or its soul (*ātman*): "That very Prajāpati, having distributed [*vidhāya*)] himself, reentered it with his *ātman*."[44]

But despite, or perhaps because of, his principal characteristic of cosmic fecundity (he is, it is said, productivity or *prajanana* itself),[45] Prajāpati often appears in the mythology as rather inept at his job. His cosmic emission initially produces a creation that is faulty in one way or another. The primordial procreative emanation engenders not a cosmos—an ordered and orderly whole—but a cosmic problem depicted in terms of the sickly nature or horrendous living conditions of the creatures: "Prajāpati emitted the creatures; these, being emitted, languished";[46] they are created without breath,[47] they suffer hunger for lack or food,[48] they are threatened by demons,[49] and they find themselves without a "firm foundation."[50]

Many of these myths of Prajāpati's failed cosmogonic efforts can be divided into two types: the cosmic emission is either insufficiently differ-

42. See also Jan Gonda's comments: "In the case of the Vedic Prajāpati creation is a process of emission and exteriorization of some being or object that formed part of, or was hidden in the creator himself, yet does not become completely independent of him, because Prajāpati, being the totality (*sarvam*), embraces his creatures. . . . The creator god is 'identical' with, that is immanent, inherent in, his creation." "Vedic Gods and the Sacrifice," *Numen* 30 (July 1983): 18.

43. ŚB 6.3.1.9; see also PB 20.4.2. At ŚB 2.5.1.5, it is said that Prajāpati emits creatures in the same way that Vāyu, the wind, enters all the quarters. Elsewhere (KB 19.2), Vāyu is proclaimed the "manifest form (*rūpa*) of Prajāpati."

44. TĀ 1.23.8.

45. E.g., ŚB 5.1.3.10, 5.1.3.12; JB 2.175. This connection between the deity and productivity leads the ritualists also to draw analogies between Prajāpati and other particularly fruitful entities such as goats and sheep, who are "most manifestly" like Prajāpati because "they bear young three times a year and produce two or three [offspring per year]" (or possibly "two [offspring] three times [per year]," *dvau trīn iti*). ŚB 4.5.5.6, 5.2.1.24; see also ŚB 3.3.3.8; TS 1.2.7.1; MŚS 2.1.4.11; BhŚS 10.17.4; ĀpŚS 10.25.12. etc., where the she-goat is said to be of the same "class" or *varṇa* as this god. The virile bull is likewise connected, for he is "Prajāpati among the animals." ŚB 5.2.5.17. The most potent (*vīryavattama*) of the gods is also linked to the most potent of the animals, the horse (ŚB 13.1.2.5). Prajāpati is thus often invoked in the ritual for the increase of the sacrificer's fertility (e.g., PB 20.4.2).

46. PB 7.10.15; see also GB 2.3.9.

47. JB 1.111.

48. TB 1.1.3.5; PB 8.8.4, 6.7.19.

49. TB 1.7.1.4.

50. PB 24.1.2.

entiated or intemperately scattered into a chaos of unconnected fragments. In other words, these two kinds of myths of defective creation explore in narrative form the two metaphysical excesses discussed above. When the story of Prajāpati's emission has the emitted creatures indistinct or overly similar, the principle of *jāmi* or excessive resemblance is recalled. When, on the other hand, the creatures are said to be dispersed and overly distinct one from another, the equally dangerous metaphysical excess of extreme differentiation, *pṛthak,* is represented. In either case, Prajāpati's procreative act results not in a cosmos but in a metaphysical mess.

The *jāmi* type of creation myth is more infrequently found, but it does appear often enough to suggest a category of similar stories. In these myths, the deity emits creatures who are formless by virtue of their cohesiveness or who are chaotically indistinguishable, being too much alike: "Prajāpati emitted the creatures. These emitted ones were closely clasped together [*samaslişyan*]," indistinct and thus without individuality or "name and form [*nāmarūpa*]."[51] Or, as another text has it, the emitted creatures are mistakenly created equal, left in a post-creation tangle marked by discord, rivalry, and cannibalism: "Prajāpati emitted the creatures. They were undifferentiated (*avidhṛtā*), at odds with one another (*asaṃjānānā*), and ate each other."[52] A creation resulting in excessive resemblance is here depicted as a nightmare of egalitarian chaos, an unstructured and homogeneous product. The acosmic primordial state of absolute oneness (Prajāpati before his emission) is thus reduplicated when the god engenders an anticosmic creation of uniformity and formlessness.

More regularly encountered are those stories in which Prajāpati's procreative act has as its consequence a universe whose parts are scattered, dispersed, separated, and utterly distinct—a *pṛthak* creation of excessive differentiation. The very act of cosmic emission is most often articulated with verbs having the dispersive prefix *vi-* (*visṛj-*, "to emit, discharge"; *vikṛṣ-*, "to scatter"), emphasizing the transition from unity

51. TB 2.2.7.1. See also TB 3.10.9.1: "Prajāpati emitted the gods. They were born bound together (*saṃdita*) with evil."

52. PB 24.11.2. This passage makes an interesting contrast to the later Hindu conception of anarchy, *matsya-nyāya* (the "law of the fishes"), whereby bigger fish devour the smaller with no other principle of order than brute size and strength. This later enunciation of disorder is one of unrestrained hierarchy, whereas the Vedic text envisions a chaos in which hierarchical order is completely absent. For another creation story that depicts Prajāpati's creatures as undifferentiated cannibals, see JB 1.117: "Prajāpati emitted the creatures, who were emitted hungry. Being hungry, they ate each other."

to diversity. But here, too, the product of the primordial creation is defective for being metaphysically excessive. Indeed, in myths of this type, creation results in a state of affairs that is equally problematic for the creator and for his creatures.

When emitted, the shattered particles of reality lie in confusion and disarray. In many texts, the creatures are said to "run away" from Prajāpati after being emanated, fearful and hungry, or they wander off disoriented.[53] In other variants, the dispersed creatures display an undisciplined independence, resisting the "superiority" (*śraiṣṭhya*) of Prajāpati, their creator and principle of order and unification.[54] Still elsewhere, we read that creatures flee from Prajāpati out of fear that he will consume them: "Prajāpati emitted the creatures. These emitted ones went away from him, fearing he would devour them."[55] Or, again, when Prajāpati had completed the creative work and was "emptied," "The creatures turned away from him. They did not remain with him as his fortune and food."[56] In these passages, the terror the creatures have of being *consumed* might be a trope for the reluctance of overly distinct elements to allow themselves to be *resumed* within a unified whole.

One of Prajāpati's postcreative problems—that is, the metaphysical problem of a universe that lacks a unifying principle—is nicely summarized in the Śatapatha Brāhmaṇa (10.4.2.3): "Having emitted all the beings, he thought to himself, 'How can I put these creatures back into my self (*ātman*)? How can I place them back into my self? How can I again be the soul (*ātman*) of all these beings?' " All these passages highlight the unstructured chaos of a creation in which the parts are excessively differentiated and thus without the order that comes from interconnection and unification.

Another of Prajāpati's quandaries is that he himself becomes totally spent and broken down after his procreative emission. Texts depicts him variously as "milked out" (*dugdha*), "drained" (*riricāna*), "exhausted" (*vṛtta*), "diseased" (*vyājvara*), or "disjointed, fallen to pieces" (*visrasta*).[57]

53. E.g., TS 2.1.2.1, 2.4.4.1; TB 1.1.5.4; PB 6.7.19; AitB 3.36; GB 2.5.9. See also TB 2.1.2.1; KS 29.9.

54. PB 6.3.9, 16.4.1–3. See also PB 17.10.2.

55. PB 21.2.1.

56. ŚB 3.9.1.1.

57. *Dugdha:* PB 9.6.7. *Riricāna:* TS 1.7.3.2, 5.1.8.3, 6.6.5.1, 6.6.11.1; MS 1.6.12; TB 1.1.10.1; ŚB 10.4.2.2; JB 2.149, 2.181, 3.282.; *Vṛtta:* TB 1.2.6.1. *Vyājvara:* GB 2.4.12. For *visrasta* and other forms of *visraṃs-* to describe Prajāpati's postcreative condition, see TB 2.3.6.1; ŚB 1.6.3.35; 4.5.4.1, 6.1.2.12; AitĀ 3.2.6; ŚānĀ 8.11. See also ŚB 1.6.3.16, where, in a version of the very ancient Vedic creation myth of Indra's slaying of the

In this sad state, the creator fears death;[58] his life force (*prāṇa*), essence (*rasa*), and luminous power (*tejas*) leave him,[59] as do the gods, the cattle, and all his progeny.[60] The dispersive quality of the faulty creation is mirrored in the dissipation of the creator.

The disarray and disconnection of Prajāpati's creatures and the dissolution of the progenitor's body are two sides of the same metaphysical coin. Prajāpati, the aboriginal One and the potential unifying power, has gone to seed, so to speak. He is broken down, emptied out, ineffectual, lying pathetically in a heap. "And truly there was then no firm foundation (*pratiṣṭhā*) here at all."[61] The constituents of the universe, Prajāpati's emitted parts, similarly are scattered in confusion and divergence; they, too, in such a condition, "found no firm foundation."[62]

Moreover, time, like space, is also defectively engendered and in much the same way. The disintegration of Prajāpati's cosmic body or self caused by his procreative emission is also envisioned as a worrisome discontinuity in the year, the temporal whole. When Prajāpati is disjointed, time is literally out of joint:

> When Prajāpati had emitted the creatures, his joints (*parvans*) became disjointed. Now Prajāpati is the year, and his joints are the two junctures of day and night, of the waxing and waning lunar half-months, and of the beginnings of the seasons. He was unable to rise with his joints disjointed.[63]

Or, again, "That Prajāpati who became disjointed is the year, and these joints of his that were disjointed are the days and the nights."[64]

As the undifferentiated One and his undifferentiated creation are seen as one form of anticosmos in one set of myths (of the *jāmi* variety), so is the dissipation of the One and the unconnected diversity of his emanation viewed as another kind of chaos in another cluster of cosmogonies. In both cases, creation is not cosmos. The natural act of

---

serpent who has the universe pent up within itself, the latter "having been hit [by Indra] lay contracted (*samvlīna*) like a leather bag which has been emptied." For some scattered comparative speculations about the meaning of Prajāpati's postcreative fatigue, see Gonda, *Prajāpati's Rise to Higher Rank,* pp. 52–54.

58. ŚB 10.4.2.2.

59. ŚB 6.1.2.12, 7.4.2.1, 7.4.2.4, 6.4.2.4, 10.1.1.1, 13.1.1.4.

60. ŚB 9.1.1.6, 8.2.3.9; PB 6.7.19; JB 3.153, 3.230; TS 2.4.4.2. For the sacrifice leaving Prajāpati, see, e.g., TS 6.1.2.4; JB 3.155, 3.274.

61. ŚB 7.1.2.2.

62. PB 24.1.2.

63. ŚB 1.6.3.35.

64. ŚB 10.1.1.2.

procreation (albeit done by a supernatural entity) results in ontological disaster, a nonbeing parallel to the nonbeing of precreation. In these stories, the moral is that all life, all being, is not produced preformed—it is, as we shall soon see, to be composed and constructed subsequent to the merely procreative act. The creation of true cosmos, otherwise put, is not simply a matter of the One becoming many but also and necessarily of the reintegration of the many into a new whole. Cosmogony, the production of an ordered universe out of a generated potential, is a secondary act in the Prajāpati myths as form is carved out of or constructed from the formless emission.

Let us take another angle on the same subject by returning for a moment to the concept of *sarva* ("all") in ancient Indian philosophy. Jan Gonda has argued that many Vedic texts make a subtle but important distinction between this word and another which is often regarded by Indologists as synonymous. *Sarva,* according to Gonda, connotes an undivided, perfectly complete, and seamless whole, as, for example, the aboriginal Puruṣa or Prajāpati. *Viśva,* often also translated as "all," carries a meaning critically distinct from *sarva,* Gonda argues, and one that might well apply to the postcreative but precosmic "all":

> The combinations of *sarva-* and *viśva-* are therefore not necessarily tautological in character . . . *viśva-* pointing out the inability to proceed after a certain total number has been counted, *sarva-* emphasizing the idea of wholeness and completeness and the inability to discern defectiveness.[65]

The creation myths we have considered, then, may also be understood as the tracing of the transition from *sarva* to *viśva,* a transformation from a perfect unity without parts to a defective totality. Another step in the metamorphosis is required for true cosmos: the reintegration of the totality (*viśva*) into a constructed whole, a composed unity of parts the texts call *samāna.* As Verpoorten has demonstrated, the move toward cosmogony and ontology in the Vedic conception is one not of return to primordial unity but rather of rebuilding a complete structure without eliminating diversity: "Behind the word *samāna* always lies a duality or a multiplicity. The unity signified by it, far from excluding multiplicity, supposes it, supports itself on it."[66]

Following the abortive attempt at cosmogony by natural means is a mopping-up operation which fashions a cosmos out of the chaos that is Prajāpati's emission. In the cosmogonic myths of the Vedas, this

65. Gonda, "Reflections on *Sarva-* in Vedic Texts," p. 54.
66. Verpoorten, "Unité et distinction," p. 81.

cosmos-building labor is signified by a shift in verbal forms. The procreative dispersal, marked by words prefixed with *vi-*, is later counteracted by action of cosmic healing, repair, and construction described with verbs beginning with *sam-*, conveying conjunction, concentration, and assembly (*samkṛ-*, *samtan-*, *samklp-*, *sampad-*, *samyuj-*, etc.).[67] Further, this constructive activity combating natural imperfection is usually said to be ritual activity. The sacrifice is a cosmogonic instrument, for the ritual process completes all the stages necessary for making an ontologically viable universe—*sarva, viśva, samāna.* Ananda K. Coomaraswamy summarizes the sacrificial structure and its connection to cosmogony:

> And what is essential in the Sacrifice? In the first place, to divide, and in the second to reunite. He being One, becomes or is made into Many, and being Many becomes again or is put together again as One.[68]

Let us now return to the creation narratives. In both of the two types we have encountered—the *jāmi* and *pṛthak* varieties—we may observe the same movement from emitted formlessness to ritually created structure.

When Prajāpati's emission is depicted as insufficiently differentiated, true cosmogony occurs when the created mass is divided into its constituents. Excessive resemblance is thereby moderated by the imposition of difference and form (*rūpa*). Creatures emitted "closely clasped together," without individuality, were made distinct when Prajāpati "entered them with form. That is why they say, 'Prajāpati is indeed form itself.' "[69] In this instance, the progenitor is also the fashioner of distinctive shapes. Elsewhere, however, Prajāpati finds a tool, the sacrificial ritual, which he then utilizes to create the essential distinctions among indistinguishable creatures. When these latter were emitted "undifferentiated, at odds with each other," and engaged in mutual cannibalism,

> This distressed Prajāpati. He saw [i.e., discovered] the forty-nine-day sacrificial session. Thereupon this [creation] became separated (*vyāvartata*). Cows became cows, horses [became] horses, men [became] men, and wild animals [became] wild animals.[70]

67. For this point, see also Silburn, *Instant et cause,* p. 56.

68. Ananda K. Coomaraswamy, "Ātmayajña: Self-Sacrifice," *Harvard Journal of Asiatic Studies* 6 (1941): 396.

69. TB 2.2.7.1; see also TB 3.10.9.1, where Prajāpati "divides" (or "releases," *vyadyat*) the gods whom he has created "bound together with evil."

70. PB 24.11.2.

Here it is pointedly the structuring effect of ritual that redeems Prajāpati's creative error. In the *jāmi* sort of creation myth, the cosmic One reproduces himself in an undifferentiated totality which must be decomposed before it can take shape as a cosmos, a constructed whole made up of distinct but related parts.

When Prajāpati's procreative act results in an excessively differentiated creation, the condition of *pṛthak* is also offset by the connective power of the sacrifice. In this case, cosmos arises out of the ritual reintegration of the splintered emitted parts. Creatures too independent and unrelated, resisting Prajāpati's "superiority," are brought back to the fold by ritual means: Prajāpati "saw that *agniṣṭoma* [soma sacrifice] and performed it. Thereupon the creatures yielded to him superiority."[71] Creatures who run away from their creator are reassimilated and oriented with the help of a rite:

> Prajāpati emitted the creatures. These emitted ones ran away from him. He saw this "undefined" (*anirukta*) morning soma pressing. With that, he went into the middle of them. They turned toward him and circled him.[72]

Or, again, creatures who flee from Prajāpati for fear of being consumed by (or resumed in) him must be returned to the creator and integrator and "eaten" in a manner that preserves distinction while interrelating and subsuming the elements within an ordered whole:

> He said, "Return to me, and I will devour you in such a way that, although devoured, you will multiply." He consumed them by means of [a certain] ritual chant and caused them to multiply by means of [another] ritual chant.[73]

The creation of cosmos requires both the fixing of Prajāpati's emission (the *sṛṣṭi,* translated by Paul Mus as "la création brute") and the repair of Prajāpati himself (*atisṛṣṭi,* "la surcréation" in Mus's terms).[74]

71. PB 6.3.9. See also, SB 3.9.1.4; "He saw that set of eleven victims [for the soma sacrifice]. Having sacrificed them, Prajāpati fattened himself again, and the creatures returned to him, and remained with him as his fortune and food. Having sacrificed in this way, he became superior (*vasīyān*)." For other instances of using ritual to resolve a disputed superiority in Vedic mythology, see TS 2.2.11.5–6 and PB 7.2.1.

72. PB 17.10.2.

73. PB 21.2.1. For Prajāpati as "eater," see also PB 17.10.2 and TB 3.8.7.1, 3.9.10.1. Other comparable passages in which ritual rectifies Prajāpati's defective creation include PB 7.10.15; 8.8.14; KS 29.9; GB 2.3.9.

74. "La création brute (*sṛṣṭi*) et la surcreation (*atisṛṣṭi*), cette dernière décrite dans les brāhmaṇa comme la reconstruction du corps de Prajāpati-Puruṣa dispersé et à qui le rite ramene symbolique ses membres (illatif), sont deux temps successifs et complèmentaires, mais en série. Ils n'adviennent pas, l'un et l'autre, qu'une seule fois." Mus, "Du Nouveau sur Ṛg Veda 10.90?" p. 182.

When Prajāpati is in a postcreative state of fragmentation and disintegration, he is made whole again and healed by the gods. They restore him when he has fallen down and put back into him the vital breath which had left him.[75] Another passage relates that when Prajāpati had fallen into pieces, his breath and energy gone out from him, "truly there was then no firm foundation here at all. The gods said, 'There is no other firm foundation apart from this one. Let us restore father Prajāpati; he will be a firm foundation for us."[76] In yet another text, the revivification of Prajāpati is depicted as a cosmic healing, performed by collecting together the luminous energy (*tejas*) and life essence (*rasa*) of all the emitted creatures, thereby simultaneously reuniting the dispersed creation (the *sṛṣṭi*) into a reconstituted unity and reinvigorating Prajāpati (the *atisṛṣṭi*) who is that unity.[77]

Several variants make explicit that this restoration or healing activity is essentially a ritual activity. The sacrificer in his ritual makes Prajāpati "whole and complete and raises him to stand upright, even as the gods once raised him."[78] Prajāpati, disjointed after procreation, begs the god of sacrificial fire, Agni, "Put me back together (*tvam mā saṃdhehi*)." Agni does so by building him up piece by piece, just as the altar of the *agnicayana* sacrifice is constructed brick by brick by the sacrificer and his officiants:

> It was five body parts of his that fell into pieces—hair, skin, flesh, bone, and marrow—and these are the five layers [of the altar]. When he builds up the five layers, it is also with those five body parts that he builds up [Prajāpati].[79]

And when Prajāpati, conceived of as the year, is "out of joint" and "unable to rise" because of the dissipating effects of the procreative act, "the gods healed him by means the *havis* offerings," the regularly performed and obligatory sacrifices of the Vedic *śrauta* sacrificial repertoire:

> With the *agnihotra* [the twice-daily sacrifice] they healed that joint [which is] the two junctures of day and night, and joined it together. With the new and full moon sacrifices, they healed that joint [which is] between thee waxing and waning lunar half-months, and joined it together. And with

75. ŚB 7.4.2.11, 7.4.2.13.

76. ŚB 7.1.2.2. See also PB 24.1.2 for the story at the level of the *sṛṣṭi:* "Prajāpati emitted the creatures. These did not have a firm foundation. With these [days of the thirty-three-day sacrificial session] they had a firm foundation. These worlds did not have a firm foundation. With these [days] they had a firm foundation."

77. TB 1.2.6.1.

78. ŚB 7.1.2.11.

79. ŚB 6.1.2.17.

the *cāturmāsyas* [quarterly sacrifices] they healed that joint [which is] the beginning of the seasons, and joined it together.[80]

Time, space, and all within them are in Vedic cosmogonies an emanation of Prajāpati and participate in his being. However, in the words of Silburn, for the ancient ritualists "neither things nor inert data exist, but only the functions and activities of synthesis."[81] Prajāpati is reconstructed in a secondary cosmogonic act of ritual construction which also shapes into form the discontinuous creatures of the cosmic emission. Unlike all the king's horses and all the king's men, the gods and men, deploying the formative and connective power of ritual, *can* put the shattered god and his creation back together again—an operation of ritually produced reintegration which Mus has cleverly called "information."

The mythology of Prajāpati also accounts for the origins of the cosmos-making tool that is the Vedic ritual. Although sacrifice is utilized to fix Prajāpati's abortive attempt at cosmogony, it is the creator god himself (who else?) who first produced the ritual that will heal him and his creatures. Prajāpati is both the creator[82] and first practitioner of the ritual, subsequently turning over the sacrifices to other deities.[83] The creator generates the individual pieces of the universal puzzle and leaves them in a chaotic jumble, but it is also he who produces the means for interlocking those cosmic fragments.

In some texts, the structure of the creation of the sacrifice replicates that of the creation of the universe as a whole. One encounters the same formula: an emission of an unorganized totality and a subsequent reintegration as the particular sacrifices are "measured out" (*udmā-),* "assigned" (*vyādiś-*), or "apportioned" (*vibhaj-*) to the appropriate deities, thus forming a systematically organized whole.[84] In other instances, however, this same distribution of the sacrifices at creation is regarded as a dangerous dispersal; it leaves Prajāpati, once again, drained or emptied until healed by yet another step in which the creator takes back into himself, by ritual means, those particular sacrifices he had disseminated among the gods.[85]

Indeed, the creation of the sacrifice is sometimes said to be as

80. ŚB 1.6.3.36; see also ŚB 1.3.5.16; 6.1.2.18, 8.7.1.1–3, 10.1.1.2–3, 10.4.3.20; 11.2.7.1–5, etc.

81. Silburn, *Instant et cause,* p. 1.

82. Or "mouth," e.g., TS 5.1.8.3; KB 13.1.

83. ŚB 2.3.1.22, 6.3.1.18; AitB 5.32.

84. TS 1.6.9.1; TB 1.3.2.5; AitB 3.13; ŚB 13.1.1.4.

85. TS 1.7.3.2, 6.6.11.1.

defective a production as the procreation of the creatures. When Prajāpati emits the sacrifice, his "greatness" (*mahi*) departs from him, and he must go searching for it;[86] or the sacrifice runs away with the demons, leaving the gods in a big jam.[87] Here, too, simple creation is insufficient and is to be followed up by an organizational effort that rectifies chaos. The sacrifice must be "restrained" by and returned to those to whom it properly belongs—who are, in the following story as elsewhere, the Brahmins:

> Prajāpati emitted the sacrifice, and after the sacrifice the *brahman* power and the *kṣatra* power were emitted. After them were emitted those creatures who eat sacrificial oblations and those who don't. The Brahmins are those creatures who eat sacrificial oblations, the Rājanyas [Kṣatriyas], Vaiśyas, and Śūdras those who don't. The sacrifice departed from them. The *brahman* power and *kṣatra* power followed after it, each with their own weapons. The weapons of the *brahman* are the horse chariot, armor, and bow and arrow. The sacrifice escaped, recoiling, from the *kṣatra*'s weapons, and the *kṣatra* did not catch it. The *brahman* followed it, caught it, and restrained it, standing from above. Caught, restrained from above, and recognizing its own weapons, [the sacrifice] returned to the *brahman*. Therefore, even now the sacrifice finds support in the *brahman* and in the Brahmins.[88]

The order-producing sacrifice, when it is itself appropriate tamed and in the hands of the priests (and not others), is not only regarded as an instrument of cosmic healing and construction; it also is sometimes said to have a procreative power supplementing that of the creator god. In some myths, Prajāpati emits the sacrifice first, and out of its parts are further generated the components of the universe:

> Prajāpati emitted the sacrifice. With the *agnyadheya* he emitted seed (*retas*); with the *agnihotra,* gods, men, and demons. With the new and full moon sacrifice, Indra was emitted. He has emitted food and drink for them from the sacrifices of vegetable oblations and the soma sacrifices.[89]

The fertility of the sacrifice at the cosmic level and its origin in the being of Prajāpati led to the frequent connection between the creator god and the creative ritual: "That sacrifice which is now being performed is Prajāpati, from whom these creatures were born; and even so

86. ŚB 13.1.1.4.
87. TS 3.3.7.1; see also TS 6.1.2.4; JB 3.155, 3.274.
88. AitB 7.19.
89. KB 6.15; see also ŚB 2.5.1.17, 2.5.2.1, 2.5.2.7, 2.6.3.4; TS 3.5.7.3.

are they born today."[90] The repeated statement in the Brāhmaṇas that "the sacrifice is Prajāpati"[91] points to the productive power of the ritual ("When he [the sacrificer] offers, he emits forth this all")[92] and indicates that Prajāpati and the ritual share the same essence. The two are counterforms of each other: "this all," which is Prajāpati, corresponds to (or results from, *anu*) the sacrifice.[93] Prajāpati emits from himself or, as one text says, "makes his *ātman*" the sacrifice,[94] and, as we have seen, the sacrificial operation in turn recreates a unified Prajāpati. Like Escher's "Drawing Hands," Prajāpati and the sacrifice bring each other into existence.

And if Prajāpati and the sacrifice are resembling forms, so too are their individual components essentially related. Either the individual sacrifices that make up the ritual repertoire are equated to Prājapati's corporal components (e.g., ŚB 12.1.4.1–3), or the parts of the "body," the rites, of one sacrifice are connected to correlative parts of Prajāpati's body or self.[95] Because of these connections based on resemblance, by putting together a sacrificial performance, rite by rite, Prajāpati (as well as his creation) is also put together.

Vedic cosmogonies, like cosmogonies everywhere, depict the origins of the present. Stories of the primeval emanation of the One into the many and of the secondary ritual act of reconstituting the creation into a constructed whole provide Vedic ritualism with its metaphysical problem (the defectiveness of the merely natural) and its ritual solution (sacrificial reclamation). Life in the historical present, no less than in the mythic time of origins, is regarded as intrinsically faulty without the formative structure only ritual can provide.

And also not unlike other myths from other religions, these myths seem to explore two remarkable—in that the study of religion too often leaves them mute—and related doctrines. First, they radically devalue the abilities of the creator god; he is portrayed as inept, the progenitor not of perfection but of a defective product. Like other myths both

90. ŚB 4.2.4.16, 4.5.5.1, 4.5.6.1, 5.1.4.1, etc.

91. Or "Prajāpati is the sacrifice." See, e.g., ŚB 3.2.2.4, 5.2.1.2, 5.2.1.4, 5.4.5.21, 6.4.1.6, 14.1.2.18; TB 3.2.3.1, 3.7.2.1. In other instances, Prajāpati is identified with the year, and the year with the sacrifice (e.g., ŚB 5.2.1.2, 5.4.5.21, 11.1.1.1; see also ŚB 11.2.7.1).

92. ŚB 3.6.3.2.

93. ŚB 3.6.3.1.

94. PB 7.2.1. See also ŚB 4.2.5.3, where Prajāpati is also said to be the *ātman* of the sacrifice.

95. See KB 6.15; ŚB 10.3.1.1; AitB 2.18; PB 13.11.18; GB 2.1.26.

within this tradition and in other religions, the god is represented as generating a world and its inhabitants which are disorganized, deficient, and degenerate (elsewhere they are termed evil in stories analyzing the problem of theodicy). Secondly, these myths legitimize the audacious assumption of enormous power on the part of certain human beings—here, the Brahmins, who are hereditary experts in the Vedic ritual and whose stories depict themselves as charged with putting together coherently what Prajāpati has so badly messed up. Human beings of a certain sort and with certain self-proclaimed privileges, together with the lesser gods, must repair the damage done by the creator god's action. It is no wonder that, with these assumed responsibilities and supposed powers, the Brahmins would (as we will see in the next chapter) call themselves human gods.

True cosmos, true reality, and true being are fabricated, continually reconstructed by sacrificial activity. This metaphysical power attributed to ritual (and to those who can manipulate it) depends on the principle of universal resemblance, to the intricacies of which we now turn.

The Metaphysics of Resemblance and Connection

Prajāpati and Puruṣa are the anthropomorphically conceived expressions of the creative source and principle of universal unification in Vedic cosmology. The sacrifice, as the resembling dynamic counterform of the Cosmic One, represents Prajāpati/Puruṣa's essence. It, too, is generative and regenerative of being, encompassing within it the universal whole, and is thus regarded as another way of speaking about the unifying force in the cosmos. When constructed properly—when rite is made to follow rite in an unbroken chain, a unity of parts—the form of sacrifice produces a formed, orderly cosmos in which all the parts are interrelated.

In other sections of Vedic ritual and philosophical literature, this unifying, constructive power is depicted as a neuter force, not unlike *mana, wakan,* or the Holy Spirit in other religions.[96] Like Prajāpati/Puruṣa the *brahman* is said to create and pervade "this all." It, too, is regarded as *sarva,*[97] and it is this feature that Gonda emphasizes when he writes, "*Brahman* is what is the whole, complete here, is what is

96. See Marcel Mauss, *A General Theory of Magic,* trans. by Robert Brain (New York: W. W. Norton, 1972).

97. E.g., ChU 3.14.1.

entire, perfect, with no parts lacking, what is safe and well etc., i.e. Completeness, Totality, the All seen as the Whole."[98] As such, the *brahman* is not different from Prajāpati himself[99] and has the same creative and ontologically formative powers. In the Śatapatha Brāhmaṇa (11.2.3.1–5), for example, the *brahman* "was in the beginning this [all]." It created the gods and organized them into their proper spheres:

> Then the *brahman* itself went to the transcendent side. Having gone there, it wondered, "How can I again return to these [immanent] worlds?" It returned again by means of name and form. . . . These are the two great manifestations of the *brahman*.

The neuter force of *brahman* is here presented as the creator, formulator, and integrative power made manifest in every one of the parts of the universe, in every immanent "name and form." The relationship between Prajāpati and his creatures is simply represented in a different idiom; for, as Maryla Falk has written,

> *nāma*s and *rūpa*s [names and forms] are the negative, mortal, differentiated condition of the one *nāma,* all-consciousness, consubstantial with the one *rūpa,* the Universe as the latter's "own form." While the *nāma* is the inner power of the individual being or thing, the *rūpa* is its sensuous appearance.[100]

As in one conception of the universe the elements of the cosmos are considered parts of a Cosmic Man, so in another but congruent notion the *brahman* creates and enters multiple reproductions of itself, thus providing their common origin and accounting for their mutually resembling forms. This point is made also in the Śatapatha Brāhmaṇa (11.2.3.6), in which the gods gain immortality through tapping the *brahman,* and the sacrificer gains the "all" and an "imperishability" through the ritual manipulation of name and form (*brahman*'s manifestation):

> In the beginning the gods were subject to death. Only when they filled themselves with the *brahman* did they become immortal. He who pours out the libation to the mind thereby obtains form—form is mind, because

98. Gonda, "Reflections on *Sarva*-in Vedic Texts," p. 64.

99. "Prajāpati is the whole (*sarva*) *brahman.*" ŚB 7.3.1.42. See also ŚB 13.6.2.8: "The *brahman* is Prajāpati, for Prajāpati has the nature of the *brahman* (*brāhma*)."

100. Maryla Falk, *Nāma-Rūpa and Dharma-Rūpa* (Calcutta: University of Calcutta, 1943), p. 19. See also Ananda K. Coomaraswamy's definitions: "forms, ideas, similitudes, or eternal reasons of things (*nāma,* 'name' or 'noumena' = *forma*) and the things themselves in their accidental and contingent aspects (*rūpa,* 'phenomenon' = *figura*)." "Vedic Exemplarism," *Harvard Journal of Asiatic Studies* 1 (1936): 44.

> it is with the mind that one knows, "This is form." And when he pours out the libation to speech he thereby obtains name—name is speech, because it is by speech that he grasps the name. As much as is name and form, that much is this all. He obtains all, and the all is the imperishable.

Brahman is, however, something of a multivalent concept within Vedism. Some shifts of the semantic range of the word can be identified as one passes from the Ṛg Veda (where the meaning tends to center on the transcendental potency of the hymn or formula), through the ritual texts (where it describes the power of sacrificial activity), to the Upanishadic literature (where it is more generally conceived as the ultimate principle of all being). Such a historical evolution should not be overly stressed, as Jan Gonda, Louis Renou, and others have shown in studies of this fundamental Vedic term.[101] The multivalence of *brahman* is explicable precisely because of its centrality; many different objects, acts, and phenomena can be "designated by the same name, because they all participate in or partake of that important and central concept."[102]

Brahman is the basis or ground of a universe or mutually resembling things and beings, a foundation in which the perpetual interplay of resemblances find their source, condition of possibility, support, and end. *Brahman* is to be understood in light of the Vedic preoccupation with continuity and stability in the face of assumed natural discontinuity and the instability of creation. Gonda rightly insists on the affinity this central metaphysical term has with other important Vedic concepts such as *āyatāna* ("base," "support," "resort"),[103] *pratiṣṭhā* ("firm foundation" in its spatial sense),[104] and *saṃsthā* ("end" or "temporal foundation"):

> It would, therefore, be easy to understand if the ancient Indian searchers for a firm ground or foundation for the universe, the human soul included, had chosen a word derived from the root *bṛh-*, "to be firm, strong, etc." to designate that ultimate foundation of all that exists. Anyhow, it is a fact that the concept of a support, that is a fundamental principle on which everything rests, and the idea of firmness and immovability are often expressed in connection with *brahman* or with God who is *brahman*.[105]

101. Jan Gonda, *Notes on Brahman* (Utrecht: J. L. Beyers, 1950); Louis Renou, "Sur la notion de *brahman*," *Journal asiatique* 237 (1949): 7–46.

102. Gonda, *Notes on Brahman*, p. 14.

103. Jan Gonda, "Āyatāna," *Adyar Library Bulletin* 23 (1969): 1–79.

104. Jan Gonda, "Pratiṣṭhā," *Samjñāvyākaraṇam, Studia Indologica Internationalia* 1 (1954): 1–37.

105. Gonda, *Notes on Brahman*, p. 47.

What is missing from Gonda's definition, however, is the active and dynamic quality of *brahman.* This force is not merely a passive, ever-present metaphysical foundation but is also a potency within all "names and forms," which, when activated, is their possibility for self-realization. Indologists of the last century liked to compare *brahman* to electricity, a latent energy that, when switched on by ritual means, produces cosmic order (*ṛta*) and individual power. Louis Renou has more recently demonstrated that it is the *connective* potency of the *brahman* that is at the heart of the Vedic concept and which links together all the meanings of the word.

Renou argues that the common semantic denominator is *brahman* as "a connective energy condensed into enigmas."[106] The enigma or mystery of the *brahman* force "is the equation between human behavior and natural phenomena, the connection between rite and cosmos."[107] The metaphysical, epistemological, and ritual are thus conjoined in a concept that is both the ground of the universe and the possibility for its establishment. "*Brahman,*" concludes Renou, "is nothing else but that form of thinking in enigmas consisting of the positing of correlation, an explicative identification: that very thing the Brāhmaṇas designate by the terms *nidāna* or *bandhu,* and eventually *upaniṣad.*"[108]

Brahman is therefore the source and foundation of all that exists—the nexus of all cosmic connections—and the connective force itself lying behind all knowledge and action that constructs ontologically viable forms. It is the fount and terminus of all potential and realized correspondences, the condition of possibility for wholeness as well as the whole itself. *Brahman,* in sum, is the connective energy that lies between apparently (and naturally) disparate elements and makes efficacious the ritual action that forges those elements into unity. *Brahman* is both the neuter counterpart to the Cosmic Man and the analogue to the sacrificial operation: "What is related to ritual activity is related to the *brahman.*"[109]

Whereas *brahman* is the ultimate nexus of and condition of possibility for *all* connections between the resembling parts of the universal whole, the *particular* resemblances are often described in terms of prototypes and counterparts, forms and images, or replicas. It is the intricate texture of these individual relationships that make up, but are not the sum of, *brahman* considered as the cosmic whole.

106. Renou, "Sur la notion de *brahman,*" p. 43.
107. Ibid., p. 12.
108. Ibid., p. 13.
109. BGS 3.13.9.

Vedic connections are of two sorts: what we might call vertical and horizontal correspondences. The former connects an immanent form and its transcendent correlative: "Deux plans, mais un être," as Mus puts it.[110] This type of connection operates between the elements of the same species located on different and hierarchically ranked cosmological levels. Horizontal connections link resembling components of two different species located within the same cosmological plane which share a similar hierarchical position within their respective classes. Here I plan to concentrate (but not exclusively) on the vertical connections within Vedic metaphysics.

One statement of the epistemological program of Vedism (which I have used as one of the epigrams to this book) is found in the Ṛg Veda (10.130.3); "What was the prototype (*pramā*), what was the counterpart (*pratimā*), and what was the connection (*nidāna*) between them?" Coomaraswamy has offered "exemplar" and "image" as translations for *pramā* and *pratimā,* respectively, "which imply in strictness 'model' and 'copy'. . . . The exemplary image, form, or idea is then a likeness in the sense of imitable prototype."[111] On the grandest level, the entire universe is the *pratimā*—literally the "countermeasure" or more freely the image, counterpart, or projection—or Prajāpati or Puruṣa, from whom all was emitted. But it is especially those phenomena that are considered "uniform" (*ekarūpa*) that are most manifestly representations of Prajāpati's nature. The year, the temporal unity, is singled out at ŚB 11.1.6.13 as the *pratimā* of Prajāpati's very self (*ātman*):

> Prajāpati reflected, "I have emitted the counterpart of my self, the year." And therefore they say, "Prajāpati is the year," for he emitted it as a counterpart of himself.

In a passage that follows shortly thereafter (ŚB 11.1.8.3), the text describes in exactly the same terms another counterpart of Prajāpati also regarded as "all," as a unified whole—the sacrifice. Elsewhere, Prajāpati is said to have "given himself" to the gods in the form of the

110. Paul Mus, *Esquisse d'une histoire du Bouddhism fondée sur la critique archéologique destextes* (Paris and Hanoi: Paul Geuthner, 1935) p. 121.

111. Coomaraswamy, "Vedic Exemplarism," p. 50. For other discussions of *pramā/ pratimá,* consult S. Schayer, "Die Struktur de magischen Weltanschauung nach dem Atharva-Veda und den Brāhmaṇa-Texten," *Zeitschrift für Wissenschaft Buddhismus* 6 (1925): esp. 275–76; and Hermann Oldenberg, *Vorwissenschaftliche Wissenschaft: Die Weltanschauung der Brāhmaṇa Texte* (Göttingen: Vandehoeck and Ruprecht, 1919), esp. pp. 114–15.

sacrifice;[112] Prajāpati is equated with the sacrifice, and the gods to whom he offers as well as the oblations with which he offers are declared to be forms (*rūpa*s) of him.[113]

Sacrifice also, then, is a *pratimā* of the Cosmic One in that the composition of parts into wholes achieved within the ritual resembles the body of Prajāpati, a similarly constructed whole and the prototype for all others. Because both the year and the sacrifice are counterparts of the same prototype, they are themselves linked: the sacrifice has "the same measure" (*sammita*) as the year.[114]

Some of the implications of regarding the sacrifice as a counterpart of the cosmic whole are obvious. The construction of a sacrifice, an ideally continuous and complete entity made out of the joining of discrete parts (rites, performers, implements, offerings, etc.), is a reconstruction of the universe itself in the sense that the one supposedly reproduces—in a different form—the other. They are not identical but resembling forms of unity, sharing the same essence but manifesting themselves differently. The sacrifice is composed of the counterparts to the cosmic prototypes (each element of the ritual being vertically connected to transcendent correlatives), and the sacrifice as a whole is the counterpart to the prototype that is Prajāpati, the universe. The sacrifice operates with "images," whereas Prajāpati's body or self is comprised of the "originals," but both participate in the same ontological essence.

Other implications also follow from the prototype/counterpart presupposition—these on the level of horizontal connections. The sacrificer and his oblation are said to be interrelated in this way, such that the sacrificer offers a form of himself when he offers clarified butter, the sacrificial cake, or an animal; for, "by virtue of the counterpart (*pratimayā*) it is the man."[115] There is no confusion here between the two, any more than there is a confusion between the transcendent god and the sacrificial ritual performed here by humans. The offering is not identical to the sacrificer but is his projected representative; and the sacrifice as a whole is, as Paul Mus puts it, "une counterpartie et un substitute personnel pour l'homme qui l'offre."[116] "The man is the sacrifice," says the Brāhmaṇa. "The man is the sacrifice because it is

112. ŚB 5.1.1.2; see also PB 7.2.1.
113. ŚB 12.6.1.1.
114. ŚB 3.1.3.17, 3.1.4.5, 3.3.3.5, 3.4.1.14, 3.9.4.11, etc.
115. KB 10.3.
116. Paul Mus, "La Stance de la plénitude," *Bulletin de l'École Francaise d'Extrême Orient* 44 (1947–50): 598.

the man who offers it. And each time he offers it, the sacrifice takes the shape of the man. Therefore the sacrifice is the man."[117] Elsewhere the "sacrifice is the man" because it is "by means of him that this all is measured," the body and its parts of the particular sacrificer being the standard of measuring various parts of the sacrifical arena.[118]

Counterparts are in this limited sense only to be regarded as "substitutes."[119] They "stand for" or "represent" their originals in that they are more or less incomplete images or emanations of them. A series of resembling forms, from the prototype to its least complete manifestation, can bring together elements within a set. The *pratimā* of Prajāpati is the year, and the counterpart of the year is the sacrifice of twelve days' duration, because "the year has twelve months, and this is the *pratimā* of the year."[120] A sacrifice lasting a whole year would, of course, be more fully the form of Prajāpati, but one of twelve days can also serve the purpose and participate in the form albeit less completely. The doctrine of counterparts makes possible not only ritual efficacy—the manipulation of ritual counterparts in order to influence cosmic prototypes—but also ritual efficiency: "The gods said, 'Find the sacrifice that will be the *pratimā* for one of a thousand years, for what man is there who could get through with a sacrifice lasting a thousand years?"[121] Man can participate in cosmic rituals through resembling sacrifices gauged to the human condition—again, not with the completeness of the original but with the efficacy and efficiency of the counterpart.

Substitutions of this type occur also between the various forms of the sacrifices in the Vedic repertoire, as we will have ample opportunity to observe in later chapters. For now, let us return to the case of the sacrificer and his oblation, a substitution within a sacrifice. The sacrificer himself, the human being, is said to be "nearest to" (*nediṣṭha*) Prajāpati, the prototype of prototypes.[122] In relation to others, however, the sacrificer himself functions as a prototype with counterparts. An animal, being more nearly resembling the sacrificer than vegetable oblations, in turn stands as the prototype in relation to the lesser forms within the series. The baked cake (*puroḍāśa*) is the counterpart of the

117. ŚB 1.3.2.1; 3.5.3.1; see also TS 5.2.5.1.

118. See, e.g., ŚB 10.2.1.2 and also cosmogonic myths such as ṚV 10.121.5, and ṚV 1.154.1 and 1.154.3, where the creator god "measures out" with his body the universe and its parts.

119. For a fuller discussion of substitution in Vedic ritualism, see Chapter 7 herein.

120. KB 25.15; KS 7.15.

121. ŚB 12.3.3.5.

122. ŚB 5.1.3.8, 5.2.1.6.

sacrificial animal (*paśu*) and, following the chain, also therefore the *pratimā* of the sacrificer.[123]

Closely related to the *pramā/pratimā* concept is that of *rūpa* ("form") and its derivatives *pratirūpa* ("image" or "counterform") and *abhirūpa* ("adaptation" or "appropriate form"). I began my treatment of Vedic metaphysics with a passage in which the transcendent *brahman* manifested itself in the immanent worlds by entering as the "name and form" of individual things and beings. Another text notes the participation of all forms in the One Form by saying that Prajāpati "became the counterform (*pratirūpa*) to every form (*rūpa*). This [all] is to be regarded as a form of him."[124]

In a recent article, Asko Parpola claims that "the world *rūpa* is used in the Brāhmaṇa texts in a meaning close to our 'symbol.' "[125] Following Hermann Oldenberg, Parpola argues, "The basic model of thought underlying the use of the term *rūpa* is . . . the distinction between a Platonic sort of idea and its physical manifestations."[126] Often indeed (although not in the example given in the previous paragraph), the distinction between *rūpa* and *pratirūpa* is akin to that between prototype and counterpart. *Rūpa* is the form and *pratirūpa* the image, or, according to Coomaraswamy, the former is the *imago imaginans* and the latter the *imago imaginata,* "reflections" or "projections" of prototypical *rūpa.*[127] The reflection of a man's form in a mirror, for example, is in several texts designated a *pratirūpa,* as is his offspring.[128]

It is not at all certain, however, that *symbol* adequately captures the usage here. And as the following citation indicates, *pratirūpa*s or resembling images are made as well as discovered, a phenomenon that tends to distinguish this conception from the Platonic one.[129] In the soma sacrifice, the sacrificer spreads out two black and white antelope skins

123. TB 3.2.8.8.

124. ṚV 6.47.18; see also BĀU 2.5.19; JUB 1.27.4–5, 1.44.1.

125. Also Parpola, "On the Symbol Concept," in H. Biezais, ed., *Religious Symbols and Their Functions* (Stockholm: Almquist and Wiksell, 1979), p. 143.

126. Ibid., p. 148, citing Oldenberg, *Vorwissenschaftliche Wissenschaft,* pp. 106ff.

127. Coomaraswamy, "Vedic Exemplarism," p. 51.

128. See ŚānĀ 6.2, 6.11; BĀU 2.1.8; GB 2.3.22; see also TB 3.9.22.2.

129. See O'Flaherty's statement on the relations between "making" and "finding" in the cosmogony and epistemology of later Hinduism: "These two kinds of creation—making and finding—are the same, for in both cases the mind—or the Godhead—imposes its idea on the spirit/matter dough of reality, cutting it up as with a cookie-cutter, now into stars, now into hearts, now into elephants, now into swans. It makes them, and finds them already there, like a *bricoleur,* who makes new forms out of *objets trouvés.*" *Dreams, Illusion, and Other Realities,* p. 212.

and touches them, saying, "You two are the works of art (*śilpa*) of the verse and the chant." The attached explanation notes, "A work of art is a *pratirūpa.* Thus what he means [when he says the mantra] is 'You two are the *pratirūpa*s of the verse and chant.' "[130]

Whereas the stress in the prototype/counterpart theory lies on the knowledge that the two participate in the same essence (though even here there is often an active *placing* of the elements on an ontological continuum), the force of the notion of *pratirūpa* is that the image of the form is constructed and made to *conform* to its model. It bears repeating here that all form in Vedism is constructed rather than given; the model and its image are equally "works of art" in this sense, though one may have been made prior to or more fully than the other.

We now come to the crucially important term *abhirūpa* ("appropriate form"), which returns us to the fact that in Vedic resemblance things can be neither exactly alike nor completely different. They are "appropriate" to their cosmological and ontological level, which distinguishes them from resembling forms at other levels, and yet they are nevertheless related by their form to correlates elsewhere. The various counterparts and images are neither identical to nor wholly distinguished from either their (vertical) prototypes or their (horizontal) formal siblings by the concept of *abhirūpa;* their particular appropriateness *locates* them.

One instance of the creation of appropriate form occurs when a formula or *mantra* is moved from one ritual context to another. The original must be modified to interlink with its new context—a formula including the word *soma,* for example, is usually modified when it is brought to a sacrifice in which there is no soma offered—and yet its form is said to persevere through the modification. "A Mantra should express the action concerned," writes S. C. Chakrabarti. "If it does, the Mantra is called *abhirūpa.*"[131]

Such appropriateness of form is indeed a general concern of Vedic ritualism. Ritual action, like all cosmogonic (or anthropogonic) processes, must avoid excess. Like Goldilocks' porridge, a ritual should be too extreme neither in one direction nor in the other, but "just right." There should be neither an "overdoing" (*atirikta*) nor a "deficiency" (*nyūna*) in the ritual performance;[132] the composition should be bal-

130. ŚB 3.2.1.5.

131. S. C. Chakrabarti, *The Paribhāṣās in the Śrautasūtras* (Calcutta: Sanskrit Pustak Bhandar, 1980), p. 135.

132. E.g., ŚB 11.2.3.9. See also Jan Gonda, "The Redundant and the Deficient in Vedic Ritual," *Vishveshvaranand Indological Journal* 21 (June–December 1983): 1–34.

anced and "well made" (*sukṛta*). In some texts the following phrase is repeated over and over again: "What is appropriate in form (*abhirūpa*) within the sacrifice is perfect (*samṛddha*)."[133]

This statement seems to be multivalent. It indicates that the sacrifice is "perfected," that is, made to resemble closely its prototype (the sacrifice of the gods, or the cosmos itself), through the inclusion within it of things, beings, and activities that are appropriate in form to that prototype; one deploys entities, objects, or acts thought to be *sayoni* ("of the same origin") as the prototype. It also might well be taken as a statement of hierarchical distinction. Particular sacrifices may attain a *relative* perfection by composing themselves of things, beings, and activities appropriate to the particular scope and purpose of the particular sacrifice—and, most importantly, appropropiate to the particular sacrificer, who is the "owner" (*svāmin*) or "lord of the sacrifice" (*yajñapati*). The sacrifice, then, is simultaneously a garment ready-made (bought off the rack, as it were) with a predetermined set of relations, and a product tailor-made for the individual sacrificer. Again, the *abhirūpa* concept makes possible both connection (to the vertically oriented prototype and the horizontally oriented elements of the composition) and distinction (the appropriate form is not identical to the prototype or to other similar structures, e.g., the rituals performed by other humans). Such a concept brings us into the very heart of what I observe to be the central principle of Vedism: hierarchical resemblance.

Having considered the nexus of all connections (*brahman*) and the important terms for those entities, objects, or acts that are connected, let us now turn to the Vedic connections in themselves. Of the many different types of linkages, the two most general are designated by the names *bandhu* and *nidāna*.[134] The first is a more or less generic term meaning "connection" or "relation" both in the sense of "relative, kin" and in the more literal sense of "bond." *Bandhu*s place different elements "in bondage" one to another. As in the theory of counterparts, *bandhu*s can be between components located on the same ontological

133. See AitB 1.16, 1.17, 1.19, etc.; KB 1.1, 3.2, 3.9, etc.; GB 2.3.6, 2.3.16, 2.4.4, etc. For a study concentrating on the appropriate form of the verses used in particular sacrifices, consult V. C. Bhattacharya, "On the Justification of *Rūpasamṛddha Ṛk-* Verses in the Aitareya Brāhmaṇa," *Our Heritage* 4 (1956): 99–106, 227–37, and *Our Heritage* 5 (1957): 119–46.

134. Others include *brāhmaṇa, upaniṣad, mithuna* ("pairing"), *sampad* and *saṃkhyāna* ("numerical agreement"), *samjñā* ("agreement" in general), *sammita* ("commensurate"), *salomata* ("congruent"), and *sayoni* ("cooriginated").

level—horizontal connections—or between resembling items on different planes altogether.[135]

Some scholars have argued that *nidāna* is used to specify that the connection is transversing cosmologically or temporally separate spheres. Louis Renou has thus defined *nidāna* as "une connexion à base d'identité entre deux choses situées sur plans differents."[136] The priest called the *āgnīdhra,* for example, is said "to be" the fire god Agni "by virtue of the *nidāna*" that puts the two in the relation of cosmic prototype and ritual counterpart.[137] In other, and comparable, cases, *nidāna*s correlate otherwise temporally distant actions. A particular offering (the *pūrṇāhuta,* "full oblation") in which the clarified butter is poured into the fire with the exclamation "*svāhā!*" is considered "the same" as the first offering Prajāpati made with that ritual utterance because of the *nidāna* joining the two.[138] This type of connection also appears at times to be what some scholars would call magic: by flinging a bunch of grass outside the sacrificial ground (the rite called *stambayajus-haraṇa*), the priest expels the demons "through the *nidāna*" of the two acts.[139]

Despite Renou's attempt to delimit the meaning of the term *nidāna* in this way, other sorts of connections not involving the linking of "choses situées sur plans differents" are labeled with the same word. To trot out again an example I have used in other contexts, the relation of resemblance between the sacrificer and the animal victim within his sacrifice is sometimes described as one in which there is a *nidāna.*[140] It might be argued that the victim, upon death, becomes the sacrifier's "representative" on another existential plane, but within the sacrifice where the connection is made it is not at all clear that the connection links elements of discrete cosmological levels.

135. See Jan Gonda, "*Bandhu-* in the Brāhmaṇas," *Adyar Library Bulletin* 29 (1965): 1–29.

136. Louis Renou, " 'Connexion' en védique, 'cause' en bouddhique," in *Dr. C. Kunhan Raja Presentation Volume* (Madras: Adyar Library, 1946) p. 57.

137. ŚB 1.2.4.13, 4.4.2.18, 5.5.1.8. See also statements that the sacrificial cow is, by the *nidāna,* the goddess of speech, Vāc, at ŚB 3.2.4.10, 3.3.1.16, 4.5.8.3–4; and that a certain pressing stone in the soma sacrifice "is" both the sun and the "out-breath of the sacrifice" for the same reason (ŚB 3.9.4.7, 4.3.5.16).

138. ŚB 2.2.1.4. See also ŚB 3.4.2.8, where the "alliance" made between the sacrificer and the priests in the soma sacrifice (the *tānūnaptra*) is connected by a *nidāna* to a prototypical alliance made among the gods.

139. ŚB 1.2.4.12.

140. See, e.g., AitB 2.11. See also ŚB 3.7.1.11, where the sacrificial stake (*yūpa*) to which the animal victim is tied is also connected, by the *nidāna,* to the sacrificer himself.

Furthermore, the bonds joining components from distinct worlds are depicted with words other than *nidāna. Bandhu,* the most general term for "connection," is often applied in precisely this sense. Perhaps the best example comes from the Ṛg Veda, where it is said that "the ancient seers discovered in their hearts the *bandhu* of the manifest (*sat*) in the unmanifest (*asat*)" (1.129.4; see also JUB 1.59.10). The word *bandhu* is indeed often defined in such a way as to put this function of relating the visible to the invisible, the immanent to the transcendent, foremost:

> In the Brāhmaṇa texts it denotes above all the mysterious connection or relation between the entities of this world and the transcendental "ideal" entities of the divine world, which are the foundation and origin of the perceptible things.[141]

Regardless of the particular term used, it is this ability to link the visible, manifest, and therefore limited counterpart to its invisible, transcendent, and unlimited prototype that is the most spectacular of the supposed effects of making connections. Placing a tangible, definite, bounded thing, being, act, or form into connection with its prototype is, as Louis Renou and Lilian Silburn write, "the effort to specify beyond well-known things, beyond definite forms, a hidden zone where the things and forms take on an inorganic aspect . . . which makes them redoubtable."[142] The "unlimitedness" (*aniruktatva*) of the transcendent is made accessible by those connections that reach out from the sacrifice, and therefore the limited is ontologically "perfected": "Applied to defined and 'structured' things, *anirukta* is what completes and perfects them. . . . According to a quite Vedic paradox, *anirukta* is that which perfectly finishes by the very fact of its being unfinished."[143]

Connections thus bring together the immanent and the transcendent in such a way that the inaccessible is made accessible by the play of resemblances, and the manifest is fulfilled by participation in the transcendent. The universal elements, emitted from the Cosmic One, attain their full, actualized reality only when linked one to another and to their point of origin. Such a composition based on connection rejoins the Cosmic One into a unity of parts in which the simple and the limited—while remaining simple and limited—participates in the whole, the un-

141. Parpola, "On the Symbol Concept," p. 150. For other definitions of *bandhu,* see Gonda, "*Bandhu-* in the Brāhmaṇas."

142. Renou and Silburn, "Nirukta and Anirukta in Vedic," p. 76.

143. Ibid., p. 77. Mus addresses the same point in *Barabadur,* p. 51.

limited. Each particular "name and form" can realize its true nature only by finding its place in this chain of resemblance—or, rather, by being placed "in bondage" with all of its counterparts under the umbrella of the prototype. Universal resemblance keeps separate while it unifies, its specific economy regulated by avoiding the extremes of identity and individuality.

4

The Ritual Construction of Being

Vedic Embryology and Other Conceptions of Human Deficiency

If, in Vedic cosmological theory, creation is not cosmos but only a flawed precondition for the ritual task of construction, so, too, at the level of human beginnings procreation is not the bringing into existence of an ontologically sound human being. Vedic conceptions of conception and reproduction reproduce the conceptions of cosmic creation examined in the last chapter: birth and anthropogony are, like creation and cosmogony, regarded as two separate moments, distinguished by the absence or presence of ritual reclamation. The bringing into existence of a viable human being is, the ritualists proclaimed, a matter of ritual rather than merely biological labor.

The procreative act of Prajāpati is the prototype of all procreative acts, including the sexual act which engenders new human life. Humans are emanated parts of the creator god and are thus subject to the natural defectiveness of all of Prajāpati's issue. And, as microcosmic versions of the macrocosmic creator, humans replicate and recapitulate in their acts of reproduction the creation of the universe as a whole. Human life is a process of ritually constructing and refining a self, an *ātman,* out of the raw materials of aboriginal creation, just as the *ātman* of Prajāpati is reconstituted (literally "remembered") by the postcreation rituals of the gods.

Unlike the unified Prajāpati of the totalistic cosmogonic process, however, the anthropogonic constructs—individual humans—are shaped into different types, made into a variety of products. Different kinds of human selves are constructed with different ontological values assigned, different degrees of the realization of completeness, different actualizations of the human ideal and potential. All selves are born defective and incomplete, but particular selves were supposed to have differing potentials for overcoming inherent defects. Birth as a male, for example, automatically qualifies one for the possibility of realizing a degree of human completeness—in the Vedic ritualistic view—not possible for females. Birth as the son of a learned Brahmin presents opportunities not available to the offspring of a Śūdra. Birth into a wealthy family holds out the potential for a self-realization different from that possible for a member of a family of lesser means.

Humans, then, are the result of both their inborn potential and their realization of it, and these two components come in unequal portions. Intrinsic, inherent potential and the actualization of that potential through a personal record of ritual performance combine to create distinctions in the "competence" (*adhikāra*) of particular individuals. And these distinctions are not regarded as merely social ones; they are rather envisioned as ontological differences in the *quality* of the human self produced in this life and of the "divine self" (*daiva ātman*) that the human will assume in the next world.

Vedic theories of conception and embryology[1] can be divided into two principal types, not coincidentally reduplicative of the two types of cosmogonic patterns identified in Chapter 3. Creation, it will be remembered, is a matter either of separating and distinguishing a formless unity or of reuniting an excessively differentiated set of emitted parts into a formed whole. In both cases it is an excess that must be moderated—an excess of similarity (*jāmi*) or an excess of difference (*pṛthak*)—in an effort to attain a structure of connected resembling parts.

The cosmic emission of Prajāpati is replicated by the emission of semen in the act of human procreation. Semen is considered the "essence" or "life sap" (*rasa*) of the man, his condensed representative: "Of created things here [in this world] earth is the essence; of earth, water; of water, plants; of plants, flowers; of flowers, fruits; of fruits, man; of man, semen."[2] When this fluid, the concentrated identity of man, is emitted into the womb of the woman, it is as if the very self of the procreator has been reproduced in the form of the new embryo:

1. See George William Brown, *The Human Body in the Upanishads* (Jubbulpore: Christian Mission Press, 1921); and Paul Deussen's discussion of the topic in his *The Philosophy of the Upanishads,* trans. by A. S. Geden (New York: Dover Publications, 1966), pp. 283–96.

2. BĀU 6.4.1.

> In a person, this one [the *ātman*] first becomes an embryo. That which is semen is the luminous power (*tejas*) extracted from all the parts [of the man]. In the self, truly, one bears another self. When he emits this into a woman, he then begets it. This is one's first birth.[3]

The male self is thus wholly, in condensed form, transmitted to and perpetuated through the male offspring, and in some texts this reduplicative view of conception seems to be regarded favorably: "The father enters the wife; having become an embryo, he [enters] the mother. When he is renewed in her, he is born in the tenth [lunar] month."[4] It is indeed generally the case that, as one text puts it, one desires a "counterpart" (*pratirūpa*) of oneself in the form of one's child, and not a "counterfeit" (*apratirūpa*).[5]

But this vision of reproduction also may be viewed as problematic, for the product of the generative act is redundant. The embryo here is an exact replica of the father. Creation so conceived recalls the macrocosmic error of *jāmi,* excessive resemblance. The fetus, a reduplication of the father, is undifferentiated until it is recast and individually shaped in the womb of the mother: "it comes into individual self-becoming (*ātmabhūya*) with the woman, just as a limb of her own. Therefore it does not injure her. She nourishes this self of his [the father] that has come to her."[6] Elsewhere the individualizing necessary to avoid the ontological flaw of *jāmi* is said to be attained by the intermingling of both male semen (the essence of the father) and female seed (the essence of the mother). The dual emission produces an independent and sufficiently distinct third entity:[7]

> A male child is born when the seed of the man is greater [than that of the woman], and a female child when the seed of the woman is greater [than that of the man]. If both are equal, a hermaphrodite is born, or a boy and a girl [i.e., fraternal twins]; and if the seed is weak or scanty, there will be a miscarriage.[8]

In any case, the male semen that carries the self of the father and creates a self which is the embryo must be tempered by, or combined

3. AitU 2.4.1; see also AitB 7.13 and AitĀ 2.5.

4. AitB 7.13; see also Manu 9.8.

5. ŚĀ 6.11; see also BĀU 2.1.8.

6. AitU 2.4.2; see also AitĀ 2.5.

7. For the relationship between male and female fluids, see Wendy Doniger O'Flaherty, *Women, Androgynes, and Other Mythical Beasts* (Chicago: University of Chicago Press, 1980), pp. 17–61.

8. Manu 3.49.

with, the female component—either in the womb itself, which provides space for an organic "self-becoming," or by means of the addition of a commingled female seed. The excessively undifferentiated semen is thus to be counteracted in some way in order to avoid the redundant sterility of *jāmi*.

In this theory of human reproduction the first ontological task is to distinguish the self of the fetus from the essence of the father's self represented by his semen. We are reminded here of the cosmogonic myths in which the emitted creatures are "clasped together" in unproductive union, "at odds with one another" in rivalry stemming from excessive similarity, and who are fearful of being "eaten" or resumed into the body of their creator.

Another theory of human origins, equally stressing the defectiveness of those origins, is also expounded in Vedic texts. This view, however, turns on the opposite ontological problem of excessive differentiation or *pṛthak*. Just as Prajāpati in the cosmic beginning emits creatures who are sometimes described as dispersed and in disarray until restructured into forms and placed into a relation one to another, so too is the human emission of semen sometimes envisioned as an act of radical dispersion and discontinuity, an act of problematical *dissemination*. The seed is described as "scattered" (*sikta*) into the womb in a microcosmic version of the macrocosmic dispersal of Prajāpati's creatures, and both microcosmic and macrocosmic fathers are depicted as "drained" after their emissions.[9]

Procreative emission here, as in the macrocosmic case, is followed by ontologically formative procedures. The semen ejaculated into the womb is subsequently "transformed" or "developed" by ritual means, in some cases with the aid of Tvaṣṭṛ, the divine builder and shaper of forms.[10] The seed is thus converted from its disseminated state and metamorphosed into a ontological composition. Through ritual manipulation, "he thereby transforms that scattered seed, and so the scattered seed is transformed in the womb."[11] And, as that same text declares, "whatever the seed is transformed into in the womb, as that is it born."[12]

The "transformation" of the unshaped (because it is either redun-

9. See, e.g., TS 6.6.5.1, where the cosmogonic act is conflated with both the human act of reproduction and the sacrificial act of generation: "Prajāpati emitted offspring. He thought himself drained. . . . He who sacrifices creates offspring. Then he [too] is drained."

10. See, e.g., KB 3.9; ŚB 1.9.2.10, 3.7.2.8, 4.4.2.16, 7.2.1.6.

11. ŚB 7.1.1.17.

12. ŚB 6.7.2.7.

dant or scattered) human potential into the reconstituted human being, beginning at conception and continuing through birth, childhood, and adolescence, is accomplished by the performances of rituals known as *saṃskāra*s. Often translated as "rites of passage," the *saṃskāra*s are really rituals of ontological healing, construction, and perfection, as we shall see in the next section. Those born into the Brahmin, Kṣatriya, or Vaiśya classes are expected to progress out of the state of inborn incompleteness and realize themselves, in different ways and to different degrees, through ritual action. A member of any one of these classes is born defective but also possesses inherent proclivities that should be actualized and exploited.

As Mircea Eliade has said in a passage that sums up much of his insight into the nature of *homo religiosus,* "every creation has a paradigmatic model—the creation of the universe by the gods."[13] Vedic ontology—the creation of human being—is a process of ritual labor and construction replicating at the anthropological level the ritual construction of the universe at the cosmological level. The fabrication of the self, like the fabrication of any or all of the "names and forms" that comprise the ordered cosmos, is a matter of lending a degree of *integrity* to an otherwise disfigured, unrealized, and unstable set of potentialities. "In this dynamic world," writes Verpoorten, "where all things at every moment flirt with effervescence, stability and continuity are the major preoccupations." For, as we have also observed, the "natural state" of all things and beings is "mere juxtaposition (*abhidhā-*)" of the parts.[14]

The movement from a condition of ontological defectiveness to that of integrated completeness which we have traced in cosmogonic myths is recapitulated in the ritual processing of individual human beings. Ritual formation and reformation of the unformed potential begins with those rites called the *saṃskāra*s. The term is derived from the Sanskrit root *kṛ-* ("to do or make"), with the integrative prefix *sam-,* and connotes, as Lilian Silburn writes, "the activity which creates forms, adapts them, and makes them perfect."[15] Or as Raj Bali Pandey puts it in his *Hindu Saṃskāras,* all of these rituals aim not only at "the formal purification of

13. Mircea Eliade, *The Sacred and the Profane,* p. 31.

14. Verpoorten, "Unité et distinction," p. 62.

15. Lilian Silburn, *Instant et cause,* p. 58. See also Jan Gonda's definition, *Vedic Ritual: The Non-solemn Rites* (Leiden: E. J. Brill, 1980), p. 364: "The untranslatable term *saṃskāra* is etymologically related to the verb *saṃskaroti* which expresses the general meaning of 'composing, making perfect, preparing properly and correctly with a view to a definite purpose.' "

the body but at sanctifying, impressing, refining and perfecting the entire individuality of the recipient."[16]

In order to understand the ontological importance of the *saṃskāra*s in Vedic ritualism, it is instructive to look at the depictions of those who have not yet undergone or do not ever (or did not when required) undergo them. These unregenerates and, therefore, in the eyes of the ritualists, degenerates are all regarded as less than really human, petrified in a state of nonbeing. Every human, as we have seen, is cast into this condition originally. Some persons and groups, however, are considered permanently faulty and incomplete. Still others are temporarily returned to the aboriginal state through neglect or illness. All again are, at death, placed into an ontological limbo complementary to that of the newly procreated fetus. In all of these instances, the "firm foundation," the structured protection that ritual activity affords against the perpetual tendency for all things and beings to deconstruct and return to their elemental formlessness—of either the *jāmi* or *pṛthak* variety—is absent or has been lost.

Although the rituals of healing and construction begin with the act of intercourse and conception, up until the time of initiation into Veda study and sacrificial ritualism (the *saṃskāra* known as the *upanayana*), the boy is considered incomplete and not yet responsible. A Brahmin, for example, who has not undergone initiation is called a "Brahmin by birth only"[17] or a "Brahmin by relation only."[18] They are in a state of nature and may therefore "act naturally," but they are also prohibited from the cultural act par excellence of sacrifice: "Before initiation [a boy] may follow his inclination in action, speech, and eating [but he shall] not partake of sacrificial offerings."[19] Such natural humans do not deserve the designation Brahmin at all; they are likened to wooden elephants or leather antelopes which "have nothing but the name" and are "equal to Śūdras"[20]—for the members of this latter class have not been "reborn" into Āryan society through the initiation and therefore are known as the "once born."[21]

The uninitiate, regardless of the class of his birth, is likened in many texts to others who are also, and for the same reasons, defective, those

16. Raj Bali Pandey, *Hindu Saṃskāras: Socio-Religious Study of the Hindu Sacraments,* 2d ed. (Delhi: Motilal Banarsidass, 1969), p. 17.

17. BGS 1.7.1; VaikhGS 1.1.

18. ChU 6.1.1.

19. GautDhS 2.1.

20. VāsDhS 3.1, 3.3, 3.11; see also Manu 2.157.

21. See Manu 10.4 and GautDhS 10.50.

who are permanently excluded from Vedic rituals and thus are permanently deficient, such as the Śūdras:

> They do not put any restrictions on the acts of [a child] before the initiation, for he is on the level with a Śūdra before his [second] birth through the Veda.[22]

> No religious rite can be performed by [a boy] before the initiation, because he is on the level with a Śūdra before his birth through the Veda.[23]

So it is that, as the Atri Smṛti declares, "By birth everyone is a Śūdra; by the performance of the *upanayana* one is called a twice-born."[24] The Śūdras live in a state of inherited and perpetual irresponsibility—they cannot perform an act serious enough to fall from position, being already at the bottom of the heap[25]—and are permanently stuck in the childlike condition of natural deficiency that members of the other classes pass through but can also pass out of by means of ritual renovation.

Whereas the defects of the Śūdra are supposedly inherited and permanent traits, others may lapse into an equivalent condition of ontological defectiveness. If a Brahmin passes his sixteenth year without undergoing initiation, if a Kṣatriya passes his twenty-second or a Vaiśya his twenty-fourth, they become "fallen ones," the *patita-sāvitrīka*s, who have lost their right to learn the Veda and to sacrifice.[26] These negligent men, bereft of and now excluded from the perfecting and healing force of ritual, degenerate instantly into a status identical to that of the Śūdra: "No one should initiate such men, nor teach them, nor perform sacrifices for them, nor have intercourse with them."[27] Elsewhere they are called "slayers of the *brahman*" and "burial grounds."[28]

In yet other texts, those who have "fallen" from the Veda and Āryan society are equated with another group in ancient India, about which little is known: the *vrātya*s.[29] Some believe these people were

22. BDhS 1.2.3.6.
23. VāsDhS 2.6; see also ĀpDhS 2.6.15.18–25.
24. Atri Smṛti 141–42.
25. Manu 10.126.
26. ŚGS 2.1.9; PGS 2.5.39.
27. PGS 2.5.40; see also JGS 1.12; ĀśvGS 1.19.9; ŚGS 2.1.10–13; VGS 5.3; GGS 2.10.6; Manu 2.40; VāsDhS 11.75.
28. ĀpDhS 1.1.1.32, 1.1.2.5.
29. For the equation of the *patita-sāvitrīka*s and the *vrātya*s, see Manu 2.39 and Yāj 1.38. The older secondary literature on the *vrātya*s is summarized in J. W. Hauer, *Der Vrātya,* 2 vols. (Stuttgart: W. Kohlhammer, 1927), I: 5–40. More recent studies include S. Biswas, "Über das Vrātyaproblem in der vedischen Ritualliteratur," *Zeitschrift der Deutschen Morgenländischen Gesellschaft* 105 (1955): 53–54; the iconoclastic study of J. C.

beyond the Āryan pale altogether, and others argue that they were a renegade branch of Āryan society; in any case it is clear that the *vrātya*s were, in the eyes of the mainstream ritualists, like the Śūdras and the "fallen" ones, defective and incomplete because of their separation from the Vedic ritual. They are depicted as strange, perverted, and lesser forms of human beings, whose practices are topsy-turvy versions of orthodox Vedism:

> Those who lead the life of a *vrātya* are defective (*hīna*) and left behind. For they neither practice the study of the Veda nor do they plough or trade. . . . Swallowers of poison are those [*vrātya*s] who eat foreign food as if it were the food of a Brahmin; who speak improperly as if it were proper; who strike the guiltless with a stick; and who, although not initiated, speak the speech of the initiated.[30]

The *patita-sāvitrīka* degenerates into a condition similar to that of the Śūdra and the *vrātya* through negligence. The physically afflicted man decomposes into much the same state when, as a result of possession, "sin," or other causes, he loses temporarily the continuity of being that ritual activity does so much to foster and protect.[31] "The vital breaths pass through him who is ill,"[32] just as they did when Prajāpati was in his postprocreative state. "Food goes forth from him,"[33] escaping from the body through the rupture that is sickness, just as the creatures run away from the weakened and "drained" Prajāpati. "He who is ill is without a firm foundation,"[34] returned to the precariousness of impaired origins, represented at the cosmic level by Prajāpati, who is collapsed in a heap awaiting reconstruction and healing.

One text, recalling the famous story of Indra's slaying of the serpent Vṛtra, compares the depleted strength of Indra after the battle to the

---

Heesterman, "Vrātya and Sacrifice," *Indo-Iranian Journal* 6 (1962): 1–37; and Radhakrishna Choudhary, *Vrātyas in Ancient India* (Benares: Chowkhamba Sanskrit Series Office, 1964).

30. PB 17.1.2.

31. The various causes of different sicknesses according to Vedic and Hindu texts are covered in G. U. Thite, *Medicine: Its Magico-Religious Aspects according to the Vedic and Later Literature* (Poona: Continental Prakashan, 1982), pp. 4–38. See also Kenneth Zysk, "Towards the Notion of Health in the Vedic Phase of Medicine," *Zeitschrift der Deutschen Morganländischen Gesellschaft* 135 (1985): 312–18; idem, *Religious Healing in the Veda* (Philadelphia: American Philosophical Society, 1986); and Johanna Narten, "Ved. *āmayati* und *āmayāvin-*," *Studien zur Indologie und Iranistik* 5–6 (1980): 153–66.

32. PB 18.5.11.

33. PB 15.13.3.

34. PB 16.13.4.

quintessential disease of depletion and rupture—diarrhea—in addition to other comparable conditions: those of an expelled king, a childless though fertile man, and the generically ill man:

> Indra slew Vṛtra. His strength went asunder in every direction. The gods searched for an expiation for him, but none would please him. Only the strong soma rite (*tivra-soma*) pleased him [and restored him strength]. He should perform [this rite] for one who drinks soma only to have it pass through him. Ruptured, as it were, is he whose soma passes through him. The performance of the strong soma rite serves to block up, to rectify the rupture. He should perform it for a king who is expelled [from his kingdom]. The subjects pass through him who has been expelled from his kingdom. The performance of the the strong soma rite serves to block up, to rectify the rupture. . . . It should be performed by one who wants offspring. Offspring pass through him who, though fertile, gets no offspring. The performance of the strong soma rite serves to block up, to rectify the rupture. . . . He should perform it for one who is ill in any way. The vital breaths pass through him who is ill. The performance of the strong soma rite serves to block up, to rectify the rupture.[35]

Finally, we may turn to the case of the recently deceased, who is situated between a former life as a man and a future existence as an ancestor. The transition is not immediately effected upon death; the spirit (*preta*) must be ritually made over time into an ancestor (*pitṛ*), just as the embryo and infant are constructed into a human being by ritual means: "The dead man does not immediately after his death and without more ado join the number of the ancestors who are worshipped; on the contrary fixed ceremonies are necessary for elevating the deceased to the rank of ancestors."[36] There is, as David Knipe puts it, a "series of bodily constructions and dissolutions the deceased undergoes before becoming established in the world beyond."[37] The rituals of death, mirroring in many ways the *saṃskāra*s of life, begin with the cremation of the body. The once integrated constituents of the human body are dissolved into their parts and redistributed throughout the cosmos:

> The voice of the dead man goes into fire, his breath into wind, his eye into the sun, his mind into the moon, his hearing into the quarters of heaven,

35. PB 18.5.2–6, 18.5.9, 18.5.11.

36. Dakshina Ranjan Shastri, *Origin and Development of the Rituals of Ancestor Worship in India* (Calcutta: Bookland, 1963), p. 62.

37. David M. Knipe, "*Sapiṇḍīkaraṇa*: The Hindu Rite of Entry into Heaven," in Frank E. Reynolds and Earle H. Waugh, eds., *Religious Encounters with Death: Insights from the History and Anthropology of Religions* (University Park: Pennsylvania State University Press, 1977), p. 111.

his body into the earth, his self into space, the hairs of his body into trees, and his blood and semen are placed in water.[38]

Man is decomposed into his natural and dispersed elements at death precisely as the Cosmic One must first become multiple before a new reformation can emerge when the parts are recomposed. And as Prajāpati, in his liminal state after procreative emission, but before ritual reconstruction, is described as depleted or "fallen to pieces," so too is the *preta,* the "gone out" or "departed" human spirit, depicted as dangerously detached before its reunification and transformation into an ancestor: "They say of the *preta,* 'He has been cut off.' "[39]

The uninitiated child, the Śūdra, the *patita-sāvitrīka,* the *vrātya,* the sick man, and the newly dead—all these conditions are comparable regressions to the primary and fundamental human condition of defectiveness. Sacrifice is in Vedism the ontological medicine to fix all deficient creations, to repair all debilitated forms. Those precluded from, without access to, or who voluntarily reject the healing balm of ritual are permanently disabled, permanently incomplete human beings from the Vedic point of view. And those who are eligible for and partake of the ontological salve that ritual provides must perpetually take precautions. The rituals must be regularly repeated to protect against the natural inclination of structured entities to deconstruct into their atomistic constituents.

Constructing Selves and Statuses

Although it is not until the Sūtras (ca. 700–300 B.C.E.) that the term *saṃskāra* is used to designate a specified set of particular rituals—beginning with one performed at the conception and ending with the death rites—other formations of *sam-* + *kṛ-* (e.g., *saṃskṛti, saṃskṛta, saṃskaroti, saṃskurute*) describing the effects of rituals on humans do appear regularly in the Veda, and with much the same meaning. As early as ṚV 5.76.2, a form of the verb appears when a certain vessel, the *gharma,* is to be made *saṃskṛta* and therefore ready for ritual use; or, again, at ŚB 1.1.4.10 an offering must be made *saṃskṛta* before it may be presented to the gods.[40]

Saṃskāra rites, in all periods of Indian history, may be performed either on things or on people. In all cases, according to the great philosopher of ritual Śabara (commenting on PMS 3.1.3), the purpose of these

38. BĀU 3.2.13; see also ṚV 10.16.3; ŚB 10.3.3.6.
39. ŚB 10.5.5.13.
40. For other examples of the use of the verb in early texts, see below, p. 101.

kinds of rites is to make the thing or being fit (*yogya*) for its function. Fitness is said to be of two kinds: that which arises by the removal of taints (especially those congenital faults stemming from biological existence) and that which arises through the ritual generation of fresh inner qualities.[41] Still another definition highlights the creative role of these rites: "Just as a work of painting gradually unfolds itself on account of the several colors [with which it is drawn], so Brahminhood is similarly brought out by *saṃskāra*s performed according to the prescribed rites."[42]

Following the ritual philosophers, then, one might best consider these rituals not as rites of passage—implying leaps from one ontologically stable condition to another—but rather both as rituals of healing (eliminating the congenital defects of the self) and as rituals of construction (adding new qualities, actualizing latent tendencies, and perfectly integrating them into an ontological composition). From conception to birth, from birth to the "second birth" of initiation, and from marriage to death, the life of the Vedic male[43] was punctuated by these rituals of healing and formation, of transformation and transfiguration.

It is unnecessary to delve here into the analytical details of all of the *saṃskāra*s.[44] A glimpse at one, and perhaps the most important, of the series might suffice to give some indication of the social and, reputedly, ontological function (what might be called the socio-ontological effect) that these rituals had for those encompassed within Vedic ritualism.

Although the *upanayana*[45] is not specifically mentioned in the Ṛg

41. The Tantravārtika on PMS 3.8.9, cited in P. V. Kane, *History of Dharmaśāstra*, 2d ed., 5 vols. (Poona: Bhandarkar Oriental Research Institute, 1968–75), II, 1: 190–91. See also the definition by the later *mīmāṃsaka* Mitramiśra, who wrote that *saṃskāra*s impart the necessary qualities for the performance of other rituals or eliminate congenital defects and impurities (also cited in Kane, p. 191); and statements to similar effect in Manu 2.26–28 and Yāj 1.13.

42. Parāśara Smṛti 8.19. The citation is also quoted in A. K. Ramanujan's afterword to his translation of U. R. Anantha Murthy's novel *Saṃskāra: A Rite for a Dead Man* (Delhi: Oxford University Press, 1978), p. 141. See also Kane, *History of Dharmaśāstra*, II, 1: p. 191: "The *saṃskāra*s had been treated from very ancient times as necessary for unfolding the latent capacities of man for development."

43. Females did not undergo all the *saṃskāra*s and were in particular prohibited from the *upanayana*.

44. The interested reader might consult Pandey, *Hindu Saṃskāras*; Kane, *History of Dharmaśāstra*, Vol. II; Gonda, *Vedic Ritual*; and H. N. Chatterjee, *Studies in Some Aspects of Hindu Saṃskāras in Ancient India* (Calcutta: Sanskrit Pustak Bhandar, 1965).

45. For this *saṃskāra*, see Karl Glaser, "Der indische Student," *Zeitschrift der Morgenländischen Gesellschaft* 66 (1912): 1–37; and Brian K. Smith, "Ritual, Knowledge, and Being: Initiation and Veda Study in Ancient India," *Numen* 33 (1986): 65–89. For the meaning of the term "*upanayana*," consult Jan Gonda, "Upanayana," *Indologica Taurinensia* 7 (1979): 253–59.

Veda,[46] it does appear as a fixed ritual already in the Atharva Veda Saṃhitā[47] and the Śatapatha Brāhmaṇa,[48] and the details of the rite given in those relatively early texts conform in most details to the initiation ritual explicated in the Sūtras. It appears that at a very early date in Vedic history the *upanayana* and subsequent period of Veda study were regarded as mandatory for the Āryan community.[49] By the time of the Sūtras, the *upanayana* was called simply the *saṃskāra*[50] to indicate its paradigmatic significance, and according to Ram Gopal the term *saṃskāra* "was gradually extended [from the *upanayana*] to all domestic rites."[51]

Upanayana initiated a young boy into the study of the Veda under the guidance of a teacher and into the performance of the sacrifice.[52] But it was also an initiation into Āryan society; he became, by virtue of the rite, "twice born" (*dvija*), a term that occurs as early as the Atharva Veda Saṃhitā.[53] In Manu, this "birth from the Veda" is explicitly contrasted with the merely biological birth from the mother and is called the "real" (*satya*) birth[54]—a blatant move to devaluate the products of women and extol the cultural/ritual labor of men. This second birth was thus claimed to be a socio-ontological birth standing in radical opposition to the defective natural birth, and was designed to rectify biological faults and construct a higher ontological existence for the young boy.

In this way, the natural birth of individual humans replicates the natural birth of the cosmos as a whole, for both are regarded as equally degenerate. And just as we understood the cosmogonic myths as statements of the ineptitude of Prajāpati, the creator god, so might we understand the denigration of natural birth as statements of the ineptitude of human mothers. The ritualists felt that only they were ultimately qualified to produce proper offspring; both the cosmos and individual hu-

46. There are references to the period of Veda study under the tutelage of a teacher, called *brahmacarya,* at ṚV 3.8.4 and 10.109.5, however.

47. AV 11.5.

48. ŚB 11.3.3, 11.5.4.

49. As early as the Taittirīya Saṃhitā (6.3.10.5), a Brahmin was said to have been born with three debts, one of which was to the primordial seers which was repaid through *brahmacarya*.

50. PGS 2.5.42–43.

51. Ram Gopal, *India of the Vedic Kalpasūtras* (Delhi: National Publishing House, 1959), p. 254.

52. For more details on these two aspects of the *upanayana* rite, see Smith, "Ritual, Knowledge, and Being."

53. AV 11.5.3; for later usage, see ĀpDhS 1.1.1.15; GautDhS 1.8; Manu 2.68.

54. Manu 2.169–70, 2.148.

mans could be "truly born" only from a womb controlled by priests, from the womb, that is, of the sacrifice.

The initiation or second birth was to occur at the age of eight for a boy born of Brahmin parents, eleven for a Kṣatriya, and twelve for a Vaiśya, the Śūdras being excluded from the rite.[55] And we have observed above the consequences of failure to undergo the ritual. Because of this "vehemence with which those who failed to undertake the *upanayana* ceremony were condemned," Jan Gonda concludes that the ritual was "more or less a compulsory institution" in Vedic India.[56] Through it one was constituted an Āryan—a true human being. But even within the order of the Āryan, the fully human, socio-ontological distinctions were made between classes. The *upanayana* generated not a generic "humanness" in the initiate but rather created humans who were thought to be of different general types. As one text puts it, the socio-ontological classes of Āryan society were distinguished not only by inborn nature (*prakṛti-viśiṣṭa*) but also by being constituted or made distinct through the ritual *saṃskāra*s (*saṃskāra-viśeṣa*).[57]

The special importance of the *upanayana,* then, was not only that it initiated the individual into human society; it was also the means by which the posited innate and distinctive class proclivities of ancient Indian groups were actualized. The class differentiations within the ritual are a predominant feature, and this is no accident (see Table 1). In hierarchical, as well as ritualistic, Vedic India, humans are ritually made different, and differently.

I have already noted that the ideal times for undergoing the initiation vary according to class—with the recommended age for the more intellectually capable Brahmin lower than those for the other classes—and so, too, is there a distinction among the ages after which initiation may not take place.[58] It is also stated that different seasons are most

55. For the ages for *upanayana,* reckoned either from conception or from birth, see ĀśvGS 1.19.1–4; ŚGS 2.1.1–5; BGS 2.5.2; BhGS 1.1; HGS 1.1.1.2–3; ĀpGS 4.10.2–3; VaikhGS 2.3; VGS 5.1–2; MGS 1.22.1; PGS 2.2.1–3; GGS 2.10.1–3; KhGS 2.4.1–6; ĀpDhS 1.1.1.19; BDhS 1.2.3.7–9; Manu 2.36; VāsDhS 11.49–51; GautDhS 1.5, 1.11. For optional ages for the attainment of different qualities, see BGS 2.5.5; VGS 5.1–2; JGS 1.12; ĀpDhS 1.1.1.20–26; Manu 2.37; GautDhS 1.6.

56. Jan Gonda, *Change and Continuity,* p. 391.

57. VāsDhS 4.1.

58. Sixteen for the Brahmin, twenty-two for the Kṣatriya, and twenty-four for the Vaiśya. See ĀśvGS 1.19.5–7; ŚGS 2.1.6–8; BGS 2.5.3–4; VaikhGS 2.3; VGS 5.3; PGS 2.5.36–38; GGS 2.10.4; KhGS 2.4.6; ĀpDhS 1.1.1.27; BDhS 1.2.3.12; Manu 2.38; VāsDhS 11.71–73; GautDhS 1.12–13.

Table 1. Class Differences in the Initiation Ritual

	Brahmin	*Kṣatriya*	*Vaiśya*
Age for initiation	8	11	12
Last age for initiation	16	22	24
Meters of Sāvitrī verse	*gāyatrī*	*triṣṭubh*	*jagatī*
Seasons for initiation	spring	hot season	autumn
Upper garment (*uttarīya, ajina*)	black antelope	spotted deer	goat or cow
Lower garment (*vāsa*)	linen or hempen	cotton or linen	woolen
Color of lower garment	reddish brown	red	yellow
Girdle (*mekhalā*)	from *muñja* grass	bowstring	woolen or hempen
Staff (*daṇḍa*)	*palāśa* or *bilva*	*nyagrodha*	*badara* or *udumbara*
Size of staff	reaches top of head	reaches forehead	reaches nose

appropriate for the performance of the ritual by different classes: Brahmins undergo the *upanayana* in the spring, Kṣatriyas in the hot season, and Vaiśyas in the autumn.[59] It is not accidental that these same correlations between socio-ontological classes and the seasons of the year appear also in the Śrauta Sūtras in discussions of the auspicious times for married householders to light the sacrificial fires.[60] As Pandey notes,

59. See, e.g., ĀpGS 4.10.4; HGS 1.1.1.4; VaikhGS 2.3; BDhS 1.2.3.10; ĀpDhS 1.1.1.19. BGS 2.5.6 and BhGS 1.1 also allow for the initiation of the *rathakāra* ("chariot-maker"), the offspring of a Vaiśya man and a Śūdra woman. His initiation should occur in the rainy season. For other stipulations on the time for *upanayana,* see HGS 1.1.1.5 and BhGS 1.1.

60. See R. N. Dandekar, ed., *Śrautakośa: Encyclopedia of Vedic Sacrificial Ritual,* 2 vols. (Poona: Vaidika Saṃśodhana Maṇḍala, 1958–82) I, 1: 1–26.

These different seasons were symbolical of the temperament and occupation of different castes. The moderation of spring symbolized the moderate life of a Brahmin; the heat of summer represented the fervour of a kṣātriya; autumn, when the commercial life of ancient India reopened after the rainy season, suggested the wealth and prosperity of a vaiśya. . . .[61]

The individual items of the uniform of the student, bestowed during the course of the initiation rites, also served to differentiate types of students and to highlight and realize the particular qualities peculiar to each. Every boy was given an upper garment, a lower garment, a belt, a staff, and, according to only some of the ancient texts, the sacred thread (*yajñopavīta*) that would become so central to later Hindu conceptions of the *upanayana*.[62]

In most cases, the differences in uniform systematically draw on ancient associations—that is, *resemblances*—between parts of nature and the qualities of the different socio-ontological classes. The upper garment, for example, is to be a skin from the black antelope if the initiate is a Brahmin, from the spotted deer if a Kṣatriya, and from a goat or a cow if a Vaiśya.[63] In the Brāhmaṇas, the black antelope is consistently connected with Brahmins,[64] the *brahman* power,[65] the "lustre of the *brahman* power" (*brahmavarcasas*),[66] and the sacrifice,[67] the workplace of the Brahmin priest. Although the connection between the Kṣatriya and spotted deer is less straightforward,[68] presumably the latter resounds with physical and royal power. This conclusion is partially confirmed by two facts. First, in a variant opinion on the proper skin for a Kṣatriya initiate, one text recommends that of the tiger.[69]

61. ". . . and the easy time of rains indicated facility for a chariot-maker." Pandey, *Hindu Saṃskāras,* p. 127.

62. It appears that the earlier practice was to use the upper garment to serve the function later taken by the *yajñopavīta.* See ĀpDhS 2.2.4.21–22 and Kane, *History of Dharmaśāstra,* II, 1: 289–91. Pandey, *Hindu Saṃskāras,* p. 132, is incorrect, however, when he writes that "None of the Gṛhyasūtras contains the prescription of wearing the Sacred Thread." See ŚGS 2.2.3; BGS 2.5.7; BhGS 1.1; VGS 5.8.

63. ĀśvGS 1.19.10; ŚGS 2.1.2–5; BGS 2.5.16; HGS 1.1.4.7; BhGS 1.1; VaikhGS 2.4; PGS 2.5.17–19; GGS 2.10.9; JGS 1.12; ĀpDhS 1.1.3.3–6; BDhS 1.2.3.14; VāsDhS 11.61–63; GautDhS 1.16.

64. AitB 7.23.

65. KB 4.11; TB 2.7.1.4, 2.7.3.3.

66. PB 17.11.8; ŚB 9.3.4.14; see also ĀpDhS 1.1.3.9 and BhGS 1.1.

67. ŚB 1.1.4.3, 3.2.1.8, 3.2.1.28, etc.

68. PB 7.5.7–10 and 12.4.24–26 associate this animal with cattle, which would suggest a connection with the Vaiśyas, not the Kṣatriyas.

69. KGS 41.13.

Second, a later commentary on a different text[70] equates the spotted deer and the tiger. The tiger (and, by inference, the spotted deer) is indeed an animal with resemblances to the Kṣatriya. It is said to be the embodiment of courage,[71] the king of the wild animals,[72] and the representative of the kṣatra power within the animal kingdom.[73] As for the relationship between the agriculturalist/merchant—the Vaiśya—and the productive and valuable cow or the prolific goat, little more need be said. Both the cowhide and the skin of the goat are symbols of "food,"[74] and the goat is said to be the very form (*rūpa*) of "increase" or *puṣṭi*.[75]

Such systematic identifications between the components of nature and those of society are also present in the case of the belt wrapped around the boy at initiation. In general, this item of the uniform is meant to protect the boy who wears it[76] and to give him strength,[77] and it may have also been a symbolic umbilical cord of the newly reborn student.[78] Most texts agree that the Brahmin's should be made of *muñja* grass (Saccharum Sara), that of the kṣatriya from the bowstring or the *mūrvā* hemp from which such strings were made (Sanseviera Roxburghiana), and the Vaiśya's from wool or hemp.[79] *Muñja* grass, it would seem, brings out the Brahmin's connection to the sacrifice, for in the ritual it is used in various capacities (for brooms, cords, seats, purifiers, and, interestingly enough, the belt tied around the body of the sacrificer's wife during the ritual). *Muñja* is quite flammable and was used in the sacrifice to make the fire blaze up,[80] thus restoring "vigor" or "life sap" (*ūrj*) to the sacrifice.[81] The resemblance between the Kṣatriya and the bowstring is obvious: "The bow, truly, is the manly strength of the Kṣatriya."[82] As for the Vaiśya, hemp appears to suggest proliferation and reproduction,[83] and

70. Rāghavānanda on Manu 2.41.
71. ŚB 12.7.2.8.
72. ŚB 12.7.1.8.
73. AitB 8.6.
74. E.g., ŚB 7.5.2.6, 7.5.2.43, 6.3.2.4.
75. TB 1.3.7.7.
76. GGS 2.10.37; PGS 2.2.8; MGS 1.22.7.
77. TS 6.1.3.3–4.
78. See, e.g., HGS 1.1.4.4.
79. ĀśvGS 1.19.12; ŚGS 2.1.15–17; BGS 2.5.13; HGS 1.1.1.17; BhGS 1.1; VaikhGS 2.4; VGS 5.7; BDhS 1.2.3.13; Manu 2.42; VāsDhS 11.5.8–10; GautDhS 1.15. See also PGS 2.5.21–23; GGS 2.10.10; JGS 1.12.
80. See, e.g., BhSS 11.3.16; MŚS 6.1.3.23; ĀpŚS 15.4.2.
81. ŚB 14.1.3.15–16; TB 3.8.1.1; TĀ 5.4.3–4.
82. ŚB 5.3.5.30.
83. It is connected to the amnion at ŚB 3.2.1.11 and to the chorion at ŚB 6.6.1.24.

wool clearly bonds the pastoralist to his domesticated animals. According to one text, the Vaiśya's belt should be made of rope used for yoking oxen to the plow, emphasizing the agricultural function of this class.[84]

The staff, too, serves to create and reinforce class differentiation and hierarchy in the boys undergoing the initiation *saṃskāra*. It is to be of varying lengths[85] and different woods according to class: *palāśa* (Butea Frondosa) or *bilva* (Aegle Marmelos) for the Brahmin, *nyagrodha* (Ficus Indica) for the Kṣatriya, and *badara* (Zizyphus Jujuba) or *udumbara* (Ficus Glomerata) for the Vaiśya.[86] Again, these prescriptions are not haphazard. In the Brāhmaṇas, *palāśa* is frequently identified with the *brahman* power[87] or with soma[88] and is said to instill luminosity (*tejas*) and the luster of the *brahman* power.[89] According to the Baudhayana Gṛhya Sūtra,[90] the staff of *palāśa* is received by the student from the teacher with the words "You are soma. Make me a soma-drinker," and that of *bilva* wood with "You are the luster of the *brahman* power. You are for the luster of the *brahman*." The *nyagrodha* or banyan tree, with its bending branches which take root in the ground, was regarded as a resembling form of the Kṣatriya:

> The *nyagrodha* is the *kṣatra* power of trees, and the Kṣatriya is the *kṣatra* power [among humans], for the Kṣatriya here dwells fastened, as it were, to the kingdom, and supported [by it]. And the *nyagrodha* is fastened to the ground, as it were, by its downward growths, and supported [by it].[91]

The staff made of this wood is taken by the Kṣatriya initiate with a *mantra* imparting physical vitality or *ojas*.[92] The Vaiśya receives the staff of *badara* with "You are increase. Put increase in me," and that of *udumbara* with "You are life sap (*ūrj*). Put life sap in me."[93] The associa-

84. ĀpDhS 1.1.2.37.

85. See ĀśvGS 1.19.13; GautDhS 1.26; VāsDhS 11.55–57; Manu 2.146; BDhS 1.2.3.15. For the inverse, however, consult ŚGS 2.1.21–23.

86. ŚGS 2.1.18–20; BGS 2.5.17; BhGS 1.1; ĀpGS 4.11.16; HGS 1.1.1.17; VaikhGS 2.4; JGS 1.12; ĀpDhS 1.1.1.38; VāsDhS 11.52–54. See also ĀśvGS 1.9.13; VGS 5.27; PGS 2.5.25–27; GGS 2.10.11; Manu 2.45; GautDhS 1.22–23.

87. ŚB 1.3.3.19, 2.6.2.8, 5.2.4.18, etc.

88. ŚB 3.3.4.10, 6.6.3.7.

89. AitB 2.1.

90. BGS 2.5.18–19.

91. AitB 7.31; see also ŚB 5.3.5.13.

92. BGS 2.5.20.

93. BGS 2.5.22–23.

tion of *udumbara* with life sap and food is well attested in the Vedic texts.[94]

Other rites within the *upanayana* besides those already mentioned also serve much the same purpose: to make socio-ontological distinctions, infuse appropriate qualities, and draw out intrinsic potentialities. According to Jaiminīya Gṛhya Sūtra,[95] the lower garment is put on the boy with *mantra*s adjusted "according to class" (*yathāvarṇa*): Brahmins are dressed with a prayer to Soma for great learning, Kṣatriyas with one to Indra for great dominion, and Vaiśyas with a *mantra* requesting Poṣa, a deity of prosperity, to deliver his goods. These varying desirable qualities are also mentioned in another rite, the entrusting of the boy to the deities, in which the *mantra*s are again appropriately modified according to the class of the boy,[96] and yet other examples could be adduced of this same phenomenon within the initiation ritual.[97]

Finally, we note a most important rite within the *upanayana,* the imparting of the *sāvitrī* verse (ṚV 3.62.10) to the newly initiated pupil. According to some texts, this *mantra* ("We contemplate the excellent glory of the divine Savitṛ; may he inspire our intellect!") was to be recited in different meters by members of the different classes. Brahmins were to learn the verse in the *gāyatrī* meter, Kṣatriyas in the *triṣṭubh,* and Vaiśyas in the *jagatī.*[98] Here again, the rules displayed in the Sūtras draw upon ancient correlations. The *gāyatrī* was directly connected to Brahmins,[99] or to the *brahman* power or luster of the *brahman,*[100] or to Agni, the priest of the gods.[101] The *triṣṭubh* was systematically associated with Kṣatriyas,[102] physical power and manly

94. E.g., AitB 5.24, 7.22; PB 5.5.2, 6.4.1; KB 25.15, 27.6; TB 1.2.6.5, 1.3.8.2; ŚB 3.2.1.33, 3.3.4.27.

95. JGS 1.12.

96. See HGS 1.1.4.8.

97. See, e.g., ŚGS 2.2.11–15 and VaikhGS 2.4. For different begging formulas used by students of different classes, see BGS 2.5.48–51; VaikhGS 2.8; VGS 5.28; PGS 2.5.2–4; BDhS 1.2.3.17; ĀpDhS 1.1.3.28–30; Manu 2.49; VāsDhS 1.1.68–70; GautDhS 2.36. For different salutes adopted by different types of *brahmacārins*, see ĀpDhS 1.2.5.16.

98. ŚGS 2.5.4–7; MGS 1.22.13; PGS 2.3.7–9; BDhS 1.2.3.11. According to other texts (VGS 5.26; KGS 41.20), wholly different Vedic verses were to be imparted to the different classes, for which consult also R. K. Mookerji, *Ancient Indian Education (Brahmanical and Buddhist)* (London: Macmillan, 1947), p. 182; and Kane, *History of Dharmaśāstra,* II, 1: 302ff.

99. PB 6.1.6; TS 7.1.1.4.

100. KB 17.2, 17.9; PB 6.9.25, 12.1.2; ŚB 4.1.1.14.

101. AitB 8.6; KB 9.2; PB 6.1.6; TS 7.1.1.4.

102. TS 7.1.1.5; PB 6.1.8.

strength,[103] and with Indra, king of the gods.[104] The *jagatī* was in like manner consistently connected to Vaiśyas in the ancient texts,[105] or to cattle,[106] prosperity in general,[107] the earth,[108] plants,[109] and the All-gods, the Vaiśya analogue in the heavenly world.[110]

Another analogy was created between the syllabic composition of the meters (the *gāyatrī* is a triplet made up of eight syllables each, the *triṣṭubh* a quartet of eleven syllables per verse, and the *jagatī* a quartet of twelve syllables each) and both the respective ideal ages for initiation of the classes (eight, eleven, and twelve) and the difference between these ages and the last ages possible for performance of the *upanayana* for each class (also eight, eleven, and twelve). Hermann Oldenberg sums up this rather complicated set of resemblances:

> The number of years given for the Upanayana of persons of the three castes (Brāhmaṇas 8–16, Kṣatriyas 11–22, Vaiśyas 12–24) is evidently derived from the number of syllables of the three metres which are so very frequently stated to correspond to the three castes, to the three gods or categories of gods (Agni, Indra, Viśve devās), etc., viz. the Gāyatrī, the Trishṭubh, and the Jagatī.

"This is a very curious example," Oldenberg goes on to opine, "showing how in India phantastical speculations like those regarding the mystical qualities of the metres, were strong enough to influence the customs and institutions of real life."[111] To put the case a bit less pejoratively, it was indeed the production of a "real" life for the initiates that the ritualists aimed for. And to do so, in the Vedic world, was to move the candidate from inborn, biological imperfection to a ritually constructed—that is, a ritually *connected*—identity.

The *upanayana* delivers a reborn Āryan, who was supposedly more really human because more fully *realized, activated* through the activity of ritual. The ritual of initiation was thus the first of many such rites designed to draw hierarchical distinctions among ritualists of different

103. AitB 4.3; KB 11.2, 16.1.

104. AitB 8.6; KB 14.3, 30.2; PB 6.1.8; TS 7.1.1.5.

105. TS 7.1.1.5; PB 6.1.10.

106. AitB 3.18, 3.25; KB 16.2, 17.2; PB 6.1.10, 18.11.9; ŚB 8.3.3.3, 12.8.3.13; TS 7.1.1.5.

107. ŚB 3.4.1.13.

108. ŚB 1.8.2.11, 6.2.1.29, etc.

109. ŚB 1.8.2.11.

110. AitB 8.6; PB 6.1.10; TS 7.1.1.5.

111. Hermann Oldenberg, *The Grihya Sūtras,* Vol. 1 (Oxford: Oxford University Press, 1886; reprint ed. Delhi: Motilal Banarsidass, 1964), commenting on ŚGS 2.1.1.

social classes, and to constitute Vedic society as a whole made up of unequal, ritually constituted groups.

The completion of the *upanayana* ritual, of the period of Veda study and tutelage under the teacher which it inaugurates, together with the performance of the equally crucial marriage *saṃskāra,* qualifies the adult householder to set his own ritual fire (or fires) and perform the Vedic sacrifices. These more complex rituals continue the ontological development and refinement of his being. If the function of the *saṃskāra*s was, as one text declares, to make fit the physical body,[112] one of the principal purposes of all Vedic rituals was to make fit the *ātman,* the self (inclusive of the body, soul, and socio-ontological identity). The construction and perfecting of the *ātman* in the sacrifice is often described in the Brāhmaṇas with the same combination of the verb *kṛ-* and the prefix *sam-* that gives us the word *saṃskāra.*

In the Aitareya Brāhmaṇa, for example, the soma sacrifice is depicted as a ritual of "self-perfection" (*ātma-saṃskṛti*) and is regarded as a "work of art" (*śilpa*).[113] The sacrificer "fashions (*saṃskurute*) his own self in a rhythmical way" through the ritual chants that are likened to seeds being poured into the womb.[114] Again, in another Brāhmaṇa, we read that in the ritual the priests construct and perfect (*saṃskurvanti*) a "heavenly self" (*daiva ātman*) for the sacrificer,[115] and in yet another text the relationship between the constructive ritual activity and the *ātman* thus constructed is recognized by the sacrificer, who knows, "This, my [new, heavenly] body is made perfect (*saṃskriyate*) by that [sacrifice]; this body of mine is procured by that [ritual]."[116]

The body of Prajāpati, the Cosmic Man, was joined together, reintegrated, and healed by the ritual acts of the gods. So also is the *ātman* of the human made whole and perfected in his sacrificial activity. Each sacrifice expresses and regenerates the sacrificer's *ātman,* and the ritual life of the individual becomes like a canvas on which is painted the picture of his self. The portrait is complete in itself at any particular

112. VaikhGS 1.1.

113. See B. M. Barua's comments on this passage in his "Art as Defined in the Brāhmaṇas," *Indian Culture* 1 (July 1934–April 1935): 120: "The substance with potentialities or possible forms is given as a work of Art Divine and the methodical realization of those possibilities is the achievement of human skill and intelligence. . . . Art consists in the intelligent working up of a desired form on a natural material, making manifest what is hidden or potential."

114. AitB 6.27.

115. KB 3.8.

116. ŚB 11.2.6.13.

sacrificial performance and is filled out over time. It is at once an index and a projection, a gauge of the relative realization of the self in this world and in the other world beyond death. Sacrifice constitutes being, on both the cosmic and human planes, through a process that is equally one of construction and of discovery, of making and of finding. As J. F. Staal writes,

> The sacrifice can now be interpreted as one of the modes of human being which constitutes being. This ontological interpretation enables us to see how it was possible (ontically, as Heidegger would say) that such importance was attached to the ritual act. . . . The transformation or consecration which is effectuated through sacrifice, is not a transformation from one being to another but the constitution of being itself.[117]

In many of the Brāhmaṇas, the second birth of the individual is not exclusively the *upanayana* but sacrifice in general.[118] For "Unborn, truly, is [the natural] man. He is really born through the sacrifice."[119] Several texts state that "man is born three times":

> First he is born from his mother and father; then, when he to whom the sacrifice inclines sacrifices, he is born a second time; and when he dies, when they put him into the [cremation] fire and he arises again, he is born a third time. Thus, they say, "A man is born three times."[120]

Sacrifice, as has often been noted by scholars of the Vedic ritual, is represented as a cycle, a series of births predicted on a series of prior deaths.[121]

"Man depends only on his own ritual work, his own *karman,*" as Jan Heesterman puts it.[122] Humans are responsible for creating an ontologically viable self for themselves and the "world" (*loka*) for that self to

117. J. F. Staal, *Advaita and Neoplatonism: A Critical Study in Comparative Philosophy* (Madras: University of Madras, 1961), p. 67.

118. For the birth symbolism surrounding the consecration rite for a soma sacrifice, the *dīkṣā* (a rite which reduplicates at a higher level the initiation or *upananyana*), see Kaelber, "The 'Dramatic' Element in Brāhmaṇic Initiation: Symbols of Death, Danger, and Difficult Passage," *History of Religions* 18 (August 1978): 54–76"; Lévi, *La Doctrine du sacrifice,* pp. 102–7; and esp. Gonda, *Change and Continuity,* pp. 315–462.

119. MS 3.6.7; see also JUB 3.14.8.

120. ŚB 11.2.1.1; see also AitĀ 2.5; JUB 3.11.3.

121. See Lévi, *La Doctrine du sacrifice,* p. 81; J. C. Heesterman, *The Ancient Indian Royal Consecration: The Rājasūya according to the Yajus Texts and Annoted [sic]* ('s Gravenhage: Mouton, 1957), p. 6; and Kaelber, "The 'Dramatic' Element in Brāhmaṇic Initiation."

122. J. C. Heesterman, "Brahmin, Ritual, and Renouncer," p. 34.

inhabit. And both self and world are ritual constructs. "Man is born into a world made by himself,"[123] a ritual world where new birth can occur. But this homemade world is also a *loka* in the sense of a status constituted by the rituals one has performed. "Born out of the sacrifice, the sacrificer frees himself from death. *The sacrifice becomes his self,*"[124] for man is the sacrifice (*puruṣo vai yajñaḥ*).[125] The dimensions of the sacrificer's self or being are correlative to the rituals he sponsors and participates in. Ritual is thus regarded as the true mother and accurate measure of being.

The *ātman,* in Vedic texts before the monistic Upanishads, represents the ritually constructed conjunction of innate and acquired potential, character, personality, and individuality: a social and ontological persona. The *daiva ātman,* or "heavenly self," to which we will return shortly, refers to the ritually constructed extracorporeal self projected into another ontological sphere, into a *loka* other than the earthly one. And *loka* here means "world" in the sense of an ontological condition or status. A *loka,* etymologically related to the English *locus,* is where the *ātman* is *placed.* As Coomaraswamy observes, "The whole world or universe . . . corresponds to the ensemble of all possibilities of manifestation, whether informal, formal, or sensible; a world (*loka* = *locus*) is a given ensemble of possibilities, a given modality."[126] Or as Gonda writes in *Loka: The World and Heaven in the Veda,*

> If "name-and-form" [*nāma-rūpa*] means the psychical and physical components of any personality, the term *loka* may denote the "place" or "room" occupied by these, wherever a personality may be found, the position (of safety) or situation in which it may be.[127]

The sacrifice is the workshop in which the sacrificer's worldly self and status are forged. But it is also said to be generative of an imperceptible "divine" self and world for the sacrificer. The *svarga loka* or "heavenly world" was, continues Gonda, "something or some state which could be, or had to be, produced by the effects of the ritual acts of the sacrificer." And, further, "The condition which for convenience may be called 'immortality' belongs to the person concerned already in his earthly existence, before his removal to the *svarga loka.*"[128] Heaven,

123. ŚB 6.2.2.7.
124. ŚB 11.2.2.5.
125. ŚB 1.3.2.1 and elsewhere.
126. Coomaraswamy, "Vedic Exemplarism," p. 45.
127. Jan Gonda, *Loka: The World and Heaven in the Veda* (Amsterdam: N. V. Noord-Hollandsch Uitgeuers Maatschappji, 1966), pp. 32–33.
128. Ibid., p. 97.

won by ritual action, is said to be "in this world": "By that which is not *svarga,*" that is to say, by the ritually created conditions in this world, "one ascends to the *svarga loka.*"[129] It is to this ritually induced—and ritually previewed—ascension to an ontological status beyond this world that we now turn.

The Sacrificial Journey to Heaven

That the Vedic ritual should be thought to have a transformative effect on those who undergo it is not entirely surprising. Participants in rituals the world over claim to be changed by them; they are consecrated, made sacred, by virtue of the power of ritual activity.

In Vedic India, however, this ritually infused sacrality is often expressed in terms of *divinity,* and the idiom can provoke confusion. What did the ritualists mean when they claimed to be gods? Did they really mean to imply an ontological identity between certain men and the gods beyond?

> There are two kinds of gods. For the gods [are gods], and the Brahmins who have studied and teach are human gods (*mānuṣya deva*s). The sacrifice of these [sacrificers] is divided into two. Oblations [are sacrifices] to the gods and sacrificial fees [are sacrifices] to the human gods, the Brahmins who have studied and teach. With oblations one pleases the gods; with sacrificial fees one pleases the human gods, the Brahmins who have studied and teach. Both kinds of gods, when pleased, place him in a condition of well-being.[130]

Not only did the Brahmin officiants claim divinity, with its economic advantages, among others; in the course of the ritual the sacrificer (regardless of class) was also said to attain a godly state. He was transformed in preliminary rites from an ordinary man into a divine entity. "He passes from the world of men to the world of the gods,"[131] and, as Henri Hubert and Marcel Mauss have written of the *dīkṣita* (one who has been consecrated for a soma sacrifice), "once his divine nature has been proclaimed, it confers upon him the rights and imposes upon him the duties of a god."[132]

129. AitB 7.10.
130. ŚB 2.2.2.6.
131. ŚB 1.1.1.4.
132. Henri Hubert and Marcel Mauss, *Sacrifice: Its Nature and Function* trans. by W. D. Halls (Chicago: University of Chicago Press, 1964), p. 21. See also Lévi's comment that 'l'homme se fait surhumain." *La Doctrine du sacrifice,* p. 9.

Furthermore, the attainment of the divine self and heavenly world—we have observed that it is one of the ontological purposes of the Vedic ritual—was claimed to be realized not only after the death of the sacrificer but also in the course of the ritual itself. In Vedic ritualism, it would seem, man became a god and entered heaven within the confines of the sacrifice, that is, in this very life.

The ritual creation of the *daiva ātman* and *svarga loka* was part of a transformative process that the texts liken to a journey, with the sacrifice itself the vehicle. The sacrificial journey corresponds to the ritual procedure which Hubert and Mauss have described as a curve. It begins with a series of consecration rites preparatory for, and instigating of, the "ascent to heaven"; it reaches a climax coincident with the offering of the principal oblation and equated with the "arrival" at the heavenly world; and then begins a "descent," a set of exit rites. This curve is followed both by the sacrificer and by the object or objects of the sacrifice, the two being linked by connections or *bandhu*s:

> The religious condition of the sacrifier thus also describes a curve symmetrical to the one traced by the victim. He begins by rising progressively into the religious sphere, and attains a culminating point, whence he descends again into the profane. So each one of the creatures and objects that play a part in the sacrifice is drawn along as if in a continuous movement which, from entry to exit, proceeds along two opposing slopes.[133]

In order to reach the world of heaven, the sacrificer is sometimes said to take the form of a bird, the ritual chants serving as wings.[134] More often, however, it is the ritual as a whole, the *yajña,* that acts as the vehicle carrying the sacrificer to yonder world. In one text, it is the sacrifice itself—and not the sacrificer—which is declared to be a bird.[135] The *yajña* is also likened to a cart,[136] the sacrificial spoons are said to be "yokemates,"[137] and the meters of the ritual utterances are equated to harnessed cattle that draw the sacrifice to the world of the gods.[138]

Another image the Brāhmaṇas frequently call upon is that of the

133. Hubert and Mauss, *Sacrifice,* p. 48. See also Lévi's description of the sacrificial journey, *Le Doctrine du sacrifice,* pp. 130–31: "Les deux temps de l'opération correspondent aux deux movements du sacrifiant: ascension au ciel et retour sur la terre. Le sacrifiant monte au ciel pour s'assurer un corps divin et immortel; en retour, il fait abandon aux dieux de son corps humain et périssable. Puis, sa place marquée et retenue au ciel, il aspire à redescendre et rachete le corps qui il avait sacrifié."

134. PB 5.1.10, 5.3.5; AitB 3.25.

135. ŚB 4.1.2.25.

136. ŚB 3.9.3.3.

137. ŚB 1.8.3.27.

138. ŚB 4.4.3.1.

sacrifice as a ship, transporting the sacrificer from the earthly to the heavenly shores. The priests are its spars and oars, "the conveyances to the heavenly world. If there is one blameworthy [priest], even that one only would make it sink. And truly, every sacrifice is a heaven-bound ship. Therefore one ought to keep a blameworthy [priest] away from every sacrifice."[139] Other elements of the ritual are also assimilated to the parts of the ship: "The Agnihotra is a ship bound for heaven. The *āhavanīya* fire and the *gārhapatya* fire are the two sides of that heaven-bound ship, the Agnihotra. The captain of the ship is the priest who offers the milk oblation."[140]

But perhaps the most frequently encountered is the comparison of the sacrifice and the chariot, the vehicle of choice in Vedic India. The introductory and concluding rites are likened to the two sides of the chariot and should be symmetrical: "He who makes them equal to one another safely reaches the world of heaven, just as one takes any desired journey by driving a chariot with two sides."[141] Similarly, another text argues that the Agnihotra should be performed after sunrise so that it will be like a chariot with both wheels: "Day and night are the wheels of the year; truly, with them he goes through the year. If he offers before sunrise, it is as if one were to go with [a chariot with] one wheel. But if he offers after sunrise, it is as if one were swiftly to make a journey with [a chariot having] both wheels."[142] In other texts, other components of the ritual are connected to the parts of the chariot—the sacrificial fees are the internal fastenings;[143] the chants are the reins;[144] and the recitations are said to be the "inner reins."[145]

The sacrifice must be a study, complete, and safely operated "vehicle," because the journey to heaven is no sure thing. It involves, the texts assure us, great difficulty and danger. The trip to the heavenly world within the sacrifice is designated a "difficult ascension" (*dūrohaṇa*), and the reasons for the difficulty begin to enlighten us about the recognized differences standing behind the proclaimed identity between gods and men.

139. ŚB 4.2.5.10.

140. ŚB 2.3.3.15; see also JB 1.166. In an interesting reversal, the Muṇḍaka Upanished (1.2.7), as part of a critique of ritualism in light of the new emphasis on mystical knowledge alone, declares sacrifices to be "leaky vessels," unfit for the true voyage—the attainment of liberation from *karma*.

141. KB 7.7.

142. AitB 5.30.

143. PB 16.1.13.

144. PB 8.5.16.

145. AitB 2.37; see also JB 1.129–30 for the most detailed of these metaphors.

In one sense, the difficulty with the ritual ascension to heaven is this: in order to ascend successfully, human ritualists are called upon to follow the steps of the gods. These inhabitants of the heavenly world also arrived at their destination, in the beginning, through ritual techniques: "It was done thus by the gods. So it is done by men."[146] Certain rites and ritual formulas have such elevating power, guaranteed by their prior ability to produce heaven for the gods: "By means of this the gods went to the world of heaven; one who desires the world of heaven should use it for reaching the world of heaven."[147]

The fundamental differences between gods and men, however, make it difficult indeed for the latter to replicate the techniques of the former. Indeed, the texts declare, the human condition is the exact opposite of the divine. In contrast to the "perfection" (*samṛddha* or *sampanna*) characteristic of divine beings, the earthly and human is said to be imperfect and "unsuccessful" (*vyṛddha*).[148] "What is 'no' for the gods is 'yes' for man," says another Brāhmaṇa[149] by way of emphasizing the utter difference between the two kinds of beings. In several passages we read that *satya,* here in the sense of ritual exactitude, is a quality of the gods, whereas *anṛta* ("error" or "disorder") is the distinguishing mark of things human.[150]

Although in the consecration rites the human sacrificer is said to acquire a godlike status within the ritual, the fact that the Brāhmaṇas call the apotheosis a "difficult ascension" implies that the authors had some doubts that man could ever entirely shed his humanity in this life and truly assume the ontological dimensions of his divine prototypes. The perfection of the gods, acquired by and realized in their ability to perform the ritual without error, was for humans an ideal rather than a realistic goal. There were simply too many things that could go wrong in the course of the performance. The sacrifice—like all created things and beings—was always inclined to fall apart, be cut, break, shatter, become defiled, inverted, or defective, as one list enumerates the possibilities.[151]

Thus, one aspect of the difficulty of the "difficult ascension" is precisely the demand for an inhuman exactitude and perfection. Walter Kaelber writes in his study of the *dūrohaṇa:*

146. TB 1.5.9.4 and elsewhere.
147. PB 2.6.2; see also PB 2.12.2, 2.15.2, 3.2.2, etc.
148. ŚB 1.4.1.35.
149. AitB 3.5.
150. ŚB 1.1.2.17, 3.3.2.2, 3.9.4.1.
151. BŚS 28.10.

> In fact, the intricacies of the ritual constitute the greatest source of danger for the sacrificer. No detail may be overlooked, no act incorrectly performed. . . . Precisely because these ritual intricacies characterize the entire sacrificial scenario, there can be little question that it constitutes a difficult passage in every sense.[152]

Even more disturbing, perhaps, is the fact that one can never be certain that ritual perfection—the timely and correct performance of every minute detail—has ever been achieved. One text nicely sums up the angst and uncertainties that the ritualists might have felt as they undertook their heaven-bound project: "The world of the gods is concealed from the world of men. 'It is not easy to depart from this world,' they say. 'For who knows if he is in the yonder world or not?' "[153]

The ascent to heaven is not only difficult; it is also perilous. One must "fall away from this world" and "arrive" at the yonder world, where the sacrifice "has its only [true] foundation, its one [true] end."[154] But the road to heaven is, in Vedism, not always envisioned as paved with gold. "Dangerous indeed are the paths that lie between heaven and earth";[155] for on either side of these roadways are eternally burning flames which "scorch him who deserves to be scorched and allow him to pass who deserves to pass."[156] The sacrifice, the vehicle transporting one to the heavenly world, is said to be "razor sharp," and success or failure is unequivocal: "Suddenly he becomes full of merit or perishes."[157] Another text refers to the "wilds and abysses of the sacrifice" and warns, "If any venture into them not knowing the ropes, then hunger and thirst, evil doers and fiends, harass them, even as fiends would harass foolish men wandering in a wild forest."[158]

Nor do the dangers cease when the journey ends. Although the

152. Kaelber, "The 'Dramatic' Element in Brāhamaṇic Initiation," p. 63. See also Lévi, *La Doctrine du sacrifice,* pp. 123–24: "Dans ce dédale de prescriptions minutieuses l'erreur est aisée et les conséquences en sont terribles. Le danger est partout qui guette le sacrifiant."

153. TS 6.1.1.1. In other texts, there is a rather specific, if variable, notion about where heaven is, if not a certainty about when one knows one has arrived there. The world of heaven takes about six months to get to (PB 4.6.17), or is some forty days' journey on horseback upward from earth, or is at a distance equivalent to the length of the Sarasvatī river (PB 25.10.16). Alternatively, "The world of heaven is as far away from this world as a thousand cows standing on top of each other" (PB 16.8.6), or "the distance [may be] also a thousand *yojana*s [about nine thousand miles], or a thousand days' journey by horse" (PB 21.1.9).

154. ŚB 8.7.4.6.

155. ŚB 2.3.4.37.

156. ŚB 1.9.3.2.

157. TS 2.5.5.6; see also Kaṭha Upanishad 3.14.

158. ŚB 1.9.3.2.

sacrificial trip to heaven is described as a difficult ascension, the perils to the sacrificer do not evaporate when he has successfully been elevated to that "world" in the ritual which coincides with the principal oblation. Rites and *mantra*s were designed not only to ensure the ascension to the heavenly world but also to establish the sacrifice and the sacrificer in that world in such a way that they do not "slip" or "fall" from it, for such would be disastrous.[159]

Paradoxically, the very success of the sacrifice, the winning of the heavenly world at the summit of the sacrificial journey, places the sacrificer in jeopardy. For the *svarga loka* is a realm which man cannot, in his present mortal state, survive. A myth of origins tells why this is so. When the sacrifice had proved effective as a conduit to the other world, "Death spoke to the gods. 'Now surely all men will be immortal. What will be my share?' They said, 'From now on, no one will become immortal with the physical body. Only when you have taken that as your share will he become immortal . . .'."[160] Because of this arrangement with death, only the disembodied win immortality and heaven on a permanent basis. Others merely rent them. The sacrificial journey places the sacrificer in the other world only temporarily, just long enough to mark out and reserve a space for the next life.

The ritual journey to heaven taken by human sacrificers, in other words, must be a round trip. For if the sacrificer wholly repeats the paradigmatic voyage of the gods and arrives at the heavenly world without descending again from it, he would, the texts postulate, die. Death would take its share, the mortal body of the sacrificer.

The gods "reached these worlds" through the sacrifice, and "having reached these worlds by means of this, they finished the sacrificial session";[161] that is to say, they did not descend again from the *svarga loka* in the declining half of the sacrificial curve. The human sacrificer, however, does not conclude the ritual at its highest point. Rather, the climax of the ritual marks the start of the second portion of the procedure, a descent from the world of heaven so laboriously won. "Having obtained the world of heaven, the sacrificers establish themselves in this world."[162] Heaven, having been attained, is quickly renounced.[163]

159. See, e.g., PB 2.6.2; KB 8.2.

160. ŚB 10.4.3.9.

161. PB 15.11.5.

162. AitB 4.21.

163. See Lévi's comment in *La Doctrine du sacrifice,* p. 88: "Le mécanisme du sacrifice est clairement répresenté par le rite du *dūrohaṇa,* 'l'ascension difficile.' Il se résume en deux periodes, l'une ascendante, l'autre descendante. Il s'agit d'élevar d'abord le sacrifiant au monde céleste; mais la terre a ses charmes, et le sacrifiant ne demande pas a

The Brāhmaṇas mince no words in their warnings to those who spurn a two-way ticket to—and from—paradise, those who do not use the return portion of the booking. The sacrificer must descend from the world of heaven or "fall away from this world" permanently;[164] he who does not leave heaven would "go to the farthest distance."[165] Those with hubris, who, like the gods, perform the ritual "in the forward direction only," "may win the world of heaven, but they will not have long to live in this world."[166] They will "vanish from this world"[167] or "go to Prajāpati,"[168] a euphemism for death.

The dangers of remaining in heaven seemed to have been particularly acute for the royal sacrificer, a king who has responsibilities for ruling over portions of this world. In the Rājasūya sacrifice, the king goes to the "world of heaven" but must return to earth, which is his "firm foundation":

> In that he is consecrated by the Rājasūya, he ascends to the world of heaven. If he did not descend to this world [however], he would either depart to a region which lies beyond human beings, or he would go mad. That ritual of shaving the hair (the *keśavapanīya*) with reversed chants is for not leaving this world. Just as he would descend [from a tree], grabbing branch after branch, so does he descend to this world with this [rite]. [The rite is] for attaining a firm foundation.[169]

The sacrificial prototype—the heaven-procuring ritual of the gods—is thus not ordinarily to be exactly repeated by men any more than the perfection of the gods' rituals can be literally realized by the human sacrificer. Just as perfection in the sense of ritual exactitude should be understood both in its transcendent, prototypical form (that of the gods) and in its relative manifestation or counterpart form (that of humans), so, too, must the perfection represented as the heavenly world be analyzed into its ideal and its humanly attainable forms. The full realization of perfection, in both cases, is not possible for humans in this life; hence Lévi's comment that "the true voyage to heaven is not accomplished until after death" and that "the only authentic sacri-

---

la quitter trop tot. Assuré de l'immortalité a venir par la première opération, il reprend par la seconde opération sa place entre le vivants."

164. KB 7.9.
165. PB 15.7.2.
166. AitB 4.2.
167. PB 4.3.5–6, 6.8.17–18.
168. PB 4.8.9.
169. PB 18.10.10; see also AitB 4.21; PB 5.5.4–5.

fice would be suicide."[170] And, as the Śatapatha Brāhmaṇa cautions, the premature death of one who is overeager to reside in the world of heaven might prove to be counterproductive: "One ought not to yield to his own desire and pass away before [he has attained] the full extent of life, for such does not make for the heavenly world."[171]

The *svarga loka* reached in the course of the ritual process is, then, not only difficult and dangerous to get to; it is also only a model of the prototypical world of heaven in which the real gods dwell. The ritually created ersatz heaven is, in other words, but a counterpart to the transcendent and paradigmatic heaven of the gods strictu sensu. The gods' world, as Jean-Marie Verpoorten has observed, is "where reigns a unity that has nothing of the constructed aggregate, but is that which is entirely indivisible"; it is characterized by its unconstructed perfection or *saṃṛddha.* The ritually produced heaven of the human sacrificers, on the other hand, is marked by *samāna,* the "constructed unity of parts," which is "the configuration (*chiffre*) of man and his ritual activity."[172] The gods live in the perfect, the whole, and the original, but man can only fabricate—through ritual labor—an inferior substitute.

If the heavenly world of the ritual and the divine status acquired by the sacrificer are not the true equivalents of those possessed by the gods, perhaps it is the case that such are attained by humans after death. Perhaps the *daiva ātman* the sacrificer makes for himself through ritual action is indeed a full-fledged divinity for those who shed the body, giving death its share, and take the final, one-way trip to the world of

170. Lévi, *La Doctrine du sacrifice,* pp. 93, 133. While, in general, Vedic texts forbid suicide, there does seem to be at least one exception. As an example of a ritual performed "in the forward direction only," there is the sacrifice called the *sarvasvāra,* described in several Brāhmaṇas and Śrauta Sūtras. It is apparently meant for an old man, probably an accomplished ritualist, "who is desirous of having an end to his life" (KŚS 22.6.1) or wishes to "go to yonder world without suffering from any disease" (PB 17.12.1; JB 2.167). When various chants designed to make him "go to the endless, to yonder world," or "from this world to the world of heaven" (PB 17.12.3–4), are completed, the sacrificer lies down between the fires, with his head covered and pointing to the south, while another chant is recited over him. "And he dies at that time. . . . The rites of the *sarvasvāra* come to an end as soon as the sacrificer dies, as there is no purpose of the sacrifice left to achieve" (KŚS 22.6.6–8). Another text instructs regarding what one should do if, perchance, death does not arrive at that time: "If he lives, he should perform the final oblation of the soma sacrifice and thereupon seek his death by starvation" (LŚS 8.8.40). For a treatment of this ritual and others, see J. C. Heesterman, "Self-Sacrifice in Vedic Ritual," in S. Shaked et al., eds., *Gilgul: Essays on Transformation, Revolution and Permanence in the History of Religions* (Leiden: E. J. Brill, 1987), pp. 91–106.

171. ŚB 10.2.6.7.

172. Verpoorten, "Unité et distinction," pp. 76, 84.

heaven, the world of the gods. Can men become gods after death, if not truly in this life? And is the world of heaven awaiting the ritualist at the end of his life the same world occupied by the Vedic deities?

Life after Death

The gods are in permanent possession of divinity and an immortal world in which to exercise it. Man, on the other hand, must work for his identity and status. He is dependent on his own ritual activity or *karman* in its original sense; he is "born into a world made by himself." Man's divinity, his *daiva ātman,* is also forged by the ontological (and transcendental) power of ritual work, and so, too, is his heavenly world—both the heaven reached in every successful sacrificial performance and the heaven to which the sacrificer ascends and in which he dwells after death.

Furthermore, the conditions of this life—one's ritually constructed socio-ontological identity and status—are accurate previews of those of the next. Both the self and the world that one builds for oneself here and those that one constructs for the afterlife are products of the rituals one performs. And they are, one might say, resembling counterparts of each other.

"Yonder world is the corresponding form (*anurūpa*) of this world," declares one text, and "this world is the corresponding form of that."[173] Because these two *loka*s "correspond," the heavenly world is presaged in this one. In this world, as Paul Mus puts it, there is "the anticipated image, or the real base, of the other world and of the immortality in that beyond."[174] Because the *svarga loka* that men enter with their *daiva ātman*s is, like more mundane *loka*s, ritually made, sacrificers with different ritual résumés realize different heavenly worlds and different divine selves.

In this universe of resemblances and interlocking forms and counterforms, the complex of self/sacrifice/status (*ātman/yajña/loka*) is projected simultaneously on different ontological planes. The self that is constructed and represented in the sacrifice is a construction/representation of the self in this world (the sacrificer's socially recognized persona) and the self of the other world (the sacrificer's *daiva ātman*). In like manner, the sacrificer's world is at once the world composed of his

173. AitB 8.2.
174. Paul Mus, *Barabadur,* pp. 135–36.

sacrifices, the social status he has attained through those sacrifices, and the individually designed heavenly world—reached temporarily at every sacrifice and attained for good after death.

Both *loka* and *ātman,* then, are particularized concepts in Vedic thought. They are intimately linked to the particular sacrificer who fabricates them in his ritual activity. Put otherwise, the "heavenly world" and the "divine self" are not, in this framework of belief and action, unitary concepts at all. They are, rather, tailored to individuals and hierarchically gauged.

The hymns of the Ṛg Veda often seem to reflect a belief in a future life in the same heaven as that inhabited by the gods.[175] But certainly in the classical texts of Vedic ritualism, the concept of *svarga loka* becomes multiple and individually shaped. A cynical view of this innovation is taken by A. B. Keith, who correctly notes that in post-Ṛgvedic texts there are "diverse degrees of good acquired by different modes of sacrifice":

> It was obviously necessary to admit that every sacrificer would receive reward by admission to the happiness of the world to come, but the Brahmans had to consider the claims of the richer of the patrons, and had to promise them more in the world to come than the poorer, who offered and gave less.[176]

A somewhat less jaded view of this shift from an egalitarian reward system to a hierarchical one lies behind Paul Deussen's summary of the way heaven is calibrated to match the achievements of individual sacrificers:

> The chief aim of the Brāhmaṇas is to prescribe the acts of ritual, and to offer for their accomplishment a manifold reward, and at the same time sufferings and punishment for their omission. While they defer rewards as well as punishments partly to the other world, in place of the ancient Vedic conception of an indiscriminate felicity of the pious, the idea of recompense is formulated, involving the necessity of setting before the departed different degrees of compensation in the other world proportionate to their knowledge and actions.[177]

In Vedic ritualism, one obtains a "good" *loka* through ritual activity, and a specifically contoured hell, a *naraka loka,* through misdeeds or failure to perform good acts. Those who spit on a Brahmin, or flick the

175. The fullest depiction of the Ṛgvedic vision of heaven occurs at RV 9.113.7–11; see also RV 10.14.10–12.

176. A. B. Keith, *The Religion and Philosophy of the Veda and Upanishads,* 2 vols. (Cambridge, Mass.: Harvard University Press, 1925), p. 572.

177. Deussen, *The Philosophy of the Upanishads,* p. 324.

mucus of their nose on him, will spend their afterlife sitting in a stream of blood, devouring their hair for food.[178] Those who consume food in this world without first sacrificing some of it to the gods will enter one of a variety of hells: "For whatever food a man eats in this world, by the very same is he eaten again in the other."[179] A person who reviles, strikes, and draws blood from a Brahmin "will not see the world of the ancestors for as many years as are the grains of dust on which the [Brahmin's] blood falls."[180] And in the myth of Bhṛgu's journey to various hells,[181] the afterlife *loka*s are described in which the punishment exactly fits the crime. Those who in this life cut down trees without sacrificing are eaten by those trees after death in one *loka*. In another, those who cook animals for themselves without sacrificing are consumed by those animals; and in yet another hell, unsacrificed rice and barley feed on the unheedful.

At death, a kind of judgment is envisioned. Good deeds (by which is nearly always meant ritual deeds) and bad ones are separated out and weighed up:

> For in yonder world they place him on the scale, and whichever of the two rises that he will follow, whether it be the good or the evil. And whoever knows this gets on the scale even in this world, and escapes being put on the scale in yonder world. For his good action rises, not his bad action.[182]

From another text we learn that "the good that man does during his life passes into his breaths, the bad into his body. When the one who knows thus departs from this world, his good deeds rise up together with his breath and his wrong deeds are left with his body."[183] Elsewhere in that Brāhmaṇa we read that the breath ascends to the heavenly world and "announces to the gods the quantity: "So much good, so much evil has been done by him,' "[184] this evidently determining the kind of *loka* the departed soul will henceforth occupy.

In the early Upanishads, too, the *lokas* comprising the universe—

178. AV 5.19.3.
179. ŚB 12.9.1.1; see also KB 11.3.
180. TS 2.6.10.2.
181. JB 1.42–44 and ŚB 11.6.1.1–13. For a translation and analysis of the JB variant of the myth, see Wendy Doniger O'Flaherty, *Tales of Sex and Violence: Folklore, Sacrifice, and Danger in the Jaiminīya Brāhmaṇa* (Chicago: University of Chicago Press, 1985), pp. 32–40.
182. ŚB 11.2.7.33.
183. JB 1.15.
184. JB 1.18.

the possible ontological and soteriological spaces and situations—are many. There is, first of all, a distinction made between the *deva loka,* the world of the gods, and the *pitṛ loka,* or world of the ancestors.[185] But we also learn of a wide variety of "worlds": those of mothers, brothers, sisters, friends, scents and garlands, food and drink, song and music, and women.[186] Elsewhere is provided a map of the ontological hierarchy of the *loka*s and their inhabitants:

> If one is fortunate among men, wealthy, a lord over others, well provided with all human enjoyments, that is the most perfect bliss of men. Now one hundred times the bliss of men is one bliss of those who have won the world of the ancestors. One hundred times the bliss of those who have won the world of the ancestors is one bliss in the world of the demigods. One hundred times the bliss in the world of the demigods is one bliss of the gods created by ritual work (*karma deva*s). One hundred times the bliss of the gods created by ritual work is one bliss of the gods by birth (*ājāna deva*s). . . . One hundred times the bliss of the gods by birth is one bliss in the world of Prajāpati. . . . One hundred times the bliss in the world of Prajāpati is one bliss in the world of Bṛahmā. . . . This is truly the highest world.[187]

Among other points of interest in this text is the clear differentiation between the "world" and "bliss" of the gods created by their own ritual labors (pulled up by their own bootstraps, so to speak) and those of the gods by birth. Here we have corroborating evidence for the position argued above: there is an unequivocal distinction in Vedic ritualism between divinity constructed and divinity eternally possessed. There is no confusion between prototypical deities and the counterpart divinity available to men who make their own divine self through sacrifice.

Man is indeed born into a world made by himself, in the afterlife as well as in this one. The particular *loka* or place a person inhabits in the

185. Already in the ṚV (e.g., 10.18.1, 10.2.7, 10.15.1–2), the path leading to the world of the ancestors is distinguished from that leading to the *deva loka.* In the ŚB, the gate to the world of the gods is said to be in the northeast (6.6.2.4), whereas that to the world of the ancestors is located in the southwest (13.8.1.5). As opposed to the celestial locale of the gods' world, the ancestors supposedly live in the atmosphere or middle space between heaven and earth (taking the form of birds, according to BDhS 2.14.9–10), or under the earth (ṚV 10.16.3; ŚB 13.8.1.20). In the Upanishads, the *pitṛ loka* is associated with the moon, darkness, sacrificial action, and rebirth (this world being a way station in the recycling of souls); the *deva loka* is connected with the sun, light, mystical knowledge, and eternal liberation (BĀU 6.2.15–16; ChU 4.15.5–6, 5.10.1–3; Kauṣītaki Upanishad 1.2).

186. ChU 8.2.

187. BĀU 4.3.33; see also TU 2.8.

next life is determined by the specifics of his actions in this life, and in every case the world humans occupy after death is distinct from the heaven of the gods by birth.

The *daiva ātman,* like the heavenly world, is also a relative term, with contours shaped by the individual. This transcendental self, however, is not to be mistaken for the biological self that emerges out of the mother's womb. The ritualists in this matter, as in the case of the second birth effected by the initiation ritual, claimed that their ritual womb brought forth superior fruit when compared to the merely natural womb of women:

> There are indeed two wombs: the divine womb is one, the human womb the other. . . . The human womb is [a part of] the human world. . . . And the *āhavanīya* fire is the divine womb, the divine world. . . . He who knows thus has two *ātman*s and two wombs. One *ātman* and one womb has he who does not know this.[188]

The divine self is "born out of the sacrifice"; that is, it is a ritual construct. And, further, the sacrifice specifies the particular dimensions of the *daiva ātman*; the ritual history of the individual sacrificer translates into the special character of the divine self: "The sacrifice becomes the sacrificer's self in yonder world. And truly, the sacrificer who, knowing this, performs that [sacrifice] comes into existence [there] with a whole body."[189] Or, again, another text declares that the sacrificer "is united in the other world with what he has sacrificed";[190] his ritual accomplishments on earth are the precise measure of his divine self in heaven. The Ṛg Veda refers to the sacrificer's "treasure," to which he will be joined at death—a kind of savings account in the next world composed of sacrificial deposits made in ritual activity—and to a "splendid body" of the sacrificer's own making: "Unite with the fathers, with Yama, with the treasure of your sacrifices in the highest heaven. Abandoning defects, return home; unite with a splendid body."[191]

Uniting with the heavenly self one has created in sacrifice is not always easy. Just as there is danger involved in the passage to heaven within the confines of the ritual, so is there a certain risk involved in the

188. JB 1.17; see also ŚB 7.4.2.20.

189. ŚB 11.1.8.6. For the emphasis on the wholeness of the *daiva ātman,* see AV 11.3.32; ŚB 4.6.1.1, 11.1.8.6, 12.8.3.31; and Jan Gonda, "Reflections on *Sarva-* in Vedic Texts."

190. TS 3.3.8.5.

191. ṚV 10.14.8.

transition from a human to a divine self after death. Self-knowledge and the ability to recognize one's "own world" when one sees it are critical:

> One man, after having left this world, knows his *ātman,* [saying,] "This am I." Another man does not recognize his own world. Bewildered by the [cremation] fire choked with smoke, he does not recognize his own world. But he who knows the *sāvitra* fire, he indeed, after having left this world, knows the *ātman,* [saying,] "This am I," and he recognizes his own world. And then the *sāvitra* fire carries him to the heavenly world.[192]

Recognizing one's own world and identifying one's true divine self, one realizes and adopts the tailor-made life after death that is the product of the ritual craft. The collective oblation one offers over the course of the years—that is, the quantity and quality of his sacrificial history—determines the *daiva ātman* as it is transformed from offering to transcendent identity: "Whatever oblation he sacrifices here, that becomes his *ātman* in the other world. When he who knows thus leaves this world, that offering which follows him calls out, 'Come here. Here I am, your *ātman.*' "[193] Alternatively imagined, the divine self is the collective sacrificial fee—which, it will be remembered, functions as the oblation to the "human gods," the Brahmins:

> He who sacrifices, sacrifices with the desire that he may obtain a place in the world of the gods. That sacrifice of his then goes forth toward the world of the gods. The sacrificial fee he gives [to the Brahmin officiants] follows after it, and holding on to the sacrificial fee [follows] the sacrificer.[194]

Indeed, there seems to have been something of a nutritive value to the various sacrifices of the Vedic ritual repertoire. Each sacrifice has a different sustaining power for the divine self in the next world. And, unremarkably, the hierarchically superior sacrifices (because they are more complicated, powerful, and rare) provide the more enduring sustenance:

> And now for the powers of the sacrifices. He who performs the *agnihotra* eats in the evening and in the morning in yonder world, for so much sustenance is there in that sacrifice. And he who performs the new and full moon sacrifice [eats] every half-month. He who [quarterly] performs the *cāturmāsya* [eats] every four months. He who [every half-year] performs the animal sacrifice eats every six months, and he who [annually] performs

192. TB 3.10.11.1–2.
193. ŚB 11.2.2.5.
194. ŚB 1.9.3.1.

> the soma sacrifice [eats] every year. But the builder of the fire altar optionally eats every hundred years, or not at all. For a hundred is as much as immortality, unending and everlasting.[195]

With this passage, we again encounter the theory that life after death correlates with the ritual performances in this world—the classical Hindu law of *karma* in the making. And also presaged here, and indeed throughout the whole of Vedic literature, is the hierarchical thought underlying, among many other classificatory schemes, the Hindu caste system.

Like the law of *karma,* Vedic ritualism is premised on the assumption that acts have consequences for those who act, both in this life and in the future. They determine who you are (in the sight of the ritualists, at least) and who you are becoming, which is what you will be. In Vedism, however, the law of *karma* is *in nuce*; for at this point in the orthodox tradition, the only acts that matter, that provoke ontological reactions, are ritual ones.[196]

And just as there is an ever-present hierarchical motif underlying Hinduism in its entirety, Vedism is also hierarchically ordered at every turn—indeed, perhaps more consistently so than in some forms of Hinduism. For, unlike the later Upanishadic and Hindu configurations, in which asceticism could turn men into gods or in which gods took on human form out of grace and love for their devotees,[197] in Vedic ritualism the gods remain gods, and men essentially remain men. While the participants in the ritual might become godlike for the duration of the ceremony, their fundamental mortality precludes anything more than a temporary counterform of true divinity. And even after death, the divine self and the heavenly world one adopts are but ritually constructed, and hierarchically differentiated, replicas of the gods' status.

195. ŚB 10.1.5.4.

196. Another critical difference between the Hindu doctrine of *karma* and the Vedic ritualists' theory of the consequences of actions is that the latter lacked the notion of transmigration of the soul into new human births until the time of the early Upanishads. Although in some of the Brāhmaṇas there is a fear of "redeath" (*punar-mṛtyu*) when the ritually acquired merit that has sent the disembodied sacrificer to heaven runs out (see, e.g., ŚB 2.3.3.9, 10.1.4.14, 10.4.3.10, 11.5.6.9; TB 3.10.11.2, 3.11.8.5–6; KB 25.1), the notion "is not to be understood as transmigration but only as a resurrecton and repeated death in the other world." Deussen, *The Philosophy of the Upanishads,* p. 327.

197. For the mythological and theological puzzles engendered by such ideas in Hinduism, see Wendy Doniger O'Flaherty, *The Origins of Evil in Hindu Mythology* (Berkeley: University of California Press, 1976), pp. 57–93; and idem, *Women, Androgynes, and Other Mythical Beasts,* pp. 65–76.

In this chapter and the preceding one, I have attempted to lay out some of the ways in which ritual, resemblance, and hierarchical presuppositions interlock to form a coherent and consistent cosmological, metaphysical, socio-ontological, and soteriological system. Articulated most fully and cogently in the Brāhmaṇa texts, Vedic philosophy results in a system of practice in which there is a correlation—that is, a relationship of mutual resemblance—between three hierarchically calibrated registers: (1) the scale of ritual performance (the relative size, complexity, duration, and especially the inclusiveness of the sacrifice both as an individual performance and as a collective term for a ritual résumé), (2) the relative quality and realization of the sacrificer's earthly self and status (the ritually constituted nexus of innate and acquired socio-ontological characteristics, comprised of inherent proclivities, ritual and educational accomplishments, and the willingness and ability to realize them), and (3) the hierarchical order of selves and worlds of the unseen spheres (ranging from the gods by birth and their worlds downward through the tiers of ritually constructed heavens of the gods created by sacrificial work to the various hells of the damned and the negligent).

The principle of hierarchical resemblance has wider application still. For when the Brahmins turned their attention to the organizing of the vast system of ritual practices in the encyclopedic Sūtras, their method there remained consistent with the explanations of the universe and its inhabitants found in the Brāhmaṇas. In the Sūtras, to which we next turn, the philosophy of hierarchical resemblance is translated into a theory of textual representation; the ritual repertoire is systematized, categorized, and ordered in a way entirely in conformity with the principles guiding other systems of Vedic classification.

5

The Organization of Ritual Knowledge

Resemblance and the Sūtra Literature

Although the latest of the Brāhmaṇa texts and the earliest of the ritual Sūtras were probably composed more or less simultaneously,[1] the difference in genre is striking. The invention of the *sūtra* format by ritualists of the Black Yajur Veda inaugurated a mode of representing and organizing knowledge that was extraordinarily influential. Both for the orthodox tradition and for emergent rivals, the Buddhists and Jains, the *sūtra* became the preferred literary form in India, most especially when traditions codified their more technical discourses.

The ritual Sūtras of the Vedic heritage, the so-called Kalpa Sūtras, are the earliest instances of this type of literature. The oldest extant text composed in *sūtra*s is the Śrauta Sūtra of the Baudhāyana school, dated to about the seventh century B.C.E. Other Śrauta Sūtras, representing the ritual according to other schools, were composed over the course of the next several centuries, together with appendages and related texts on the domestic ritual (the Gṛhya Sūtras) and, finally, on all aspects of life—inside and outside the ritual—the Dharma Sūtras.

The Kalpa Sūtras, then, form the corpus of knowledge most inti-

1. The ritual Sūtras, with a few very late exceptions, can be dated between 800 and 300 B.C.E., according to C. G. Kashikar, *A Survey of the Śrautasūtras* (Bombay: University of Bombay, 1968), p. 161. Ram Gopal's dates of 800–500 B.C.E. end too early. See his *India of the Vedic Kalpasūtras* (Delhi: National Publishing House, 1959), p. 89.

mately connected to the practice and implications of the Vedic ritual. Other sciences of the orthodox tradition, however, also codified into Sūtras, emerged out of the necessities related to correct ritual performances—grammar, phonology, prosody, and etymology, on the one hand, to ensure the proper preservation and recitation of Vedic *mantras*; and astrology, on the other hand, to guarantee precision in the calculations for timing the occurrences of various rituals. Together with the Kalpa Sūtras, these six sciences are known collectively as the Vedāṅgas, the "subsidiaries to the Veda." And while the interrelations among these six ancient Indian subjects remain little studied—and would handsomely repay investigation—it is likely indeed that the different Sūtras of the Vedāṅga share similarities not only in form but in epistemological assumptions as well.[2] In all cases, the Sūtras are testimonies to the systematizing instincts of the ritual science; they are far better understood as taxonomies than as handbooks or manuals for practice.[3]

Another unprobed, and almost certainly significant, area of ancient Indian history is the relationship between the Sūtras of the orthodox tradition and those of Buddhism and Jainism. Why were the earliest scriptures of these dissenting groups written in the same genre as that of the Vedic ritualistic literature? Otherwise put, what is the meaning of the fact that the composition of the Kalpa Sūtras tended to precede, and then coincide with, the rise of the heterodox religions? How much should be made of the fact that the new religions utilized the *sūtra* format to represent their founders' sayings and aphorisms, whereas in the Kalpa Sūtras the aphorisms are those of the various teachers within a ritual school? The answers to these questions are outside the scope of this study, but it would seem possible that the Jains and Buddhists consciously composed their texts as Sūtras in order to place them in relation to those of the ritualists—a relation of imitation, competition, or, most likely, both.

2. For an example of partial and preliminary scholarship in this area, see Louis Renou's comparative study of the ritual and grammatical Sūtras, "Les Connexions entre le rituel et la grammaire en sanskrit," *Journal asiatique* 233 (1941–42): 105–65, reprinted in J. F. Staal, ed., *A Reader on the Sanskrit Grammarians* (Cambridge, Mass.: MIT Press, 1972), pp. 435–69.

3. In the case of the Kalpa Sūtras, this point is attested to by the fact that a subsequent body of literature—comprised of both commentaries on the Sūtras and derivative texts known as *prayogas*—was produced to guide the actual performance of the rituals the Sūtras refer to. The rules for the ritual given in the Sūtras, in other words, are far too cursory and lacking in detail to function adequately as manuals of practice.

As for the composers of the orthodox ritual Sūtras, they were consciously in dialogue with the literature of the tradition out of which they had come: the Veda. As opposed to the prolix style of the Saṃhitās, Brāhmaṇas, Āraṇyakas, and Upanishads, however, the Sūtras are by definition concise, sometimes to the point of being nearly unintelligible to the outsider. Literally translated as "thread," the *sūtra* designates both a brief proposition and the ensemble of propositions which comprise a work.

Brevity and concision are certainly characteristic of individual aphorisms making up the Sūtras, but the way the contents of the work as a whole are interrelated is perhaps even more definitive of the genre. Unlike the Brāhmaṇas, for example, the Sūtras organize their subject matter not in a linear manner but rather into a peculiarly methodical, systematic, and didactic structure.[4] Such a difference in style may indicate a more general shift, as Louis Renou has speculated:

> Different styles, due to different needs, may be ascertained: that of speculation, formulaic and enveloped in mysterious symbols, with a clear bent toward an archaic and emphatic prose style; and that of the description of rites, with a realistic, objective prose.[5]

In any case, in the Sūtras the "threads" are woven together into a whole rather than tied sequentially into a linear chain. Indeed, Renou considers the succinctness of the individual propositions less important to the definition of the Sūtra genre than the unique way in which individual propositions are related one to another:

> The genre of *sūtra* is defined by its relation more than by its content: a *sūtra* (in the sense of "rule" or "aphorism") is primarily an element dependent on context, even though it is grammatically autonomous; it is determined by the system and . . . [is] correlative to the group which surrounds it.[6]

In both style and the form in which the contents interrelate, then, the Sūtra departs from its Vedic literary predecessors. Still, it would be a mistake to overemphasize these differences. The Sūtras wholly presuppose the philosophy of hierarchical resemblance enunciated—in a different format—in the Brāhmaṇas, and extend its application to the literary form itself. The primary distinction between the earlier Vedic texts and

4. Jan Gonda suveys the stylistic and organizational features of the ritual Sūtras in his *The Ritual Sūtras,* pp. 629–47.

5. Louis Renou, *Les Écoles Védique,* p. 211.

6. Louis Renou, "Sur le genre du *sūtra,*" p. 166.

the ritual Sūtras is merely one of idiom, not ideology. It is the principle of resemblance that governs both.

Although, as Renou has noted, an individual *sūtra* derives much of its meaning from its surrounding context, the Sūtras also employ certain general rules that permeate the entire text and supplement particular aphorisms. Knowledge of the ritual as it is codified in these works depends on prior knowledge of a set of "first principles," "general rules," or "metarules." These kinds of *sūtra*s, whose reach extends over all other *sūtra*s, are called in Sanskrit *paribhāṣā*s.[7] The development of a series of metarules has been cited as one factor in dating the ritual Sūtras.[8] The earliest, the Baudhāyana Śrauta Sūtra, only occasionally gives general rules, and scatters them throughout the text (the Paribhāṣā Sūtra which is appended to the BŚS is almost certainly a late addition). An apparently late work such as the Kātyāyana Śrauta Sūtra, on the other hand, provides a set of *paribhāṣā*s at the very beginning of the Sūtra.[9]

For the novice—then and now—the *paribhāṣā*s are the key to unlocking an otherwise often cryptic Sūtra. Their general applicability[10] clarifies the text as a whole, just as a light placed in a corner illuminates the entire room.[11] "A *paribhāṣā* of a Śrautasūtra," writes S. C. Chakrabarti, "means a general principle that facilitates the correct interpretation of the work."[12] Indeed, a set of metarules makes possible an individual *sūtra* which is maximally succinct, a highly desirable goal for the authors of the Sūtras; a man was said to take as much delight in the saving of a single syllable in his Sūtra as he did in the birth of a son.[13]

The metarule enables such economy in exposition because it states once what thereafter can be assumed throughout the text unless specifically contradicted. In the ritual Sūtras, for example, metarules state that unless otherwise noted, the reward for a sacrifice is the attainment of

7. For the following discussion, I am greatly indebted to S. C. Chakrabarti's pioneer study, *The Paribhāṣās.* For the *paribhāṣā*s in the Sūtras of grammar, see K. V. Abhyankar, "On *Paribhāṣā* Works in Sanskrit Grammar," *Annals of the Bhandarkar Oriental Research Institute* 36 (1955): 157–62.

8. See, e.g., Kashikar, *A Survey of the Śrautasūtras,* pp. 153–57.

9. For some reservations on depending too heavily on this criterion for dating the Sūtras, consult Staal, *The Science of Ritual,* p. 21.

10. See, e.g., ŚŚS 1.2.29.

11. The image is taken from the grammarian Patañjali. See S. D. Joshi, ed. and trans., *Patañjali's Vyākaraṇamahābhāṣya* (Poona: University of Poona, 1968), on Pānini 2.1.1.

12. Chakrabarti, *The Paribhāṣās,* p. 27.

13. Cited in Staal, *The Science of Ritual,* p. 22.

heaven, the fire will ordinarily refer to the *āhavanīya* fire (in the Śrauta Sūtras), the usual oblation is that made of rice paddy or barley, and so on. Once the metarule has been laid down, the persons and objects subject to the ritual rule are often subsequently referred to only by pronouns, and the reader must know the metarule in order to know whom or what is meant by the pronoun at hand.

The principle of the metarule introduces the systematic mode of presentation characteristic of the ritual Sūtras and serves as the first instance of the ways the Sūtras assume and extend the general Vedic principle of hierarchical resemblance. For the underlying force of the metarule is the assumption of the resemblances of particulars to the overarching generality. Put another way, the notion encountered here is that knowledge of the particulars can be inferred from knowledge of their archetype. To know the archetype—the metarule—is thus to know all the manifestations of the archetype—the particular resembling instances. Resemblance, however, is not identity. A metarule on metarules states that the distinctiveness of the particular overrides the general application of the metarule. Thus, "a specific injunction is stronger than a general one."[14]

This interplay between the general and the specific is the heart of the science of ritual as it is represented in the Sūtras. And this science is guided by much the same assumptions as those guiding the metaphysics of the Brāhmaṇas. For here, too, the discourse is delimited by the excesses of identity and difference. The excess of resemblance (*jāmi*) is found in the erroneous view that the particular is *identical* to the general; hence the metarule cited above that overrides the general when particular distinctions are encountered. The excess of difference (*pṛthak*) finds its transformed expression in the Sūtras as well. There are cases when there is no specific indication of to which genus or class a particular species of rite or ritual belongs; it appears unique, unconnected, and different from all others. As we will see shortly, the concept of resemblance (*sāmānya*) developed in the Sūtras makes it possible to avoid this epistemological danger and to link any particular to its paradigm.

In Vedic philosophical discourse, the general and the particular are expressed in terms of "prototypes" and "counterparts," "forms" and "counterforms." In the organizational structure of the ritual Sūtras, a comparable contrast is set up between paradigms (*prakṛti*s) and variations of the paradigm (*vikṛti*s). Entire rituals, individual rites, and specific offerings within rites are thus constituted either as paradig-

14. ĀśvŚS 1.1.22.

matic guides to resembling variants or as modified variants of another paradigm. Whereas in the Brāhmaṇas prototypes are the hierarchically superior and fuller forms and counterparts the inferior and less complete versions thereof, in the Sūtras the paradigm is the basic model out of which variations are generated. Thus, for example, the *agniṣṭoma* is the simplest form of the soma sacrifice, but also the paradigm for all more developed, more complicated, and hierarchically superior soma sacrifices.

But although the variants are more fully developed versions of their ritual paradigms, the economy of explanation in the Sūtras reverses the relationship between the two and replicates more exactly the hierarchical element of the prototype/counterpart relation in the Brāhmaṇas. For in the Sūtras the paradigm is much more completely explicated—just as the prototype is the more completely realized instance of its class. The variation is only partially explicated in the text, for the previously given specifics of the model are assumed and extended to the variant.

The explanatory form of the Sūtras thus reverses the hierarchical value of the sacrifices it is explaining, working from the most basic to the most highly developed rather than from the superior to the inferior. The relationship between the general and the particular—between the paradigm and the variation—is described as one between what is "prior" (*pūrva*) and what is "subsequent" (*uttara*) and therefore dependent: "How should one know what is the precedent ceremony and what is subsequent? That which is the paradigm (*prakṛti*) is the precedent, and that which one creates from it is subsequent."[15] The interdependence of the *agniṣṭoma* and its more complex variations is depicted in the same manner: the latter are "subsequent" forms of the "prior" paradigm.[16] One definition of the paradigm emphasizes this epistemological priority in terms of the powers of extension it has; "Paradigm is the name of that which is transferable."[17]

But the science is complex. For what functions as a variation of one paradigm can simultaneously act as a paradigm for variations of another class. The rite of animal sacrifice to Agni-Soma in the soma sacrifice is a variation of the paradigmatic new and full moon sacrifice; and it is also the paradigm for other animal sacrifices within soma rituals. In this way and others, the Sūtras fabricate a chain of intricate connections as they organize the variety of rituals into a systematically interlinked whole.

15. BŚS 24.5.
16. BŚS 24.5: *jyotiṣṭomaḥ somānāṃ pūrvā tatiḥ sarve somā uttarā tatiḥ.*
17. ŚŚS 1.16.2.

At the highest level of its operation, the principle of paradigms and variations acts to relate all sacrifices one to another. The metarules declare that the *agnyādhāna* ritual, in which the sacrificer's fires are first lit, is the paradigm for the *punarādhāna* or reestablishment of the fires should they become extinguished. The new and full moon sacrifice is the paradigm for all other sacrifices in which the oblation is made from vegetable matter (the *iṣṭi*s) and for the animal sacrifice dedicated to Agni-Soma. The *agniṣṭoma* serves as the paradigm for all soma sacrifices up to those of twelve days' duration; the *dvādaśāha* soma sacrifice is paradigmatic for soma sacrifices of twelve days or more. In this manner, all rituals find their place in the explanatory chain.[18]

The new and full moon sacrifice is perhaps the most important of all the paradigmatic rituals. Knowledge of its structure is essential to knowledge of nearly all other rituals—including, as we will see, the rituals at the domestic level (the *gṛhya* sacrifices)—and the Sūtras constantly refer back to it or assume its details. The Śrauta Sūtras open either with a list of metarules or, more frequently, with a detailed account of the new and full moon sacrifice which serves much the same purpose as the set of metarules—it provides transferable knowledge for the performance of any sacrifice in the repertoire. The Sūtras, then, in nearly every instance follow an epistemological rather than a chronological order, the paradigmatic new and full moon sacrifice preceding the ritual for lighting the fires.[19]

The Āśvalāyana Śrauta Sūtra, to take but one example, opens with some short statements of purpose (to demonstrate the ritual application of the verses from the Ṛg Veda and to detail the procedure for the *śrauta* rituals beginning with the *agnyādhāna*). It then provides an explanation of why the following account will begin with the new and full moon sacrifice, and not with the ritual of the lighting of the fires: "We will explain the new and full moon sacrifice first because the teaching on the basic ritual framework (*tantra*) is known from it."[20] The inferential epistemological possibilities of the paradigmatic sacrifice take priority over the chronological necessities of the ritual life in the Sūtra organizational scheme.

18. For a full list of the paradigmatic rituals and their variations as they are given in the Sūtras, consult Chakrabarti, *The Paribhāṣās,* p. 136.

19. Two exceptions are the late Vaikhānasa Śrauta Sūtra and the poorly transmitted and fragmentary text of the Vādhula school, both of which begin with an account of the Agnyādhāna.

20. ĀśvŚS 1.1.3.

It is indeed the establishment of a system of inferences that is fundamental to the Sūtra literature. When the paradigm is known, inferences to the variations are guided by what is transferable from the former to the latter and what is not. But when there is no indication of what is paradigmatic for a particular case, other metarules aid the ritualist. The general rule for tracing an unknown paradigm from a known variation invokes a principle that operates in many other situations in the Vedic mental universe. "In case of doubt, the rule is to be inferred from resemblance (*sāmānya*)";[21] other texts lay down a similar proposition, stating that "The modification (*vikāra*) is known from the resemblance."[22] The resembling features of different sacrifices make possible both the inferences between them and the discovery of the appropriate paradigm from which to infer. Resemblance brings together rules and rites of a common type, linking paradigms and variations, in the ritual Sūtras, just as resemblance relates prototypes and counterparts in the metaphysics of the Brāhmaṇas. The intricacies of this web of ritual resemblances in the Sūtras will engage our attention in what follows.

The Organizational Economy of Resemblance

We have already encountered some of the technical terms employed in the Sūtras to analyze and structure the ritual system: "paradigm" (*prakṛti*), "variation" (*vikṛti*), and the key concept of *sāmānya,* which I have translated as "resemblance." Before proceeding deeper into the organizational fabric of the Sūtras, it will be necessary to introduce a few more of these critical terms.

All variations of a common paradigm utilize the same set of what are known as "subsidiary rites" (*aṅga*), which are described fully only in the Sūtra's treatment of the paradigm. Taken together, the subsidiary rites constitute the sacrificial framework (*tantra*), and it is indeed by virtue of the shared framework that rituals are classified together as variations of a paradigm. In the procedure of any one of these variations, the framework is followed up to the point of the "principal rites" (*pradhāna*) of the individual sacrifice and is again adopted after those principal rites are concluded. There is thus a "prior framework" (*pūrva tantra*) and a "subsequent framework" (*uttara tantra*) common to related

21. ŚŚS 1.16.18.
22. BhŚS 6.15.9; HŚS 3.8.

rituals, located on either side of a distinctive center comprised of the principal rites.[23]

It is the "insertion" (*āvāpa*) of the set of principal rites in the middle of otherwise resembling sacrifices that gives each variation of a common paradigm its unique identity. The principal rites are the procedures taken for offering oblations to particular deities who are invoked for the success of the sacrifice. This is why it is said that the principal rites are the critical part of the ritual; it is with them that the desired results or "fruit" of the particular ritual are produced. Therefore, the subsidiary rites are merely subservient adjuncts to the main event of any ritual performance; their characteristic "mark" is their role in helping to achieve the purpose of the principal rites.[24] In summary, as Chakrabarti writes,

> The principal offerings constitute the principal component part of a sacrifice, whereas the other acts that subserve them are treated as their subsidiaries. The subsidiary acts constitute the *tantra,* "the sacrificial framework," and the principal part is known by the term *āvāpa.*[25]

With this arsenal of technical terms now in hand, we are ready to progress further into the workings of the ritual science. The ritual is organized in the Sūtras on the basis of a series of judgments regarding the basic similarity or difference between the various sacrifices.

One form of similarity is known as "extended application by analogy" (*atideśa*), and we have already seen one way in which it is deployed: the ritual framework of the paradigm is extended by analogy to all the variations of that paradigm. As a general principle, extended application helps the Sūtra writers to minimize words by tapping connections and resemblances:

> The sacrifices some of the particulars of which are not specified borrow them from other similar sacrifices that are enjoined with all the details. This process of extended application of details by analogy is called *atideśa,* by which the subsidiaries prescribed in connexion with one sacrifice are made applicable beyond that sacrifice and transferred to similar sacrifices. The sacrifice from which the subordinate rites are transferred is called an

23. For more details on the specific rites that constitute the *pūrva tantra* and the *uttara tantra* and the exact location for the insertion of the principal rites, consult ŚŚS 1.16.3–6.

24. ŚŚS 1.16.6.

25. Chakrabarti, *The Paribhāṣās,* p. 124.

archetype (*prakṛti*) and the sacrifice to which they are so transferred is called an ectype (*vikṛti*).[26]

Such extensions on the basis of similarity or analogy are further analyzed into two kinds. The first is a kind of interior extension whereby the purpose of a particular sacrifice extends from the center—from the principal rites—to the periphery or subsidiary rites. The second type of extension by similarity is the extension of details from one whole ritual to another, from the paradigm to the variation.

The first of these two types involves the extended application of the purpose (*artha*) of a particular ritual from the center (which is directly concerned with the fulfillment of that purpose) to the subsidiary rites, which, by themselves, produce no results. They derive their purpose, by extended analogy, entirely from the principal rites they subserve. The purpose of a sacrifice in this way radiates outward to the otherwise purposeless subsidiary rites.

To take one text as a case in point of this phenomenon, the Kātyāyana Śrauta Sūtra makes it quite clear that the principal rites are the critical actions in the ritual procedure for the attainment of the purpose and "fruit." Rites which do not produce results are by definition subsidiary to others;[27] and the principal rites, by contrast, may generate results without their subsidiaries "because of the separation" between the two.[28] Because the purpose of the ritual is independent of the subsidiary rites, these latter may in some cases be performed in any order at all.[29]

It is more often stated, however, that the principal and subsidiary rites are interdependent. Multiple oblations to several deities occurring during the principal rites of a single sacrifice are subserved by a common set of subsidiary rites which are performed only once. This is because, it is said, the subsidiaries "make possible the purpose" fulfilled by the principal rites, because both the subsidiary and principal rites share "one purpose," and because the Veda has made authoritative judgments regarding their "union."[30] Subsidiaries, although unable to produce results inde-

26. Ibid., p. 131. See also S. G. Moghe, "The Evolution of the Mīmāṃsā Technical Term *Atideśa*," *Annals of the Bhandarkar Oriental Research Institute* 58–59 (1977–78): 777–84.

27. KŚS 1.2.4.

28. KŚS 1.2.18–19.

29. KŚS 1.5.1–2.

30. KŚS 1.7.1–2.

pendently, are "attracted" to the purpose of the principals they serve; they are called *parārthatva,* "subservient to the purpose of another."[31]

Another way in which the texts present the interdependence of the subsidiaries and principals and the extension of purpose within the interior of the ritual from center to periphery is in terms of a "commonality of context" (*prakaraṇa*):

> The subsidiary acts are linked with the principal ones enjoined in the same context by *prakaraṇa,* which means a mutual desire to be united with each other. . . . The principal offerings of a sacrifice produce the result only when they are duly accompanied by the subsidiary rites, and hence they look for the latter. On the other hand, the subsidiary rites, which cannot produce the main result independently, become fruitful by subserving the purpose of the principal offerings. This mutual desire unites the principal and the subsidiary components of a sacrifice, which, as a whole, leads to the desired results.[32]

The "commonality of context" thus provides a mutual attraction between subsidiary rites and principal ones; it also bonds together the different principal oblations within the center of a single sacrifice. The various principal oblations are said to "share a common procedure" when they share a common context.[33]

In the interior of the ritual procedure, then, the extended application on the basis of analogy or similarity works in several different ways. It transfers the purpose of the ritual from the principal rites to the subsidiaries, it makes possible a common subservient framework for several different principal oblations, and it links those different principal oblations together into a "common context."

The second type of extended application by analogy is that by which the features of the paradigmatic sacrifice are extended to the structure of the dependent variant sacrifices. Whereas the first type of extended application functions *within* one ritual, this second type operates *between* two or more rituals, and in the latter case as in the former, the principle works in several different ways.

The extended application may transfer knowledge of the subsidiary rites of the paradigmatic ritual to the variant rituals of the class. All variations resemble each other in that they share the framework of subsidiary rites found in their paradigm. Thus, for example, the ritual

31. See, e.g., KŚS 1.6.10. For the *mīmāṃsā* analysis of this concept, see PMS 3.1.2–6 and Mādhva's *Jaiminīyanyāyamālā* (Poona: Ānandāśrama, 1892), 3.1.5.

32. Chakrabarti, *The Paribhāṣās,* p. 126.

33. ĀpŚS 24.2.26–27.

framework of the new and full moon sacrifice is extended by analogy to all the variations (the *iṣṭi*s and the animal sacrifice) "because of the commonality of purpose" which that framework serves in all rituals of the class.[34] Similarly, many features of the *agniṣṭoma* extend to the soma sacrifices of one to twelve days' duration "because of the appearance of the same auxiliary acts" in both the paradigm and the model.[35] An alternative way of stating this same principle is to say that the distinctive principal oblations of a variant ritual are performed "with the support" of the subsidiary rites extended from the paradigmatic sacrifice of the class.[36]

Another form that extended application between sacrifices may take is to transfer the rules for the principal oblation themselves from the paradigm to the variation. Thus, one text states that the rules for offering the principal oblations of the new and full moon sacrifice extend over all the "subsequent" sacrifices, with a few exceptions noted.[37]

Extended application on the basis of similarity or analogy—working either within a sacrifice or between sacrifices—is a frequently encountered organizational principle in the ritual Sūtras and is one way in which the Sūtra writers adapted the fundamental Vedic principle of resemblance. But resemblance, as we have had ample occasion to witness, not only makes possible a set of connections based on similarities but also requires differentiation. The principles by which the ritual scientists distinguished sacrifices from one another comprise the flip side of the same coin that made it possible for them to forge connections between similar sacrifices.

Some of the ways in which rituals are distinguished have already been noted. Different classes of sacrifices are so categorized on the basis of the different subsidiary rites which form a definitive ritual framework for the class. This distinctive framework is taken from the paradigmatic sacrifice of each class and extended over the variants, constituting them all as distinctive from other classes of rituals. Within each class, moreover, each member maintains its individuality (and thus avoids the excess of resemblance the Brāhmaṇas call *jāmi*). For, although every ritual within the set shares the same subsidiary rites (the ritual framework), every one also has distinctive and, again, definitive principal rites. As Chakrabarti puts it, "The procedure cannot, however, be *identical* because the ritual proce-

34. KŚS 4.3.2.
35. KŚS 12.1.1; see also KŚS 13.1.1.
36. KŚS 1.5.4.
37. HŚS 3.8.

dure varies with the principal offerings, and the difference in principal offerings distinguishes one sacrifice from another."[38]

Finally, we have already seen that within the ritual organization of the Sūtra texts the general rule is overriden by the particular. Extended application on the basis of the similarity between the paradigm and the variation occurs only in cases where no specific injunction to the contrary is encountered with the variant. A specification in the variant requires a cessation of the extended application, as, for example, in the case of the different deities to which the principal oblations are offered:

> In all cases where deities are specified, the gods of the paradigmatic sacrifice should be withdrawn [from the procedure of the variant]. Divinities between those of the two oblations of clarified butter and the offering to Agni Sviṣṭakṛt [i.e., the deities of the principal oblations] are then replaced [by those specified for the variant sacrifice].[39]

There are other grounds for the cessation of the extended application from the paradigm to the variation; there are, in other words, other methods for constituting differences between the rituals of a class. One text rules that "the [extensions from] the paradigmatic sacrifice [to the variations of it] are annulled on three grounds: by counterinjunction, prohibition, or loss of purpose."[40] Examples of counterinjunction would include not only the declaration of distinctive principal oblations to the appropriate deities within the variant but also the specification of different materials used for those or other oblations. A prohibition means that in the variant it is explicitly required that certain of the otherwise extended rites from the paradigm be dropped. Loss of purpose (*arthalopa*) refers to cases of superfluity. For example, when the variant ritual calls for an oblation of rice gruel instead of the usual cake, the rites for preparing the cake are dropped from the variant procedure because they no longer serve any purpose.

Other Sūtras provide other lists of occasions when the extended application ceases. The Bhāradvāja Śrauta Sūtra[41] includes "accomplishment" (*siddhi*) along with others already mentioned, which may very

38. Chakrabarti, *The Paribhṣās,* p. 132; emphasis added. J. M. Verpoorten, in "Unité et distinction," p. 82, echoes the point: "Le début et la fin du rite doivent former une unité. Ils seront semblables l'un à l'autre, se réspondront à tous égards par delà une zone intermédiaire, un centre, qui, par sa consistance propre, les séparera, les distinguera, et permettra ainsi de parer au reproche de *jāmi,* de répétition superflue."

39. ĀśvŚS 2.1.22–23.

40. ĀpŚS 24.4.2.

41. BhŚS 6.15.6.

well be equivalent to the "change in purpose" listed in another text.[42] For, as yet another text explains, "The modification in the ritual framework of sacrifices not mentioned here [in a section on the paradigmatic sacrifices] should proceed out of consideration for the particular purpose [of those sacrifices]."[43] Sacrifices are distinguished by their principal rites, and the individualized purpose of sacrifices is brought about by those principal rites; therefore, a change in the center will sometimes require a change in the subsidiary framework, to conform with a "change in purpose" and to make possible the "accomplishment" of that new purpose.

These, then, are some of the reasons for annulling the extension of the procedure from the paradigm to the variant, some of the rules for knowing where and how to distinguish the variant from the paradigm. We come now to a somewhat different problem, the solution to which brings us to the crucial concept in the Sūtras of resemblance or *sāmānya.* When there is no particular injunction specified in the variant, and when there are competing claims of analogy within the paradigm, how does one decide which of the similarities take priority for the procedure of the variant sacrifice? What is at issue here is how to sort out competing claims of resemblance which have caused a "contradiction" (*virodha*) or confusion in a system based on inferences and transferences based on resemblance.[44]

The solution to the problem requires an understanding of the way the ritualists analyzed resemblance. The general rule for inferential knowledge from the paradigm to the variant is that the "modification" (*vikāra*) required is known from resemblance, that is, by finding the most analogous instance in the paradigm. The general rule is further refined, however, by an analysis of resemblance into three kinds: resemblance of the number of potsherds on which sacrificial cakes are baked,

42. Others included in ŚŚS (9.1.3–7) are "appellation" (*nāmadheya*), prohibition, "number" (*parisaṃkhyā*), and "addition" (*upajana*). It is not clear what is meant by most of these terms, however. See Caland's notes to these *sūtra*s found in his translation of the text. For other instances in which extended application is to be annulled, consult KŚS 4.3.8, 4.3.22.

43. ĀśvŚS 2.14.14.

44. In some text places (e.g., ŚŚS 1.16.18; ĀpŚS 24.3.46), this "contradiction" in claims of analogy is designated by the term *sāmānya,* which I have translated as "resemblance." In those passages, it would seem as if one must translate the term in much the same manner as I have suggested for the Brāhmaṇic word *jāmi*—that is, as "excessive resemblance" or, perhaps, "a conflict in resemblance." *Virodha* is, in any case, the usual designation for the problem at hand.

resemblance of divinity, and resemblance of oblation material.[45] These three kinds of resemblance establish paradigmatic rites located in a variety of particular rituals. The extended application is thus from a paradigmatic rite rather than from a portion of the paradigmatic ritual, and the modification is based on that rite regardless of the class to which the variant ritual belongs.

The first type of resemblance is fundamentally one of numerical analogy. Thus, "when there is no specific injunction" regarding the procedure required in the variant, the following guidelines come into play: all cases in which there are cakes baked on eight potsherds are modifications (*vikāra*s) of the procedure followed in the rite of the preparation of the cake dedicated to Agni in the new and full moon sacrifice; all instances of cakes baked on eleven potsherds are modifications of the preparation of the cake dedicated to Agni-Soma in the full moon sacrifice; and so on.[46]

The second sort of resemblance is that of the deity, and here, too, the analogy is often purely numerical. Offerings in a variant sacrifice for a single deity (for which there are no specific instructions to the contrary) follow the rites accompanying the offering to Agni in the new and full moon sacrifice. Offerings to two or more deities are modifications of either the cake offered to Agni-Soma in the full moon sacrifice or that dedicated to Indra-Agni in the new moon sacrifice.[47] Within this category of resemblance, however, there are cases of analogy which are not simply numerical. Thus, for example, if the variant sacrifice calls for an offering to Indra as part of the principal oblations, the inferences for the procedure are not based on the paradigmatic offerings to a single deity; rather, they are to be modifications of the offering to Indra-Agni (a dual deity) because of Indra's appearance in both cases.[48] Here we begin to see the possibility of conflicting resemblances and the resolution of the conflict. Resemblance between the number of divinities receiving offerings conflicts with the resemblance established by virtue of the fact that the same deity appears in two cases. The conflict in this case is solved by giving priority to the latter; it is the "stronger" of the two resemblances.

The third type of resemblance the Sūtras recognize is that of the oblation material. The rite of preparing the offering of porridge for

45. BŚS 27.14; see also HŚS 3.8.
46. BŚS 27.14; see also ĀpŚS 24.3.38–39.
47. BhŚS 6.15.9; ĀpŚS 24.3.41–44; HŚS 3.8.
48. BhŚS 6.15.10; ĀpŚS 24.3.45; HŚS 3.8.

Soma in the *cāturmāsya* ritual is paradigmatic for all offerings of porridge in which there are no specific injunctions. Oblations of curds, milk, the mixture of coagulated and fresh hot milk (*āmikṣā*), and offerings of animal parts all are modifications of the rites for preparing and offering the milk mixture for Indra at the new moon sacrifice.[49]

It is now time to return to the question of conflicting claims of resemblance. It should come as no surprise that in the Sūtras, as in other texts of the Vedic tradition, the hegemonic principle of resemblance is modulated by the equally important principle of hierarchy. Conflicting claims of resemblance are arbitrated by the establishment of a hierarchical order of precedence, centering in this case on the perceived import to the effectiveness of the sacrifice. Thus, of the three types of resemblance analyzed above, the resemblance of potsherds is determined to be the least important and is overruled by either a competing resemblance of divinity or one of oblation. And between deity and oblation, it is the latter that prevails, for it is said to be "stronger."[50] Elsewhere, the hierarchical superiority of the resemblance of oblation is justified "because of the intimate union of the material" from which the oblation is made and the sacrifice as a whole.[51] Other texts concur in stating that the resemblance of oblation overrides competing claims to resemblance by virtue of its "strength."[52]

Hierarchical ordering adjudicates other kinds of conflicting claims in the system of resemblances, linkage, and transferences so elaborately woven in the Sūtras. In one text, a series of metarules provides just such a hierarchy of resemblance for determining the means for inferential knowledge within the ritual universe. In the event of a contradiction between the instructions for performing the subsidiary rites of the paradigmatic sacrifice and those for the variant sacrifice, the former prevail. The "multiplicity" of the principal oblations in the variation may require overruling the rules for performing the subsidiary rites transferred from the paradigm, and the "position" of the principal oblations in the ritual sequence overrides the demands stemming from their multiplicity. And a direct injunction regarding the principal oblation takes precedence over the inferences made on the basis of the considerations listed

49. BŚS 27.14. The fact that the meatless new and full moon sacrifice is regarded as the paradigmatic ritual for, among other variants, the animal sacrifice is explained by this less than apparent analogy between the milk libation in the former and its modification, the offering of the omentum of the animal, in the latter. See BhŚS 7.6.9 and KŚS 4.3.14–16.

50. BŚS 27.14.

51. KŚS 4.3.9.

52. See ĀpŚS 24.3.46; HŚS 3.8; ŚŚS 1.16.17.

above.[53] The hierarchical order of the authoritative strength of the claim thus moves from the most general to the most specific.

In all instances of such hierarchies within the Sūtra's organization of the ritual, the underlying consideration is the most direct way to achieve the "purpose" (*artha*) of the particular sacrifice. This concept of purpose stands at the apex of considerations regarding the relations between rites and rituals; it is the standard against which all others are gauged.

The resemblance of oblation takes precedence over other types of resemblance because it is more directly and effectively connected with the fulfillment of the purpose of the ritual. But even the resemblance of oblation is overpowered by other and more pressing instances of "resemblance of purpose" (*arthasāmānya*), that is, an even more powerful analogy between the goals of two sacrifices: "When there is a contradiction of resemblance between the oblation material and the purpose, it is the resemblance of purpose that is more important because that [the oblation] is for the sake of the other [i.e., the purpose]."[54] Other texts note that the oblation "depends on" the ritual act[55] and that the ritual act is what brings about the accomplishment of the purpose of the oblation.[56] Chakrabarti sums up the view of the Sūtras by observing, "A material is prescribed for serving some purpose, and not simply for the sake of being introduced. Hence a material is less important than the purpose it has to serve."[57] As we will observe in a later chapter, the overriding consideration of purpose makes possible any number of substitutions within a ritual. Here it is enough to observe the hierarchical superiority of purpose within a scale of resemblances constituting a web of connections linking rites and rituals. Indeed, one text makes this principle the most important of all for guiding the ritualist: rules specified in the paradigm are to be modified in the variant rituals "according to the purpose" of the individual sacrifices.[58]

This brief survey of the inner workings of the ritual science as it is represented in the Sūtras does not pretend to be comprehensive.[59] Rather, this overview of the nuts and bolts of the metarules and their

53. HŚS 3.8.
54. KŚS 1.4.16; see also KŚS 1.5.5; ĀpŚS 24.3.48.
55. HŚS 3.8.
56. BŚS 24.2.
57. Chakrabarti, *The Paribhāṣās*, p. 176.
58. KŚS 4.3.20.
59. The rules for applying and transferring *mantras*, for example, provide another context for witnessing the ritual scientists at work. See Chakrabarti, *The Paribhāṣās*, pp. 132–36, 154–65.

applications was meant to underline two points. First is the fact that the organization of ritual knowledge in these highly technical texts proceeds in ways comparable to the philosophical discourse of the Brāhmaṇas. Although there are obvious differences in genre, age, authorship, and goal distinguishing the earlier texts from the Sūtras, there are more fundamental continuities extending between them. Vedism—a religion represented in *both* the Vedas per se and the ritual Sūtras—is in every one of its textual productions characterized by the dominance of the principle of hierarchical resemblance.

The second point, which will be developed in the next section, concerns the implications of the metarules for evaluating the relations between two of the components that comprise a Kalpa Sūtra—the Śrauta Sūtra, which covers the large-scale *śrauta* sacrifices, and the Gṛhya Sūtra, whose subject concerns the simpler rituals at the domestic level. The principle of hierarchical resemblance, as it was recast into a classificatory and literary tool in the ritual Sūtras, links these two main components of a Kalpa Sūtra in much the same way as individual rites and rituals are connected and differentiated. In other words, I will explore the way the epistemological connections the Sūtras formulated *within* a text were also extended *between* texts of the same ritual school.

The Śrauta Sūtra of the school appears first in the textual corpus and functions in much the same way as the paradigmatic ritual, which is also epistemologically prior. The Gṛhya Sūtra, in which chronologically prior rituals are described, is dependent on the Śrauta Sūtra in ways redolent of the manner in which the depiction of the variant sacrifice depends on the paradigm in the Sūtra's exposition.

Intertextual Connections

In the Śrauta Sūtras, metarules direct the ritualist in making necessary inferences when there is insufficient information given in the text itself. These metarules, helpful as they are, do not succeed in filling in all the gaps. The Sūtras are not adequate guides in themselves to ritual practice; they are not self-contained texts.

It is thus misleading to refer to these literary productions, as some do, as handbooks or manuals of ritual practice. It is impossible, as revivalists in modern India have discovered, to carry out any *śrauta* sacrifice completely and properly when one has only the Sūtra. There is simply too much left out and too much taken for granted in the interest of a succinct representation. Modern practitioners rely exclusively on the *prayogas* for such supplementary information. These texts, many quite recent, are true manuals of performance; their step-by-step instructions for the execution of the ritual go into exhaustive detail. Some scholars speculate about the existence of similar kinds of ritual handbooks, complementing and augmenting the Sūtras, in ancient India, although no instances of genuine antiquity have survived.[60]

The ancient ritualists may have relied on *prayogas* to fill in the lacunae of detail left by the Sūtras, but they certainly depended on the earlier ritual texts of their tradition, the Vedas. Like all types of Sūtra, the Śrauta Sūtras are classified as *smṛti,* "traditional" or "remembered" knowledge originating in human teachers, and not *śruti,* the "revealed" and canonical knowledge springing from transcendent sources. The dependence of the *smṛti,* and especially the ritual Sūtras, on the *śruti* is profound. Renou considers the Vedāṅga as a whole as being "at the same time without and within the Veda," though he further notes that "from the Indian point of view, it is a line of rigorous division" separating the two classes of texts.[61] The line is at its fuzziest, however, when the Śrauta Sūtras are considered. As C. G. Kashikar points out, "The Śrautasūtras deal with the Vedic sacrifice in a systematic and detailed manner almost strictly following the Saṃhitās and the Brāhmaṇas including the Āraṇyakas."[62] More than any other example of the Sūtra literature, perhaps, the Śrauta Sūtras are thematically and epistemologically dependent on, and a continuation of, the Veda.

One source, then, for supplementary knowledge for the Sūtras—for what I will call here intertextual inferences or connections—is the Veda. Every Śrauta Sūtra assumes a certain knowledge of the *śruti* texts of the school. The portions of those earlier texts which present the rules of the ritual (the *vidhis*) are most often either wholly repeated or simply assumed in the Sūtra's representation of the ritual; and the philosophical or explanatory aspects of the Brāhmaṇas (the *arthavādas*) are entirely presupposed. Furthermore, the Sūtras also assume knowledge of the Saṃhitā of the school in which are located the verses which are utilized

60. For such speculations, see Kashikar, *A Survey of the Śrautasūtras,* p. 29; and Jan Gonda, *Vedic Literature,* p. 339.

61. Renou, *The Destiny of the Veda in India,* p. 16.

62. Kashikar, *A Survey of the Śrautasūtras,* p. 3; see also p. 15: "Broadly speaking, therefore, there is no difference between the rituals represented by the Brāhmaṇas and those represented by the Śrautasūtras." For the relations between these two genres, see Naoshiro Tsuji, *On the Relation between Brāhmaṇas and Śrautasūtras* (in Japanese with an English summary) (Tokyo: Tôyo Bunko, 1952). Tsuji's work supersedes R. Löbbecke, *Über das Verhältnis von Brāhmaṇa und Śrautasūtren* (Leipzig; Kreysing, 1908).

in the ritual as mantras. In the Sūtras, these mantras are almost always given in what is known as the *pratīka* form: only the first few words of the complete verse are provided, the remainder to be supplied by the already memorized text in the Saṃhitā.

Another outside source for the details of ritual practice supplementing the Sūtra is the actual procedure adopted by authoritative ritual experts. This, too, might be regarded as a kind of intertextual connection—the other "text" being the memories and practices of human beings to whom the Sūtras refer in cases of doubt or controversy or simply out of the interest in conciseness of exposition.

Both the Veda and the ritual experts are included in a list of authoritative sources for supplementary knowledge of the ritual provided at the beginning of one Sūtra's collection of metarules: "One should look toward five authorities for help in knowledge of the ritual—the mantra, the Brāhmaṇa, evidence, inference, and the interchangeability of aspects of rituals of the same class."[63] The passage goes on to illustrate each of these methods. By "mantra" the Sūtra means that the order of verses and formulas in the Saṃhitā may serve as an indication of the order of performance of the rites using those mantras. Brāhmaṇa refers to the section of rules given in that text specifying the correlation with particular mantras and ritual acts, as well as those rules which indicate that certain rites are to be performed without the recitation of mantras. The method called "evidence" involves the evidence of ritual procedure as it is laid out in a Veda other than one's own. Thus, in this case, the ritual of the Yajur Veda is sometimes further supplemented by the rules given only in the Sāma or Ṛg Vedas. Inference, the text explains, means this: "When, given the authoritative sacrificial framework, one cannot make [the usual] authoritative inference, one should resort to [the ritual experts] of the villages, [thinking] 'This is the way of undertaking [the ritual] taught by the knowledgeable ones here.' " Finally, the interchangeability of aspects of rituals of the same class is explained in terms of legitimate substitutions based on resemblances between the elements of variant rituals following the same paradigmatic sacrifice. Such are the methods the Śrauta Sūtras themselves devised to complete an exposition of ritual practice they left incomplete.

But what might be the ways in which the Gṛhya Sūtras, equally succinct representations of the domestic rituals of the Vedic repertoire, supplement themselves by establishing linkages to authorities outside the text? Unlike the Śrauta Sūtras, the Gṛhya texts can make no claim of

63. BŚS 24.1.

close association with the ritual described in the Veda.[64] *Śrauta,* after all, means "relating to the *śruti*"; one of the alternative names for the *gṛhya* ritual is *smārta,* "relating to the *smṛti,*" indicating a rather different point of reference.

Because the domestic sacrifice is not the ritual the *śruti* revolves around, neither the order of the mantras in the Saṃhitā nor the application of the mantras to ritual action found in the rules of the Brāhmaṇas provides a useful method for augmenting a Gṛyha Sūtra. That is, the Gṛhya Sūtra does not, by and large, explicitly cite the authority of the *śruti* to justify ritual rules, nor does it depend on the Vedic texts for inferential knowledge concerning ritual procedure. When a Gṛhya Sūtra utilizes the verses of the Saṃhitā as mantras in the domestic ritual, it usually draws them out of their original context; the order of verses as they are found in the Saṃhitā is therefore not usually crucial—and is often irrelevant—for supplementing knowledge of the *gṛhya* rites as it is transmitted in the Gṛhya Sūtras.

There are, however, more or less indirect claims of linkages to the Veda issuing forth from the Gṛhya Sūtras. One text of domestic ritualism goes so far as to declare that the rules for the *gṛhya* sacrifices were once also given in Brāhmaṇas, but unfortunately those texts have disappeared. Still, the text maintains, a *śruti* origin for the domestic ritual may be inferred on the basis of "performance" (*prayoga*).[65] A related Sūtra states at its opening that "Here [are laid out] those rituals [i.e., the domestic sacrifices] which are known from practice (*ācāra*)."[66]

What is meant by these references to performance or practice? There are several possibilities. The texts may be speaking of a localized body of knowledge and traditional custom which remains outside the exposition of the ritual in the Sūtra. Such a practice would then be the means for completing the practice outlined in the Gṛhya Sūtra. Support for this possibility comes from one text's section on the marriage ritual in which the Sūtra notes that "the ways of different regions and of different villages are various indeed and should be followed at the wedding. We will explain here only those that are commonly prescribed."[67]

64. This apart from the fact that the Gṛhya Sūtras patterned the rituals they describe after the *śrauta* ceremonial. See Chapters 6 and 7 herein; and also Ram Gopal, "Influence of the Brāhmaṇas on the Gṛhya Sūtras," *Vishveshvaranand Indological Journal* 1 (1963): 291–98.

65. ĀpDhS 1.4.12.10.

66. ĀpGS 1.1.1.

67. ĀśvGS 1.7.1–2.

Another possible explanation is the often cited authority of the "practice of the learned," that is, of the ritual experts who, in this case, have mastered the performative details of the domestic ritual. These experts, "who are properly trained in the Veda and its supplements and who know how to make inferences from the *śruti,*"[68] are to be consulted, to take one example, regarding the times not specified in the Gṛhya Sūtra for discontinuation of the study of the Veda.[69]

As seen in the definition above, these authorities on the domestic ritual are learned in the Veda and the texts dependent on it, that is, the entire corpus of instruction on the Vedic sacrifice. It is arguably the connections and dependent relations that the Gṛhya Sūtras maintain with these other texts that led one writer to infer a lost *śruti* source dealing with the domestic ritual per se.

It is certainly the case that the later commentators on the Gṛhya Sūtra passages at issue thought that the practice the text referred to as a supplementary source of information on the domestic ritual was the practice of the *śrauta* sacrifices. One commentator explicates the *sūtra* which reads, "Here [are explained] those rituals which are learned from practice." He glosses the text by writing, "So that the domestic rituals might be intelligible in terms of the Veda, and inferable in terms of well-known practice, and so that these [domestic rituals] might be properly observed, there has been a prior explanation of the *śrauta* rituals [in the Śrauta Sūtra of the school]."[70] The commentator goes on to observe that the full disclosure of all the details for a complete discussion of the domestic ritual would involve "too much repetition." They have already been set out in the Śrauta Sūtra and are to be extended to the Gṛhya text: "The practice should extend from the parts to the whole." The other commentator on the text, Haradatta, speaks of the "continuity" of the teachings on the *śrauta* and *gṛhya* rituals and of the "dependence" of the latter on the former.[71]

There is, then, a strong sense in which the Gṛhya Sūtra and the ritual represented in it function as a kind of "subsequent" component dependent on and following the "precedent" which is the Śrauta Sūtra of the school and the ritual with which it is concerned. This relationship is

68. BDhS 1.1.1.6.

69. GGS 3.3.29.

70. Sudarśana on ĀpGS 1.1.1: *yat eva ācārānumeyavedāvagamyāni gārhyāṇi karmāṇi, ata eva tebhyah prathamamanuṣṭheyebhyo'pi pūrvaṃ śrautānām vyākhyānāṃ kṛtam.*

71. Haradatta on ĀpGS 1.1.1: *atrāthaśabdena śrautopadeśānantaraṃ smārtopadeśaṃ kariṣyāmīti vadan tadapekṣāmasya darśayati.*

highly reminiscent—indeed, I would argue, merely a reduplication—of the relationship between the paradigmatic sacrifices and their variants as constituted by the composers of the Sūtras, the epistemological wing of the Vedic ritualist world. Just as knowledge of "prior" and "subsequent" rituals depicted within a Sūtra is dependent on knowing how to extend what is said about the former to the latter, so is there established a series of intertextual connections and inferences moving from the Śrauta Sūtra to the Gṛhya Sūtra.

These two components of a Kalpa Sūtra, taken together, form a unified and multidimensional body of knowledge on the Vedic ritual system as a whole. The two types of ritual Sūtra divide up their interdependent referents; the *saṃskāras* and other domestic rituals presupposed by the *śrauta* ceremonial are described in the Gṛhya Sūtras, but the sacrifices on which many of the domestic rituals were modeled and assume knowledge of are given only in the Śrauta Sūtra. The relationship between the rituals (and those who perform them) at the *śrauta* and *gṛhya* levels is the subject of the next two chapters. I wish here only to observe that the *texts* describing these two types of Vedic ritual are also interrelated and interconnected—and in a manner entirely consistent with the organizational scheme that structures the contents of the individual Sūtra.

Chapters 6 and 7 are exercises in reapplying some of the organizational principles of the Sūtras discussed in this chapter. I will demonstrate how two major lines of inquiry into Vedic ritualism open up when imagined in terms of the paradigm/variant model articulated in the Sūtras. In Chapter 7 we will investigate the relationship between the *śrauta* and the *gṛhya* sacrifices by arguing that the latter are to the former as the variations are to the paradigm. This will help to underscore the relations of resemblance the ritualists established between the "subsequent" variation (the domestic ritual) and the "prior" paradigm (the *śrauta* ceremonial). In Chapter 6, however, I turn the model on its head in order to take a different angle on the relationship between the two levels of Vedic ritualism. I will argue that, just as the paradigmatic ritual is usually a simple and basic version of the more elaborated variations, the *gṛhya* sacrifice is a reduced and elementary form of the more protracted *śrauta* sacrifice.

And although the paradigm/variation model will be used in two different ways in order to bring out two different kinds of features of the relationship of resemblance between the domestic and the *śrauta* rituals (and those who engage in them), in both cases we will not lose sight of the hierarchical aspect of the relationship.

6

The Organization of Ritual Practice

The Unity of Ritual

A major assumption made in the ritual Sūtras, and itself largely assumed by me in Chapter 5, is that there is what one text calls a "unity of ritual" (*kalpaikatva*) extending among the three great classes or levels of Vedic ritual praxis: the domestic or *gṛhya* sacrifice, the *śrauta* sacrifice (properly called the *haviryajña*), and the rituals in which soma is offered and consumed.[1] The Vedic ritual is thus conceived as a whole comprised of three hierarchically ordered and formally analogous levels (within each class there are seven subclasses).[2]

For our purposes, however, the three great classes might be coalesced into two by collapsing the soma sacrifices into the *śrauta* ritual. This move may be justified by the fact that the Vedic ritualists discuss both (but not the domestic ritual) in the same texts, the Śrauta Sūtras. In any event, the point I wish to reiterate and follow through new material is this: the domestic ritual was included within a totalistic system in the ritual Sūtras, it participated in the web of interrelations linking the components of that system, but it was also the lowest level possible within the Vedic ritual universe—or, more precisely, within the Vedic ritual universe as it was mapped out in the ritual Sūtras.

1. ŚGS 1.1.13–15.

2. For this typology of the ritual into three classes, each with seven subclasses or *saṃsthās*, see BŚS 24.4; LŚS 5.4.23–24; GB 1.5.7, 1.5.23, 1.5.25; VaikhGS 1.1; BDhS 2.2.4.23; GautDhS 8.19–20. BGPariS 1.6.22 concludes an extended metaphor in which the Vedic ritual is likened to a tree by referring to the three great classes as the "roots" (*mūlas*), that is, the fundamental categories.

Before the Sūtras, the last textual layer of Vedism per se, the domestic ritual is largely undocumented. The Saṃhitās and Brāhmaṇas ignore it almost entirely (though not without some intriguing if somewhat ambiguous references). Because the domestic ritual is not much treated in these early texts, some have been led to speculate that in this period the domestic cult was the province of a "popular piety" apart from the "élite" religion of sacrificial Vedism. The Sūtras, insofar as they for the first time include domestic ritualism in their systematic treatment of the Vedic ritual in its entirety, might thus represent a kind of "domestication" of the domestic cult itself.

In this scenario, the Sūtras are evidence that the Brahmins enveloped the household sacrifices into their own well-established ritual corpus, systematizing it to conform to their own *śrauta* sacrifice. A. B. Keith, for example, writes:

> The priests . . . appear to have aimed, as time went on, at absorbing *en masse* the popular rites and decking them out with their own poetry and their ritual elaboration. . . . So far from the texts hinting at distaste for the popular ritual, they rather exhibit the priests determined to secure their participation in it to the fullest extent, at the expense of the field of action which first lay open to the head of the family as his own domestic priest.[3]

This is, however, only a hypothesis, and not the only one possible. As I will note below, the admittedly scanty references to something like domestic ritualism in the earlier era of the Saṃhitās and Brāhmaṇas may indicate that a simplified form of Vedic ritualism, formally similar to that of the later Gṛhya Sūtras and formally distinguished from other kinds of Vedic ritualism, was at least known and possibly already systematized before the composition of the Sūtras.[4] It is, at any rate, just as possible to posit an origin within Vedic ritualism for the domestic sacrifice as to imagine it "absorbed" by Vedic ritualism; but the question remains unresolved and will not preoccupy us here.

On the other side of things—that is, after the time of the ritual Sūtras—the domestic rites were (again?) largely divorced from the increasingly anachronistic and abandoned *śrauta* ceremonial. Domestic ritualism of Vedic coinage survived, and continues to survive, in Hinduism long after the *śrauta* rituals had been discontinued by all but the

3. A. B. Keith, *The Religion and Philosophy of the Veda,* I: 56.

4. See below, pp. 161–67. Mention might also be made of AitB 8.10, which instructs the *purohita* of the king to make certain oblations into a domestic fire (*gṛhyāgni*). Also note that at least one particular domestic rite of the *gṛhya* cycle, the *upanayana,* was already outlined in some detail in AV 11.5 and ŚB 11.3.3 and 11.5.4.

occasional king and pockets of Brahmins in peripheral and isolated areas of the subcontinent.

When detached from their relations to the *śrauta* sacrifice, domestic rites could take on new functions and significances (a topic to which I will return in the next chapter). But in the context of the "unity of ritual" established in—and perhaps *by*—the Sūtras, the domestic ritual cannot be properly understood other than in situ.

In this chapter, I will explore the "situation" of the domestic sacrifice within Vedic ritualism. I will first present an analysis of the connotations behind one of the principal generic names used in the Sūtras for the domestic ritual as one class of rites in relation to others: the *gṛhyayajña* or "sacrifice of the household." Next, I look at the domestic ritual, as it appears in the Sūtras, as a feminine counterpart to the masculine prototype. I will conclude with a discussion of the meanings behind a second classificatory designation for this type of Vedic ritual: the *pākayajña,* sometimes translated as the "cooked sacrifice" but more often meaning a "small" or "feeble" sacrifice. Both of these terms (*gṛhyayajña* and *pākayajña*) I will maintain, do not so much refer to a way of sacrificing in itself but rather to one that has consciously been constituted *in relation to* other levels of the Vedic ritual repertoire.

I begin by briefly outlining some of these relations. First and foremost—and generative of others—was the fact that domestic ritualism was *basic* to the ritualism of the ancient Vedic Indians. By this I mean several things. Some of the rituals included under the heading of the domestic class were prerequisites for the *śrauta* sacrifices. The *saṃskāras* of childhood and adolescence, and most especially the initiation and marriage rites, were one component of the necessary qualifications for those who would enter into the next level of Vedic ritualism, the higher *śrauta* cult, and thus were chronologically prior.[5]

Others of the rituals included within the rubric of domestic ritualism might be considered basic in the sense of being complementary to the *śrauta* ritual. House-building ceremonies, rites relating to childbirth, domestic animals, and many others complemented rituals at the *śrauta* level and would be performed by the *śrauta* sacrificer as occasions came

5. For a general discussion of the importance of these two *saṃskāras* for the *śrauta* sacrifice, consult Madeleine Biardeau, *Le Sacrifice dans l'Inde ancienne* (Paris: Presses Universitaires de France, 1976), pp. 36–38. See also P. V. Kane, *History of Dharmaśāstra,* II: 190–95. The question of which of the *saṃskāras* were required, which were optional, and when, historically, such decisions began to be made, is largely unexplored to my knowledge. The Sūtras themselves do not appear to address the topic.

up.[6] The domestic sacrifice was therefore basic also in the sense of being fundamental to the necessity of properly maintaining the household.

A third way in which the *gṛhya-* or *pākayajña* might be considered basic to Vedism is in a hierarchical sense. The domestic ritual had preparatory purposes and domestic functions to serve within the "unity" of Vedic ritualism. It would appear that the *gṛhya* ritual was preeminently suited not only for certain jobs but also for certain persons who were also defined by their participation in it. And, we shall see, in form as well as function, the domestic sacrifice was most often represented as a condensed counterpart—a *pāka* version—of larger, more complete, and yet still resembling sacrifices. So, too, therefore, a hierarchical evaluation of those relegated to the domain of domesticity was made in the Vedic texts.

One might also see the relationship between the domestic and *śrauta* rituals, as I suggested at the end of Chapter 5, as a replication of the relationship between the fundamental (and prior) paradigmatic sacrifice and the often more complex (and subsequent) variation (*gṛhya : śrauta :: prakṛti : vikṛti*). And like most cases of the paradigm/variant relation, the domestic ritual is elemental in the sense of hierarchically inferior to the more developed ritual (in this case, the *śrauta* sacrifice as a whole). The *gṛhya* ritual's association with home and family (and especially with the wife) served only to reinforce a hierarchical inferiority within the Vedic ritual, and within a socio-ontological system.

Domestic Ritualism and Domesticated Ritualists

The domestic ritual or *gṛhyayajña* is, unsurprisingly, so designated because of its close ties to the domestic realm. It is the cycle of rites oriented toward the needs and wants of the household; or, as one authority puts it, the domestic sacrifice is "of the world."[7] The intimate connections among the household fire, the sacrifices offered in it, the household in general, and the householder, his wife, and his children in particular, are brought out clearly in the commentators' glosses on the Gṛhya Sūtras and in other

6. See, e.g., BGPariS 1.16.1–2: "When he intends to set the [*śrauta*] fires . . . he extinguishes [the domestic fire] and thereafter prepares this [domestic fire] from ritual to ritual [i.e., only when necessary]."

7. ĀpGS 1.2.9.

later writings. Devasvāmin, for example, explicating ĀśvGS 1.1.1 ("Having already expalined the *śrauta* rituals, we will now explain the *gṛhya* rituals") writes:

> The *gṛhya* rituals are those done with regard to the home. The word "home" here is used in three senses: [rituals] concerning the wife, those concerning the domicile, and [rituals] concerning the stage in life [*āśrama*; i.e., householdership].[8]

Other later authorities of the tradition concur, emphasizing one or another of these components of domestic ritualism. Gobhilaputra, who composed a manual based on the Gobhila Gṛhya Sūtra, explains the purpose of the domestic ritual in terms of the household (*gṛhya*), which he defines as the wife, sons, and daughters, together with presently conceived unborn children and unborn children not yet conceived: "These are considered the household, the kin relations of the sacrificer. . . . Therefore the ritual law [pertaining to the domestic ritual] is called *gṛyha*."[9] Commenting on ĀpGS 2.5.14 ("The domestic fire is perpetually maintained"), Haradatta Miśra writes in a similar vein but underlines especially the connection with the sacrificer's wife (which will be explored in more detail in the next section). "This fire," writes that commentator, "set at the time of marriage, is perpetually, that is, eternally maintained for the purpose of rituals closely connected to the wife."[10]

In the ritual texts, the domestic fire (the *śālā-* or *gṛhyāgni,* the "fire of the house"; also known as the *aupāsana* or *aupāsada* fire, the "fire for worship"; and *vaivāhikāgni,* "the marriage fire") serves as something of a metonym for domestic ritualism as a whole. It is distinguished from the ordinary cooking fire of the home (the *pacanāgni*) and is sacred in relation to any other "worldly" fire (*laukikāgni*). And the Sūtras generally assume that all domestic rituals will be done with this sacred, set-apart domestic fire.[11]

8. *gṛhe bhāvani yāni karmāṇi tāni gṛhyāni. tatrāyaṃ gṛhaśabdastriṣvartheṣu vartte bhāryāyāṃ śālāyāmāśrama iti.*

9. M. Bloomfield, ed. and trans., *Das Gṛhyasamgrahapariśishṭa des Gobhilaputra* (Leipzig: G. Kreysing, 1881), 1.35–36.

10. *eṣa vaivāhiko'gnirnityaḥ śāśvatiko dhāryaḥ patnīsambandhānāṃ karmaṇāmarthāya.*

11. In some texts, however, certain of the *saṃskāra*s require separate fires. Many schools require a so-called *sutikāgni* for performance of the birth and naming ceremonies (*jātakarman* and *nāmakarman*); see PGS 1.16.23; VGS 2.11; HGS 2.3.4–6; BhGS 1.26;

It is important to note that this fire used for the domestic ritual is to be established inside the house itself; it is to be placed and then maintained on a square mound of earth (called the "home of the fire," *agniśālā*) located in the eastern or northeastern section of the family's home.[12] The details of this shrine within the home are, unfortunately, only vaguely described in the Gṛhya Sūtras, but what is noteworthy for us is, first, its location within the house (reemphasizing the domesticity of the ceremonial performed with it as the centerpiece) and, second, its situation in the northeastern quarter. This latter detail is significant because it, too, reiterates the strong bonds the domestic fire and sacrifice maintain with the home and household. It is in the northeastern corner, according to one authority, where *bali* offerings are placed daily for the "deities of the home" (*gṛhadevatās*), the "deities of the site of the house" (*āvasānadevatās*), and the "lord of the site of the house" (*āvasānapati*).[13] The domestic fire, in sum, is located where the invisible beings most directly involved with the affairs of the house are concentrated. The association of the fire (and the ritual cycle it recapitulates) and the home is in this way made manifest in part by the very location of the domestic fire.

The time this fire is first established differs according to different schools,[14] but in all cases it coincides with the attainment of a degree of independence. The setting of one's own domestic fire is preconditioned on and signals a change from the status of a dependent member of another's household to an assumption of lordship over some domain of one's own, limited though it might be.[15] A qualified male, one who has been initiated and has learned some portion of the Veda, may set his own domestic fire at the time when he separates from or takes control of his patriarchal family. This time usually coincides with marriage. The

---

VaikhGS 3.15. Generally, this fire is extinguished and the domestic fire rekindled before the conferring of the name on the child (HGS 2.4.8; BhGS 1.26), but see ŚGS 1.25.11 and Oldenberg's note in his translation for a school which expects the *sutikāgni* to be kept for a full year after the birth of the child.

12. See KhGS 1.2.1; ĀpGS 2.6.10; BGS 3.4.6, 3.4.9.

13. BGS 2.8.25.

14. For the texts on this subject, consult Kane, *History of Dharmaśāstra,* II: 678–80; and H. W. Bodewitz, *The Daily Evening and Morning Offering (Agnihotra) according to the Brāhmaṇas* (Leiden: E. J. Brill, 1976), pp. 194–95.

15. This point challenges J. C. Heesterman's intriguing thesis that the domestic fire symbolizes the householder's dependence on and antagonistic relations with others in society. See his "Other Folks' Fire" in J. F. Staal, ed., *Agni,* II: 76–94.

fire and the cycle of rites inaugurated at the wedding subsequently act as palpable signs of the ties between husband and wife and the family they will produce and also signals new spheres of influence and power for both man and woman.

For the groom, the lighting of the domestic fire marks a new independent status as he separates from his father's household and becomes head of his own. Other recommended occasions for lighting a new domestic fire are either when the patriarch dies and the assets of the household are divided among the male members or when the death of the patriarch occurs and the family stays together. In the latter case, the eldest son moves into the vacated position of leadership within the family, a move accompanied by the creation of a new domestic fire. He thereby becomes "chief" of the domain (*parameṣṭhin*), as one text puts it,[16] or "personally superior" (*svāyam jyāyan*) to other members of the household, as it is phrased in another text.[17]

Another option, and the one that is apparently favored only by the schools of Baudhāyana and Bhāradvāja, concerns the pupil who has finished Veda study and is about to take the concluding bath of the graduate and become a *snātaka* (literally "one who has bathed"). He is to take as his domestic fire the fire he has established at the initiation and maintained throughout the period of scholarship:

> In the fire that he establishes at the time of the *upanayana,* in that [fire he offers oblations] at the time of the observance of the vows [for learning different sections of the Veda]; in that [he offers] at the bath concluding studentship; in that [he offers] at the marriage ceremony; and in that [same fire he offers the oblations of] the domestic rituals.[18]

In this case, the continuity of the domestic sacrifice stretches over the entire ritual life of the sacrificer, beginning with the initiation that

16. GGS 1.1.12. See also Bloomfield, *Das Gṛhyasamgrahapariśishṭa des Gobhilaputra,* 1.77.

17. ŚGS 1.1.5.

18. And, the text continues, "according to some," this domestic fire is also the one used for all optional domestic rituals (*kāmyāni karmāṇi*) and the *saṃskāras* performed on the children of the household (BGS 2.6.17–18; BGPariS 1.16.4; see also BGPariS 1.16.15–16). For similar statements in the Bhāradvāja literature, see C. G. Kashikar, "On the Bhāradvaja Gṛhyasūtra and Its Commentary," *Bulletin of the Deccan College Research Institute* 35 (1975): esp. 68: "Bhāradvāja prescribes that it is the fire established at the Upanayana which is to be maintained and on which all subsequent rites including the marriage ceremony are to be performed. The boy who has undergone the Upanayana-ceremony should make offerings on his fire every morning and evening, and in the evening

constitutes the child into a responsible being and member of society. Each stage in the ritual process, however, is carefully distinguished from the following ones as the boy only gradually attains greater degrees of independence.

The student, under the lordship of his teacher (who in some cases was also his father), is allowed to sacrifice only with the fuel sticks and with the minimal ritual utterances known as the *vyāhṛti*s (these are the exclamations "*oṃ*," "*bhūḥ*," "*bhuvaḥ*," and "*svaḥ*," which are said to represent either the essences of the Vedas or the spatial worlds of the cosmos). Beginning with the graduation bath and continuing up until the time of marriage, the *snātaka* is independent of the teacher/father but is not yet a householder with a family of his own. During this period, the daily oblations into the fire are only those of clarified butter, again with the *vyāhṛti*s in place of full mantras. Only from the marriage onward, when the *snātaka* has been reconstituted as a *gṛhasthin* or householder, is the daily sacrifice made with food oblations, put into the fire by hand, and accompanied by mantras of direct address to the gods: "To Agni, *svāhā*! To Prajāpati, *svāhā*!"[19]

In this way, the relative completion of the individual and the degree of his command over a domain (a *loka* or "world," one might say) is ritually calibrated by his differing prerogatives vis-à-vis the domestic fire. Even the newly initiated boy may participate in the realm of domestic sacrificial action, but it is only the married householder who fully engages in the domestic cult in all its completeness.

The *gṛhyayajña* is, by way of summary, broadly characterized by its particular association with the household and its inhabitants, by its location within the home, and by its representational qualities as the sign of the householder's lordship over his own domestic domain. But, as I have said above, the full meaning of domestic ritualism becomes apparent only when placed in relation to the *śrauta* ceremonial. When compared to the *śrauta* sacrificer, it becomes clear that the *gṛhya* ritualist is limited to the domestic domain and the form of sacrifice appropriate to it, just as the household fire is literally confined within the home.

---

he should consign that fire into himself and cause it to descend upon the actual fire the next day. At his marriage he should cause the consigned fire to descend upon the actual fire, and perform the rites on it. After the marriage, however, the householder cannot consign the fire into himself; he must maintain it permanently."

19. BGS 2.6.19–21 = BGPariS 1.16.5–9.

The Baudhāyana Śrauta Sūtra[20] defines the domestic sacrifice as one which is offered in a fire other than those located in the *vihāra,* the sacrificial grounds of the *śrauta* ritual.[21] *Vihāra* means "separation" and refers primarily to the separation of the three or five *śrauta* fires that are enkindled in that space. It is possible, however, that *vihāra* also connotes a domain of ritual action separate from the home, that is, set apart from—and beyond—the arena of domestic ritualism. The *vihāra* is typically near, but not inside, the sacrificer's house.[22]

Whereas the domestic sacrificer, who is also called an *ekāgni* ("having one fire"), performs rituals with a single domestic fire located within the domicile, the *āhitāgni* or *śrauta* sacrificer performs "expanded" or "extended" (*vaitāna*) sacrifices with three or five fires located outside the home.[23] If the *gṛhyayajña* is characterized by its domesticity, the *śrautayajña* is distinguished by this expansive, even imperialistic and colonizing, spirit. The *vihāra* is an extension, as well as a superseding, of the household domain in which the *ekāgni* is confined for his ritual activities.

As we will see in more detail later, the *śrauta* ritual is an "extended" version of the domestic sacrifice, and the domestic is a condensed counterpart of the *śrauta,* in more ways than one. For now, in addition to the number of fires and all they represent, mention might be made of the fact that in the *gṛhya* rites the ritual labor done by a multitude of priests at the *śrauta* level is handled by the domestic sacrificer himself, with the optional help of the *brahman* priest.[24] The sacrificial gifts or fees

20. BŚS 24.4.

21. *yacca kim cānyatra vihārāddhūyate sarvāsthās pākayajñasaṃsthā iti.*

22. See BhŚS 5.2.11; ĀpŚS 5.3.22; and HŚS 3.2, where a settled householder (*śālīna*) is instructed to set his fires at a place outside the house (to the east or north of it, according to HŚS). A frequent traveler (*yāyāvara*), however, should establish the fires in a place inside the house. See Louis Renou's comment in his *Vedic India,* trans. by P. Spratt (Delhi: Indologoical Book House, 1971), p. 99: "The Vedic cult knows no temple. The ceremonies take place either in the sacrificer's house or on a plot of ground close by . . . on which the three altars are arranged."

23. For the *śrauta* sacrifice as a whole depicted as *vaitāna,* see, e.g., ĀśvŚS 1.1.1 and ĀŚvGS 1.1.1. The term especially denotes the "expansion" of the *vihāra* as the *śrauta* fires are established.

24. The *gṛhya* sacrificer always does the work of the *adhvaryu,* the priest charged primarily with ritual manipulations, and according to some texts he is specifically said to perform also the duties of the *hotṛ* (who recites many of the mantras). The *brahman* priest, the overseer of the entire sacrifice, is not required at the domestic ceremonial (GGS 1.6.21; KhGS 1.1.23; BGPariS 1.5.5; ŚGS 1.8.6 with Oldenberg's note; ĀśvGS 1.3.6); and if he is not present, the sacrificer also "does the work both of the *hotṛ* and the *brahman*" (see GGS 1.6.21, 1.9.8–9; and KhGS 1.1.17–18).

(*dakṣiṇā*) owed to this latter officiant, if he is even present, are minimal as opposed to the significant donations required at the *śrauta* rituals.[25]

A married man who has sired a son and who is not yet old (his hair must still be dark),[26] who is of the proper class (the servant class or Śūdras being excluded), who is learned in the Veda, physically fit, and relatively affluent (he must own at least two cows for the performance of even the simplest *śrauta* ritual, the daily *agnihotra*),[27] may establish the three or five *śrauta* fires and perform sacrifices in them. He thereby becomes an *āhitāgni,* "one who has laid [the *śrauta*] fires."

These *śrauta* fires are first established by expanding, although with intermediaries, the domestic fire (*gṛhyāgni*) into the "householder's fire" (*gārhapatyāgni*),[28] which is said to be five times more powerful.[29] This new fire, like the old domestic fire from which it is kindled and which it now supersedes, must be perpetually kept lit from this time forward.[30] From the *gārhapatya* fire embers are carried to the places of the other two *śrauta* fires, the *āhavanīya* used for sacrifices to the gods and the *dakṣiṇa* or "southern" fire employed for offerings to the ances-

25. See GGS 1.9.10–11: "A full vessel is the lowest *dakṣiṇā* at a domestic sacrifice. The highest is unlimited." See also MGS 2.2.28; KhGS 2.1.30; JGS 1.4; and GGS 1.9.6. BGS 1.4.38 prescribes the gift of a cow; a horse or a cow is to be given according to VGS 1.38; and ĀśvGS 1.10.27 suggests only the remnant of the oblation material as *dakṣiṇā.*

26. BDhS 1.2.3.5: "A *śruti* passage says, 'Let him light the *śrauta* fires while his hair is [still] black.' " See Kane, *History of Dharmaśāstra,* II: 350–51.

27. Kane, *History of Dharmaśāstra,* p. 979: "The daily agnihotra required the maintenance of at least two cows, besides thousands of cow-dung cakes and fuel-sticks. For the maintenance of agnihotra and the performance of *darśapūrṇamāsa* (in which four priests were employed) and the Cāturmāsyas (where five priests were required) the householder was required to be well-to-do." Some indication of the enormous expenses incurred by the sponsor of the greater, and optional, Vedic rituals may be gathered by studying the operating budget for the 1975 performance of the *agnicayana* in Kerala. Leaving aside costs for the foreign observers, the sacrifice entailed expenditures of Rupees 160,810. See Staal, "The Agnicayana Project," in *Agni,* II: 457–63. A *vājapeya* was done in Poona in 1955 for approximately a quarter of the cost of the *agnicayana,* still a hefty price tag far out of the reach of any but the very wealthiest and most powerful. For other qualifications constituting the competency (*adhikāra*) for one who would light the *śrauta* fires, see Chakrabarti, *The Paribhāṣās,* pp. 142–47.

28. A succinct description and interpretation of the setting of the *śrauta* fires may be found in Heesterman's "Other Folks' Fire."

29. See MŚS 8.23.1–3, where the wife of a deceased *āhitāgni* takes "a fifth portion" of the *gārhapatya* fire (before it, along with the other *śrauta* fires, is used to cremate the sacrificer and then is extinguished) as a new domestic fire. "She should tend this new domestic fire according to the *pākayajña* procedure" (MŚS 8.23.7).

30. One authority, KŚS 4.13.5, requires the perpetual maintenance of all three fires by the *gataśrī,* "one who has become rich." See also ĀpŚS 6.2.12.

tors. In this way the continually maintained *gārhapatya* fire is daily "extended" or "spread out" (*vi* + *tan*) into the other two fires.[31]

Notice here the continuity of the fire as one takes the single household fire, transforms and empowers it, and then reestablishes it as a "householder's fire," the *gārhapatya*. The old domestic fire may now be extinguished and rekindled only when needed for special circumstances (as noted above), or, according to some authorities, the *śrauta* sarificer may, if he wishes, continue to offer the regular domestic sacrifices in the *dakṣiṇa* fire.[32]

As Heesterman points out, in many respects the "southern" fire of the *śrauta* ritual "stands in opposition to the others. In contradistinction to the *gārhapatya* and *āhavanīya,* which are situated on a line running from west to east, the heaven-going direction, the *dakṣiṇāgni* is placed to the south. It marks the north-south direction that is concerned with the fathers, i.e., predominantly with men."[33] In this way,

31. In addition to these three *śrauta* fires, some schools require two more of the *āhitāgni.* These are the *sabhya* ("the fire of the house of assembly") and the *āvasathya* ("the fire of the rest house"). See Alfred Hillebrandt, *Vedic Mythology,* 2 vols., trans. by S. R. Sarma (Delhi: Motilala Banarsidass, 1981), II: 81–82; and Frederick Smith, "The Āvasathya Fire in the Vedic Ritual," *Adyar Library Bulletin* 46 (1982): 73–92.

32. See VGS 1.6. According to HGS 2.6.16.2, the annual sacrifice to the serpents (*śrāvaṇa*) should be done either with the domestic fire or on the *dakṣiṇāgni* if the sacrificer is an *āhitāgni.* See KGS 47.1–2, where it is said that the domestic sacrifices are to be performed either in the "wedding fire" (*agni vaivāhana*), which can only be the domestic fire, or in the *aupāsada,* which the commentators gloss as the *śrauta dakṣiṇāgni.* The relationship between the two fires—at two different levels of Vedic ritualism—is indeed a close one, as Heesterman has pointed out in "Other Folks' Fire", p. 83.

33. Heesterman, "Other Folks' Fire," p. 83. On pp. 81–82 of that article, Heesterman writes that "the fires for the *śrauta* ritual . . . form in a complicated way the extension of the domestic fire." He emphasizes, however, the connection of the domestic fire not with the *gārhapatya* but rather with the *dakṣiṇāgni,* and highlights those texts that provide the option of kindling those fires from embers taken from another's fire. He thus sees the fires as a symbolic link to social life in general in "a time of scarcity." In a "preclassical" or "agonistic" period, "the *dakṣiṇāgni* is associated with both the domestic fire and with others' fires. The meaning is, quite simply, that for the business of life one needs the others." But this dependence involves conflict, and "thus the social aspect of the fire is inextricably bound up with strife and violence" (p. 86). The continuity of the domestic and *śrauta* fires and the ties they both maintain to social life thus presents a problem, according to Heesterman, and one that was solved in the "classical" period in part by the radical separation of the *gṛhya* and *śrauta* fires: "Now . . . the *śrauta* fire had to be permanently attached to and identical with the sacrificer. This meant, in the first place, that the *śrauta* fire had to be rigorously dissociated from the domestic, which inevitably remained bound up with marriage and household—and hence with society" (p. 92). This interpretation obviously runs counter to the one put forward here and tends to ignore the "domestic" and

the domestic ritual is effectively and symbolically encompassed within the *śrauta* ceremonial.

But the continuities between the two realms of Vedic ritualism, represented by the continuities between the fires with which they are performed, should not cloud the hierarchical distinctions between them. The *gārhapatya* fire is often equated with the home,[34] with this world,[35] and with things "related to the human" (*mānuṣya*)[36]—just as is the domestic fire. But as the superordinate and individualized version of the comparatively weak *gṛhyāgni* with its homey associations, the *gārhapatya* fire is also homologized to the earthly realm in its entirety (and not merely to the householder's domestic domain), while the other two *śrauta* fires are connected to the cosmological worlds of atmosphere and heaven.[37] Extending the fires is thus an extension of the *śrauta* sacrificer's sphere of influence, an enlargement of the *āhitāgni*'s lordship and domain of ritual action. With the *śrautayajña,* one "conquers" or "wins" all worlds; with the *gṛhyayajña,* one is circumscribed and domesticated. The complementarity and continuity of the two does not obscure the hierarchical relationship that constitutes them into inferior and superior forms of Vedic ritualism.

The Feminization of the Domestic Ritual

With the exception of the two schools of Baudhāyana and Bhāradvāja, whose position was delineated above, the Vedic ritualists held that it was with marriage that domestic ritualism within Vedism was inaugurated. It will be recalled that one of the names for the domestic fire was the *vaivāhikāgni,* the fire relating to marriage, and many of the Gṛhya Sūtras underline the importance of the wedding by including within their descriptions of that rite of passage the rules for the standard procedure (*tantra*) common to all domestic sacrifices. The marriage ritual, in other words, acts as a paradigm for all other sacrifices at the domestic level;

"social" aspects of the "classical" *śrauta* cult. I have tried to keep these connotations intact with an expandable conception of the terms *household, domain, sphere of influence,* and *lordship*.

34. ŚB 1.1.1.18–19.

35. TS 6.1.8.5, 6.4.2.5, etc.

36. TS 1.6.7.1.

37. The *brāhmaṇa*s on this point are brought together by Hillebrandt in *Vedic Mythology,* II: 66–69.

and whereas the initiation transforms the child into an Āryan, it is the wedding that establishes the male as something of a free agent, independent of teacher and father, with a household domain under his umbrella.

The wedding ceremony also transforms the socio-ontological status of the bride. Marriage, as it is conceptualized by the authors of the ritual Sūtras, is for women the counterpart of the initiation or *upanayana*;[38] it draws her into a relationship with the Veda and with fire sacrifice through the bond to the new husband. As the young boy gains access to, and a modicum of control over, ritual activity only by first placing himself within the socio-ontological realm of the teacher, so does the woman, by taking a place under the authority of her husband, both subordinate herself to the lordship of another and connect herself to the domestic fire and the rituals done in it.

The importance of the wife to the ritual is not unacknowledged by the Sūtra writers. Her presence is required for the proper performance of both the domestic and *śrauta* sacrifices of her husband and, indeed, is regarded as an essential part of the householder's very being: he is "completed" by her.[39] She is integral to the householder's lordship, and together "they two become yoked like oxen in the sacrifice."[40]

The particularly close association of the wife and the domestic ritual, touched on above, also serves to diminish its relative importance in the eyes of the (male, need it be said) ritualistic writers. The "feminization" of the domestic sacrifice, implemented through the connections the ritualists drew between it and the wife, had as one of its purposes to denigrate it in comparison to the *śrauta* ritual.

Let us first briefly review the ritual of lighting the domestic fire at the wedding ceremony. The fire for this latter ritual—which will thereafter serve as the couple's domestic fire—is kindled by rubbing together two sticks of wood; or, alternatively, it is taken from the domestic fire of a Vaiśya, thus reemphasizing its connection to the earth, fecundity, and

38. See, e.g., Manu 2.67: "The rule relating to the wedding is stated to be the *saṃskāra* of the Veda [i.e., the initiation] for women; serving her husband is [the counterpart of] the residency with the teacher; and maintaining the home is [the counterpart of] the worship of the fire."

39. See Manu 9.45 and BĀU 1.4.17. See also Paul Mus, "The Problematic of the Self, West and East, and the Mandala Pattern," in C. A. Moore, ed., *Philosophy and Culture, East and West* (Honolulu: University of Hawaii Press, 1960), esp. p. 601; and Orlan Lee, "From Acts—To Non-Action—To Acts: The Dialectical Basis for Social Withdrawal or Commitment to This World in the Buddhist Reformation," *History of Religions* 6 (May 1967): 289–92.

40. TB 3.7.5.11.

domesticity; or, as yet another option, it is first established from embers borrowed from the fire of a *śrotriya,* a learned ritualist who maintains the three *śrauta* fires and who is famous for his sacrificial achievements.[41] The householder's domestic fire is set up at this time either by performing a simple rite as part of the wedding ceremonial or by the performance of a condensed version of the ritual known in the *śrauta* ritual as the Agnyādhāna.[42] When the wedding ritual is concluded, this fire is encased in a vessel, and the newly wedded couple carry it with them to their home.

From that time forward, the fire is perpetually maintained according to all the Gṛhya Sūtras. Although it is primarily the duty of the householder himself to offer into this fire on a daily basis, thereby fulfilling the obligation to "worship" (*upasthāna*) the fire continually for as long as he lives, some texts also allow other members of the household to offer the daily sacrifices in this fire that is so closely bound to the home and its inhabitants: "Beginning from marriage, he [the householder] himself should worship the domestic fire, or his wife, his son, his daughter, or his pupil."[43] If the fire should go out, the text continues, the wife must fast as part of the expiation and preliminary to the reestablishment of the domestic fire.

In another Sūtra, the teacher first follows the more conservative path and prohibits the wife and uninitiated sons from offering the oblations, but then adds as an equally valid option a rule that allows the wife to make the offerings (without recitation of the mantras).[44] Such is also the ruling according to unnamed ritual teachers quoted by Gobhila Gṛhya Sūtra and Khādira Gṛhya Sūtra; the wife may by herself perform the twice-daily Agnihotra sacrifice at the *gṛhya* level: "For the wife is the

41. For a survey of these and other alternatives for generating the wedding/domestic fire, see Heesterman, "Other Folks' Fire," pp. 79–80. The author rightly notes that "these alternatives all have one feature in common: the fire has to be procured from elsewhere, or rather from someone else, whose willing or unwilling cooperation is therefore necessary. And, strangely, it is nowhere said that one should continue maintaining one's paternal or ancestral fire. In fact, there does not seem to be such a thing as an ancestral fire, because the fire ends with the life of the householder and is last used in his cremation. After that his son has to set up his own fire." In this instance, and with the reservations expressed above, we may agree that "here, in ritual terms, we encounter the paradox we already noticed, namely, that of permanence and instability, continuity and discontinuity" (pp. 80–81).

42. For such replicas at the *gṛhya* level of certain *śrauta* rituals, see Chapter 7 herein.

43. ĀśvGS 1.9.1; see also ŚGS 2.17.3. The issue of whether anyone other than the householder was qualified to make oblations in the domestic fire was, however, controversial. See Kane, *History of Dharmaśāstra,* II: 683–84.

44. BhGS 3.12.

house (*gṛha*) and this fire is domestic (*gṛhya*)."[45] In many texts, the *agnihotra* is followed by a distribution of rice balls to various household deities, spirits, and other beings. Some of the authorities specify that the evening distribution is to be done by the wife—again, without the recitation of Vedic mantras.[46]

To appreciate the significance of the fact that the relationship between the wife and the domestic ritual was regarded as so strong as to persuade some teachers to allow the wife to perform the sacrifice on her own, let us turn to the *śrauta* ritual. There are some rites that the wife performs in that ceremonial under the guidance of the priests, but the Śrauta Sūtras are adamantly opposed to the notion that she is capable of any independent ritual action. In the *śrauta* sacrifices, the wife is a necessary but dependent performer; she participates in them only conjointly with her husband.[47]

There are, however, some unusual circumstances under which even in the *śrauta* ceremonial the wife is empowered to offer the rituals on her own. A look at these exceptions, however, only proves the rule: it is the domestic ritual that is more properly the field of action of women, in addition to domesticated men.

The occasions in which the wife may carry out sacrificial performances ordinarily assumed by the *āhitāgni* are when he is away on a journey, when he is physically incapacitated, or when he is dead. The first two of these circumstances are covered in the following citation from the Mānava Śrauta Sūtra:

> Together do these two [husband and wife] constitute a couple; together do these two maintain the sacred fires; together do these two procreate and obtain progeny. The eastern world pertains to the husband, the western world to the wife. Since the wife takes upon herself the responsibility of maintaining the vow of the husband who has gone out on a journey or who has become incapacitated, therefore she is entitled to half [of the ritually acquired merit]. Women are [in these instances] qualified to perform sacrifices.[48]

The text goes on to say that in the *śrauta* sacrifice, "whatever one offers on the *āhavanīya* fire relates to the sacrificer, and whatever is offered on the *gārhapatya* fire relates to the sacrificer's wife." In this, the tag line justifying the woman's qualifications to assume the sacrificial vow when

45. GGS 1.3.15; KhGS 1.5.17.
46. GGS 1.4.5; VaikhGS 6.17; Manu 3.121; see also ŚGS 2.17.3.
47. For this point, consult Chakrabarti, *The Paribhāṣās,* p. 142.
48. MŚS 8.23.10–14.

her husband cannot (it is half hers), the portion of the sacrifice which is specifically the wife's is that which is offered in the superpowered *śrauta* version of the domestic fire, the *gārhapatya*.

The death of the *āhitāgni* or his wife provides another situation in which the characteristic linkages of both to certain of the fires which represent their spheres of influence is made clear. Here, once again, the texts present domestic ritualism as the special province of the woman. Upon its demise, the body is cremated as a final oblation into the fire or fires kept during one's lifetime. In the case of the domestic sacrificer (the *ekāgni*) who dies before his wife, the procedure is as follows: he is burnt in the domestic fire he has faithfully maintained, and when that fire has finished its last duty, it is allowed to go out, never again to be rekindled. The texts do not make specific references to any subsequent ritual responsibilities for the widow of a domestic sacrificer. Presumably there is none. She takes her place within the household of a son or another male relative and at the time of her own death is cremated in a fire set especially—and exclusively—for this purpose, a fire regarded by the authorities as "worldly," that is, secular.

The case of the death of a *śrauta* sacrificer or his wife is more complicated. The general rule is that whoever dies first is to be cremated in the combined three fires. Both husband and wife, as we have seen, are intimately tied to these fires, and both have claims to their efficacy. So it is that should the wife of an *āhitāgni* precede him in death, she is cremated (together with the sacrificial implements) in the *śrauta* fires, which are then extinguished.

And what does the surviving husband do when his fires have been thus used up? Baudhāyana Pitṛmedha Sūtra[49] gives several alternatives, all of which emphasize the importance of the domestic fire for the continuity of the household even after it has suffered the loss of the female partner. One option is to rekindle new *śrauta* fires out of the domestic fire of the first marriage. If this domestic fire has not been maintained after the time of establishing the three *śrauta* fires, it is rekindled from a portion of the old *gārhapatya* fire—before, of course, the latter has been used in the cremation ceremony for the wife. Having obtained a domestic fire (either employing the one he has always kept or reigniting one he had left behind), he may remarry, using the domestic fire at the second wedding. With his new wife, he may then generate new *śrauta* fires out of the old domestic one.

In this text, interestingly enough, there is no mention of the possibil-

49. BPS 2.4.2–17.

ity of the widowed *āhitāgni* "downgrading" himself to the level of the domestic ritualist. Having once set the *śrauta* fires, he can no longer go back to the *gṛhya* ceremonial exclusively. He must either remarry and reset the three fires or discontinue life as a householder altogether and renounce the world and all sacrifices other than those done purely meditatively. The domestic cycle of rituals, it would seem, is too intimately associated with a particular household, and a particular wife, to be continued when that wife has passed away.

The text also covers the case of the wife whose *āhitāgni* husband has died. Unlike the widower, the widow is not allowed to remarry; there is therefore no possibility of reestablishing the *śrauta* fires and continuing sacrifices of that class. But also unlike the widower, the surviving wife of an *āhitāgni* is permitted to continue, on her own, the sacrificial rituals at the domestic level. She is to maintain the domestic fire she once shared with her husband and perform the rituals so closely related to the household. Before having her husband cremated in his three fires, the woman takes a fraction of the *gārhapatya,* returns it back into a domestic fire, and performs the regular cycle of *gṛhya* sacrifices in it until the end of her life. This option is given in the Mānava Śrauta Sūtra and is attributed to a teacher known as Māruka:

> Śākalya says that after the husband has died a woman becomes devoid of sacred fires and is unfit to perform any sacrifice. But Māruka has explained how she should tend a fifth portion [of the *gārhapatya* fire] with proper service. If the wife [of the deceased] is observing the contemplated vow [i.e., to maintain the fire sacrifice], the officiating priest should say to her, "Attend upon the domestic fire." . . . She should tend the domestic fire according to the procedure of the domestic sacrifice.[50]

Wearing soiled clothing and with other signs of her widowhood, the woman is instructed henceforth to make daily oblations of clarified butter (and not the oblations of grain that are usually prescribed) into the domestic fire. At the end of her life, she is cremated in the domestic fire she has in this way maintained.[51]

The "feminization" of the domestic ritual—that is, its bonds to the wife, especially when compared with the more "virile" *śrauta* sacrifice—highlights both its domesticity and, in a patriarchically oriented society, its relative limitations. The ceremonial performed in the home and with

50. MŚS 8.23.1–3, 8.23.7.

51. This is from BPS 2.4.3. The Mānava text requires that she be cremated in a special fire set for that purpose.

the domestic fire is so simple and so basic that even those, who in the eyes of the ritual authorities, had minimal competency for Vedic ritualism could carry it out. The *ekāgni* is put on a par with the wife of the *āhitāgni*. The domestic ritualist's one fire is regarded as the equivalent of but one-fifth of the "householder's fire" at the *śrauta* sacrifice. And this *gārhapatya* fire is itself relegated to oblations "that pertain to the sacrificer's wife" and are thus encompassed within the larger ritual domain of the sacrificer.

Basic Vedic Ritualism

Another generic term for the domestic sacrifice as a type, in addition to the *gṛhyayajña,* was *pākayajña*. And this, too, was a designation designed to indicate the relative inferiority of this class of rituals in relation to other, more complete, and more realized types.

Whereas the "sacrifice of the home" was contrasted to the "extended sacrifice," the *pākayajna* or "small sacrifice" was so called because there were *mahāyajña*s or "great sacrifices."[52] The nomenclature highlights the elemental and basic nature of domestic ritualism within Vedism; the *pākayajña* was conceived and represented as a diminutive, condensed form of its larger model, the *śrauta* ritual.

The word *pāka* in this context is not to be derived, as is sometimes done, from the verb *pac-*, "to cook, bake, or roast."[53] Rather, the term here is formed from the root *pā-*, "to suck," with the diminutive *-ka* suffix.[54] It is thus best translated as Manfred Mayrhofer has suggested: "*pākaḥ*: einfach, arglos, rechtschaffen, unwissend; sehr jung, m. Tierjunges/simple, honest, ignorant; very young, m. the young of an animal."[55]

52. I use the term here only in its literal sense. As a technical term, it is used to classify the *aśvamedha* (TS 2.2.7.5; KS 10.9; MS 2.2.9) or the soma sacrifice (TS 3.2.2.2.; ŚB 2.4.4.14), among others of the major *śrauta* rituals. The *mahāyajña*s were reincarnated in five simple domestic rites in later texts, as we shall see in Chapter 7 herein.

53. See, e.g., Hermann Oldenberg's translation of "*pākayajña*" as "boiled offering." *The Grihya Sūtras,* I:xxiii. Pierre Rolland offers "sacrifices de maturité" in his translation of the VGS, playing on the two possible meanings of the word *pāka*.

54. V. V. Bhide, *The Cāturmāsya Sacrifices* (Poona: University of Poona, 1979), p. 210, citing Bhaṭṭabhaskāra's commentary on TB 1.6.6.

55. Manfred Mayrhofer, *Kurzgefasstes etymologisches Wörterbuch des Altindischen* (A Concise Etymological Sanskrit Dictionary, 4 vols. (Heidelberg: Carl Winter Universitätsverlag, 1957), II: 243.

The word employed in this sense can be traced to the earliest texts of the Vedic tradition.[56] It often appears as semantically in opposition to various terms for "knowledgeable." Different forms of *pāka* are contrasted with *dhīra* ("intelligent, wise, expert"),[57] *gṛtsa* ("clever, judicious"),[58] and *vidvas* ("knowing, learned").[59] Elsewhere, *pāka* is glossed by various terms meaning "ignorant." At ṚV 10.7.6, for example, *pāka* is juxtaposed to *aprecetas* ("foolish"), whereas at ṚV 1.164.5–6, it is found together with *avijānant* ("ignorant") and *acikitvas* ("unknowledgeable"). Finally, an interesting context in which one finds *pāka* in the older texts, and one which foreshadows its later use as a technical term within the ritual vocabulary, is ṚV 10.2.5, where the term is placed next to *dīnadakṣa* ("a defective ability to act").

Given this etymological and semantic history, the designation of certain kinds of rites and rituals as *pāka* is readily explicable. It is with the connotations of "simple, small, uncomplicated, feeble, and weak" that the ritualists composing the Sūtras deployed the word to classify the domestic sacrifice: "The word *pākayajña* is used to describe these rituals because of their smallness or feebleness (*hrasvatva*), for '*pāka*' indeed means 'small' or 'feeble' (*hrasva*)."[60] Later commentators on various ritual texts in which the term comes up concur in glossing *pāka* in these contexts with the synonym *alpa* ("little, easy").[61]

Although, as stated above, there is no systematic treatment of the domestic ritual in the texts before the Sūtras, there are a few references to *pākayajña*. And in all such cases, the term is employed to label certain simplified rites within the *śrauta* ritual which have direct connections to domesticity. One example of this is when the *gṛhamedhīya* rite of the *cāturmāsya* sacrifice (in which offerings are made to the Maruts who are called "householders") is referred to as a *pākayajña*,[62] in part because of its associations with the household and domestic animals and in part because of its abbreviated format.[63] In the *gṛhamedhīya* rite, which is a

56. For *pāka* and its derivatives in the ṚV, consult Louis Renou, *Etudes védique et pāninéennes*, 17 vols. (Paris: Publication de l'ICI, 1955–69), IV: 129, VII: 90, 93, XII: 6.

57. ṚV 1.164.21, 2.27.11, 10.1.18, 10.86.19, 10.100.3; AV 4.19.3, 10.1.18; TS 2.1.11.5.

58. ṚV 4.5.2, 10.28.5.

59. ṚV 1.31.14.

60. VGS 1.2–3.

61. E.g., Sāyana on TS 1.7.1; Haradatta on ĀpGS 1.2.9; Devasvāmin on ĀśvGS 1.1.3; and Śrīnivāsa on JGS 1.1.

62. TB 1.6.6 simply calls this rite *pākatrā* ("concise").

63. MS 1.10.15 and KS 36.9. See also Bhide, *The Cāturmāsya Sacrifices*, pp. 89–91.

pākayajña, certain rites from the usual paradigmatic procedure of the *śrauta* ceremonial are dropped: the fore- and after-offerings which surrounded the principal oblation, and the so-called kindling verses recited by the *hotṛ* priest (the *sāmidhenīka*). In its discussion of the *darvīhoma,* which is not accidentally another name used by the Gṛhya Sūtras for the domestic ritual as a class,[64] the Kātyāyana Śrauta Sūtra characterizes that type of rite by noting the same adjustments, and adding others, to the normal *śrauta* ritual procedure:

> *Darvīhoma*s are to be done in a single fire. They do not have fore- and after-offerings, and do not have the "kindling verses." There are no calls of instruction by the *adhvaryu* priest (the *nigada*s) in *darvīhoma*s. They are to be offered by uttering the name of the deity [in the dative case] with the exclamation "*svāhā*!" [and not "*vaṣat*!" as in the usual *śrauta* format].[65]

These references, in the texts concerned with the higher levels of Vedic ritualism, to a condensed and simplified *pākayajña* or *darvīhoma* within the *śrauta* ceremonial itself foreshadow the descriptions given in the Gṛhya Sūtras of the domestic ritual. It is surely no coincidence that the very same features of the *śrauta pākayajña* and *darvīhoma* are those characteristic of the domestic ritual as it is systematized in the Gṛhya texts. The domestic ritual is depicted there as also employing but one fire, and the ritual framework (*tantra*) for such classes of Vedic ritual is an adaptation and condensation of the *śrauta* new and full moon sacrifice (which supplies the *tantra* for all other *śrauta* sacrifices).[66] The particular omissions specified in the Gṛhya Sūtras are the exclusion of the fore- and after-offerings and the dropping of the "kindling verses" and "calls of instruction," and some texts also specify the omission of the *iḍā* rite in the domestic procedure.

This last detail is of some interest, for, oddly, in the earlier texts[67] this *iḍā* rite (in which the oblation material is divided into portions that are distributed among and subsequently consumed by the officiating priests and sacrificer) is also labeled a *pākayajña.*[68] In this instance, as

64. E.g., BGS 1.4.39; HGS 1.1.3.1.

65. KŚS 6.10.20–24.

66. See, e.g., ĀpGS 3.7.23: "By the ritual procedure relating to the new and full moon sacrifice, other rituals are explained."

67. E.g., AitB 3.40; TS 1.7.1.1; ŚB 1.7.4.19, 1.8.1.1ff.

68. The specific exclusion of the *iḍā* from the domestic ritual (e.g., ŚGS 1.10.5) might be understood in the same way as one understands the rule that the domestic fire is to be extinguished when it has been reconstituted into the *śrauta gārhapatya* fire. The *iḍā,* like the *gārhapatya,* is the representative of the *pākayajña* in the *śrauta* ritual, but it is a supercharged representative. It therefore transcends domestic ritualism because it represents it in the higher *śrauta* ceremonial.

with the *gṛhamedhīya* rite, the direct associations with food, cattle, fecundity, and the home—that is, with the concerns of the domestic realm—seem to lie behind the designation. And also connoted by the label is the fact that the *iḍā* rite is simple, diminutive, feeble, and inferior when compared to other rites of the *śrauta* sacrifice.

The great commentator on Vedic texts, Sāyana, explains the link between the *iḍā* and the *pākayajña* by emphasizing the eating of and connections to food in both.[69] The connection to food is, however, only one of a series of associations between the *iḍā* in particular and the *pākayajña* as a class—a network that includes as nodes food, cattle, fecundity, the house, and all things human and earthly. Thus, for example, one text explains the fact that the oblation is consumed rather than offered in the *iḍā* rite by drawing on the equally important connection between the rite and animals: "They [the priests and sacrificer] eat it and do not offer it into the fire lest they throw the animals into the fire."[70]

Iḍā is not only a rite in the Vedic ritual; she is also a goddess whose essence is projected into the rite which is her namesake.[71] And, following the chain, the *iḍā* rite is, in its turn, the essence of the *pākayajña*: "He invokes the goddess Iḍā. The *pākayajña*s have as their resembling form the *iḍā* rite (*iḍāvidhā*). Through the *iḍā* rite whatever *pākayajña*s there are are included within the soma sacrifice."[72] The mythology of this goddess, then, may be instructive for our understanding of the *pākayajña* in the Brāhmaṇas.

This goddess's creation is related as part of the story of the first man, Manu, who is deluged by a great flood and is saved from drowning by a fish he had previously cared for.[73] The fish pulls an ark with Manu in it to a mountaintop, rescuing Manu (and the human race as a whole) from a watery doom: "The flood swept away all creatures and Manu alone remained here."

Manu, reprising the role of the creator god Prajāpati, desires offspring and deploys the usual Vedic mythological methods for unilateral procreation: austerity and sacrifice. The latter, according to the text, was a "*pākayajña* consisting of an offering of ghee, curds, whey, and the mixture of coagulated and fresh milk, placed into the waters." After a year passes, the solidified form of the oblations, the goddess Iḍā, arises,

69. Commenting on ŚB 1.7.4.19: *pākayajñeṣu hutaśeṣo bhakṣyate, iḍāhutaśeṣo bhakṣyate; tena pākayajñārthetyucyate.*

70. ŚB 1.8.1.38.

71. ŚB 1.8.1.11.

72. AitB 3.40.

73. ŚB 1.8.1.1 ff.

and the text depicts her as the daughter of Manu. She addresses her progenitor by saying:

> Those offerings of ghee, curds, whey, and the mixture of coagulated and fresh milk—which you made in the waters—with you and them you have engendered me. I am the blessing [procured from the sacrifice] and therefore am suitable for use in the [*śrauta*] sacrifice. If you use me in the sacrifice, you will become rich in offspring and cattle.

Manu then invokes Iḍā at the sacrifice, incorporating the *iḍā* rite within the procedure, and thus he "generated this human race, the race of Manu."

Iḍā, the goddess of nourishment; *iḍā,* the rite in which food from the cooked oblations are consumed by humans; and the *pākayajña,* the first sacrifice of Manu and the womb of the goddess—all are in this text (and elsewhere) associated with sustenance, fecundity, and cattle.[74] All are also connected to humanity, to the sphere of Manu and his race—that is, to the earthly realm in contradistinction to the heavenly worlds of the gods. Iḍā is the daughter of Manu and is thus described as *mānavin,* "belonging to humans." She is one of three goddesses ruling the three worlds: Bhāratī oversees the highest realm of heaven, Sarasvatī looks after the intermediate region, but it is Iḍā who rules over the *bhūloka,* the earthly realm, and exerts influence over offspring, cattle, rain, food, and, in sum, all aspects of domestic life.[75]

In other situations within the *śrauta* ritual, the texture of strands connecting Iḍā to the *pākayajña* also displays both as inextricably bonded to the domestic arena. In the *agnihotra,* for instance, Iḍā is explicitly related to the house (the locus of the *pākayajña* from which she was created) in addition to other connections to offspring, cattle, and so on. One of the prayers included within the litany of the daily worship of the fires[76] is to be recited while looking at the house.[77] The *brāhmaṇa* on this

74. For other texts on the goddess Iḍā, consult S. K. Lal, *Female Divinities in Hindu Mythology and Ritual* (Pune: University of Poona, 1980), pp. 31–40; and J. R. Joshi, *Some Minor Divinities in Vedic Mythology and Ritual* (Pune: Deccan College Postgraduate and Research Institute, 1977), pp. 50–54.

75. TB 2.6.10.4, 3.6.13.1, etc. For the reincarnation of Iḍā as the later Hindu goddess Annapūrṇā—a buxom deity of nourishment significantly depicted iconographically with a *darvī* ladle in her hand (the principal utensil for offering the *pākayajña*s)—see Lal, *Female Divinities,* p. 40, with the plates on pp. 276–78.

76. TS 1.5.6.1: "I gaze on offspring, the offspring of Iḍā who belongs to Manu; may they all be in our home."

77. BŚS 3.8; ĀpŚS 6.16; KŚS 4.12.1–4; ŚŚS 2.11.2–5; MŚS 1.6.2; see also BhŚS 6.2.5.

passage reads, " 'I gaze on offspring,' he says; truly he [thereby] wins all the domesticated animals."[78] Another *brāhmaṇa,* this one on the *iḍā* rite itself, identifies both the rite and the man with domestic animals: "[With the *iḍā*] he firmly established domestic animals in domestic animals."[79] Taken together, the constellation of connections indicates that the *iḍā,* and therefore the *pākayajña* which is encapsulated in that rite, was regarded as ritual activity most especially concerned with earthly and domestic prosperity.

In yet another context, the series of interrelations among the *pākayajña,* food, cattle, fecundity, the home, the human, and the this-worldly is restated through a focus on another related element: the Vaiśya class. As part of the consecration vow for a soma sacrifice, sacrificers of the different classes consume different substances which correspond to their socio-ontological natures. The Brahmin drinks milk, for it is said to be full of luminous power; the Kṣatriya consumes rice mash (*yavāgū*), "for rice mash is harsh, and is the form of the thunderbolt." The Vaiśya, the agriculturalist and tiller of the land, ingests *āmikṣā,* curds and milk, for this substance is declared the "form of the *pākayajña* and is for obtaining earthly prosperity (*puṣṭi*)."[80]

Just as the Vaiśya is the lowest of the three twice-born classes, the *pākayajña* is at the bottom of the ritual chain. The hierarchical inferiority of this class of Vedic sacrifices is also brought to the fore in texts dealing with the *iḍā,* which represents the *pākayajña* as a whole.

As we have seen, the *iḍā* is linked to Manu, the first human, and is thereby contrasted to the more efficacious and totalistic sacrifice of the gods: "With a whole sacrifice (*sarvena yajñena*) the gods went to heaven. Manu labored [here on earth] with the *pākayajña* and Iḍā went to Manu."[81] The earthly and relatively incomplete *iḍā* rite within the "divine" *śrauta* ceremony is thus a bit problematic: "Those who, in the middle of the sacrifice, perform the *iḍā* rite, break it apart and injure it." The *brahman* priest, the physician of the sacrifice, is called upon to heal and restore to full strength the ritual which has in this way been weakened by the inclusion of the *iḍā.*[82] Another passage from that Brāhmaṇa uses the adjective *pākayajñīya* ("like a *pākayajña*") to depict the *iḍā* rite as the weak link in the sacrificial chain: "This [part] of my sacrifice, this

78. TS 1.5.8.1.
79. TB 3.3.8.2.
80. TS 6.2.5.2–4.
81. TS 1.7.1.3.
82. ŚB 1.7.4.19.

iḍā rite which is like a *pākayajña,* is the very weakest (*taniṣṭha*). The demons must not injure my sacrifice at this time."[83]

Other early references to a *pākayajña* in the Saṃhitās and Brāhmaṇas also tend to underwrite its connotations in the Sūtras as the most basic and hierarchically inferior ritual within the system. Yājñavalkya, the iconoclastic teacher of the White Yajur Veda, is quoted in one text as stating that the daily Agnihotra is a *pākayajña,* and not a full-fledged *śrauta* ritual, because of certain ritual features which are indeed reminiscent of the domestic sacrifice outlined in the Gṛhya Sūtras.[84] These features, the teacher claims, are "of the *pākayajña,*" and the text goes on to note that the *agnihotra* is the "form" (*rūpa*) of domestic animals; and furthermore, "the *pākayajña* is related to domestic animals."[85]

Here again we encounter an early connection between the *pākayajña* type of ritual and domesticity. And what Yājñavalkya does here, and what others do elsewhere, by calling rites and rituals of the *śrauta* ceremonial by this term is also to point to a "small" sacrifice in comparison to other, "greater" forms of ritualism. In another passage from the Śatapatha Brāhmaṇa, we come across the phrase "the *pākayajña*s and the rest" to refer to the whole set of Vedic sacrifices beginning with the lowest, the most basic, and moving "on up": "Agni is indeed all sacrifices. All sacrifices are performed in him, the *pākayajña*s and the rest."[86]

The Aitareya Brāhmaṇa[87] also considers the *pākayajña* to be the simplest type of ritual still within the pale. In a passage whose point is to extol the virtues of the soma sacrifice, the ritual is said to contain the essences of all Vedic sacrifices,[88] both the "later" (higher) forms of the soma sacrifice and the "earlier" (lower) forms of rituals which do not use the soma juice as the oblation material. Among these "earlier" sacrifices are the various *śrauta* rituals beginning with the *agnihotra.* But the list of

83. ŚB 1.8.1.16, 1.8.1.18.

84. E.g., the injunction *juhoti* rather than the usual *śrauta* injunction *yajati,* and the eating of the remains of the oblation material (ŚB 2.3.1.21). See also KŚS 6.10.27–28. For a further comparison of the *śrauta agnihotra* and the domestic ritual, see ŚB 2.3.1.18 and TB 2.1.4.5 on the one side; and BGS 1.4.40–42; BGPariS 2.1.39–44; and ĀpGS 1.2.10–11 on the other.

85. ŚB 2.3.1.21.

86. ŚB 4.5.1.13; see also ŚB 1.4.2.10.

87. AitB 3.40–41.

88. For this feature of Vedic ritualism, whereby a more complex sacrifice is said to contain within it representative fragments of less complicated rituals, see Frits Staal, "Ritual Syntax," and G. U. Thite, *Sacrifice in the Brāhmaṇa Texts,* pp. 52–54: "A sacrifice is shown to include (mystically) many other sacrifices and then the importance of that particular sacrifice is established."

rituals said to be encompassed within the soma sacrifice begins with the *pākayajña,* placed at the very start of a hierarchical enumeration that moves from the simplest to the most complex.

These early references are too few and too vague to allow us to conclude that already in the Saṃhitās and Brāhmaṇas a full-blown domestic cult similar to that depicted in the later Sūtras existed side by side with the *śrauta* ritual. They do indicate, however, that some simplified rites and rituals within the *śrauta* cycle were from ancient times designated by a term that was later used for the domestic ritual as a whole, and that these *śrauta* rites and rituals so labeled as *pākayajña*s also were associated with matters particularly within the sphere of domesticity. The later use of the term *pākayajña* in the Gṛhya Sūtras was, at the very least, consistent with and a perpetuation of the older semantics.

The simplicity and domesticity of the domestic ritual—as it is depicted in texts of all periods in Vedism—is in harmony with the relatively feeble ritual capacities and limited spheres of influence of those who perform it. Principally, of course, I am speaking of the domestic (and domesticated) sacrificer himself, but also the wife and the son or pupil, all of whom for one reason or another are precluded from the sacrifices at the *śrauta* level. The domestic ritualist, the *ekāgni,* is, by virtue of lack of sufficient wealth, knowledge, opportunity, or desire, relegated to a delimited sphere of ritualism—a level of praxis associated in the texts with the home (and not the cosmos), the earthly (and not the heavenly), the human (and not the divine), the "womanly" (and not the "virile"). The wife, because of the supposed liabilities of her gender, does not have the competence to learn the Veda or perform sacrifices that require the recitation of Vedic mantras. But because of her situation within a chain of interconnected concerns and arenas of interest (the earth, fecundity, prosperity, food, animals, and the home), she is allowed to participate independently in Vedism on the *gṛhya* plane. The young boy or Veda student is not yet out from under the control and lordship of his teacher and father, and is not yet fully adept in either the Vedic texts or the ritual procedure. The domestic ritual for him functions as a kind of ritual training ground, preparing him for future ritual activity at the same or higher levels.

In the Sūtras, *pākayajña* describes a formally condensed and relatively inferior class of Vedic rituals, the domestic sacrifices. Its simplicity is in conformity with its basic goals and purposes, all of which revolve around the prosperity and protection of the household. It is because of its fundamental nature within the "unity" of Vedic ritualism that I have called attention to the analogies it has to the conceptualization of the paradigmatic (*prakṛti*) sacrifices in the Sūtras' organization of ritual knowledge. Formally simple, prior (either chronologically or epistemologically), and the base on which more developed or "extended" rituals are formed, both the domestic sacrifice and the paradigmatic sacrifice function as "elementary forms" of the Vedic ritual system.

As we shall observe in the next chapter, the framework or *tantra* for carrying out the *pākayajña* was a contracted version of the more expanded framework of the *śrauta* sacrifice. The domestic procedure was, in other words, a counterpart to the prototypical *śrauta* format, upon which it was based. Turning around the comparison made in this chapter, the *gṛhya* ritual was dependent on the *śrauta* ritual as the modified sacrifice (*vikṛti*) is dependent on the paradigm (*prakṛti*).

Furthermore, with this compacted ritual framework, the domestic sacrificer was obliged to perform regularly sacrifices paralleling those obligatory to the *āhitāgni*. In this way, the same rituals could be performed at either the *śrauta* or *gṛhya* levels, bringing the different orders of ritual praxis into a relationship of resemblance and complementarity which itself harmonizes with Vedic metaphysics, epistemology, and the principles of ritual and textual organization and representation.

7

Ritual Hierarchy, Substitution, and Equivalency

Is the Simple the Equivalent of the Complex?

Within the context of a "unity" subsuming several discrete, if interrelated and resembling, levels of Vedic ritualism and ritualists, the domestic ritual is linked to higher forms through the relations of complementarity and correlativity discussed at the beginning of Chapter 6. As we have seen, however, these relations are further specified by the oppositions of domesticated/expanded, "female"/"male," simple/complex, and, above all, the hierarchical relation of inferior/superior. The Vedic ritual may be a "unity" composed of mutually related *śrauta* and *gṛhya* cycles, but the two are clearly differentiated and differently valued.

Later I will return to the issue of just how—and why—the ritual experts constituted the domestic sacrifice as simultaneously a condensed counterpart and an inferior resembling form of the *śrauta* ceremonial; and how, ironically, such machinations made it possible in the course of time for the *gṛhya* ritual to replace, for all intents and purposes, its prototype and survive within a different "unity," that of Hinduism.

For now, let us call up once again the model that was useful for discussing the relationship between the two levels of Vedic ritualism, the model, that is, of paradigm (*prakṛti*) and variation (*vikṛti*). When the domestic ritual, within Vedism, is seen as a kind of modification or variation of the *śrauta* ritual, the *śrauta* acts as the paradigm for the domestic ritual. Just as in the metarules provided in the Sūtras the *vikṛti* sacrifices are presented in a shorthand, condensed summary while the *prakṛti* rituals are described more fully and completely, so, too, is the domestic sacrifice an abbreviated, condensed, and adapted version of the more complete, expanded, and prototypical *śrauta* sacrifice. This type of interrelation between the two levels of Vedic ritualism is stressed by Jan Gonda when he writes, "There is no denying that the domestic cult as described in the *gṛhya* manuals was to a considerable extent influenced by, *and even modelled on,* the *śrauta* rites which in some cases run parallel."[1] As we also will observe later in this chapter, domestic rituals are systemized in the Sūtras in large part by being represented as miniature replicas of *śrauta* models.

Having come this far, however, in this explication of the Vedic ritual system (a system which, I have claimed, was based on principles of resemblance and hierarchical distinction), we must now confront an apparent discrepancy. For there is another possible relation between the *śrauta* and *gṛhya* levels of the Vedic "unity of ritual," which, if left unexplained, would seem to undercut the very basis of the system I have been describing.

Because of the parallels and strong bonds connecting the domestic sacrifice to the *śrauta* ritual—the web of *bandhu*s the ritualists fabricated in the process of constructing their ritual "unity"—it may appear that the relation between the two is really one of *equivalency.* As Madeleine Biardeau puts it, "It seems that the *gṛhya* rites with their one fire may be . . . to a very large degree *substitutes for śrauta rites.*"[2] Were the domestic rituals within the Vedic ritual system (which were, as I argued in Chapter 6, inferiorized in relation to the more complex *śrauta* sacrifices) also substitutes in the sense of being equivalent replacements for the rituals on which they were modeled and to which they were linked?

The question cannot be easily dismissed. For in the ritual Sūtras themselves, the locus classicus of the Vedic ritual unity, passages are found in which the case for equality between simple domestic ritualism and the complex *śrauta* sacrifice is apparently made in unequivocal terms. One rather late ritualistic text equates the domestic fire with the three or five *śrauta* fires, seemingly overturning the careful distinctions and qualitative differences drawn between them by other texts in Chapter 6:

> The [*śrauta*] fires are incorporated into the domestic fire, and the domestic fire into the sacrificer. Therefore one should not swerve from [the regular

1. Jan Gonda, *The Ritual Sūtras,* p. 549; emphasis added.
2. Biardeau, *Le Sacrifice dans l'Inde ancienne,* p. 39; emphasis added.

performance of sacrifices into] the domestic fire. . . . There is no distinction (*vivecana*) between the domestic fires and the *śrauta* fires.[3]

Similar statements may be found in even the older Gṛhya Sūtras. The Bhāradvāja Gṛhya Sūtra, quoting a (now lost) Śāṭyāyani Brāhmaṇa,[4] notes that because the deities are the same in the *agnihotra* of both the *śrauta* and *gṛhya* cycles, the domestic sacrificer reaps the same benefits from his small-scale version of the ritual as does the *āhitāgni* whose performance is much more complicated, time-consuming, and expensive:

> Because of the prescribed deities [in both versions of the ritual], and because of the results promised in the Veda, the same deities as are found in the [*śrauta*] *agnihotra* are worshipped in the ritual performed in the domestic fire. The practice of the *āhitāgni* is the practice [for the domestic sacrificer of the *agnihotra*]; the world (*loka*) of the *āhitāgni* is [the same as] that of him who offers in the domestic fire.[5]

Another claim to such equivalency appears in a different text, this one also equating the domestic and *āhitāgni* sacrificers:

> The fire [which is maintained] from the marriage is called the domestic fire. In that are performed all rituals relating to the household. Through his regular service [to that fire, accomplished through the daily performance of the *agnihotra,* he attains] the state of the *āhitāgni.* And by the oblations sacrificed on the new and full moon days, [he attains] the state of the [*śrauta*] sacrificer of the new and full moon sacrifice.[6]

How are we to understand these seemingly straightforward equations between what the ritualists have elsewhere hierarchically distinguished? Is the simple really the equivalent of the complex in these ritual texts? Is the domestic sacrifice within the Vedic ritual system a true and full substitute for paralleling *śrauta* rituals in these texts? And, if so, why would anyone go to the considerable trouble and expense of performing the complicated and costly *śrauta* rites? The very raising of questions

3. Bhāradvāja Pariśeṣa Sūtra 188. The text and translation of this work are included in C. G. Kashikar, trans. and ed., *The Śrauta, Paitramedhika and Pariśeṣa Sūtras of Bhāradvāja,* 2 vols. (Poona: Vaidika Saṃshodana Maṇḍala, 1964). Kashikar dates this text to the first centuries C.E.

4. Remnants of this Brāhmaṇa have been published in B. K. Ghosh, ed., *Collection of the Fragments of Lost Brāhmaṇas* (Calcutta: Modern Publishing Syndicate, 1935).

5. BhGS 3.18.

6. HGS 1.7.26.1–3. See also BGPariS 1.16.14: "With this [domestic new and full moon sacrifice, he attains] the state of the [*śrauta*] sacrificer of the new and full moon sacrifice." Similar claims for the equivalency of the domestic and *śrauta* sacrificers of the animal sacrifice may be found at BGPariS 2.1.27.

such as these shake what we have assumed to be the systematically formulated and implemented foundations of the Vedic religious, ritual, and social hierarchy. Do texts such as the ones cited above represent dissenting voices (perhaps of the economically dispossessed)? The changed circumstances of a different historical era? Or can they be comprehended in terms of the mainstream and ancient Vedic "unity of ritual"?

To begin grappling with these serious queries, let us turn to the subject of substitution, for the answers may turn on how we understand the meaning of substitution and its operation. First, we will analyze the nature of substitution within those rituals found the world over which we call sacrifices; and, second, we will look specifically at substitution within Vedic ritualism.

Sacrifice and Substitution

Substitution, the placing of a stand-in for an original which then represents it, is at the very heart of sacrifice. Such, in any case, is the common conclusion drawn by any number of scholars of the subject who have approached the topic from a wide variety of methodological angles.

Henri Hubert and Marcel Mauss, in their classic *Sacrifice: Its Nature and Function,* contend that "the very nature of sacrifice" is "dependent, in fact, on the presence of an intermediary, and we know that with no intermediary there is no sacrifice."[7] This "intermediary" so crucial to, even defining of, the sacrificial ritual is the ritual victim who represents (and substitutes for) both the divine recipient of the offering and the human being who is offering:

> Sometimes there is a direct and natural representation: a father is represented by his son, whom he sacrifices, etc. In general, since a sacrifier [sacrificer] is always obliged to undertake the expenses in person, there is, by virtue of this very fact, a more or less complete representation. But in other cases this association of the victim and the sacrifier is brought about by a physical contact between the sacrifier (sometimes the priest) and the victim. . . . Through this proximity the victim, who already represents the gods, comes to represent the sacrifier also. Indeed, it is not enough to say that it represents him: it is merged in him. The two personalities are fused together.[8]

7. Henri Hubert and Marcel Mauss, *Sacrifice: Its Nature and Function,* p. 100.
8. Ibid., pp. 31–32.

It is, according to these authors, through the victim (who is the full representative of and substitute for both the giver and the recipient of the sacrifice) that the "communication" between the sacred and profane realms is effected (and this is the "nature and function" of sacrifice according to Hubert and Mauss). The purpose of sacrifice is, therefore, to bridge the chasm between the sacred and profane worlds, and its mechanism for doing so involves a kind of double substitution: the victim stands in for both the sacrificer and the deity and thereby draws them together.

Many scholars have noted that all sacrifice is a kind of symbolic self-sacrifice; as Ananda K. Coomaraswamy puts it, "To sacrifice and to be sacrificed are essentially the same."[9] The sacrifice is a symbolic transformation of the self as one immolates a "lower" self and gains a "higher" identity:

> In other words, the appetitive soul, the greedy mind, is the Sacrifice; we, as we are in ourselves, seeking ends of our own, are the appropriate burnt offering. . . . The sacrificer's "death" is at the same time his salvation; for the Self is his reward.[10]

And insofar as the self-sacrifice which is sacrifice remains "symbolic," a substitute victim is obviously required. Sylvain Lévi has thus termed sacrifice a "subterfuge," and he states his position forcefully: "The only authentic sacrifice would be suicide."[11] The substitution of another for the self might thus serve to distinguish sacrifice from other related phenomena: suicide, martyrdom, and all other literal forms of self-death.

Others have emphasized another function of sacrificial substitution: displaced violence toward another. In this view, sacrifice is defined not in relation to other forms of self-death but rather in relation to other forms of murder—and in either case it is by virtue of the substitute that sacrifice is distinguishable from other killings.

Sigmund Freud, in his brief but extraordinarily important series of reflections on sacrifice at the end of *Totem and Taboo,* understood the sacrificial victim as only *consciously* the substitute for the sacrificer (although the element of the sacrificer's "renunciation"—of the egoistic and selfish will as well as of healthy independence—he found very significant indeed, and characteristic of religion as a whole). He argued, however, that the victim was also an *unconscious* representation of or substi-

9. Ananda Coomaraswamy, "Ātmayajna," p. 359.
10. Ibid., pp. 375, 376.
11. Sylvain Lévi, *La Doctrine du sacrifice,* pp. 32–33.

tute for the deity, the figure of authority, the idealized, all-powerful father figure. Sacrifice is thus simultaneously a conscious renunciation of independence, performed out of guilt generated from repressed feelings of hostility and resentment toward the authority figure, and an unconscious display of those same feelings as the authority figure, in the guise of the victim, is slaughtered and consumed:

> We find that the ambivalence implicit in the father-complex persists in totemism and in religions generally. Totemic religion not only comprised expressions of remorse and attempts at atonement, it also served as a remembrance of the triumph over the father. . . . Thus it became a duty to repeat the crime of parricide again and again in the sacrifice of the totem animal, whenever, as a result of the changing conditions of life, the cherished fruit of the crime—appropriation of the paternal attributes—threatened to disappear.[12]

For Freud, in sum, sacrifice is shot through with ambivalence toward authority, and most especially toward the father. It is stimulated by guilt stemming from Oedipal wishes, and it alleviates that guilt by providing a means for renouncing such wishes; but it also perpetuates and reproduces guilt by giving expression to the Oedipal fantasy of killing the father by means of killing the substitute, the sacrificial victim.

A more recent work, indebted in many ways to Freud, on sacrifice and substitution is René Girard's *Violence and the Sacred.* Girard, like Hubert and Mauss and like Freud, places the concept of substitution at the very center of sacrifice and, again like the others mentioned, speaks of a "double substitution" in the ritual. Following Freud, Girard sees violence (repressed and expressed) as the key to sacrifice, and he writes of a "fundamental truth about violence; if left unappeased violence will accumulate until it overflows its confines and floods the surrounding area. The role of sacrifice is to stem this rising tide of indiscriminate substitution and redirect violence into 'proper' channels."[13]

The substitute or victim, who represents the community as a whole, provides such a target for the acceptable expression of violence. But it is here that a complicated "double substitution" comes into play. The "original" or "real" victim is nothing other than the communal violence inherent in society—and this must be expunged for the survival and harmony of the group. A "surrogate victim"—a scapegoat, in other words—substitutes for the community. But then, according to Girard, a

12. Sigmund Freud, *Totem and Taboo,* trans. by James Strachey (New York: W. W. Norton, 1950), p. 145.

13. René Girard, *Violence and the Sacred,* trans. by Patrick Gregory (Baltimore: Johns Hopkins University Press, 1977), p. 10.

"ritual victim" substitutes for the "surrogate victim" in order to preclude revenge for the death of the surrogate. The cycle of violence is thus short-circuited by the double substitution which at once conceals and represents the real victim[14] as it transfers the violence from the real victim to a surrogate and then again to a ritual substitute. This byzantine chain of displacement and replacement is explained thus:

> The ritual victim is never substituted for some particular member of the community or even for the community as a whole: *it is always substituted for the surrogate victim.* As this victim itself serves as a substitute for all the members of the community, the sacrificial substitute does indeed play the role that we have attributed to it, protecting all the members of the community from their respective violence—but always through the intermediary of the surrogate victim. . . . Ritual sacrifice is founded on a double substitution. The first, which passes unperceived, is the substitution of one member of the community for all, brought about through the operation of the surrogate victim. The second, the only truly "ritualistic" substitution, is superimposed on the first. It is the substitution of a victim belonging to a predetermined sacrifical category for the original victim.[15]

Whether conceived as a transaction leading to communication between the sacred and the profane (Hubert and Mauss), or as a self-death leading to a transformation of the self, or as a violent expression and displacement of hostility toward another (the father with Freud, the community and its members with Girard), the general conclusions regarding sacrifice coincide. For all, sacrifice is defined by substitution. It is, in the first place, a substitute for an impossible or prohibited real act, such as the actual coalescence of the divine and the human, suicide[16], or violent aggression and murder. All substitutions within a sacrificial

14. Girard's position is that there is both a concealment and a necessary memory of the original victim for the sacrifice to be efficacious: "Once we have focused attention on the sacrificial victim, the object originally singled out for violence fades from view. Sacrificial substitution implies a degree of misunderstanding. Its vitality as an institution depends on its ability to conceal the displacement upon which the rite is based. It must never lose sight entirely, however, of the original object, or cease to be aware of the act of transference from that object to the surrogate victim; without that awareness no substitution can take place and the sacrifice loses all efficacy." Ibid., p. 5.

15. Ibid., pp. 101–2.

16. See now also Jan Heesterman's "Self-sacrifice in Vedic Ritual." Heesterman concludes, "What emerges from the ritual and from ritualist speculation is that self-sacrifice as such is invalid. . . . Sacrifice, on the other hand, cannot be valid by immolating just any victim that presents itself. The person, animal, or substance that is immolated must be that part of the sacrificer that defines him as such, namely the goods of life he has acquired by risking his own life. . . . Without this bond uniting the sacrificer and his victim, sacrifice would be as invalid as self-sacrifice is *per se*" (p. 105).

ritual are therefore substitutions for a prior, and defining, substitution. Secondly, all emphasize the critical importance of the victim to the sacrificial process, and all see this victim as a multivalent substitute and symbol for a pair of opposites: the sacred and the profane, god and man, recipient and giver, higher and lower selves, father and son, society as a whole and its individual members. The substitute victim is, as a symbol, a representative of two (or more) different and even contradictory things or beings.

And because it is a symbol, it is not critical to the efficacy of the sacrificial process itself who or what is selected to act as the symbol, the victim. It could be, and in the comparative view is, almost anything: humans (of any number of culturally constituted types), animals, vegetables, nonsentient physical objects, physiological functions (as in the "sacrifice of breath" in the Upanishads), even ideas ("individuality," "desire," "faith," "truth," etc.) can and do function as the symbolic victim.

This is not to say, however, that within particular cultures and particular religious traditions the choice of the appropriate victim is left to the whims of individuals. Far from it. The appropriate sacrificial victims are, as Girard says, "predetermined." They are also often hierarchically ordered and valued.[17] Such is certainly the case in Vedic ritualism—or is it?

Vedic ritualism in its entirety, like sacrifice as a category within religion, is based on substitution. The theology, metaphysics, and ontology created by the Vedic ritualists presume the inaccessibility of transcendent prototypes and the necessity, therefore, of ritual action using counterparts or "symbols" for the "real thing." Indeed, the sacrifice as a whole is a counterpart of the transcendent Cosmic One, Prajāpati or Puruṣa, who has created the ritual as a *pratimā* of himself.

I have pointed out elsewhere that in Vedism—as in sacrifice generally—the victim simultaneously represents the deity and the sacrificer, just as the ritual as a whole mediates between macrocosmos and

17. For a dicussion, inter alia, of the hierarchies of sacrificial victims in Indo-European myth and ritual, see Bruce Lincoln, *Myth, Cosmos, and Society: Indo-European Themes of Creation and Destruction* (Cambridge, Mass.: Harvard University Press, 1986), esp. pp. 65–86. More specific treatments of the topic in the Indo-European contexts are E. Mayrhofer-Passler, "Haustieropfer bei dem Indoiraniern und den andern indogermanischen Volkern," *Archiv Orientalini* 21 (1953): 182–205; Gerard Capdeville, "Substitution de victimes dans les sacrifices d'animaus à Rome," *Melanges d'archéologie et d'histoire de l'École Francaise de Rome* 83 (1971): 283–323; and Jean Puhvel, "Victimal Hierarchies in Indo-European Animal Sacrifice," *American Journal of Philology* 99 (1978): 354–62. My thanks to Bruce Lincoln for bringing these studies to my attention.

microcosmos. The often mentioned equation of Prajāpati and the sacrifice (*prajāpatir vai yajñaḥ*), and that of the sacrificer (and/or the Cosmic Man) and the sacrifice (*puruṣo vai yajñaḥ*), may also be formulated with "victim" (*paśu*) plugged in for "sacrifice."

But all counterparts are not created equally, and so, too, are sacrificial victims not all equal in their ability to represent most fully the prototype. The victim, mediating between and simultaneously representing both god and sacrificer, comes in different varieties with different capacities to manifest the complete form. One list of the appropriate victims for sacrifice is found in a passage whose purpose is to explain the etymology of the term *paśu:*

> Prajāpati turned his attention to the forms (*rūpa*s) of Agni. He searched for that boy who had entered into the [various] forms [of Agni]. Agni became aware [of this and thought], "Father Prajāpati is searching for me. I will take a form unrecognizable to him." He saw those five sacrificial victims: man, horse, cow, ram, and goat. Because he saw (*paśyat*) [them], they are therefore *paśu*s. He entered these five sacrificial victims and became these five sacrificial victims.[18]

Later in that same text, another passage makes it clear that the order in which the *paśu*s are listed is not accidental but rather is calibrated to the relative "excellence" of each:

> He offers [*alabhate,* literally "seizes" or "possesses"] the man first, for man is the first of the *paśu*s; then [he offers] the horse, for the horse comes after the man; then the cow, for the cow comes after the horse; then the ram, for the ram comes after the cow; then the goat, for the goat comes after the ram. In this way he offers them, in hierarchical succession (*yathāpūrvam*) according to their relative excellence (*yathāśreṣṭham*).[19]

Man (*puruṣa*) is generally proclaimed in the texts to be the highest of all possible sacrificial victims. Not only is man listed first in various enumerations of the *paśu*s; he is also extolled by texts which place him closest to Prajāpati. In an account of a sacrifice sponsored and performed by the gods, the list of *dakṣiṇā*s given to the divine priests includes the gift of a man to Prajāpati[20]—for, as we read elsewhere, "Man is the nearest to (*nediṣṭham*) Prajāpati [of all creatures]."[21] The

18. ŚB 6.2.1.1–3. The "boy" alluded to in the second sentence seems to refer to the Ṛg Vedic myth in which the child of Agni is lost, searched for, and found (ṚV 5.2). My thanks to Wendy Doniger O'Flaherty for this reference.

19. ŚB 6.2.1.18.

20. TB 2.2.5.3; see also PB 1.8.14.

21. ŚB 5.1.3.8, 5.2.1.6.

human being in another account is said to be superior because "man is all *paśu*s," that is, encompasses them all by virtue of his hierarchically superior rank (note also, again, the order in which the *paśu*s are listed):

> Prajāpati at first was one. He desired, "May I emit food, may I be reproduced." He measured out the *paśu*s from his breaths. From his mind [he measured out] the man; from his eye, the horse; from his breath, the cow; from his ear the ram; from his voice, the goat. And since he measured them out from his breaths, they say "The *paśu*s are the breaths." And since he measured out the man from his mind, they say "The man is the first, the most potent (*vīryavattama*) of the *paśu*s." The mind is all the breaths, for all the breaths are firmly established in the mind. And since he measured out the man from his mind, they say, "The man is all *paśu*s," for they all become the man's.[22]

In yet another narrative concerning the types and relative ranking of the sacrificial victims, this same order—from man, the highest form of *paśu,* to the goat, the lowest on the scale—is reiterated. The enumeration appears in the course of relating how the quality that constitutes all of these animals as worthy of sacrifice (their *medha*) entered into and then left them, creating in its wake new but defective forms of each. In this text, we are also introduced to another component of the Vedic theory of substitution. For although it is clear that the *paśu*s are ranked here, as they are elsewhere, the lowest on the hierarchical ladder is also said to be the victim most often used and, in some ways, the best victim:

> The gods offered man as sacrificial victim. Then the sacrificial quality (*medha*) passed out of the offered man. It entered the horse. Then the horse became fit for sacrifice and they dismissed him whose sacrificial quality had passed out of him. He [the former man, now devoid of the sacrificial quality] became a defective man (*kimpuruṣa*).[23] They offered the horse, and the sacrificial quality passed out of the offered horse. It entered the cow. . . . It [the former horse] became the white deer. They offered the cow. . . . The sacrificial quality entered the ram. . . . It [the

22. ŚB 7.5.4.6.

23. The *kimpuruṣa* is synonymous with the *kinnara* (Manu 1.39), the *puruṣa mṛga* ("wild man," TS 5.5.15.1; MS 3.14,16; VS 24.35) and the *mayu* (at ŚB 7.5.2.32 the *kimpuruṣa* and the *mayu* are explicitly equated). Various translations have been offered for these terms, ranging from "monkey" or "ape" to "dwarf," "savage" or "mock-man." See, e.g., Eggeling's note on ŚB 1.2.3.9. For the *kimpuruṣa* as a "horizontal androgyne," half equine and half human, consult Wendy Doniger O'Flaherty, *Women, Androgynes and Other Mythical Beasts* (Chicago: University of Chicago Press, 1980), pp. 216, 309. It seems probable that in Vedic texts it is the tribal peoples living outside of the Āryan settlements to which all the terms, *kinnara, kimpuruṣa, puruṣa mṛga,* and *mayu,* refer.

former cow] became a gayal. They offered the ram. . . . The sacrificial quality entered the goat. . . . It [the former ram] became the camel. It [the sacrificial quality] stayed the longest in the goat; therefore the goat is the *paśu* most often used [as sacrificial victim].[24]

The least "excellent" of the *paśu*s, the goat, is here presented as not only the one "most often used" but also the one most saturated with the quality that constitutes a sacrificial victim as such, the *medha.* This peculiar virtue of the least desirable and hierarchically most inferior victim is corroborated in other texts as well. One, for example, displays the goat to advantage by claiming that it possesses the essences of all the other (and hierarchically superior) *paśu*s—thus turning on its head the earlier cited text which claimed, in accord with the expected, that man, the highest *paśu,* encompasses all other victims. In the text at hand, however, the offering of a relatively lowly goat in sacrifice is "equivalent" to the offering of all the possible victims:

In this *paśu* [the goat] is the form (*rūpa*) of all *paśu*s. The form of man [incorporated in the goat] is what is hornless and bearded, for man is hornless and bearded. The form of the horse is what is possessing a mane, for the horse possesses a mane. The form of the cow is what is eight-hoofed, for the cow has eight hoofs. The form of the ram is what possesses ram-hoofs, for the ram possesses ram-hoofs. What is the goat, that is [the form] of the goat. Thus, when he offers this [goat], all those *paśu*s are offered by him.[25]

The least worthy substitute is thus said to recapitualte all members of the class of substitutes. Nor does this process of concentrating the sacrificial quality into lower and more easily expendable objects in the category stop with the goat.

When, according to the myth, the sacrificial quality finally left the goat after its longish residency, "it entered this earth. They searched for it by digging. They found it as those two, rice and barley (*vrīhi* and *yava*). Thus even now they find those two by digging." And further, these lowly victims, these vegetable *paśu*s, are said to "possess as much potency (*vīryavat*) as all the sacrificed *paśu*s would have."[26] This text is echoed by another, which equates the vegetable oblation with the animal offering. "When they also offer a cake [made from rice or barley] in the animal sacrifice [it is with the thought], 'Let our sacrifice be with a

24. AitB 2.8; see also ŚB 1.2.3.6, 1.2.3.9.
25. ŚB 6.2.2.15.
26. ŚB 1.2.3.7.

sacrificial victim possessed of the sacrificial quality; let our sacrifice be with a fully constituted (*kevala*) victim.' "[27]

Such texts from the Brāhmaṇas seem not so much to solve the problem we began with—whether inferior domestic sacrifices substitute for, in the sense of acting as the full equivalents of, complex *śrauta* rituals—as they appear merely to restate the quandary. The revaluation of the lowest *paśu*s as the recapitulation and apparent equal of the highest sacrificial victims seems to indicate that here, as in the case of the equations drawn between domestic and *śrauta* rituals, the hierarchical order of things has been overturned and rendered meaningless—perhaps by rival groups within the Vedic ritual milieu who competed for ritual status and social position by changing the economic rules of the game.

But perhaps also there is a simpler answer to this puzzle of substitution and "equivalency," one that emerges with consistency from within the established Vedic system of ritual and resemblance itself. In order to explicate the principles at work here, we must expand the discussion to substitution of all sorts in Vedic ritualism, and we might again take our cue from the *paribhāṣā*s or "general rules" on the topic as they are prescribed in the Sūtras.

Vedic Principles of Substitution

The passages from the Brāhmaṇas on substitutions for the victim in sacrifice are but one dimension of a more comprehensive theory of substitution within the Vedic texts. And although such a theory is rooted in the Brāhmaṇas, it is fully and systematically developed only in the ritual Sūtras.[28]

In addition to treating the various kinds of substitutes for animal victims, the Brāhmaṇas occasionally provide rules for substituting for other oblation materials used in the ritual. To take only one example, many of these older texts allow for the use of the *pūtīkā* plant and others

27. AitB 2.8.

28. The best study I know of to date on the intricacies of the Vedic ritual theory of substitution, and one to which I am indebted for what follows here, is Frederick Marcus Smith's *The Vedic Sacrifice in Transition: A Translation and Study of the Trikāṇḍamaṇḍana of Bhāskara Miśra,* Ph.D. dissertation, University of Pennsylvania, 1984. For an interesting overview of the philosophy of substitution in Vedic ritual texts, see Heesterman's "Self-sacrifice in Vedic Ritual."

in place of soma[29]—suggesting, perhaps, that the original soma was unknown, or often unavailable, or possibly never existed at all.[30] Soma, one might say, had become a transcendent prototype early on; in this case, as in others, both the "original" and the "substitute" were counterparts of an inaccessible prototype.[31]

Such instances of rulings on substitution in the Brāhmaṇas—confirming general theories of "double substitution" surveyed above—became authoritative precedents for the authors of the Sūtras. *Śruti* legitimization, in other words, provided one kind of authorization for substitution.[32] Conversely, previous explicit statements in the Veda prohibiting certain substitutions delimited those allowed by the Sūtras. Thus, nothing that is prohibited in the *śruti* can be used as a substitute "because of the unacceptability" of such innovation.[33]

The *śruti* was, however, not sufficiently explicit and comprehensive in its rulings on substitutions to function as the sole guide for all the instances in which substitutes might be necessary. Other standards were also observed by the ritualists, such as the authority of learned Brahmins.[34] But the most important of these aids were certain general principles which directed the specifics of substitutions in all cases.

One of the chief reasons for substitution in sacrifice, according to the Sūtras, is to enable the "accomplishment" or "completion" of an obligatory (*nitya*) ritual which otherwise would not be performed.[35] Replacing a specified element of the ritual with an acceptable substitute is justified by the "purpose" or "end" (*artha*) of the ritual as a whole, and in the case of the *nitya* or obligatory sacrifices, the very performance is the ritual's purpose. "*Nitya* rituals," it is said in one Sūtra, "are those which, when left unperformed, bring damage (*doṣa*) and worldly re-

29. E.g., ŚB 4.5.10.1ff; TB 1.4.7.5ff; JB. 1.354; PB 9.5.2ff.

30. The standard work on the question of the original soma remains R. Gordon Wasson and Wendy Doniger O'Flaherty, *Soma: Divine Mushroom of Immortality* (New York: Harcourt, Brace and World, 1968). The authors conclude that soma was originally a mountain mushroom called the fly agaric which eventually became inaccessible to the ritualists as they moved away from the Himalayas. That an "original" soma never existed at all is a speculation that has not been put forward by Indologists and perhaps deserves consideration.

31. See AitB 2.14 and TB 3.12.5.12 for the substitution of ghee for gold, "for both are nectars of immortality."

32. See, e.g., KŚS 1.4.4–5, 1.6.11.

33. KŚS 1.6.8; see also HŚS 3.1; ĀpŚS 24.4.1.

34. See, e.g., BGS 4.9.15.

35. See, e.g., ŚŚS 3.19.2; HŚS 3.1.

proach [to the sacrificer]."[36] "One should be forever bound to the performance of obligatory sacrifices," states another text. "He whose obligatory sacrifices are interrupted . . . takes an evil path. He does not go to heaven, but rather falls."[37] And so, the Sūtra continues, *nitya* sacrifices may be done with any number of substitutions, as long as they are done: "Thus, with a root, some fruit, honey or meat, the obligatory sacrifices are to be performed continually. And [thereby] one does not interrupt the obligatory sacrifices." We may be here observing, by the way, one of the early roots of the later Hindu theory of *āpad dharma,* in which the normal duties of the various castes are suspended in "times of emergency." Indeed, the laws of *dharma* and the laws of ritual are both extremely complex, detailed, and demanding; perhaps for this very reason the lawmakers provided various escape hatches to allow for their human frailty and the vagaries of life.

Substitutions may be made before beginning an obligatory sacrifice—the reasons for doing so include, as in the case of *āpad dharma,* various exigencies in times of distress or the unavailability of certain required materials[38]—or after the sacrifice has already been started (e.g., when certain of the necessary materials have become spoiled, lost, or otherwise rendered unusable).[39] The situation is different, however, in the optional or *kāmya* rituals of the Vedic ritual repertoire. There, because the "purpose" or "end" of the sacrifice is the attainment of "desired" or optional goals, there is much more emphasis placed on doing the ritual with the required materials. "In the absence of a prescribed [substance], one should not begin [an optional sacrifice], for its proper accomplishment depends on that [prescribed substance]."[40] Unlike the obligatory sacrifices, an optional ritual should not be undertaken if the materials for it are unavailable; substitution here is allowed only if the required substances become unusable in the course of the sacrifice. In those cases, a replacement may be brought in in order to avoid "incompletion" and the "blemish" (*doṣa*) the sacrificer would otherwise acquire.[41]

36. HŚS 3.1.
37. BŚS 28.13.
38. See, e.g., BŚS 29.8, for the "times of distress" which may preclude the performance of the *agnihotra:* a disturbance within the whole country; becoming afflicted with disease; being away on a journey; living at a teacher's house; unfavorable conditions regarding place, time, and materials; and "circumstances in which other things are unavailable."
39. HŚS 3.1.
40. KŚS 1.4.1.
41. KŚS 1.4.3–4.

Substitutions are therefore prohibited in cases where there is a direct *śruti* injunction to that effect and in the case of an optional sacrifice not yet begun. Other prohibitions are generated, however, out of the general principle of the importance of the purpose of the ritual and the subservience of other concerns to it. One reads that no replacements may be made for the sacrificial fire, the deity to whom the offerings are made, the mantra which accompanies an oblation, or the ritual act itself.[42] All these components, it would seem, are too intimately connected to the purpose of the ritual to be tampered with. As Chakrabarti puts it, "Transcendental results are produced by the sacrificial fires, deities, Mantras, and acts. If they are replaced by substitutes, the result of the sacrifice cannot be achieved."[43] All the Sūtras are agreed that there can also be no substitute for the sacrificer himself. The "lord" (*svāmin*) of the sacrifice is also too closely connected to the "fruit" of the ritual, that is, the result or "end" of the sacrifice, to be replaced by another.[44]

But if substitution is, in some cases at least, allowable on the grounds of the fulfillment of the purpose of the sacrifice, how is one to know what exactly may be substituted for an unavailable or unusable original? "A substitute should be taken on the basis of resemblance (*sāmānya*)," that is, resemblance to the original;[45] and "this is the guiding method (*dharma*) for all substitutions."[46] As in the epistemological standards for linking paradigmatic rites and rituals to variations of them, the fundamental principle for proper substitutions revolves around the

42. KŚS 1.6.6–7; ĀpŚS 24.4.1; HŚS 3.1. Another list (HŚS 3.1) also disallows substitutes for the son of the sacrificer and the place and time of the ritual.

43. Chakrabarti, *The Paribhāṣās,* p. 177. See also KŚS 1.6.6, where the reason for the prohibition against substituting for these items is "because of their subservience to the purpose of another (*parārthavat*)."

44. KŚS 1.6.9; see also HŚS 3.1; ĀpŚS 24.4.1. Some exceptions to this rule are allowed, however. A substitute for one of the sacrificers in a *sattra,* should he die before the ritual is completed, is legitimate (KŚS 1.6.11–12); and it would appear that the presence of the sacrificer is not required during the performance of those subsidiary rites not directly concerned with the production of the "fruit" of the ritual. In this latter case, the officiating priest also acts in the place of the sacrificer. See the oblique *sūtra*s at KŚS 1.6.9–10 and BGS 1.3.13. And, of course, in a very real sense, the victim serves as a substitute for the sacrificer, thus obviating the need to substitute further.

45. KŚS 1.4.2; MŚS 3.1.3; ĀpŚS 24.3.52; HŚS 3.1; ŚŚS 3.20.9; PMS 6.3.27.

46. ŚŚS 3.20.10. See Frederick Smith's translation of the "Trikāṇḍamaṇḍana of Bhāskara Miśra," 2.26 (p. 453): "[Substitutes should be selected on the basis of] similarity of effect (*kārya*), form (*rūpa*), color (*varṇa*), sap (*kṣīra*), flowers (*puṣpa*), fruit (*phala*), smell (*gandha*), and taste (*rasa*). In the absence of the former [attribute], the next in the list should be accepted."

concept of resemblance. As Chakrabarti notes, "Similarity with the original material is the determining factor in choosing the substitute, so that the substitute may be capable of serving the purpose of the original substance."[47] No substitute may "conflict" with the original, and, again as in the discussion on paradigms and variations, an order of resemblances applies here, too, in cases of conflicting claims to resemblance. It is the "resemblance of purpose" that is supreme and overruling when it comes to otherwise equally resembling options.[48]

The question of which option to select for a substitute when there are several available is addressed at KŚS 1.4.14. The *sūtra* states that one of them should be chosen at the start of the sacrifice (picked on the basis of its availability and for its "resemblance of purpose" to the original) and should then be employed for the duration of the ritual. The other options then cease to be options. If the substitute for an original should for some reason become unusable in the course of the performance, the secondary substitution should be made on the basis of its resemblance to the original, and not on the basis of a similarity to the substitute.[49] "There can be no substitute for a substitute," as Chakrabarti notes.[50] On this point, we may be faced with a Vedic exception to Girard's general rule. In his theory of ritual substitution, it will be recalled, the "ritual substitute" substitutes for a "surrogate victim" or scapegoat which is itself a substitute for a "real victim." The Vedic rule, by prohibiting substitutes for substitutes, seems to disallow—at least at a purely syllogistic level—Girard's formula.

Also consistent with the principles of Vedism as they are manifested in other situations is the fact that a substitute is considered a resembling, but not identical, counterpart to its prototypical original. Thus, on the one hand, the replacement is to be regarded and treated in the same way as the original would have been. All the characteristic features, and all the preparatory rites which make the substance fit for sacrifice, are transferred to the substitute.[51] The mantras recited for the original also remain unchanged when there is a replacement: references in the prescribed verse to the original (e.g., soma or goat) are unexpunged even

47. Chakrabarti, *The Paribhāṣās,* p. 175.
48. HŚS 3.1; KŚS 1.4.16.
49. KŚS 1.4.15.
50. Chakrabarti, *The Paribhāṣās,* p. 176. See PMS 6.3.9, 6.3.35–36, and Śabara's commentary.
51. ĀpŚS 24.3.53.

when a substitute is being used (e.g., *pūtīkā* for soma, or a cake for a goat).[52]

On the other hand, however, it is clear that some substitutes more nearly resemble the original than others, and it is here that we pick up the threads of the earlier discussion on the hierarchical ranking of elements within a class. The Sūtras, when listing the possible replacements for any given original component of the sacrifice, do so with a clear order of preference based on the strength of the resemblance of the species to the genus.

Take, for example, the substitutes given for clarified butter (a staple of virtually any Vedic ritual). BŚS 28.13 notes that the genus here is the ghee made from cow's milk, and the replacements for it ("if it is unattainable") are then listed: ghee made from buffalo's milk, or from that of a goat; oil of sesame seeds, of *jartila* seeds, of flax seed, of safflower seeds, or of mustard seeds; resin from a tree; or flour of rice, barley, or *śyāmāka* mixed with water. Or, again, observe the progression in the list of substitutes for fire if it has gone out and cannot be regenerated. One may, in that case, use an ordinary (*laukika*) fire, or offer in the right ear of a female goat (because, according to ŚB 7.5.2.6, Prajāpati created the goat from his ear?), in the right hand of a Brahmin (where the "oblations" of sacrificial gifts, *dakṣiṇā*s, are also placed), on a cluster of *darbha* grass, or in water.[53]

It must be emphasized again that such lists of substitutes are not randomly registered as equally valued alternatives. One Brāhmaṇa gives as substitutes for the milk at the Agnihotra the following in descending order of suitability: oblations of rice and barley (such as are standard in other rites) or of other domesticated plants in general or of wild plants, fruits from trees, water, or an oblation of "truth in faith" (*satyam śraddhāyām*).[54] The hierarchical nature of such lists is perhaps most obviously exemplified in the discussion of substitutes for the *dakṣiṇā* or "sacrificial fee" offered to the officiating priests by the sacrificer.[55] In

52. ŚŚS 3.20.11; ĀśvŚS 3.2.19; KŚS 1.4.9–10.

53. See ĀpŚS 9.3.3–16; BhŚS 9.4.5–9.5.5; HŚS 15.1.51–64.

54. ŚB 11.3.1–4; see also MŚS 8.10.4 for a substitute sacrifice of "truth" in the *agnihotra*.

55. For the *dakṣiṇā*, which is not really a "fee" as much as another kind of oblation offered to the Brahmins, the "human gods" of the sacrifice, see Charles Malamoud, "Terminer le sacrifice: Remarques sur les honoraires rituels dans le brahmanisme," in Biardeau and Malamoud, *Le sacrifice dans l'Inde ancienne*, pp. 155–204; Klaus Mylius, "*Dakṣiṇā*: Eine Studie über den altindischen Priesterlohn," *Altorientalische Forschungen* 6

Baudhāyana Śrauta Sūtra,[56] it is said that the standard *dakṣiṇā* for a sacrifice is comprised of a cow, some gold, and a garment—obviously a gift of some expense (and in some sacrifices the *dakṣiṇā*s are far more costly). If these items are "unavailable," the text continues, a much more modest (and inferior) substitute is prescribed: a gift of edible fruits and roots. "If even this not [within reach of the sacrificer]," the teacher concludes (perhaps with some exasperation), "he should not offer the sacrifice." Just as one could not offer a sacrifice to the gods without providing some (indeed, almost any) oblation in the fire for them, so one is prohibited from sacrificing without offering something to the Brahmin priests, the "human gods." And it may not be out of place here to recall who the creators of these ritual rules were.

Condensation and Hierarchical Resemblance

Let us now turn again to the problem of certain claims for the domestic ritual as an equivalent substitute for *śrauta* sacrifices, having gained some perspective on the issue through an overview of the Vedic theory of substitution. As we have seen, substitutes in general in the Vedic ritual are regarded as resembling, but not identical, counterforms of their original prototype. As such, they are certainly connected to the prototype (because of the shared participation within a class) but are also clearly hierarchically distinguished as well (the species is not the genus, the counterpart is not the prototype, and one counterpart is not the same as any other). Such are the by now familiar workings of the Vedic theory of resemblance, operating between the two poles of the exactly the same (the equivalent, the identical, *jāmi*) and the completely different (the unique, the disconnected, *pṛthak*).

Still, one might ask, how does all this make sense of statements which seem to equate the lower with the higher, the lowly goat with the "most excellent" *paśu,* the simple domestic ritual with the intricate *śrauta* sacrifice? Is not hierarchical distinction eclipsed by these claims of equivalent substitution?

Again, I think, a general overview informs the specific case. For, as we have seen, substitution in the ritual texts entails not only a subsequent assumption of equivalency (the substitute is treated in the ritual as

---

(1979): 141–79; and Jan Heesterman, "Reflections on the Significance of the *Dakṣiṇā,*" *Indo-Iranian Journal* 3 (1959): 241–58.

56. BŚS 28.13.

if it were the original) but also is in every case a simplification. In all the instances treated in the Sūtras, the chain of acceptable substitutes moves from the most complex, highly valued, and rare to the simpler, less costly, and more common. Such chains always end with the minimally acceptable. And this is, I suggest, precisely what is assumed in and lies behind those texts that speak of the "identification" between the *gṛhya* and *śrauta* ceremonials within Vedic ritualism.

A larger perspective—that is, one that looks at the system as a whole—puts the particular in its proper place. Minimalism presented as equivalency is not unique to the situation perplexing us. The representation of the smaller, the less adequate, and the abbreviated as the "equal" of the larger, the fully appropriate, and the unabridged is an integral feature of Vedic ritualism. In one sense, the whole of Vedic ritualism is founded on such a notion.

The "equation" of obviously inferior rituals to higher ones was not invented by the authors of the Gṛhya Sūtras. It was a relatively common means of expression long before. Claims of equivalency between sacrifices of different values were made in the Brāhmaṇas between rituals within the *śrauta* cycle and between hypothetical and prototypical rituals and their human counterparts. "Find the sacrificial ritual which is the counterpart of that one of a thousand years' duration," say the gods in one text. "For what man is there who could complete a thousand-year ritual?"[57] The text continues with a string of equations between rituals of greater length and those done more economically, concluding with the *Tāpaścita* sacrifice which is said to be the counterpart of the thousand-year sacrifice. The phenomenon, when it deals with sacrifices within the realm of human possibility, most often takes the form of "equating" lesser rituals to the soma sacrifice. This latter ritual is often said to be the "most excellent" or "best" or "first" among all rituals; that is, it is the highest and most nearly complete and perfect of the Vedic rituals.[58] It is, therefore, the sacrifice other sacrifices replicate. The Ṣaḍviṃśa Brāhmaṇa,[59] for example, goes to great lengths to demonstrate how the rites of the simplest of the *śrauta* sacrifices, the *agnihotra,* are "really" the same as those comprising the soma sacrifice. The *cāturmāsya* ritual is in like manner said to be the "form" (*rūpa*) of the soma sacrifice,[60] and the animal sacrifice, one text claims, is not to be categorized among the

57. ŚB 12.3.3.5.
58. See ŚB 6.6.3.7; TS 7.1.1.4; ĀpŚS 10.2.3.
59. ṢaḍB 4.1.6,9–11.
60. BhŚS 8.25.13.

lesser rituals but rather as a "great sacrifice" or *mahāyajña,* that is, a soma sacrifice.[61] In similar fashion, another passage in that Brāhmaṇa equates the new and full moon sacrifice with the soma sacrifice, concluding with a declaration that cannot help but recall the passages in question in the later Sūtras: "By performing the new and full moon sacrifice, he wins as much as is won by performing a soma sacrifice. The [ritual] thus becomes a great sacrifice (*mahāyajña*)."[62]

Vedic resemblance thus allows for two different kinds of ritual condensations, both of which entail a kind of synecdochic reductionism (whereby a part of the whole represents the whole) but differ regarding what kind of part is made to represent the whole.

The first type of this synecdoche, which we have seen at work before and which is readily understandable in hierarchical terms, is the encompassment (or claim of encompassment) of the condensed essences of lesser rituals within greater ones—a condensation *upward,* so to speak. I observed above such a claim for the human victim, which is said to encompass within it all other *paśu*s, and for the soma sacrifice, which contains within it all other sacrifices, both the lower and the higher.[63] Elsewhere the soma sacrifice is said to be the "the most perfect" (*sampannatama*) of all Vedic rituals on account of its all-encompassing nature.[64] Other rituals are similarly advertised. The rites within the Agnicayana are assimilated into the rituals of the Vedic repertoire, and thus "he obtains all the sacrifices with the Agnicayana."[65] The Rājasūya has the same capacity: "He who offers the Rājasūya envelopes all sacrificial rituals."[66] Such great rituals make their claim to superiority in part

61. ŚB 11.7.2.2

62. ŚB 2.4.4.11–14. See TS 1.6.9.1–2, where one "who knows thus" is said to obtain the results of the *agniṣṭoma,* the *ukthya,* and the *atirātra* by offering, respectively, the *agnihotra,* the full moon sacrifice, and the new moon sacrifice. See also G. U. Thite, *Sacrifice in the Brāahmaṇa-Texts,* pp. 49–50. The author observes, "In order to elevate any sacrificial rite efforts were made to show how the rite has some connection with Soma." For equations between the hierarchically lowest *śrauta* ritual, the *agnihotra,* and the soma sacrifice, see H. G. Bodewitz, *The Daily Evening and Morning Offering,* pp. 125–35. For claims of equivalency between various rites of the domestic *upanayana* and the subsequent period of Veda study on the one hand and the *śrauta* rituals on the other, see Brian K. Smith, "Ritual, Knowledge, and Being," pp. 79–80, and Chapter 8 herein.

63. AitB 3.40–41.

64. AitĀ 2.3.3.

65. ŚB 10.1.5.1–3.

66. ŚB 5.2.3.9.

by virtue of the fact that they encompass within them the condensed kernels of all other Vedic sacrifices.[67]

The second form of condensation within Vedic resemblance is less obviously in harmony with hierarchical presuppositions. This is the type we have been observing in this chapter: a condensation *downward* of the essences of superior victims or superior sacrifices which are reprised within inferior "equivalents." Claims of equivalency between "great" prototypes and their condensed counterparts, in the Sūtras as well as in the Brāhmañas, can also be explicated in terms of hierarchical resemblance. They serve to unite Vedic ritualism from top to bottom, and vice versa. The homologies are not intended to collapse distinctions but rather to strengthen connections between interrelated phenomena. In such a system, even the smallest and relatively weakest rite or ritual may function as a resembling counterpart to the greatest and most complete version of the rite or ritual. The inferior is not here regarded as an equivalent replacement for but rather only as a condensed representative of its superior relative within a class. It is in this sense, and in this sense only within the context of the "unity of ritual" that is Vedism, that one may speak of the domestic rituals as "substitutes."

There is another, more practical end served by drawing links between the great and the small, the expanded and the condensed. Recalling that it is the "resemblance of purpose" (*arthasāmānya*) which is the most important and overriding form of resemblance in Vedism, and that substitution is most especially legitimate when it is necessary to bring about the completion of the obligatory (*nitya*) sacrifices, we may now turn again with new understanding to obligatory domestic rituals that replicate obligatory *śrauta* rituals. For it would seem that one important function of domestic replicas is to act as substitutes for *nitya* rituals for those ritualists at the lower levels of the Vedic ritual—and social and economic—system; and the supreme resemblance, the resemblance of purpose, is the one that links obligatory rituals at the two levels. Resemblance, it would seem, served as the glue for a certain kind of systemic solidarity, binding together within a ritual, social, and economic whole all the levels of the hierarchy.

By at least the time of the Gṛhya Sūtras, if not before they were so

67. For the performance of lesser *śrauta* rituals in the course of the performance of the soma sacrifice, see Jan Gonda, *The Haviryajnāḥ Somāḥ: The Interrelations of the Vedic Solemn Sacrifices. Śānkhāyana Śrauta Sūtra 14, 1–13. Translation and Notes* (Amsterdam: North-Holland, 1982).

documented, certain of the *nitya* sacrifices of the *śrauta* cycle were performed, in condensed forms, as part of the obligatory rituals of the domestic cycle. Two of the most important of these, for both cycles, were the daily *agnihotra* and the bimonthy new and full moon sacrifice. Called by the same name, based on the same ritual procedures, and connected by the "resemblance of purpose," the *agnihotra* and the new and full moon sacrifice were to be performed by both the *ekāgni* and the *āhitāgni.*

The *agnihotra* ritual was correlated to the rising and setting of the sun, and, among its other purposes, it was vital to the perpetual maintenance of the fire(s) (the "fire worship" or *agnyupasthāna*). With the daily *agnihotra,* the ritualist nurtures the continuity of fire, of sacrifice, and, in the minds of the ritualists, of life itself.[68] H. W. Bodewitz, who believes that the ritual was primarily meant as a transference of solar light into the fire, also recognizes that "the fires are related to the *āhitāgni* himself, the hearth is connected with the head of the family, and the fires are identified with the *prāṇāḥ* [life breaths] of the sacrificer. As a result the daily *agnihotra* offered in these fires may be explained as a daily confirmation of this relationship."[69]

Equally essential for the maintenance of the sacrificial vow and for the continuity of the sacrificer's ritually constituted being was the new and full moon sacrifice. It is required of the *āhitāgni* for "as long as he lives, or for thirty years, or until he becomes too old."[70] Whereas the *agnihotra* is synchronized to the daily rising and setting of the sun, the new and full moon sacrifice, as its name suggests, is calibrated to the lunar cycle. And the latter, like the former, "once begun should never be discontinued."[71] The *agnihotra* and the new and full moon sacrifices are the most important of the obligatory *śrauta* rituals and must be continuously performed by *āhitāgni*s of all ranks.[72]

68. P.-E. Dumont writes, "The daily obligation to offer the *agnihotra* is essential, for it seems that one of the principal objects of the *agnihotra* is to perpetuate both the continuity of the sacrifice and the continuity of the race of the sacrificer." *L'Agnihotra: Description de l'agnihotra dans le rituel védique* (Baltimore: Johns Hopkins University Press, 1939), p. vii.

69. Bodewitz, *The Daily Evening and Morning Offering,* p. 2.

70. ĀpŚS 3.14.10.

71. BhŚS 3.13.11.

72. See, e.g., HŚS 3.1: "[For the Brahmin, Kṣatriya, and Vaiśya] the *agnihotra* and new and full moon sacrifices are obligatory. A soma sacrifice [is also obligatory] for the Brahmin. From the time the fires are set up, the *agnihotra* and new and full moon sacrifices are obligatory. For a non-Āryan chief (*niṣāda*) and a chariot-maker (*rathakāra*), the *agnihotra* and new and full moon sacrifices become mandatory from the time the fires

These two obligatory *śrauta* sacrifices, among others, were replicated in domestic ritualism with a formally simplified and relatively inferior procedure. The framework (*tantra*) for the performance of all domestic rituals was a contracted rendition of the more expanded and full framework of the *śrauta* sacrifice. With this condensed procedure, the *ekāgni* performs rituals that parallel those of his prototype, the *āhitāgni,* and that allow him to participate in the Vedic cult of fire sacrifice and all that it entailed.

In one Gṛhya Sūtra,[73] a reduced and domesticated version of the establishment of the fires (*agnyādheya* or *agnyādhāna*) is enjoined for the *ekāgni*. The procedure for its performance, the text notes, is known from the *śrauta* procedure: "All [rites here are performed as in the ritual] that contains the eating of the *cātuṣprāśya* food," by which is clearly meant the *agnyādheya* depicted in the school's Śrauta Sūtra. Other domestic Sūtras give instructions for reestablishing the fire (the *punaragnyādheya*) should it go out or be neglected for twelve days or more. For this ritual, too, the texts refer back to the *śrauta* model, noting also the adaptations necessary when applying the model to the domestic situation.[74]

The domestic *agnihotra* and new and full moon sacrifices are similarly adaptations—and condensations—of *śrauta* prototypes. Although the *agnihotra* is performed at the same time and offerings are made to the same deities at both levels of Vedic ritualism, the oblation in the domestic sacrifice is not the milk obtained from the "*agnihotra* cow" every *āhitāgni* is required to own. Rather, here the prescribed oblation consists only of uncooked rice and barley grains, offered with the hand (and not with a ladle) by the sacrificer himself (and not by an officiating priest).[75] I have already noted (in Chapter 6) some of the rites eliminated and abbreviated in the condensed performance of the domestic version of the new and full moon sacrifice. Other modifications include a simple offering of cooked food in a dish (*sthālīpāka*) to Agni, replacing

are set up." Most texts list seven *nitya* sacrifices for the *āhitāgni,* regardless of class: the *agnyādheya* (establishing the fires), the *agnihotra,* the new and full moon sacrifices, the seasonal *āgrāyana* sacrifices of first harvests, the quarterly *cāturmāsyas,* the twice-yearly animal sacrifice, and an annual soma sacrifice. For this last obligatory sacrifice as only so mandated for Brahmins, see HŚS above and KŚS 1.2.12 ("according to some").

73. PGS 1.2.1–13.

74. See, e.g., HGS 1.7.26.4–18.

75. For these and other differences between the *śrauta* and *gṛhya agnihotras,* consult Bodewitz, *The Daily Evening and Morning Offering,* pp. 191–204.

the *śrauta* requirements of cakes to Agni, Agni-Soma, and Indra, and an offering of clarified butter to Prajāpati.[76]

In addition to these, the most fundamental and necessary of the obligatory sacrifices, other *nitya* rituals are also replicated in domestic miniatures. The seasonal sacrifices (*āgrayaṇa*s) are performed at the same times, and offerings are made to the same deities, by both the *āhitāgni* and the *ekāgni.* But in this case, as in all others, the domestic ritual is a much abridged variant of the more complete *śrauta* model.[77] Animal sacrifices at the domestic level, including the yearly *śūlagava* (a sacrifice of an ox or cow to Rudra) and the *aṣṭakā*s (in which a cow is sacrificed for the ancestors), are directly based on—and are collapsed forms of—the twice-yearly *śrauta* animal sacrifice.[78]

In one remarkable section from a domestic ritual text of the Baudhāyana school,[79] instructions are given for domestic versions of the full complement of obligatory *śrauta* rituals. Some general rules for making the proper adjustments necessary for the domestic replication of these sacrifices are noted:

> Where there [in the *śrauta* ritual] there are cakes, here [in the domestic replica] there are oblations of cooked rice porridge (*caru*). The divinities, the proper invitation verse (*puroṇuvakya*) and sacrificial verse (*yājya*) are the same [in both versions]. Where there there is the cry "*vaṣat*!" at the time of offering, here there is the exclamation "*svāhā*!"[80]

Specific details are also provided in the text for the miniature performance of the particular rituals of the *śrauta* cycle, including the method for offering a vegetarian "animal sacrifice" (which makes the domestic ritualist "the equal of the sacrificer of the animal sacrifice") and the way to offer a *gṛhya* "soma sacrifice" accomplished without the use of soma.

All these obligatory sacrifices were performed in their fullness only by the *āhitāgni* utilizing the full array of three to five empowered fires,

76. Descriptions of the deities and offerings that comprise the principal oblations at the *śrauta* new and full moon sacrifices may be found in Alfred Hillebrandt's *Das Altindische Neu- und Vollmondsopfer* (Jena: Gustav Fischer, 1879), pp. 107–16; and in Urmila Rustag's more recent work, *Darśapūrṇamāsa: A Comparative Ritualistic Study* (Delhi: Bhāratīya Vidyā Prakashan, 1981), pp. 235–46. For the domestic version of the ritual, see Jan Gonda, *Vedic Ritual,* pp. 346–53.

77. The domestic Āgrayaṇa is performed with a *sthālīpāka,* and not a cake as in the *śrauta* ritual, made from the newly harvested grains of each season. See Kane, *History of Dharmaśāstra,* II: 827–29; and Gonda, *Vedic Ritual,* pp. 430–32.

78. See ĀśvGS 1.11; MGS 2.4; KGS 51.

79. BGPariS 2.1.

80. BGPariS 2.1.37.

sacrificing the proper oblation material to the full number of relevant divinities, and performing the entire ritual according to the more complex and inclusive *śrauta* procedure. The domestic replicas, condensed substitutes at a lower level, are but bleached-out simplifications of their prototypical models.

As integral components of a unified and comprehensive Vedic ritual system, the domestic rites were resembling "equivalents" or "substitutes" for those who could do no better; for those who, because of lack of wealth, education, experience, or interest and desire, were unqualified for participation in the *śrauta* cult. Within the "unity of ritual," that is, when seen in relation to *śrauta* ritualism, the domestic sacrifice takes its place as the simple and basic form of Vedic ritualism, a formally resembling but impoverished and incomplete manifestation of superior ritual expressions. But as condensations of those higher ritual forms, the domestic sacrifices (and those who engaged in them) also found a place, humble though it was, within the Vedic world of hierarchical resemblance.

From the Inferior to the Replacement: The Domestication of the Vedic Sacrifice

It is not at all an easy thing to pinpoint when, historically, the Vedic unity began to crumble and new systems of religious belief and practice overshadowed and replaced it. As I have argued in Chapter 2 and as I will maintain again in Chapter 8, there is a real sense in which Vedism never did die but merely transmigrated into new bodies. Still, there is no question that the subsequent incarnations of Vedism were significantly different from the original (as counterparts differ from their prototypes), and, by way of concluding this survey of that original form of Vedism, it might be useful to reflect on the first signs of its death and its earliest rebirths.

One possible site for locating the first shift from one system, one set of religious assumptions and organizing principles, to another is the forest of sixth-century B.C.E. India—the locale of the world renouncers of both the "orthodox" and "heterodox" traditions. The latter, principally those that eventually emerged as what we call Buddhism and Jainism, radically broke away from the Vedic ancestor in the course of time, although they did not and could not ignore its legacy. The "orthodox" traditions of world renunciation, most especially those based on principles of monism (later to be designated Vedānta), are even more complicated cases of continuity and change vis-à-vis the Vedic system focused on here.

To some scholars it would appear that Vedic resemblance, governing a plethora of interlocking hierarchical registers, found its necessary end in the monistic thought represented in the early Upanishads. For these students of Indian history, the latter texts are continuous with, and are the teleological conclusion of, the earlier ritualistic thought. In the Upanishads, universal resemblance is brought to its logical terminus: universal identity. The complex system of connections between resembling phenomena, the web of *bandhu*s integral to Vedic ritualism, and hierarchical distinctions are collapsed in monistic thought into the ultimate connection: the equation of self and cosmos (without the ritual intermediary) formulated as the identity and full equality of *ātman* and the *brahman*.

In this view, the ritualists are retrospectively seen as seeming "to circle a final, long-sought identity, preferring to postpone recognition of that ultimate correspondent in which all oppositions cease."[81] Jan Heesterman, in his seminal article "Brahmin, Ritual, and Renouncer," takes a somewhat different view of the continuity between the ritualistic texts (the Brāhmaṇas and Sūtras) and the texts of the world renouncers. Heesterman argues that ritualistic thought developed through three discrete periods: a largely hypothetical "preclassical" period characterized by agonism and reciprocity; a "classical" era in which the ritual is "individualized" and reciprocal exchange eliminated; and, as the culmination of the Vedic sacrificial ideology, a third period of "interiorization" and world renunciation represented by the Upanishads. According to Heesterman, ritualistic thought

> had to advance to its logical conclusion, that is the interiorization of the ritual which makes the officiants' services superfluous. . . . It would seem to me that here we touch the principle of world renunciation, the emergence of which has been of crucial importance in the development of Indian religious thinking.[82]

Heesterman has made what is probably the best case to date for the "orthogenetic, internal development of Vedic thought" extending to and climaxing in the absolute independence of the sacrificer by means of philosophical monism and renunciation of social existence. "The point I

81. David Knipe, *In the Image of Fire: Vedic Experiences of Heat* (Delhi: Motilal Banarsidass, 1975), p. 33.

82. Jan Heesterman, "Brahmin, Ritual, and Renouncer," p. 39.

want to stress," he writes, "is that the institution of renunciation is already implied in classical ritual thinking. The difference between classical ritualism and renunciation seem to be a matter of degree rather than of principle."[83] /

Perhaps the case for a certain discontinuity, for the Upanishads as emblematic not of an extension of Vedic ritualism but of its demise as the dominant worldview of ancient India, can be made on the basis of my work here. I have located the heart and soul of Vedic ritualism in a principle at odds with that underlying monism. In the Upanishads, one might be witnessing the conclusion of Vedism not in the sense of its culmination but in the sense of its destruction. In the proto-Vedāntic view, the universe and ritual order based on resemblance has collapsed, and a very different configuration based on identity (abhorred by the Vedic ritualists as the "excess of resemblance," *jāmi*) has emerged. Upanishadic monism, one might say, blew the lid off a system contained, as well as regulated, by hierarchical resemblance.

The formulation of a monistic philosophy of ultimate identity—arguably one indication of Vedism dissipating and reforming into a new systematic vision of the world and its fundamental principles—was born outside of normative classification schema of Vedic social life and became institutionalized as a counterpoint to life in the world. But another locus of Vedism in transition and transformation might also be identified. It might be maintained that Vedic ritualism survived the Vedic period by becoming a part of a larger whole, Hinduism, and did so not by being excluded from social life but by being thoroughly integrated in it, that is, by being domesticated. Perhaps Vedism culminated not in the forest but in the home.

Beginning at approximately the same time as the first appearance of the world renouncers and their new philosophies, and coinciding with the production of the ritual Sūtras, new forms of political power put the older ideological hegemony of the Brahmin ritualists in jeopardy. The Buddhist influence at the highest levels of polity, most dramatically realized in but not ceasing with Aśoka Maurya and his pan-Indian reign, in all likelihood made the continued performance of large and ostentatious Vedic sacrifices (with their overt statements of overlordship) impolitic at best, if not simply impossible. The adherents of and successors to the Vedic ritual system may have had to make some adjustments and accommodations in light of these political and religious changes.

Through the time of the composition of all but the most recent

83. Ibid., p. 41.

Gṛhya Sūtras, the domestic ritual was presented as in the shadow of the *śrauta* cult. Somewhat later, and perhaps under the very different circumstances suggested here, the domestic ritual is represented rather differently. In texts such as the Manu Smṛti (ca. second century B.C.E. or later), one of many literary productions of the classical Hinduism oriented around caste duty and the obligations of the householder, the domestic sacrifice or *pākayajña* appears not as an inferior version of other and greater rituals but rather as the epitome of and effective replacement for them; and the whole system of domestic ritualism itself was concentrated into five daily activities of the householder.

The orthodox Hindu strategists inherited the means to rethink and revalue domestic ritualism from Vedic ritualism: condensation, minimalism, and the representation of the simple as the complex through synecdochical reductionism. Set within a context in which the *śrauta* rituals—and especially the greatest of these, the soma sacrifices and the royal rituals—were largely anachronisms, these features of an older hierarchical system took on new significances.

As early as the Śatapatha Brāhmaṇa[84] and the Taittirīya Āraṇyaka,[85] one reads of five "great sacrifices" (*mahāyajña*s) by which a householder daily acquits himself of his ritual obligations to the gods, the ancestors, the spirits, his fellow human beings, and the *brahman*. These "great sacrifices" are also labeled "great extended sacrificial sessions" (*mahāsattra*s), but only "by way of laudation," as one text notes.[86] For within the hierarchical system, these "great" sacrifices, like other domestic rituals also so designated, were in fact extremely simple forms of Vedic ritualism:

> He should daily offer [an oblation into the fire] with the exclamation "*svāhā*!" even if it is done only with a stick of wood. That fulfills the sacrifice to the gods. He should daily offer [an oblation to the ancestors] with the exclamation "*svadhā*!" even if it is only a vessel of water. That fulfills the sacrifice to the ancestors. Daily he should pay respect [to the spirits], even if it is only [by offering them] some flowers. That fulfills the sacrifice to the spirits. Daily he should give food to Brahmins, even if it is only some roots, fruits, or vegetables. That fulfills the sacrifice to humans. And every day he should recite [a portion of] the Veda, even if it is only the syllable "*om*". That fulfills the sacrifice to *brahman*.[87]

84. ŚB 11.5.6.1 ff.
85. TĀ 2.10.
86. ĀpDhS 1.4.12.15: "In reference to these [five sacrifices] there is the laudatory statement (*saṃstuti*) [that refers to them as] '*mahāyajña*s' and '*mahāsattra*s.' "
87. BDhS 2.6.11.2–6; see also ŚB 11.5.6.2; TĀ 2.10.

As Charles Malamoud puts it, "The lesson of the five great sacrifices is that there exists a minimum ritual necessary and sufficient so that the daily religious obligation may be completely accomplished."[88] The recipients of these five great sacrifices are the sum total of all eligible "eaters of oblations" in Vedic ritualism; by concentrating sacrifices to them into one daily sequence, the *mahāyajñas* in effect represent a minimalistic form of Vedic ritualism as a whole for householders with limited means. P. V. Kane writes, "Every man could not afford to celebrate the solemn *śrauta* rites prescribed in the Brāhmaṇas and Śrauta Sūtras. But every one could offer a fuel-stick to fire that was deemed to be the mouth of the great Gods of Heaven and thus show his reverence and devotion to them."[89]

And if the five *mahāyajñas* were the minimal condensed forms of Vedic ritualism as a whole, they were also, even within the hierarchical Vedic ritual system, the representations of the domestic cycle of sacrifices in its entirety. In one classification of the different types of *gṛhya* rituals, the subclasses or *saṃthās* comprising the domestic level of sacrifice, the categories are suspiciously akin to four of the five daily "great sacrifices":

> [A domestic ritual is designated] a *huta* by virtue of the daily *agnihotra* oblation [to the gods]; an *ahuta* by virtue of the rice ball offerings [to the spirits]; a *prahuta* by virtue of the rites to the ancestors; and a *prāśita* is the oblation made in [the mouth of] a Brahmin.[90]

The only *mahāyajña* not potentially covered in this classification scheme, this fourfold typology of the domestic ritual as a whole, is the "sacrifice of speech" or the daily Vedic recitation, a sacrifice that may very well be considered as included within other rituals in the form of the accompanying mantras. Although the correlation here between the types of domestic ritualism and the five daily great sacrifices is not explicit, it is, I think, implied. The domestic ritual, the *pākayajña,* itself the diminutive representative of the Vedic ritual system, is represented in this text as further

88. Charles Malamoud, *Le Svādhyāya: Recitation personnelle du Veda* (Paris: Institut de Civilisation Indienne, 1977), p. 14.

89. Kane, *History of Dharmaśāstra,* II 697–98.

90. ŚGS 1.10.7; see also ŚGS 1.5.1; PGS 1.4.1; JGS 1.1; KGS 13.2. The classification at ĀśvGS 1.1.2 is similar. Another and competing method of classifying the types of domestic rituals organizes them into seven categories, paralleling the seven subclasses of the *śrauta* and soma ritual. See BŚS 42.4; BGS 1.1; GB 1.5.23,25; VaikhGS 1.1; GautDhS 8.18; and Sudarśana's commentary on ĀpGS 1.1; Sāyana's commentary on TS 1.7.1.1; and Kane, *History of Dharmaśāstra,* II: 194n.

reduced into its quintessential kernel—five "great" sacrifices that may be performed with a piece of wood, a glass of water, some flowers and fruits, and by saying "*om.*"

The correlation of the divisions of the domestic sacrifice and those of the "great sacrifice," made only implicitly in the Śankhāyana Gṛhya Sūtra cited above, is explicitly formulated in Manu Smṛti.[91] In that post-Vedic and classical Hindu text, one reads:

> Teaching the Veda is the sacrifice to *brahman,* the offerings of food and water [the *tarpaṇa*] is the sacrifice to the ancestors, the oblation in the fire is the sacrifice to the gods, the rice ball offering is the sacrifice to the spirits, and the honoring of guests is the sacrifice to humans. . . . These five sacrifices are [also] known as the *ahuta,* the *huta,* the *prahuta,* the *brāhmyahuta,* and the *prāśita. Ahuta* is the repetition of the Veda, *huta* the oblation offered in fire, *prahuta* the rice ball offering to the spirits, *brāhmyahuta* the reception of twice-born [guests], and *prāśita* the satiating of the ancestors.[92]

In this text, the condensation of the whole domestic ritual, in all its typological forms, into the five simple daily sacrifices of the householder is complete. But what is at least as significant is the fact that the rationale for the performance of the *mahāyajña*s is different here. In the Gṛhya Sūtras and other texts of Vedic ritualism, the five great sacrifices were a minimalistic method for the domestic sacrificer to pay back, sacrificially, his "debts" to the various classes of beings in the universe. In Manu, however, as Madeleine Biardeau observes, "The new idea—which is added without replacing the old idea of 'debts'—is that the life of the householder implies an inevitable 'violence' with regard to living beings."[93] The householder, we are informed, has five "slaughterhouses" in the home: the hearth, the grinding stone, the broom, the mortar and pestle, and the water vessel. These five daily "bind" him with the sin of killing. It is, according to Manu, for the purpose of

91. It is likely that the similarity between the classification system in the ŚGS and that in Manu is not just coincidental. Ram Gopal, in "Manu's Indebtedness to Śānkhāyana," *Poona Orientalist* 27 (1962): 39–44, analyzes a number of parallel passages in the two texts and concludes that "the author of the Manu Smṛti who drew upon the Śānkhāyana Gṛhya Sūtra . . . was probably a follower of the Śānkhāyana Śākhā of the Ṛg Veda and not a follower of Maitrāyaṇīya Mānava Śākhā." The question of Manu's Vedic affliation, if any, remains controversial, however.

92. Manu 3.70, 3.73–74.

93. Biardeau, *Le Sacrifice dans l'Inde ancienne,* p. 42.

"redemption" (*niṣkṛtyartha*) that the five great sacrifices, the essence of the domestic ritual as a whole, are daily prescribed.[94]

"The main point of the religious activity of the Brahmins," writes Biardeau, "amounts to a system of expiations."[95] The domestic sacrifice is transformed—through its new guise as the five great sacrifices—from a small-scale resembling form of ritual activity conceived of as constructive activity to a defensive countermeasure against the "sin" of killing, of *hiṃsā* (perhaps under the influence of Buddhist and Jain valorizations of *ahiṃsā*).

With this new vision of the purpose of sacrifice, and with this new use of the old strategies of condensation and minimalism, we have perhaps crossed the invisible boundary that sets Vedic ritualism apart from its Hindu successors. Texts such as the Manu Smṛti present the domestic sacrifice as the quintessential sacrifice and the five great sacrifices as the quintessence of the domestic sacrifice, and they do so in order to domesticate the Vedic sacrifice and encompass it within a new religious configuration. Furthermore, the daily life of the domesticated householder takes on new meanings when it is no longer evaluated in relation to the being and praxis of the *āhitāgni,* the *śrauta* sacrificer. "The ideal image of the *yajña* is the superior *yajña,*" writes Charles Malamoud. "The domestic *yajña* ordinarily is a reduced and impoverished copy." But by epitomizing the domestic sacrifice by five "great" sacrifices, texts such as Manu's "present the copy as superior to the model."[96] Resemblance here, too, as in the proto-Vedāntic Upanishads, gives way to identity as the inferior substitute becomes, perhaps out of a certain necessity, the effective replacement.

Biardeau has argued that with the development of the meaning and practice of the five great sacrifices we are confronted with "un usage dérivé, symbolique" of the term *sacrifice* in Indian history, "une première extension de l'application du terme *yajña.*"[97] As will be seen in the next chapter, this was indeed only the beginning of the Hindu appropriation of the category of sacrifice, and it is in this manner, finally, that the real destiny of Vedic ritualism may be traced.

94. Manu 3.68–69.
95. Biardeau, *Le Sacrifice dans l'Inde ancienne,* p. 42.
96. Malamoud, *Le Svādhyāya,* p. 21.
97. Biardeau, *Le Sacrifice dans l'Inde ancienne,* p. 41.

8

The Destiny of Vedism

Vedism: Dead or Alive?

The Vedic sacrifice in post-Vedic India has been pronounced dead by Indologists often and early, too early. The pioneers of Western knowledge of the Vedic ritual—Hillebrandt, Lévi, Caland, and others—assumed their subject matter was speaking to them from the grave. Those experts regarded performances of Vedic sacrifices recorded in the nineteenth and early twentieth centuries as, at best, a kind of necrophiliac theater performed by Brahmins reading from a script.

Scholars more recently—C. G. Kashikar, Frits Staal, Frederick Smith, Asko Parpola, Michael Witzel, and David Knipe, to mention a few—have demonstrated that the *yajña* was relegated to a historical tomb a bit prematurely. To paraphrase Mark Twain's reply to the Associated Press, evidence of enclaves of Vedic ritualists in present-day India has proved that such reports of death are greatly exaggerated. Vedic rituals are in no sense popular or widespread in contemporary South Asia, but fieldwork data are now being accumulated which reveal a surprisingly large number of living traditions of Vedic ritualists throughout India.[1]

Too often, however, fieldwork on current performances and performers of Vedic *yajña*s has tended merely to repaint the death mask

1. See, e.g., C. G. Kashikar and Asko Parpola, "Śrauta Traditions in Recent Times," in Frits Staal, ed., *Agni: The Vedic Ritual of the Fire Altar,* 2 vols. (Berkeley: Asian Humanities Press, 1983), II: 199–251. Other reports from the field should be forthcoming shortly.

rather than strip it off. Contemporary exempla of Vedic ritualism have been too frequently presented as surviving fossils of the distant past, wholly irrelevant to the religions of India now—and to those of the past two millennia. The *yajña,* it is said with a certain commonsensical persuasiveness, is at most an antique relic for post-Vedic religions; when it is not simply ignored as a museum piece of no contemporary interest or usefulness, it is sadly misunderstood. The now world-famous Agnicayana held in Kerala in 1976 attracted crowds of South Indian Hindus who betrayed their ignorance of the ritual, at least in the eyes of the congregated foreign scholars taping and filming the event, by mistakenly perceiving the *yajña* as a strange kind of *pūjā.* They are reported to have come to the sacrifice

> in a spirit and mood of devotion. Among these outsiders [*sic!*] there was a strong tendency to conceive of the ritual enclosure as a kind of temple or place of pilgrimage, where devotees could receive "darshan" (a glimpse of a presiding deity), make a donation, perform a circumambulation, and return home with freshly acquired religious merit.[2]

The experts winced in embarrassment for the sad naiveté of Hindus who in this way so blatantly manifested their misperception of the "true meaning" of the Vedic sacrifice.

The *yajña,* it would seem, does not participate in what continuity there is in the three-thousand-year-old Vedic religious heritage. When Jan Gonda published his *Change and Continuity in Indian Religion,* he included chapters on *māyā,* the "Īśvāra idea," gift-giving, the guru, and even the number sixteen as exempla of continuity—but no chapter on sacrifice. Similarly, W. Norman Brown, in his quest for those cultural entities "which in each successive periodic reincarnation of the civilization [have] caused the new existence of the civilization," did not enumerate among them the ideology and practice of *yajña.*[3]

Sacrifice, as a fossilized archeological datum discrete from post-Vedic Hinduism, is also not found in those definitional statements on Hinduism examined in Chapter 1 which focus on certain pan-Hindu religious themes. As observed above in the discussion of various approaches to defining Hinduism, scholars of one school are persuaded that the unity of the religion is to be found in certain shared religious or

2. Frits Staal, "The Agnicayana Project," in Staal, *Agni,* II: 469.

3. W. Norman Brown, *Man in the Universe.* Similarly, Franklin Edgerton, in "Dominant Ideas in the Formation of Indian Culture," *Journal of the American Oriental Society* 62 (1942): 151–56, does not count *yajña* as such a "dominant idea."

philosophical themes. Some forms of this strategy for defining Hinduism identify the concepts of transmigration (*saṃsāra*), *karma,* and liberation from transmigration and *karma* (*mokṣa, mukti,* etc.) as definitive of the religion. Other versions of this type of the thematic approach to defining Hinduism explore "key concepts" such as *brahman* and *dharma* in addition to *saṃsāra, karma,* and *mokṣa.* In none of these sorts of attempts to define Hinduism thematically, however, does *yajña* figure in the array of definitional themes,[4] and the way the recently discovered continued existence of Vedic ritualism is being encoded (archaic, peripheralized, and ultimately irrelevant to Hinduism) will not convince anyone of its definitional importance to the configuration that is Hinduism. The Vedic sacrifice, despite its newly discovered ongoing existence in certain traditions of present-day India, is for all intents and purposes regarded by observers today—as it was by the scholars of the past—as a relic of the dead past.

In this concluding chapter, I present a short argument for the past and continued importance of *yajña* in India—and not just as a ritual performed by a few offbeat Brahmins. I will begin with evidence that *yajña* is indeed an entity that has transmigrated throughout the history of post-Vedic Indian religious discourse, in a variety of historical settings and divergent traditions. It has done so, in the first place, as a category of explication and, subsequently, as a category of traditionalization. It must be included, I will maintain, in any discussion of the possible "continuities" stretching over the millennia in Indic civilization. Secondly, sacrifice often plays a crucial role in the self-definition of Hindu religious institutions and practices as Hindu. It is perhaps one of only two such categories that can perform such a canonical function in Hindu religious life, the other being the category Veda.

My argument depends on viewing *yajña* in the history of post-Vedic Indian religions not so much as a ritual act or set of acts (the purpose of which might be constructive, expiatory, propitiary, purifying, cathartic, etc.) but rather as a *category that acts to provide explanatory power, traditional legitimacy, and canonical authority*.

It has been said that the essential function of sacrifice the world

4. One might partially exempt Madeleine Biardeau's *Le Sacrifice dans l'Inde,* which has as its thesis that sacrifice is "un tronc commun de l'hindouisme" (p. 13) and "que l'action rituelle, sans cesse répétée, est le modèle même de toute action, et que le sacrifice, mode de communication de la terre avec le ciel, en est le centre. Tout peut devenir sacrifice" (p. 153). Biardeau's claims for the continuity of sacrifice in Indian religious history differ from those presented here, however, and she is reluctant to go so far as to say that *yajña* is a definitional element of post-Vedic Hinduism.

over is to consecrate, to make sacred; and, indeed, the etymology of the word *sacrifice* testifies on behalf of this position (*sacer-facio,* "to make sacred"). Sacrifice, as a category in Indian religious thought, does indeed make sacred: it projects traditional and canonical meaning onto a potentially infinite set of human religious activities and doctrines, thereby consecrating and legitimizing them. One might say that the imaginary entity called the Indian mind often thinks with a sacrificial consciousness.[5]

Hindu Uses of the Vedic Sacrifice

Let us begin with a survey of history of *yajña* as an *explanatory category:* a mode of classification that renders phenomena explicable by connecting them to an already assimilated precedent. For Indian writers and thinkers from Vedic times to the present, *yajña* is, contrary to some Western opinions, in a real sense a datum or known quantity. It might appear from what follows that sacrifice functions as a metaphor in Indian religious discourse, but it could equally be said that from the Indian point of view other beliefs, actions, and phenomena are metaphors of the sacrifice. That is to say, it is quite as reasonable to regard the Vedic sacrifice as a model *for* understanding other phenomena as it is to assume that it is only a model *of* other phenomena.[6]

The projection of the sacrifice from its ritual confines onto various aspects of human life and of the world at large begins, of course, in the Veda itself. The theory of ritual in Vedic texts, as we have seen in Chapters 3 and 4, centers on the notion that sacrifice is not only the activities of the priests (the *adhiyajña* level of meaning) but is also the means for explaining the workings of the cosmos (the *adhidevatā* level of meaning, "relating to the macrocosmos") and the human self (the *adhyātman* level of meaning, "relating to the self, the microcosmos"). Sacrifice is thus the primary category of knowledge in both Vedic cosmology and Vedic anthropology, as is indicated in the frequently encountered phrase *puruṣo vai yajñaḥ,* "man [cosmic and human] is the sacrifice."

5. The phrase *sacrificial consciousness* I owe to my friend and colleague Holland Hendrix, who employs it in reference to the development of early Christian doctrine and practice.

6. *Model of* and *model for* are, of course, Clifford Geertz's terms for what he regards as the two principal functions of religion in cultural life: to provide both intellectually plausible and emotionally satisfying modes of living. Consult his "Religion as a Cultural System," in *The Interpretation of Cultures: Selected Essays by Clifford Geertz* (New York: Basic Books, 1973), pp. 87–125.

The sacrifice as an explicatory model for understanding the cosmos is dramatically exemplified in the well-known Puruṣa Sūkta, ṚV 10.90, in which the creation of the universe is represented as the primordial sacrifice and dismemberment of the Cosmic Man. This myth—as well as the related cosmogonic myths of Prajāpati's fragmentation of sacrificial reconstruction discussed in Chapter 3—provides a blueprint etched by the *yajña* for tracing the origins of the cosmos.

But it is the epistemological function of the Vedic sacrifice, in the cosmological mode, that interests us at this juncture. This function of the sacrifice serves to explain the cosmos in both its origins and its ongoing operations. These latter are also comprehended through application of the sacrificial paradigm, as the early Upanishad testifies:

> The world [of heaven] over there, Gautama, is a fire. The sun is its fuel, the rays of the sun are its smoke, the day is its flame, the moon its coals, the stars its sparks. Into this fire the gods offer faith, and from that oblation king Soma is born. The rain cloud, Gautama, is a fire. The wind is its fuel, the mist its smoke, lightning its flame, the thunderbolt its coals, and the roar of the thunder its sparks. Into this fire the gods offer king Soma, and from that oblation rain is born. The earth, Gautama, is a fire. The year is its fuel, space its smoke, night its flame, the four directions its coals, the four intermediate directions its sparks. Into this fire the gods offer of rain, and from that oblation food is born.[7]

Such a sacrificial comprehension of the workings of the cosmos often assumes a reciprocal arrangement among the cosmic forces, one sacrificing to another in order to keep the universe functioning in its regularity:

> The fire here [on earth] offers itself in the rising sun; the setting sun offers itself in the fire; the night also offers itself in day, and the day [offers itself] in night; the in-breath [offers itself] in the expiration, and the expiration [offers itself] in the in-breath. These six sacrifice themselves each in the other.[8]

Indeed, as the Śatapatha Brāhmaṇa puts it, "this all (*tat sarvaṃ*) participates in (*ābhakta*) the sacrifice,"[9] and "this all" is made explicable when conceived in such a manner.

The sacrificial arena as the model both of and for the organization of the cosmos persists long after the Vedic age has come to a close, providing us with examples of the post-Vedic exercise of the "sacrificial

7. ChU 5.4.1–5.6.2.
8. KB 2.8.
9. ŚB 3.6.2.26.

consciousness." The Buddhist *stūpa,* a cosmological mapping centered on a Cosmic Man of another sort, the Buddha, is made up of parts whose names are borrowed from the terminology of the Vedic sacrifice.[10] So, too, when Hindu temples appear in the middle of the first millennium C.E., dedicated to gods propelled to glory by the *bhakti* movement, they, too, patterned themselves on the plan of the Vedic sacrificial arena.[11] The Vedic sacrifice, as the Indian *ur*-model of the cosmos, thus is superimposed on post-Vedic worship centers and microcosms of both the Buddhist and Hindu varieties.

But it is at the level of *adhyātman,* making sense of the human self and human life, that the Vedic sacrifice most obviously and continually reappears throughout the history of Indian religions. The projection of the sacrifice onto the human *puruṣa* and his or her existence, the meaningful overlay of the concept of sacrifice onto human existence, also begins in the Veda itself. The human body is understood as a reduplication of the sacrificial arena, for at the microcosmic level, too, *puruṣo vai yajñaḥ:*

> Man, Gautama, is a fire. Speech is his fuel, breath his smoke, the tongue his flame, the eye his coals, the ear his sparks.[12]

Or again:

> The sacrificial site (*vedi*) is indeed his breast, the sacrificial grass is his hair. The *gārhapatya* fire is his heart, the *dakṣiṇa* fire is his mind, the *āhavanīya* fire is his mouth.[13]

The generation of human bodies depicted in sacrificial terms under this paradigm is envisioned as a process of sacrificial oblations of male seed into the "fire" that is woman. Into the "fire" that is man, the gods make an "offering of food," from which semen is produced. The semen, in turn, is poured into the woman to produce a new life. For not only is man depicted as a sacrifice, but "Woman, Gautama, is a sacrificial fire. The vagina is her fuel, foreplay her smoke, the womb her flame, the penetration her coals, and pleasure her sparks. Into this fire the gods

10. Consult L. A. Govinda, *Psycho-Cosmic Symbolism of the Buddhist Stūpa* (Emeryville, Calif.: Dharma Publishing, 1976).

11. See L. A. Ravi Varma, "Rituals of Worship," in Haridas Bhattacharya, ed., *The Cultural Heritage of India,* 4 vols. (Calcutta: Ramakrishna Mission Institute of Culture, 1956), IV:448; and esp. Stella Kramrisch, *The Hindu Temple,* 2 vols. (reprint ed., Delhi: Motilal Banarsidass, 1976), I: 1–17, 67–97, 139–44.

12. ChU 5.7.1.

13. ChU 5.18.2.

make an offering of semen, and from that oblation the embryo is born."[14]

The body's dissolution at death is likewise regarded in sacrificial terms in Vedic texts, a final and complete offering of the corpse into the cremation fire. Replicating the cosmogonic sacrificial dispersion of the body of Puruṣa/Prajāpati, the human body, too, is sacrificially disintegrated and reintegrated into the cosmos:

> The voice of the deceased enters the fire, his breath [enters] the wind, his eye the sun, his mind the moon, his ear the cardinal directions, his flesh the earth, his *ātman* the atmosphere, his body hair the plants, the hair on his head the trees, and his blood and semen are deposited in the waters.[15]

As Bruce Lincoln writes by way of summarizing this and other related Indo-European visions of death as sacrifice, "Like all sacrifice, death is a repetitive, ritual act. Each death repeats every other death and every other sacrifice: above all the first death, which was also the first sacrifice."[16]

When the new doctrine of rebirth first appears in the early Upanishads, it is not surprisingly cast in the mold that is the Vedic sacrifice. The earliest formulation of transmigration and the reincarnation of *ātman* explains the process of rebirth as a series of oblations in five fires, culminating in the oblation of male seed into the womb fire of the female:

> Thus in the fifth oblation, water comes to have a human voice. When the embryo has lain inside there for ten months or nine months, or however long, covered with the membrane, then he is born. When he is born, he lives as long as his allotted life-span. When he has died, they carry him to the appointed place and put him in the fire, for that is where he came from, what he was born from. . . . Those who worship in the village, concentrating on sacrifices and good works and charity, they are born into the smoke, and from the smoke into the night, and from the night into the other fortnight, and from the other fortnight into the six months when the sun moves south. They do not reach the year. From these months they go to the world of the fathers, and from the world of the fathers to space, and from space to the moon. That is king Soma. That is the food of the gods. The gods eat that. When they have dwelt there for as long as there is a remnant [of their merit], then they return along that very same road that they came along, back into space; but from space they go to wind, and when one has become wind he becomes smoke, and when he has become

14. ChU 5.8.1–2.
15. BĀU 3.2.13.
16. Bruce Lincoln, *Myth, Cosmos, and Society*, p. 127.

smoke he becomes mist; when he has become mist, he becomes a cloud, and when he has become a cloud, he rains. These are then born here as rice, barley, plants, trees, sesame plants, and beans. It is difficult to move forth out of this condition; but if someone eats him as food and then emits him as semen, he becomes that creature's semen and is born.[17]

And just as both the origins and the ongoing functions of the cosmos are represented in sacrificial tones in the Veda, so is the ongoing process of human life—in addition to the origins and ends of that life—depicted as a *yajña.* According to the Chandogya Upaniṣad, human existence is to be understood as a kind of soma sacrifice, with its three periods of youth, maturity, and old age corresponding to the three pressings in the morning, midday, and evening.[18]

The sacrificial paradigm is also applied in discussions of the critical moments of that sacrifice which is the life of humans. The "second birth" or initiation into Vedic society (*upanayana*), which was briefly analyzed in Chapter 4, is one of the few rituals of Vedism that persists more or less unchanged throughout the history of Vedism—and has always been represented as a sacrifice. As Jan Gonda has demonstrated, the *upanayana* is both conceived as and modeled on the initiation and consecration of the sacrificer, the *dīkṣā,* and initiation into the cult throughout the history of Indian religions, orthodox and heterodox alike, preserves and reduplicates this sacrificial origin.[19]

Upanayana also inaugurates the study of the Veda (*brahmacarya*) which is likewise understood as a kind of sacrifice. From the Śatapatha Brāhmaṇa we read that "He who enters upon *brahmacarya* enters into a long sacrificial session (*dīrgha-sattra*). The stick of fuel he places on the fire is the opening offering; and that [which he places on the fire] when he is about to bathe is the concluding offering; and what [sticks of fuel] there are [placed on the fire] between these, are his [offerings] of the sacrificial session."[20] A comparable passage has *brahmacarya,* through etymological machinations, as mysteriously a sacrifice:

What people call "sacrifice" (*yajña*) is really *brahmacarya,* for only through *brahmacarya* does he who is knower (*yo jñatā*) find that [knowl-

17. ChU 5.3.1–10, trans. in *Textual Sources for the Study of Hinduism,* ed. and trans. by Wendy O'Flaherty with Daniel Gold, David Haberman, and David Shulman (Manchester: Manchester University Press, 1989).

18. ChU 3.16–17.

19. Jan Gonda, *Change and Continuity,* pp. 315–462. See also Brian K. Smith, "Ritual, Knowledge, and Being," pp. 79–80.

20. ŚB 11.3.3.2.

edge]. And what people call a "sacrificial oblation" (*iṣṭa*) is really *brahmacarya,* for only after having searched (*iṣṭvā*) through *brahmacarya* does one find the *ātman.* And what people call the "protracted sacrificial session" (*sattrāyaṇa*) is really *brahmacarya,* for only through *brahmacarya* does one find the protection (*trāṇa*) of the real (*sat*) *ātman.*[21]

The various individual components of the life of the student are similarly comprehended in the language of the sacrifice. Alms which are begged by the pupil and brought to the teacher are regarded as "oblations" (*havis*) placed into the *āhavanīya* fire which is the mouth of the preceptor,[22] and the portion of the alms consumed by the student is called "the remnants of the sacrificial oblations" (*havirucchiṣṭha*).[23] Already in the Śatapatha Brāhmaṇa, the daily recitation of the Veda is regarded as a "sacrifice to the *brahman*" (*brahma-yajña*), one of the five "great sacrifices" (*mahāyajñas*) or "great sacrificial sessions" (*mahāsattras*)[24] that in the later Dharma Śāstras become the centerpiece of the daily religious life of post-Vedic Brahmanism. The *svādhyāya* or personal recitation of the Veda is equated with the actual performance of the Vedic ritual:

> Now for the sacrifice to the *brahman.* The sacrifice to the *brahman* is one's daily recitation of the Veda. Speech is the *juhū*-spoon of this sacrifice; mind is the *upabhṛt.* The eye is the *dhruvā,* intelligence the *sruva.* Truth is its concluding bath, the heavenly world its concluding rites.[25]

The conclusion of the period of Veda study is, as expected, homologized with the conclusion of the Vedic sacrifice: the gift to the teacher presented by the departing student is specifically termed a *dakṣiṇā* or sacrificial fee,[26] and the ceremonial bath at the end of *brahmacarya,* the *samāvartana,* recalls the concluding bath of the sacrifice (the *avabhṛtha*).

The notion that the accumulation of religious knowledge is a kind of sacrifice together with the conceptualization of human physiology in sacrificial terms combine to make possible the representation of world renunciation (in the Upanishads and other texts) as yet another version of the *yajña.* But the very act and subsequent life of renunciation—which includes renunciation of sacrifice, of ritual action or *karman*—is

21. ChU 8.5.1–2.

22. ĀpDhS 1.1.3.43–44; see also Manu 2.231. For teacher as sacrificial fire, see ĀpDhS 1.1.3.42; VāsDhS 7.5–6; GautDhS 3.6–8.

23. ĀpDhS 1.1.4.2–4.

24. ŚB 11.5.6.

25. ŚB 11.5.6.3; see also ŚB 11.5.6.4–9; BDhS 2.6.11.7; ĀpDhS 1.4.12.3; ĀśvGS 1.1.5.

26. ĀpDhS 1.2.7.19; JGS 1.12.

presented in the texts as a "higher" or "truer" sacrifice. The renouncer, or "sacrificer," "sacrifices only in himself (*ātmanneva yajati*),"[27] and such a sacrifice is envisioned by the monistic Upanishadic thinkers as a means to obtain mystical union in a pantheistic conception of that oneness: "His offering is made in all worlds, in all beings, in all selves."[28]

This identification of the life and physiology of the renouncer—who has resumed within himself the sacrificial fires which are then extinguished[29]—and the ritual of sacrifice creates homologies between all the functions of life and the functions of ritual. The consumption of daily meals becomes an *ātmayajña* or "sacrifice to and in the self."[30] Even the breathing of the renouncer is considered to be an "inner sacrifice" (*antara-agnihotra*) or "sacrifice to and in the life-breaths" (*prāṇā-agnihotra*):[31]

> After the *brahmādhāna* [the ritual in which the sacrificial fires are "interiorized" and life as a world renouncer is begun] the sacrificer himself [has within him] the sacrificial fires. The inhalation (*prāṇa*) is the *gārhapatya* fire, the exhalation (*apana*) is the *anvāhāryapacana* [the *dakṣiṇa*] fire, the circulation in the body (*vyāna*) is the *āhavanīya* fire, and the cerebral circulation (*samāna*) is the *sabhya* and *āvasathya* fires. These five fires are in the self (*ātman*). He offers in the self alone.[32]

In this way, every moment of the life of the world renouncer is regarded as sacrifice, every breath an "oblation," and life as a whole is considered a "continuous" and "uninterrupted" *yajña:*

> As long as a person is speaking, he is not able to breathe. Then he is sacrificing breath in speech. As long as a person is breathing, he is not able to speak. Then he is sacrificing speech in breath. These two are unending, immortal oblations; whether waking or sleeping one is sacrificing continuously, uninterruptedly.[33]

27. Maitri Upanishad 6.9.

28. ChU 5.24.2.

29. For the rite of the "interiorization" of the sacrificial fires, see, e.g., BDhS 2.10.17.19.

30. For the *ātmayajña,* see Ananda Coomaraswamy, "*Ātmayajña*"; and H. W. Bodewitz, *Jaiminīya Brāhmaṇa I, 1–65* (Leiden: E. J. Brill, 1973), pp. 213–18.

31. For the *prāṇāgnihotra,* see Bodewitz, *Jaiminiya Brāhmana;* J. Varenne, ed. and trans., *La Mahānārāyana Upaniṣad* (Paris: E. de Boccard, 1960), pp. 69ff.; and the following texts: ChU 5.19–24; BĀU 1.5.23; AitĀ 3.2.6; ŚānĀ 10; Kauṣītaki Upanishad 2.5; Maitri Upanishad 6.3; VaikhGS 2.18; BDhS 2.10.18.

32. BDhS 2.10.18.8.

33. Kauṣītaki Upanishad 2.5.

The taking of *sannyāsa* is, as Louis Dumont,[34], Patrick Olivelle,[35] and others have shown, a renunciation of the *yajña* itself; and, as claimed in Chapter 7, the Upanishadic monistic philosophy is in dramatic opposition to the principles of Vedic resemblance. But in most texts world renunciation is not presented as a renunciation of the *concept* of sacrifice; the category has simply been appropriated in order to extol the virtues of a very different set of beliefs and practices. The *ātma-yajñin,* the "sacrificer to the self," is indeed said to be superior to the *deva-yajñin,* "the sacrificer to the gods"[36]—but although his "sacrifice" may be better, it is still presented as a sacrifice.

In the Upanishads the *yajña* was transformed and redefined—but nevertheless preserved—as new religious practices—meditation, yoga, and contemplation on the ultimate nature of the self—were equated to it. Some scholars, seen in Chapter 7, argue that world renunciation represents an "orthogenetic, internal development of Vedic thought."[37] In the Upanishads there was, however, "a redefining of the place of sacrifice within the total religious scheme."[38] Or, as Heesterman rightly observes, "The question that occupies religious thought appears not to be: sacrifice or rejection of sacrifice, but rather what is the true sacrifice."[39]

The Upanishadic redefinition of the "true sacrifice" might be best seen not as the logical outcome of Vedic ritual thinking but rather as a valuable *objet trouvé* useful to assimilate the foreign to the traditional. Eliade has argued that the equating of practices such as *tapas* (ascetic austerity) and yoga—both of which he regards as extra-Āryan in origin—to the Vedic sacrifice allows for flexibility and change within the Brahmanic tradition:

> For *tapas,* too is a "sacrifice." If, in Vedic sacrifice, the gods are offered *soma,* melted butter, and the sacred fire, in the practice of asceticism they are offered an "inner sacrifice," in which physiological functions take the place of libations and ritual objects. . . . The concept of this "inner sacri-

34. Louis Dumont, "World Renunciation in Indian Religions," *Contributions to Indian Sociology* 4 (1960): 33–62; reprinted in *Religion/Politics and History in India: Collected Papers in Indian Sociology* (The Hague: Mouton, 1970), pp. 33–60.

35. Patrick Olivelle, "A Definition of World Renunciation," *Wiener Zeitschrift für die Kunde Südasiens* 19 (1975): 75–83; idem, "Odes of Renunciation," *Wiener Zeitschrift für die Kunde Südasiens* 20 (1976): 91–100.

36. Already in ŚB 11.2.6.13–14; see also BĀU 1.4.10.

37. Heesterman, "Brahmin, Ritual and Renouncer," p. 40.

38. Thomas B. Goman and Ronald S. Laura, "A Logical Treatment of Some Upaniṣadic Puzzles and Changing Conceptions of Sacrifice," *Numen* 19 (April 1972): 62.

39. Heesterman, "Brahmin, Ritual and Renouncer," p. 42.

fice" is a fertile one, which will permit even the most autonomous ascetics and mystics to remain within the fold of Brahmanism and later of Hinduism. . . . The practical consequence of homologization is substitution (which it justifies). Thus asceticism becomes equivalent to ritual, to Vedic sacrifice. Hence it is easy to understand how other yogic practices made their way into the Brahmanic tradition and were accepted by it.[40]

Regardless of whether the representation of the practices of world renouncers in sacrificial terms is interpreted by its scholars as the organic development of Vedic ritualism or as a strategy for incorporating within the orthodox tradition practices of extraneous origin, the function is the same: to conceptualize and articulate the new in terms of the old. The category of *yajña* thus serves to *explain the unknown* (its explicative function as a category); and, we might safely say, it also acts to *traditionalize the innovative.*

Sacrifice was, indeed, such a valuable category in the discourse of ancient India that even the ostensibly anti-Vedic heterodox traditions seemed compelled to argue that their religious practices, too, were sacrificial. By doing so, these anti-Vedic movements could simultaneously represent themselves as connected to the ancient Vedic practices and as superseding them. In the early Jaina and Buddhist Sūtras (which also sometimes simply dismiss the Vedic sacrifice as worthless and heinous), there are texts in which the issue is, as Heesterman has pointed out, What is the *true* sacrifice? The edifying Jaina story of Harikeśa,[41] an outcaste (*cāṇḍāla*) and a Jaina monk, has him approach a Vedic sacrificial site. The monk scrupulously reproaches the Brahmin priests, who are depicted as "stuck up by pride of birth, those killers of animals, who did not subdue their senses, the unchaste sinners." Harikeśa informs them that they are incorrectly performing the sacrifice: "You [use] *kuśa*-grass, sacrificial poles, straw and wood; you touch water in the evening and in the morning; thereby you injure living beings, and in your ignorance you commit sins again and again." The Vedic ritualists, portrayed here as being remarkably quick to admit the error of their ways, inquire of the Jain, "How should we sacrifice, o monk, and how avoid sinful actions?"

The answer, of course, is to take up the practices of the Jain monk: noninjury to living beings and renunciation of property, women, pride,

40. Mircea Eliade, *Yoga: Immortality and Freedom,* 2d ed., trans. by Willard R. Trask (Princeton, N.J.: Princeton University Press, 1969), pp. 111–12, 113.

41. H. Jacobi, trans., *Jaina Sūtras,* 2 vols. (Oxford: Clarendon Press, 1884–85; reprint ed. New York: Dover, 1968), II: 50–56.

and so on. The Brahmins then pose another question and receive a reply in which the "true" sacrifice is disclosed:

> "Where is your fire, your fireplace, your sacrificial ladle? Where is the dried cowdung [used as fuel]? Without these things, what kind of priests can the monks be? What oblations do you offer to the fire?" "Penance is my fire; life my fireplace; right exertion is my sacrificial ladle; the body the dried cowdung; *karman* is my fuel; self-control, right exertion, and tranquility are the oblations, praised by the sages, which I offer."

A similar tale is told in an early Buddhist text, the Kūṭadanta Sūtra,[42] in which the Buddha is cast as a Vedic priest attached to a king (a *purohīta*) in one of his previous lives. The Buddhist-Vedic priest instructs his patron in the proper mode of sacrifice, performed with appropriately Buddhist nonviolence (*ahiṃsā*):

> At that sacrifice neither were any oxen slain, neither goats, nor fowls, nor fatted pigs, nor were any kinds of living creatures put to death. No trees were cut down to be used as posts, no Dabha grasses mown to strew around the sacrificial spot. . . . With ghee, and oil, and butter, and milk, and honey, and sugar only was that sacrifice accomplished.

What follows in the text is a hierarchy of "sacrifices" even better than this bloodless one, each one "less troublesome, of greater fruit and of greater advantage" than the last. At the very top of the hierarchy, the highest "sacrifices" are the (very nonviolent) meditational practices of the Buddhist monk.

In these texts, the heterodox traditions unveil their new doctrines and religious activities in the guise of "higher" or "truer" forms of the Vedic ritual. The latter is made to appear as relatively ineffectual in comparison with newly revealed "sacrifices." But what is important for our purposes is the fact that even the heterodox religions found it expedient to call up the category of sacrifice as a hermeneutical device: new doctrines and practices were made understandable by being encoded in the already ancient and well-known vocabulary of sacrifice; and they were made to appear old but lost up until now.

By the time of the Bhagavad Gītā (ca. second century B.C.E. or later), a text that manifests a syncretistic and emerging Hindu orthodoxy, any number of traditional as well as heterogeneous and non-Vedic

42. Found in T. W. Rhys Davids, trans., *Dialogues of the Buddha,* 3 vols. (London: Pali Text Society, 1899; reprint ed. London: Routledge and Kegan Paul, 1973–77), I: 160–85.

practices are synthesized into Hindu religious life by identifying them with *yajña:*

> Some *yogins* offer only sacrifice to the gods; others offer the sacrifice with the sacrifice in the fire of *brahman.* Others offer the senses beginning with hearing in the fires of self-restraint; and others offer the objects of sense, beginning with sounds, in the fires of the senses. Others [offer] all acts of the senses and acts of the breaths in the fire, kindled by wisdom, of the yoga of self-restraint. Others [offer] material sacrifice, the sacrifice of austerities, or the sacrifice of yoga; and [others offer] sacrifices of Veda-recitation (*svādhāya*) and mystical knowledge (*jñāna*)—world renouncers whose vows are keen. Some offer the inhalation of breath in the exhalation of breath, and the exhalation of breath in the inhalation of breath, controlling them both, intent on breath-control. Others restrict their meals and offer the breaths in the breaths. All these are knowers of the sacrifice, their defilements erased by sacrifice.[43]

And with the Gītā we also witness a new extension of the category of sacrifice. Isolating and generalizing the component of the ritual called the *tyāga* (the "giving up" or "renunciation" of the offering), the Gītā teaches the doctrine of *karma-yoga* as sacrificially oriented everyday action whereby "all attachment and all the fruits [of action] are renounced."[44] For, the text says, "this world is bound by the bonds of *karma* except where that action is done sacrificially."[45]

In other texts more or less contemporaneous with the Gītā (as well as in the Gītā itself), this conception of sacrifice is also used to redeem the function of kings and warriors whose professions otherwise contravene the newly emergent Hindu doctrine of *ahiṃsā:*[46] "A king who protects [all] beings through *dharma,* and who executes those sentenced, daily sacrifices with sacrifices having thousands of sacrificial fees."[47] The Mahābhārata as a whole, as Alf Hiltebeitel among others has shown,

43. Bhagavad Gītā 4.25–30.

44. Bhagavad Gītā 18.6.

45. Bhagavad Gītā 3.9.

46. A comparable example of this phenomenon—applying the category of "sacrifice" to a practice that might otherwise be judged abhorrent and in opposition to religious principles—is the custom of widow-burning or *satī.* See, e.g., Śiva Purāṇa 2.2.7.4–6, where Sandhyā enters the sacrificial fire as an act of *satī:* "Her body itself became the *puroḍāśa* [the sacrificial cake] in that sacrifice." My thanks to Paul Courtright for this reference.

47. Manu 8.306; see also Manu 5.93, where a king is compared with those engaged in an extended sacrificial session.

presents war as a "sacrifice of battle":[48] "He obtains the world of heroes who offers up in battle his own body as an oblation."[49] Sacrifice, in cases such as these, is called upon to reconcile conflicting Hindu doctrines (*ahiṃsā* and the necessity for kings and warriors to fulfill their duties) through reformulating the new problem as an old answer.

In yet another move that will have great consequences for the subsequent development of devotionalistic Hinduism, the Gītā introduces the new teaching of *bhakti* in the guise of the reinterpreted "true sacrifice":

> A leaf, or a flower, or a cup of water that a pious soul may offer Me with *bhakti,* that do I accept, for it was *bhakti* that made the offering. Whatever you do, whatever you eat, whatever you offer or give away, whatever austerity you may perform, consign it to Me. You will be liberated from those bonds which *karma* creates, whose fruits are good and bad. Your *ātman* yoked by renunciation and yoga, fully liberated, you will come to Me.[50]

In later texts of Hindu sectarian and devotionalistic traditions, sacrifice continues to be a leitmotif long after it has ceased to be performed by anyone other than the occasional king (seeking Vedic legitimacy) or Brahmins stuck in the backwaters of South Asia. The ritual of *pūjā* to the image of Viṣṇu, Śiva, the Goddess, or one of their avatars simultaneously replaces the *yajña* while it incorporates within itself many rites from the Vedic sacrifice. The *smārta* Hindu *pūjā* ritual structure encompasses within it Vedic rites of the fire sacrifice (mostly at the *gṛhya* level) but makes them subservient to more recent principal rites of service to the image. Vedic ritualism, recapitulated in its most compact form now functions as merely a subsidiary rite within a ritual oriented around a different center and purpose.[51]

Already in the Mahābhārata,[52] Kṛṣṇa is said "to be" the sacrifice, just as Viṣṇu was even in Vedic texts. The image of Viṣṇu, in a Hindu Pañcarātra Vaiṣṇava text, is equated with the Vedic sacrifice—the parts

48. *Raṇayajña,* e.g., Mbh 5.57.12; 5.154.4 See Alf Hiltebeitel, *The Ritual of Battle: Krishna in the Mahābhārata* (Ithaca, N.Y.: Cornell University Press, 1976). For one of the books of the Mahābhārata as "a coherent whole structured from beginning to end by the entire Rājasūya," see pp. 95–101; and J. A. B. van Buitenen, "On the Structure of the Sabhāparvan of the Mahābhārata," in J. Ensink and P. Gaeffke, eds., *India Maior: Congratulatory Volume Presented to J. Gonda* (Leiden: E. J. Brill, 1972), pp. 68–84.

49. Mbh 18.1.14.

50. Bhagavad Gītā 9.26–28.

51. See T. Goudriaan, "Vaikhānasa Daily Worship," *Indo-Iranian Journal* 12 (1970): 161–215.

52. E.g., Mbh 3.13.44, 14.70.20.

of the body identified with the components of the ritual—and the worship of the image (*pūjā*) is said to procure for the devotee "the fruits of a hundred sacrifices."[53] In a Śaivite text, the Śivadharma, we read that "the ritual greeting [to the image of Śiva, *namaskāra*] is superior to all sacrifices, and having made the ritual greeting to Mahādeva he obtains the fruit of a horse sacrifice."[54]

Certain Hindu texts do indeed "have as their sole object," as wrote A. Barth, "to teach a sort of cult at a discount, procuring the same fruits as the great sacrifices."[55] Or, as Kamaleswar Bhattacharya observes, "the rewards that the Vedic ritualists aimed for can now be obtained at a smaller expense."[56] In these cases, the Vedic sacrifice provides later Hinduism with a kind of standard of worth by which non-Vedic religious practices might be gauged. In the Mahābhārata,[57] to cite another example of this frequently encountered phenomenon, the rewards of visiting various Hindu pilgrimage spots are couched in terms of the old sacrificial system. The mere appearance at one or another *tirtha* wins for the pilgrim "the fruit of a soma sacrifice" or "the fruit of a horse sacrifice." Results which once entailed great expense and painstaking labor, and which were in all likelihood available only to the religious, political, and economic élite, are now easily obtainable by all thanks to the full equation of the later version of the original. In this way, the new and relatively simple religious practices of Hindu worship are said to resume in themselves the power of the most complex Vedic sacrifices, just as certain domestic rites came to contain the essence of the *mahāyajñas*. And identification of the simple and the complex puts the former in a better light: why bother to undertake massive and obsolete sacrificial endeavors when their "fruits" can be efficiently (and economically) obtained through new and improved techniques?

But the purpose of shrouding new Hindu practices in sacrificial clothing is not simply to prove the superiority of the new to the old, but first and foremost to present the new *as* the old. Sacrifice has functioned

53. Ahirbudhnya Saṃhitā, chap. 37, cited in Kamaleswar Bhattacharya, "Le 'Védisme' de certains texts hindouistes," *Journal asiatique* 225 (1967): 200–201.

54. Cited in ibid., p. 211. Compare a much earlier text, the ĀśvGS (1.1.5), in which, after a discourse in which *śraddhā* ("faith") is extolled as the true sacrifice, the passage ends by quoting an (unspecified) Brāhmaṇa by way of equating sacrifice and *namaskāra* (*yajño vai namaḥ iti hi brāhmaṇa*).

55. A. Barth, *Les Religions de l'Inde: Extrait de l'Encyclopédie des sciences religieuses* (Paris: G. Fischbacher, 1879), p. 60.

56. Bhattacharya, "Le 'Védisme' de certains texts hindouistes,' p. 211.

57. Mbh 3.80–83.

throughout Indian religious history as a marker for traditionalism and as a means for acceptable innovation. The very radical movement of Tantricism, too, does not neglect to codify its practices in orthodox sacrificial terminology. The partaking of the five "forbidden" (to the orthodox, that is) substances is represented in Tantric texts as oblations to various deities located within the body of the practitioner.[58]

Sacrifice thus serves as a stake for traditionalism and as a means for acceptable innovation within the boundaries of orthodoxy, and the strategy of reforming by appeal to the category of *yajña* is still at work in the modern period in India. Tagore preached his secularized humanism in a dramatic vehicle entitled "Sacrifice,"[59] and Gandhi's redefinition of *yajña* in light of his own philosophy summarizes a process that has been at work throughout Indian religious history—the search to find a "deeper" and new meaning in the archaic Vedic concept:

> [Y]*ajña* has a deeper meaning than the offering of ghee and other things in the sacrificial fire. *Yajña* is sacrifice of one's all for the good of humanity, and to me these offerings of *āhutis* have a symbolic meaning. We have to offer up our weaknesses, our passions, our narrowness into the purifying fire, so that we may be cleansed.[60]

Yajña as a Canonical Category

Enough has been said here to indicate that the Vedic sacrifice is indeed a candidate for inclusion in the repertoire of entities constitutive of the Indic cultural and religious continuity. In all times and in the most diverse traditions comprising the Indic religious configuration, the concept of sacrifice has been an old skin into which new wine is poured.

But the deployment of the category of *yajña* is also a means to make Hinduism Vedic; and to make something Vedic in Hinduism, as argued above in Chapter 1, is to make it canonical and orthodox. It is in this sense that the Vedic sacrifice in Hinduism might be regarded as one mode of defining Hindus; it is because of the integral connection be-

58. See Agehananda Bharati, *The Tantric Tradition* (New York: Samuel Weiser, 1975), pp. 260–62.

59. Rabindranath Tagore, "Sacrifice," in *A Tagore Reader,* ed. by Amiya Chakravarty (Boston: Beacon Press, 1966), pp. 125–48.

60. Mohandas Gandhi, *In Search of the Supreme,* comp. and ed. by V. B. Kher (Ahmedabad: Navajivan Publishing House, 1961), p. 276.

tween *yajña* and Veda that sacrifice might be called a *canonical category* in Hinduism.

Hindus, also as already seen in Chapter 1, appear to use only the "outside" of the Veda, oblivious to what is "inside." And what is the subject matter found inside the covers of the Veda? The mantras, rules (*vidhis*), and explanations (*arthavādas*) of the Vedic sacrifice. The paradox of Hindu orthodoxy defined as adherence to the canonical authority of the Veda which is not understood reduplicates the paradox of Hindu practices presented in the guise of the Vedic sacrifice which is, by and large, no longer performed.

The Hindu use of the Veda to claim orthodox authority for post-Vedic texts and the Hindu representation of post-Vedic practices as *yajña*s thus appear as two aspects of the same phenomenon. Sacrifice is perhaps the only category in Hindu discourse that reduplicates the possibilities of the category of Veda.[61] When Hindus represent post-Vedic practices as "sacrifices," or equivalent to sacrifices, or as new forms of sacrifice, they appear to be doing the same thing—and for the same ends—as representing post-Vedic texts in various ways as "Veda." Veda as canon and sacrifice as a canonical category are touchstones to orthodoxy in the Hindu religion.

In both cases, however, the paradox that concerns scholars of Hinduism arises only when the Veda is regarded as a set of ancient texts and the *yajña* as a set of ancient ritual acts. If, on the other hand, we envision both Veda and *yajña* as categories for creating orthodoxy, the Hindu preoccupation with them ceases to be so mysterious. Hinduism might then be considered a *process* of innovation through traditionalization and canonization, and with perhaps more than one "unchanging" point of reference by which one *returns* in order to progress within the boundaries of Hinduism.

Both the Veda and the sacrifice have been represented by Indologists as irrelevant and misunderstood by Hindus—the ancient scripture because it is unread and the ancient ritual because it is unperformed and "meaningless." One conclusion we might draw from this study is that Hinduism could very well have inherited more from the ancient Vedic religion than just the outside of an unread Veda and an empty shell of the Vedic sacrifice. What I would like to suggest as we terminate this projection into the ideology and practice of Vedic ritualism is what I suggested in the opening chapter: what we have termed the "strategies

61. "Brahmin" is possibly the only other category with the same persistence and centrality for the tradition. See J. C. Heesterman, "Brahmin, Ritual and Renouncer"; and esp. Jan Gonda, *Notes on Brahman* (Utrecht: J. L. Beyers, 1950).

of orthodoxy" in post-Vedic Hinduism are indeed Vedic in origin. Put succinctly, the necessary obsession to constitute as "derivative" Hindu texts, practices, and institutions, and to connect them to Vedic originals (this text is really the Veda, this practice is really a sacrifice, etc.) is itself a Vedic mode of thought.

Inside the pages of the Veda, in the interior of the ideology and practice of Vedic ritualism, one finds—in never-ending abundance—connections, or *bandhus,* linking components of various planes of reality to one another. The Vedic sacrifice is the workship for forging such *bandhus,* and one principal type of connection links manifest counterparts to their transcendent prototypes. The Vedic ritual device of connecting, for example, the three fires with the three worlds is replicated in Hindu strategies for orthodoxy—such as connecting a well-known Purāṇa and an unread Veda, or an oft-performed *pūjā* and a neglected fire sacrifice.

The metaphysics of the Veda are set forth in terms of forms (*rūpas*) and counterforms (*pratirūpas*), prototypes (*pramā*s) and counterparts (*pratimā*s), and the organization of the ritual structure itself reduplicates this metaphysics. In the *paribhāṣā sūtra*s, the ritual system is depicted as a set of paradigmatic models (*prakṛti*s) and derivative variants (*vikṛti*s). And the epistemological program of Vedic thought, we recall, is nicely summed up at ṚV 10.130.3: "What was the prototype, what was the counterpart, and what was the connection between them?"

This Vedic quest for linkages between archetypes and resembling manifestations of the archetypes seems to hold the key to understanding the strategies for orthodoxy observed in Hinduism. The Veda and the sacrifice function as categorical prototypes for all subsequent texts, practices, and institutions. These latter are represented as counterparts through the forging of connections—*bandhu*s or *nidānas*—back to the Veda, back to the *yajña,* back to Vedic ritualism. The significance of the Veda and the Vedic sacrifice for subsequent Hindu thought and praxis might in this manner be traced to the Veda itself. Hindus think about the Veda in ways that seem reduplicative of Vedic thought; and Hindus use the canonical category of sacrifice in ways that might be interpreted as "sacrificial" in the original Vedic sense: as a connective, constructive activity. The principles and philosophy of Vedic ritualism, which I have tried to represent in this book, seem to have survived Vedism and become the instruments for creating and transforming orthodoxy in Hinduism. Vedic connections are, in sum, the very means by which Hinduism is connected to Vedism.[62]

62. In his conclusion to *The Ritual of Battle,* Hiltebeitel makes much the same argument: "The epic poets would thus emerge not so much as programmers, transposing

Conclusion

"Analogies," wrote Sigmund Freud, "it is true, decide nothing, but they can make one feel more at home."[63] Domesticating the chaos of the unknown by categorizing it, classifying it, and making it *conform* altogether to the familiar—this is, I think, an adequate description of the work of religion, and of the work of those who study it. The method I have called, in the Vedic context, resemblance (and what Freud and others call analogy, or homology, or a system of ideal connections) appears to be a very effective way by which both the religieux and their observers make themselves at home.

Religion is an exercise of the creative power of the imagination. Religion is one of the most persuasive attempts, with its claims to absolute and eternal truth, to empower illusions with living reality; it is one of the ways in which humans have made meaningful a world in which meaning always must be imposed and overlaid. Human beings are generally encountered here taking responsibility for the entire cosmos about them, just as the ancient Vedic Brahmins did within their ritual. They are *making sense* of it—and this is what might be called the *art of transformation,* the "making and finding" epistemological step common to all who desire to live in a comprehensible world.

In Vedic ritualism, to a degree not always seen, the guidelines for constructing categorical connections (analogies, homologies, etc.) were explicitly formulated and, in the ritual itself, set into motion and activated. Here the art of transforming the unknown into an instance of the already known, transforming the unique and disconnected into a member of a class, followed the articulated rules of the Vedic brand of hierarchical resemblance.

Locating all reality between the poles of unitary identity and wholly differentiated individuality, the ritualists posited a series of models which made possible knowable particulars: prototypes accumulated their resembling counterparts; counterforms of forms were made and found; paradigms organized the elements of the whole into categorized

one set of information into another form, but as *ṛṣis,* in this case the *ṛṣis* of the 'Fifth Veda' whose school is covered by the name of the elusive but ever-available *ṛṣi* Vyāsa. By calling attention to this term for visionaries and poets, I refer in particular to the *ṛṣis* faculty of 'seeing connections,' 'equivalences,' 'homologies,' and 'correspondences.' This faculty of 'seeing connections' would have involved the epic poet, not only with correlations between myth and epic, but also between epic and ritual—especially that of the Brāhmaṇic sacrifice. Thus the 'mythic exegesis' must coexist with a 'ritual exegesis' " (pp. 359–60).

63. Sigmund Freud, *New Introductory Lectures on Psychoanalysis,* trans. and ed. by James Strachey (New York: W. W. Norton, 1965), p. 72.

variants. Resemblance between a set of particulars and the archetypical, and the hierarchical differentiation of the particulars into more and less complete realizations of the archetype, provided an epistemological tool that could be reapplied to any number of situations. The universe at large, this world and its inhabitants, the other worlds and their denizens, representations of ritual practice, and the ritual practice itself and those who participated in it—all were systematically organized with this transformative methodology.

Resemblance made possible a system of connections which, as we have seen, was never confused within Vedic ritualism with a system of identities. Connections were forged horizontally between analogues in different hierarchical registers (between the various social classes and particular animals or food, for example); and they were made between higher and lower elements within the same hierarchical order (between prototypes and counterparts and between the counterparts themselves).

In this latter type of connection, the vertically directed bondings between superior and inferior forms, we have also observed two different types of strategies, both utilizing synecdoche whereby a part stands for the whole. First, there was what I have called an "upward condensation," whereby the lower is encompassed within the higher (e.g., the essences of the lesser sacrificial victims or rituals are subsumed within the hierarchically superior forms). But, secondly, there was also the possibility of making vertical connections between the superior and the inferior in such a way that the essence of the higher is reprised within the lower: a "downward condensation" or synecdochic reduction that could easily be, and has been in the past, confused with true equivalency and full replacement. Apparent homologies between the higher and the lower were not meant, within Vedism, to overturn the hierarchical order of things but rather to strengthen the relations among the elements within the hierarchical order. As stated above, "equations" in this system were not intended to *collapse distinctions* but rather to *strengthen connections* among interrelated elements on a vertically oriented, and hierarchically calibrated, scale.

Nor were these "mere ideas," if there are such beasts. The overweening preoccupation of the ancient Indians with ritual led to belief that these ideas could be and were put into effect. The Vedic ritualists attempted to *realize* their epistemological constructs by ritually constructing the universe, heavens, this world, and society; a metaphysics was produced through the ritual activation of an epistemology. Human beings were likewise ritually constituted, in various forms and hierarchically gauged realizations of form, both in this life and in the projected afterlife. An ontology was thus also a product of the ritual activation of the epistemology of hierarchical resemblance.

But Vedic religion, far from being a *mysterium tremendum* created by different minds a long time ago and far away, appears (and perhaps *only* appears, perhaps *must* appear, and perhaps *should* appear) to us to be a variation of a familiar human phenomenon. Their connections between prototypes and counterparts, forms and counterforms, paradigms and variants, are, at the very least, resembling versions of the categories we deploy and the instances of them we then discover in the course of the study of religion (among other disciplines within the modern academy). We, too, as an epistemological necessity, imagine ideal (and, one might say, prototypical) categories ("religion," "myth," "ritual," "Vedism," "Hinduism," and so on) in order to organize a world of otherwise chaotic particulars (or "counterparts"). The process of transforming the disconnected and sui generis into instances of the general categories ("the Hindu *religion,*" "the *myth* of the Cosmic Man," "the *ritual* or *sacrifice* which is *yajña*") is not at all dissimilar from the Vedic system of connections or *bandhus.* To acknowledge these kinds of resemblances is to begin to engender a truly humanistic sense of commonality (which is not, of course, simple identity), which could help overturn previous assumptions—conscious and unconscious—of radical difference between the objects and subjects of study.

Moreover, the process of knowing also involves the process of *learning,* of reimagining the categories and what is imagined to be contained within them. This is what we might label the ongoing *reformational work* which complements and perpetually corrects the *transformational art* of discovery. Here, too, we have encountered interesting—and comparable—reflections of the study of religion in the religious data reflected upon in this work.

There is little doubt that over the course of the many centuries during which the Vedic ritualists were composing the texts they have left us, they, too, were adjusting the nature of their prototypes, forms, and paradigms as they rethought the counterparts, counterforms, and variants that could be connected to them. But such historical manifestations of reformational work are more clearly visible when we observe the relationships established between later Hinduism and its Vedic forebear. The orthodox offspring of Vedism, in their appropriation and reworking of their ancestor, display quite plainly the activity of reforming the old in light of the new.

Hindu doctrine and practice are presented as the already asserted, the already believed, the already done. Hinduism was (and continues to be) presented, in other words, as Vedism or neo-Vedism—and in either case as a faithful rendition of the established prototype. The authoritative texts of the various Hindu sects are associated, in one way or another, with the prototype of all authoritative texts of the tradition: the Veda. While claiming to have discovered, in the process of exercising the transformational art, a new (and supposedly better) version of the old, Hindus have, from the outsider's point of view, been engaged in the reformational work of revising the category in light of new particulars in need of connection. The particulars, in this case, are the ever-changing detritus of history: new teachings on the nature of the universe, the place of human beings in it, the praxis of a powerful and effective life, the ideals of perfection. And they, by being assimilated into the "unchanging" ("It is in the Veda"), provoke a revision in what the Veda *was* in light of what it *has become.* The Veda, indeed, may be among the most rethought and reworked items in the orthodox Hindu tradition.

Another Indian archetype that might, however, at least compete on this score is the Vedic *yajña,* "sacrifice." I noted above that *yajña,* like the Veda which first describes it, persists in the imagination of Hindus (and others), and for many of the same reasons—not because of what *yajña* and Veda once were but because of what they continually can be. Hindus have *worked* with these categories, they have engaged their creativity *through* them, because they have not abandoned them. These categories have been continually reinfused with the prestige of the archaic and the fundamental and are thus preserved. Sacrifice no less than Veda has been a rubric which has made possible the creation of new instances of it—because it has not ceased to be viable as a classificatory tool. The work of reformation, it would seem, always presupposes a certain illusion that some categories don't change.

Such an illusion, necessary for maintaining the continuity and orthodoxy of religious traditions, is not one that is appropriately reduplicated in scholarship about those traditions, however.

The theory that Vedic ritual—or any other—is without meaning (or has "intrinsic meaning," or is "transcendent" of historical and human meaning and reality) simply reenlivens an essentially religious conception which is protected from discussion, disputation, and interpretation. Indeed—so it is maintained, at any rate—discussion, disputation, and interpretation are precisely what the Vedic ritual sought to eliminate as it supposedly became purposeless and without meaning outside itself. While this may or may not be true for the Vedic ritualists (and I have tried in this work to present evidence that it is not), it is disingenuous for historians of religion to reposition such notions as scholarly conclusions.

Any thesis for the "meaninglessness" of any human creation, as I have stated above, is a meaningful interpretation of a previously improperly understood phenomenon—and thus is itself a paradox that cries for a solution. Ironically, what appears to some philologically trained Indologists as meaningless—and therefore denied a purpose and a history—cannot be other than meaningful, and for more reasons than one.

In the first place, to designate a set of actions as *yajña,* sacrifice, ritual, or anything else, is to give them meaning they otherwise do not have. Of course, these actions have no intrinsic meaning—*nothing* has intrinsic meaning. So much is obvious (and hardly cause for a new and improved theory of ritual). Meaning is always imposed on "naturally" meaningless phenomena—this is what human beings do, and must do, or face chaos and insanity. Humans abhor meaninglessness in much the same way as nature abhors a vacuum.

Secondly, once a set of actions has been transformed into a meaningful entity by virtue of concepts such as *yajña,* sacrifice, ritual, and so on, the set and the individual acts within the whole serve as signifiers for any number of other signifieds. The *yajña,* for example, can signify the cosmos, and individual activities within the ritual can signify various cosmic phenomena.

That the meaning given to both the concept of *yajña* and the individual acts subsumed under the concept can and does change is also obvious. The "meaninglessness of ritual" school ignores the competing and shifting meanings of *yajña* while making a mountain out of the molehill which is the fact that there is no intrinsic and changeless meaning in the term, in the actions the term makes meaningful, or in what those actions then come to signify.

For these reasons, the Vedic ritual, *yajña,* was never meaningless and is not meaningless for those who write (meaningful) scholarly articles and books about it. It was understood in different ways by different people even in Vedic times and remained open to *new* interpretations and *new* meanings in post-Vedic Hinduism (and in the study of Vedism itself). The "transcendence" or privileged place of the Vedic sacrifice did not, in fact, imply its eternal "meaninglessness" but rather its infinite possibilities for meaning.

What cannot be ignored, however, is the fact that there is an unbridgeable discrepancy between the claims of the religious and the historical sensibilities that the scholar cannot suspend. Religion, and not just Vedic or Hindu religion, might be regarded as—among other things, need it be said—a perpetual denial of the fact that the unchanging ideals it imagines are unrealizable (that, e.g., Hindu texts, beliefs, and practices are eternally faithful to Vedic texts, beliefs, and practices). But, unless we are willing to imagine humans vastly different in their commonsensical recognition of reality when they see it, religion must also be conceived of as the perpetual reminder to the all-too-human practitioners of it that their imagined ideals *are* unrealizable in a real world of change and imperfection. It is this very fundamental—and ultimately intractable—incongruity in religious belief and practice that religions seek to overcome, in vain. Religion is a never-ending search for *reconciliation* between the real and the ideal; it is a continual attempt to coordinate the two.

In addition to the *transformational art* of religion (and now, I might add, religion as both the academic subject and object of study) and the *reformational work* of religion (again, in both senses of *religion*), one might also speak of a *coordinative value* of religion. By way of conclusion, we might now reflect on whether and in what ways religion as an object—exemplified here by Vedism and Hinduism—might reveal something about this aspect of the subject of religion within the academy.

There is a certain sense in which what I have called Vedic resemblance might just as well be labeled coordination. The system of *bandhus*—linking macrocosm, sacrifice, and microcosm (*adhidevatā, adhiyajña,* and *adhyātman*)—was a strategy to *co-order* the planes of reality (or, from our point of view, the planes of the real and the ideal) and place them in a relation of mutual resemblance (Chapter 3). Other reapplications of the philosophy of Vedic ritualism and resemblance had much the same end. The organization of human beings (Chapter 4); the organization of the ritual repertoire in the *paribhāṣā* sections of the Śrauta Sūtras (Chapter 5); the organization of Vedic ritualists (Chapter 6) and ritual practice (Chapter 7); as well as the organization of orthodox Hinduism (Chapters 1 and 8)—all these exempla of Vedism in action reveal the same impulse to reflection, reduplication, or, if you will, coordination.

But it was not, in any of these instances, an *egalitarian* set of interrelations and transformations. Vedism (and Hinduism insofar as it inherited certain definite and possibly defining features of Vedism) is a system based not only on mutual resemblance but on *hierarchically calibrated distinctions*. It is, in other words, a system based on judgments of better and worse, more and less complete, higher and lower realization of form. And the hierarchical yardstick was unfailingly applied to human beings—the most obvious, and too often heinous, ramification being the Indian caste system. In India, resemblance was posited not only on difference (which is the necessary precondition for making connections) but on differences differently valued.

On the other hand, egalitarianism does have one ubiquitous incarnation in India, but it is one that seems to destroy rather than to democratize the system of resemblances. Vedāntic philosophy, in nuce in certain ancient Upanishads and in full bloom in the *darśana* that carries it through Hinduism, pushes Vedic-Hindu resemblance, based on hierarchical distinctions, into identity based on egalitarianism. The Vedic-Hindu world is reconstituted by Vedānta into a false world of *māyā,* and the truth of unity is attained only at the price of the *denial* of its applicability in human life within society. Egalitarianism, in India, has almost always entailed renunciation or *saṃnyāsa.*[64]

I have attempted in this book as a whole to reimagine Vedism and Hinduism in a way that highlights the similarities between the object studied and the subject who studies; to underline the points of resemblance while not confusing them with identities; to rethink the assumed differences without denying all difference; to make a product of the human imagination there and then, and a product of the human imagination here and now, reflect each other. Whether one can do so in an egalitarian mode, without ceding the right to make hierarchical value judgments, is, one might say, the dominant and as yet unsolved problem that plagues all humanistic studies in our age.

64. See Dumont's important essay, "World Renunciation in Indian Religions."

Bibliography

Sanskrit Texts and Translations

Ritual Literature

Āgniveśya Gṛhya Sūtra. Ed. by L. A. Ravi Varma. Trivandrum Sanskrit Series, no. 144. Trivandrum: University of Travancore, 1940.

Aitareya Āraṇyaka. Ed. and trans. by A. B. Keith. Oxford: Clarendon Press, 1909; reprint Oxford: Oxford University Press, 1969.

Aitareya Brāhmaṇa. 2 vols. Ānandāśrama-saṃskṛta-granthāvaliḥ, granthānkḥa 32. Poona: Ānandāśrama, 1931.

———. 2 vols. Ed. and trans. by M. Haug. Bombay: Government Central Book Depot, 1863.

———. Trans. by A. B. Keith. In *Rigveda Brāhmaṇas,* Harvard Oriental Series, Vol. 25. Cambridge: Harvard University Press, 1920; reprint Delhi: Motilal Banarsidass, 1971.

Aitareya Upaniṣad. Ed. by V. P. Limaye and R. D. Vadekar. In *Eighteen Principal Upaniṣads.* Poona: Vaidika Saṃśodhana Maṇḍala, 1958.

———. Trans. by Robert Hume. In *The Thirteen Principal Upanishads,* 2d ed. Oxford: Oxford University Press, 1931.

Āpastamba Dharma Sūtra. Ed. by U. C. Pandeya. Kashi Sanskrit Series, no. 93. Varanasi: Chowkhamba Sanskrit Series Office, 1969.

———. Trans. by Georg Bühler. In *The Sacred Books of the Āryas.* Sacred Books of the East, Vol. 2. Oxford: Clarendon Press, 1879; reprint Delhi: Motilal Banarsidass, 1965.

Āpastamba Gṛhya Sūtra. Ed. by U. C. Pandey. Kashi Sanskrit Series, no. 59. Varanasi: Chowkhamba Sanskrit Series Office, 1971.

———. Trans. by Hermann Oldenberg. In *The Grihya Sūtras.* Sacred Books of the East, Vol. 30. Oxford: Oxford University Press, 1886; reprint Delhi: Motilal Banarsidass, 1964.

Āpastamba Śrauta Sūtra. 3 vols. Ed. by R. Garbe. Calcutta: Royal Asiatic Society of Bengal, 1882–1902.

———. 3 vols. Trans. into German by W. Caland. Calcutta: Vandenhoeck and Ruprecht, 1921; reprint Wiesbaden: Dr. Martin Sändig, 1969.

Āśvalayana Gṛhya Sūtra. Ed. and trans. by N. N. Sharma. Delhi: Eastern Book Linkers, 1976.

———. Trans. by Hermann Oldenberg. In *The Grihya Sūtras.* Sacred Books of the East, Vol. 29. Oxford: Oxford University Press, 1886; reprint Delhi: Motilal Banarsidass, 1964.

Āśvalāyana Śrauta Sūtra. Ed. by R. Vidyaratna. Calcutta: Asiatic Society of Bengal, 1874.

———. Incomplete trans. by H. G. Ranade. Poona: R. H. Ranade, 1981.

Atharva Veda Saṃhitā. 4 vols. Ed. by V. Bandhu. Hoshiarpur: Vishveshvaranand Vedic Research Institute, 1960–62.

———. 2 vols. Trans. by W. D. Whitney. Harvard Oriental Series, Vols. 7 and 8. Cambridge: Harvard University Press, 1905; reprint Delhi: Motilal Banarsidass, 1962.

Atri Smṛti. Ed. by Manmatha Nath Dutt. In *The Dharma Śāstra Texts.* Calcutta: M. N. Dutt, 1908.

Baudhāyana Dharma Sūtra. Ed. by U. C. Pandeya. Kashi Sanskrit Series, no. 104. Varanasi: Chowkhamba Sanskrit Series Office, 1972.

———. Trans. by Georg Bühler. In *The Sacred Books of the Āryas.* Sacred Books of the East, Vol. 14. Oxford: Clarendon Press, 1879; reprint Delhi: Motilal Banarsidass, 1965.

Baudhāyana Gṛhya Sūtra and Paribhāṣā Sūtra. Ed. by R. Shama Sastri. Mysore: Government Branch Press, 1920; reprint New Delhi: Meharchand Lachhmandas, 1982.

Baudhāyana Śrauta Sūtra. 3 vols. Ed. by W. Caland. Calcutta: Asiatic Society of Bengal, 1904–24; reprint New Delhi: Munshiram Manoharlal, 1982.

Bhāradvāja Gṛhya Sūtra. Ed. by H. J. W. Salomons. Leyden: E. J. Brill, 1913; reprint Delhi: Meharchand Lachhmandas, 1981.

Bhāradvāja Śrauta Sūtra. 2 vols. Ed. and trans. by C. G. Kashikar. Poona: Vaidika Saṃśodhana Maṇḍala, 1964.

Bṛhadāraṇyaka Upaniṣad. Ed. by V. P. Limaye and R. D. Vadekar. In *Eighteen Principal Upaniṣads.* Poona: Vaidika Saṃśodhana Maṇḍala, 1958.

———. Trans. by Robert Hume. In *The Thirteen Principal Upanishads,* 2d ed. Oxford: Oxford University Press, 1931.

Chandogya Upaniṣad. Ed. by V. P. Limaye and R. D. Vadekar. In *Eighteen Principal Upaniṣads.* Poona: Vaidika Saṃśodhana Maṇḍala, 1958.

———. Trans. by Robert Hume. In *The Thirteen Principal Upanishads,* 2d ed. Oxford: Oxford University Press, 1931.

Drāhyāyana Gṛhya Sūtra. Ed. by T. U. N. Singh. Muzaffarpur: Shastra Publishing House, 1934.

Gautama Dharma Sūtra. Ed. by Manmatha Nath Dutt. In *The Dharma Śāstra Texts.* Calcutta: M. N. Dutt, 1908.

———. Trans. by Georg Bühler. In *The Sacred Books of the Āryas.* Sacred Books of the East, Vol. 14. Oxford: Clarendon Press, 1879; reprint Delhi: Motilal Banarsidass, 1965.

Gobhila Gṛhya Sūtra. Ed. by Chintamani Bhattacharya. Calcutta: Metropolitan Printing and Publishing House, 1936.

———. Trans. by Hermann Oldenberg. In *The Grihya Sūtras*. Sacred Books of the East, Vol. 30. Oxford: Oxford University Press, 1886; reprint. Delhi: Motilal Banarsidass, 1964.

Gobhilaputra Gṛhyasaṃgrahapariśiṣṭa. Ed. and trans. into German by Maurice Bloomfield. Leipzig: G. Kreysing, 1881.

Gopatha Brāhmaṇa. Ed. by R. Mitra and H. Vidyabhusana. Calcutta: Bibliotheca Indica, 1872; reprint Delhi: Indological Book House, 1972.

Hiraṇyakeśin Gṛhya Sūtra. Trans. by Hermann Oldenberg. In *The Grihya Sūtras*. Sacred Books of the East, Vol. 30. Oxford: Oxford University Press, 1886; reprint Delhi: Motilal Banarsidass, 1964.

Hiraṇyakeśin Śrauta Sūtra and Gṛhya Sūtra. 10 vols. Ed. by K. Agase and S. Marulakara. Poona: Ānandāśrama, 1907–32.

Jaiminīya Brāhmaṇa. Ed. by R. Vira and L. Chandra. Nagpur: Sarasvati Vihara Series, 1954.

———. Incomplete trans. by H. W. Bodewitz. In *Jaiminīya Brāhmaṇa I: 1–65*. Leiden: E. J. Brill, 1973.

———. Incomplete trans. into German by W. Caland. Amsterdam: Johannes Müller, 1919; reprint Wiesbaden: Dr. Martin Sändig, 1970.

Jaiminīya Gṛhya Sūtra. Ed. and trans. by W. Caland. Punjab Sanskrit Series, no. 2. Lahore: Moti Lal Banarsi Dass, 1922; reprint Delhi: Motilal Banarsidass, 1984.

Jaiminīya Śrauta Sūtra. Included in *Jaiminīya-Śrauta-Sūtra-Vṛtti of Bhavatrāta*. Ed. by Premnidhi Shastri. Śata-Piṭaka Series, Vol. 40. New Delhi: International Academy of Indian Culture, 1966.

Jaiminīya Upaniṣad Brāhmaṇa. Ed. and trans. by Hanns Oertel. *Journal of the American Oriental Society* 16 (1896): 79–260.

Jaiminīyanyāyamāla of Mādhva. Ānandāśrama Sanskrit Series, Vol. 24. Poona: Ānandāśrama, 1892.

Kaṭha Upaniṣad. Ed. by V. P. Limaye and R. D. Vadekar. In *Eighteen Principal Upaniṣads*. Poona: Vaidika Saṃśodhana Maṇḍala, 1958.

———. Trans. by Robert Hume. In *The Thirteen Principal Upanishads,* 2d ed. Oxford: Oxford University Press, 1931.

Kāṭhaka Gṛhya Sūtra. Ed. by W. Caland. Lahore: Research Depts., D.A.V. College, 1925.

Kāṭhaka Saṃhitā. Ed. by V. Santavalekar. Bombay: Bhāratamudraṇālayam, 1943.

Kātyāyana Śrauta Sūtra. Ed. by Albrecht Weber. Chowkhamba Sanskrit Series, no. 104. Reprint Varanasi: Chowkhamba Sanskrit Series Office, 1972.

———. Trans. by H. G. Ranade. Pune: Dr. H. G. Ranade and R. H. Ranade, n.d.

Kauṣītaki Brāhmaṇa. Ed. by H. Bhattacharya. Calcutta Sanskrit College Research Series, no. 73. Calcutta: Sanskrit College, 1970.

———. Trans. by A. B. Keith. In *Rigveda Brāhmaṇas*. Harvard Oriental Series, Vol. 25. Cambridge: Harvard University Press, 1920; reprint Delhi: Motilal Banarsidass, 1971.

Kauṣītaki Upaniṣad. Ed. by V. P. Limaye and R. D. Vadekar. In *Eighteen Principal Upaniṣads*. Poona: Vaidika Saṃśodhana Maṇḍala, 1958.

———. Trans. by Robert Hume. In *The Thirteen Principal Upanishads,* 2d ed. Oxford: Oxford University Press, 1931.

Khādira Gṛhya Sūtra. Ed. by A. M. Sastri and L. Srinivasacharya. Mysore: Government Branch Press, 1913.

———. Trans. by Hermann Oldenberg. In *The Grihya Sūtras*. Sacred Books of the East, Vol. 29. Oxford: Oxford University Press, 1886; reprint Delhi: Motilal Banarsidass, 1964.

Lāṭyāyana Śrauta Sūtra. Ed. by Anandachandra Vedantavagisa. Calcutta: Asiatic Society of Bengal, 1972.

Maitrāyaṇī Saṃhitā. 4 vols. Ed. by L. von Schroeder. Leipzig: F. A. Brockhaus, 1883–86; reprint Wiesbaden: Franz Steiner Verlag, 1970–72.

Maitrāyaṇī Upaniṣad. Ed. by V. P. Limaye and R. D. Vadekar. In *Eighteen Principal Upaniṣads*. Poona: Vaidika Saṃśodhana Maṇḍala, 1958.

———. Trans. by Robert Hume. In *The Thirteen Principal Upanishads,* 2d ed. Oxford: Oxford University Press, 1931.

Maitri Upaniṣad. Ed. by V. P. Limaye and R. D. Vadekar. In *Eighteen Principal Upaniṣads*. Poona: Vaidika Saṃśodhana Maṇḍala, 1958.

———. Trans. by Robert Hume. In *The Thirteen Principal Upanishads,* 2d ed. Oxford: Oxford University Press, 1931.

Mānava Gṛhya Sūtra. Ed. by R. H. Shastri. Reprint Delhi: Meharchand Lacchmandas, 1982.

———. Trans. by M. J. Dresden. Groningen: J. B. Wolters Uitgevers, 1941.

Mānava Śrauta Sūtra. Ed. and trans. by J. M. van Geldner. Śata-Piṭaka Series, Vol. 27. New Delhi: International Academy of Indian Culture, 1963.

Manu Smṛti. 5 vols. Ed. by J. H. Dave. Bhāratīya Vidyā Series. Bombay: Bhāratīya Vidyā Bhavan, 1972–82.

———. Trans. by Georg Bühler. Sacred Books of the East, Vol. 25. Oxford: Clarendon Press, 1886; reprint New York: Dover Publications, 1969.

Muṇḍaka Upaniṣad. Ed. by V. P. Limaye and R. D. Vadekar. In *Eighteen Principal Upaniṣads*. Poona: Vaidika Saṃśodhana Maṇḍala, 1958.

———. Trans. by Robert Hume. In *The Thirteen Principal Upanishads,* 2d ed. Oxford: Oxford University Press, 1931.

Pañcaviṃśa Brāhmaṇa. 2 vols. Ed. by P. A. Cinnaswami Sastri and P. Pattabhirama Sastri. Kashi Sanskrit Series, no. 105. Benares: Sanskrit Series Office, 1935.

———. Trans. by W. Caland. Bibliotheca Indica, no. 255. Calcutta: Asiatic Society of Bengal, 1931.

Parāśara Smṛti. Ed. by Manmatha Nath Dutt. In *The Dharma Śāstra Texts*. Calcutta: M. N. Dutt, 1908.

Pāraskāra Gṛhya Sūtra. Ed. by M. G. Bakre. Bombay: Gujrati Printing Press, 1917; reprint Delhi: Meharchand Lachhmandas, 1982.

———. Trans. by Hermann Oldenberg. In *The Grihya Sūtras*. Sacred Books of the East, Vol. 29. Oxford: Oxford University Press, 1886; reprint Delhi: Motilal Banarsidass, 1964.

Purvamīmāṃsā Sūtras of Jaimini. 2 vols. Ed. and trans. by Mohan Lal Sandal. In *Mīmāṃsā Sūtras of Jaimini*. Reprint Delhi: Motilal Banarsidass, 1980.

Ṛg Veda Saṃhitā. 4 vols. Ed. by F. Max Müller. Chowkhamba Sanskrit Series, Vol. 99. Reprint Varanasi: Chowkhamba Sanskrit Series Office, 1966.

———. 4 vols. Trans. into German by Karl Friedrich Geldner. Harvard Oriental Series, Vols. 33–36. Cambridge, Mass.: Harvard University Press, 1951–57.

———. Partial trans. by Wendy Doniger O'Flaherty. New York: Penguin Books, 1981.

Ṣaḍviṃśa Brāhmaṇa. Ed. by B. R. Sharma. Kendriya Sanskrit Vidyapeetha Series, no. 9. Tirupati: Kendriya Sanskrit Vidyapeetha, 1967.

———. Trans. by W. B. Bolle. Utrecht: Drukkerij A. Storm, 1956.

Śānkhāyana Gṛhya Sūtra. Ed. and trans. by S. R. Sehgal. Delhi: Munshiram Manoharlal, 1960.

———. Trans. by Hermann Oldenberg. In *The Grihya Sūtras*. Sacred Books of the East, Vol. 29. Oxford: Oxford University Press, 1886; reprint Delhi: Motilal Banarsidass, 1964.

Śānkhāyana Śrauta Sūtra. 2 vols. Ed. by A. Hillebrandt. Reprint New Delhi: Meharchand Lachhmandas, 1981.

———. Trans. by W. Caland. Nagpur: International Academy of Indian Literature, 1953; reprint Delhi: Motilal Banarsidass, 1980.

Śatapatha Brāhmaṇa. 5 vols. Bombay: Laxmi Venkateshwar Steam Press, 1940.

———. 5 vols. Trans. by Julius Eggeling. Sacred Books of the East, Vols. 12, 26, 41, 43, 44. Oxford: Clarendon Press, 1882–1900; reprint Delhi: Motilal Banarsidass, 1963.

Taittirīya Āraṇyaka. 2 vols. Ānandāśrama-saṃskṛta-granthāvaliḥ, granthānkha 36. Poona: Ānandāśrama, 1981.

Taittirīya Brāhmaṇa. 3 vols. Ānandāśrama-saṃskṛta-granthāvaliḥ, granthānkha 37. Poona: Ānandāśrama, 1979.

———. Partial trans. by P.-E. Dumont. In *Proceedings of the American Philosophical Society* 92, 95, 98, 101, 107, 108, 109, 113.

Taittirīya Saṃhitā. 8 vols. Ānandāśrama-saṃskṛta-granthāvaliḥ, granthānkha 42. Poona: Ānandāśrama, 1978.

———. 2 vols. Trans. by A. B. Keith. Harvard Oriental Series, Vol. 18 and 19. Cambridge, Mass.: Harvard University Press, 1914; reprint Delhi: Motilal Banarsidass, 1967.

Taittirīya Upaniṣad. Ed. by V. P. Limaye and R. D. Vadekar. In *Eighteen Principal Upaniṣads*. Poona: Vaidika Saṃśodhana Maṇḍala, 1958.

———. Trans. by Robert Hume. In *The Thirteen Principal Upanishads,* 2d ed. Oxford: Oxford University Press, 1931.
Tantravārttika of Kumārila Bhaṭṭa. Ed. and trans. by G. Jha. Calcutta: Bibliotheca Indica, 1924.
Vaikhānasa Gṛhya Sūtra. Ed. by W. Caland. Bibliotheca Indica, no. 242. Calcutta: Asiatic Society of Bengal, 1927.
———. Trans. by W. Caland. Bibliotheca Indica, no. 251. Calcutta: Asiatic Society of Bengal, 1929.
Vaikhānasa Śrauta Sūtra. Ed. by W. Caland. Bibliotheca Indica, no. 265. Calcutta: Royal Asiatic Society of Bengal, 1941.
Vārāha Gṛhya Sūtra. Ed. and trans. into French by Pierre Rolland. Aix-en-Provence: Publications universitaires de lettres et sciences humaines, 1971.
Vārāha Śrauta Sūtra. Ed. by W. Caland and R. Vira. Reprint Delhi: Meharchand Lachhmandas, 1971.
Vāsiṣṭha Dharma Sūtra. Ed. by Manmatha Nath Dutt. In *The Dharma Śāstra Texts.* Calcutta: M. N. Dutt, 1908.
———. Trans. by Georg Bühler. In *The Sacred Books of the Āryas.* Sacred Books of the East, Vol. 14. Oxford: Clarendon Press, 1879; reprint Delhi: Motilal Banarsidass, 1965.
Vedānta Sūtras. With commentaries of Śankarācārya and Rāmānuja. Trans. by George Thibaut. Sacred Books of the East, Vols. 34, 38, 48. Oxford: Oxford University Press, 1904; reprint Delhi: Motilal Banarsidass, 1962.
Yājñvalkya Smṛti, 2d ed. Ed. by Mahamahopadhyaya T. Ganapati Sastri. New Delhi: Munshiram Manoharlal, 1982.

Other Texts and Collections

Ācārya, Rāma Śarmā, ed. *Matsya Purāṇa.* Bareli: Saṃskṛti Saṃsthāna, 1970.
Bühler, Georg, trans. *Sacred Laws of the Āryas.* 2 vols. Sacred Books of the East, Vols. 2 and 14. Oxford: Clarendon Press, 1879–82; reprint Delhi: Motilal Banarsidass, 1965.
Dandekar, R. N., ed. *Śrautakośa: Encyclopedia of Vedic Sacrificial Ritual.* 2 vols. Poona: Vaidika Saṃśodhana Maṇḍala, 1958–82.
Datta, Bhagavad, ed. *Nirukta Śāstram.* Amritsar: Ramalal Kapur Nikshepa Trust, 1965.
Dutt, Manmatha Nath, ed. *The Dharma Śāstra Texts.* Calcutta: M. N. Dutt, 1908.
Ghosh, B., ed. *Collection of the Fragments of Lost Brāhmaṇas.* Calcutta: Modern Publishing Syndicate, 1935; reprint Delhi: Meharchand Lachhmandas, 1982.
Gupta, Sri Anand Swarup, ed. *The Kūrma Purāṇa.* Varanasi: All-India Kashi Raj Trust, 1972.

———. *The Vāmana Purāṇa*. Varanasi: All-India Kashi Raj Trust, 1968.

Hume, Robert Ernest, trans. *The Thirteen Principal Upanishads,* 2d ed. Oxford: Oxford University Press, 1931.

Jacobi, H., trans. *Jaina Sūtras*. 2 vols. Sacred Books of the East, Vols. 22 and 45. Oxford: Clarendon Press, 1884–85; reprint New York: Dover Publications, 1968.

Limaye, V. P., and R. D. Vadekar, eds. *Eighteen Principal Upaniṣads*. Poona: Vaidika Saṃśodhana Maṇḍala, 1958.

Oldenberg, Hermann, trans. *The Grihya Sūtras*. 2 vols. Sacred Books of the East, Vols. 29 and 30. Oxford: Oxford University Press, 1886; reprint Delhi: Motilal Banarsidass, 1964.

Rhys Davids, T. W., trans. *Dialogues of the Buddha*. 3 vols. Sacred Books of the Buddhists, Vols. 2–4. London: Pali Text Society, 1899; reprint London: Routledge and Kegan Paul, 1973–77.

Śāstri, Pandit Hṛishikeśa, ed. *The Vārāha Purāṇa,* 2d ed. Varanasi: Chaukhamba Amarabharati Prakashan, 1982.

Shastri, J. L., ed. *Brahmavaivarta Purāṇa*. 2 vols. Delhi: Motilal Banarsidass, 1984.

———. *Linga Purāṇa*. Delhi: Motilal Banarsidass, 1980.

———. *Bhāgavata Purāṇa*. Delhi: Motilal Banarsidass, 1983.

———. *Brahmāṇḍa Purāṇa*. Delhi: Motilal Banarsidass, 1973.

Sukthankar, Vishnu S., ed. *The Mahābhārata*. 19 vols. Poona: Bhandarkar Oriental Research Institute, 1933–60.

Van Buitenen, J. A. B., ed. and trans. *The Mahābhārata*. 3 vols. Chicago: University of Chicago Press, 1973–78.

Zaehner, R. C., trans. *The Bhagavad Gītā*. New York: Oxford University Press, 1969.

Secondary Sources (Indological)

Abhyankar, K. V. "On *paribhāṣā* Works in Sanskrit Grammar." *Annals of the Bhandarkar Oriental Research Institute* 36 (1955): 157–62.

Apte, V. M. *Social and Religious Life in the Gṛhyasūtras*. Ahmedabad: V. M. Apte, 1939.

Aquilar, H. *The Sacrifice in the Ṛgveda*. Delhi: Bharatiya Vidya Prakashan, 1976.

Banerjea, A. C. *Studies in the Brāhmaṇas*. New Delhi: Motilal Banarsidass, 1963.

Banerjee, Santi. "Prajāpati in the Brāhmaṇas." *Vishveshvaranand Indological Journal* 19 (June–December 1981): 14–19.

Barnett, L. D. *Hinduism*. London: Constable, 1913.

Barth, Auguste. *Les Religions de l'Inde: Extrait de l'Encyclopédie des sciences religieuses*. Paris: G. Fischbacher, 1879.

Barua, B. M. "Art as Defined in the Brāhmaṇas." *Indian Culture* 1 (July 1934–April 1935): 118–20.

Basu, J. *India in the Age of the Brāhmaṇas.* Calcutta: Sanskrit Pustak Bhandar, 1969.

Bedekar, D. K. "The Revelatory Character of Indian Epistemology." *Annals of the Bhandarkar Research Institute* 29 (1948): 64–84.

Bergaigne, Abel. *Recherches sur l'histoire de la liturgie védique.* Paris: Imprimerie nationale, 1889.

———. *La Religion védique d'après les hymnes du Rig-Veda.* 3 vols. Paris: F. Vieweg, 1878–83.

Bhankarkar, Ramakrishna Gopal. "The Veda in India." *Indian Antiquary* 3 (May 1874): 132–35.

Bharati, Agehandana. "The Hindu Renaissance and Its Apologetic Patterns." *Journal of Asian Studies* 29 (February 1970): 267–88.

———. *The Tantric Tradition.* New York: Samuel Weiser, 1975.

Bhargava, P. L. *India in the Vedic Age: A History of Aryan Expansion in India,* 2d ed. Aminabad: Upper India Publishing House, 1971.

Bhattacharji, S. "Rise of Prajāpati in the Brāhmaṇas." *Annals of the Bhandarkar Oriental Research Institute* 64 (1983): 205–13.

Bhattacharya, D. "Cosmogony and Rituo-Philosophical Integrity in the Atharvaveda." *Vishveshvaranand Indological Journal* 15 (March 1977): 1–12.

Bhattacharya, Jogendra Nath. *Hindu Castes and Sects.* Calcutta: Editions Indian, 1968.

Bhattacharya, Kamaleswar. "Le 'Védisme' de certains texts hindouistes." *Journal asiatique* 225 (1967): 199–222.

Bhattacharya, V. C. "On the Justification of *rūpasamṛddha ṛk-* Verses in the Aitareya Brāhmaṇa." *Our Heritage* 4 (1956): 99–106, 227–37; 5 (1957): 119–46.

Bhide, V. V. *The Cāturmāsya Sacrifices.* Pune: University of Poona, 1979.

Biardeau, Madeleine. "L'Inde et l'histoire." *Revue historique* 234 (1965): 47–58.

Biardeau, Madeleine, and Charles Malamoud. *Le Sacrifice dans l'Inde ancienne.* Bibliothèque de l'École des Hautes Études, Sciences religieuses, vol. 79. Paris: Presses Universitaires de France, 1976.

Biswas, S. "Über das Vrātyaproblem in der vedischen Ritual-literatur." *Zeitschrift der Deutschen Morgenländischen Gesellschaft* 105 (1955): 53–54.

Bloomfield, Maurice. *The Atharva-Veda and the Gopatha Brāhmaṇa.* Strassburg: Karl J. Trübner, 1899; reprint New Delhi: Asian Publication Services, 1978.

———. *The Religion of the Veda.* New York: G. P. Putnam's Sons, 1908.

Bodewitz, H. W. *The Daily Evening and Morning Offering (Agnihotra) according to the Brāhmaṇas.* Leiden: E. J. Brill, 1976.

Bonazzoli, Giorgio. "The Dynamic Canon of the Purāṇas." *Purāṇa* 26 (July 1979): 116–66.

Bouquet, A. C. *Hinduism.* London: Hutchinson's University Library, 1948.

Brown, Cheever Mackenzie. *God as Mother: A Feminine Theology in India.* Hartford, Vt.: Claude Stark, 1974.

———. "Purāṇa as Scripture: From Sound to Image of the Holy Word in the Hindu Tradition." *History of Religions* 26 (1986): 68–86.

Brown, G. W. *The Human Body in the Upanishads.* Jubbulpore: Christian Mission Press, 1921.

Brown, W. Norman. "The Creation Myth of the Ṛg Veda." *Journal of the American Oriental Society* 62 (1942): 85–98.

———. *Man in the Universe: Some Cultural Continuities in Indian Thought.* Berkeley: University of California Press, 1970.

———. "The Sources and Nature of Puruṣa in the Puruṣa Sūkta." *Journal of the American Oriental Society* 51 (1931): 108–18.

———. "Theories of Creation in the Ṛg Veda." *Journal of the American Oriental Society* 85 (1965): 23–34.

Caland, Wilhelm. *Die Altindischen Todten- und Bestattungs-gebräuche.* Amsterdam: Müller, 1896; reprint Wiesbaden: Martin Sändig, 1967.

———. *Altindischer Ahenenkult: Das Śrāddha nach den verschiedene Schulen mit benutzund handschriftliche quellen dargestellt.* Leiden: E. J. Brill, 1893.

———. "On the Relative Chronology of Some Ritualistic Sūtras." *Acta Orientalia* 9 (1931): 69–76.

———. *Über das rituelle Sūtra des Baudhāyana.* Abhandlungen für die Kunde des Morgenländes herausgegeben von der Deutschen Morganländischen Gesellschaft, Vol. 12, no. 1. Leipzig: F. A. Brockhaus, 1903.

Caland, Wilhelm, and V. Henry. *L'Agniṣṭoma: Description complete de la forme normale du sacrifice de Soma dans le cult védique.* 2 vols. Paris: Ernest Leroux, 1906.

Chakrabarti, S. C. *The Paribhāṣās in the Śrautasūtras.* Calcutta: Sanskrit Pustak Bhandar, 1980.

Chakrabarti, S. K. "On the Transition of the Vedic Sacrificial Lore." *Indo-Iranian Journal* 21 (1979): 181–88.

Chatterjee, H. N. *Studies in Some Aspects of Hindu Saṃskāras in Ancient India.* Calcutta: Sanskrit Pustak Bhandar, 1965.

Chauduri, Nirad C. *The Continent of Circe.* Bombay: Jaico Publishing House, 1965.

Choudhary, Radhakrishna. *Vrātyas in Ancient India.* Chowkhamba Sanskrit Studies, Vol. 38. Benares: Chowkhamba Sanskrit Series Office, 1964.

Coburn, Thomas B. *Devī Māhātmya: The Crystallization of the Goddess Tradition.* Columbia, Mo.: South Asia Books, 1985.

———. " 'Scripture' in India: Towards a Typology of the Word in Hindu Life." *Journal of the American Academy of Religion* 52 (September 1984): 435–59.

———. "The Study of the Purāṇas and the Study of Religion." *Religious Studies* 16 (1980): 341–52.

Coomaraswamy, Ananda K. "Ātmayajña: Self-Sacrifice." *Harvard Journal of Asiatic Studies* 6 (1941): 358–88.

———. "Vedic Exemplarism." *Harvard Journal of Asiatic Studies* 1 (1936): 44–64.

Das, Veena. "Language of Sacrifice." *Man* (new series) 18 (September 1983): 445–62.

Derrett, J. D. M. *Religion, Law and the State in India.* London: Faber and Faber, 1958.

Deussen, Paul. *Philosophy of the Upanishads.* Trans. by A. S. Geden. New York: Dover Publications, 1966.

Devasthali, G. V. *Religion and Mythology of the Brāhmaṇas.* Poona: University of Poona, 1965.

Dimock, Edward C. *The Place of the Hidden Moon.* Chicago: University of Chicago Press, 1966.

Dimock, Edward C., Edwin Gerow, C. M. Naim, A. K. Ramanujan, Gordon Roadarmel, and J. A. B. van Buitenen. *The Literatures of India: An Introduction.* Chicago: University of Chicago Press, 1974.

Drury, Naama. *The Sacrificial Ritual in the Śatapatha Brāhmaṇa.* Delhi: Motilal Banarsidass, 1981.

Dumont, Louis. *La Civilisation indienne et nous.* Paris: Armand Colin, 1975.

———. *Homo Hierarchicus: The Caste System and Its Implications,* complete rev. English ed. Trans. by Mark Saisbury, Louis Dumont, and Basia Gulati. Chicago: University of Chicago Press, 1980.

———. *Religion/Politics and History in India: Collected Papers in Indian Sociology.* The Hague: Mouton Publishers, 1970.

———. "World Renunciation in Indian Religions." *Contributions to Indian Sociology* 4 (1960): 33–62. Reprinted in *Religion/Politics and History in India: Collected Papers in Indian Sociology.* The Hague: Mouton Publishers, 1970, pp. 33–60.

Dumont, P.-E. *L'Agnihotra: Description de l'agnihotra dans le rituel védique d'après les Śrautasūtras.* Baltimore: Johns Hopkins University Press, 1939.

———. "The Agnihotra (or Fire-God Oblation) in the Taittirīya-Brāhmaṇa: The First Prapāṭhaka of the Second Kāṇḍa of the Taittirīya-Brāhmaṇa with Translation." *Proceedings of the American Philosophical Society* 108 (1964): 337–53.

———. "The Animal Sacrifices in the Taittirīya-Brāhmaṇa: The Part of the Hotar and the Part of the Maitrāvaruṇa in the Animal Sacrifice." *Proceedings of the American Philosophical Society* 107 (1962): 246–63.

———. *L'Aśvamedha: Description du sacrifice solennel du cheval dans le culte védique d'après les textes du Yajurveda blanc.* Paris: P. Geuthner, 1927.

———. "The Full-moon and New-moon Sacrifices in the Taittirīya-Brāhmaṇa." *Proceedings of the American Philosophical Society* 101 (1957): 216–43; 103 (1959): 584–608; 104 (1960): 1–10.

———. "The Horse-Sacrifice in the Taittirīya-Brāhmaṇa: The Eighth and Ninth Prapāṭhakas of the Third Kāṇḍa of the Taittirīya-Brāhmaṇa with Translation." *Proceedings of the American Philosophical Society* 92 (1948): 447–503.

———. "The Human Sacrifice in the Taittirīya-Brāhmaṇa: The Fourth Prapāṭhaka of the Third Kāṇḍa of the Taittirīya-Brāhmaṇa with Translation." *Proceedings of the American Philosophical Society* 107 (1963): 177–82.

———. "The Iṣṭis to the Nakṣatras (or Oblations to the Lunar Mansions) in the Taittirīya-Brāhmaṇa with Translation." *Proceedings of the American Philosophical Society* 98 (1954): 204–23.

———. "The Kāmya Animal Sacrifices in the Taittirīya-Brāhmaṇa: The Eighth Prapāṭhaka of the Third Kāṇḍa of the Taittirīya-Brāhmaṇa with Translation." *Proceedings of the American Philosophical Society* 113 (1969): 34–66.

———. "The Kaukilī-Sautrāmanī in the Taittirīya-Brāhmaṇa: The Sixth Prapāṭhaka of the Second Kāṇḍa of the Taittirīya-Brāhmaṇa with Translation." *Proceedings of the American Philosophical Society* 109 (1965): 309–41.

———. "The Special Kinds of Agnicayana (or Special Methods of Building the Fire-Altar) according to the Kaṭhas in the Taittirīya Brāhmaṇa: The Tenth, Eleventh, and Twelfth Prapāṭhakas of the Third Kāṇḍa of the Taittirīya Brāhmaṇa with Translation." *Proceedings of the American Philosophical Society* 95 (1951): 628–75.

———. "Taittirīya-Brāhmaṇa 3.7.7–10 and 3.7.12–14: Seven Anuvākas of the Seventh Prapāṭhaka of the Third Kāṇḍa of the Taittirīya-Brāhmaṇa with Translation." *Proceedings of the American Philosophical Society* 107 (1963): 446–60.

Edgerton, Franklin. "Dominant Ideas in the Formation of Indian Culture." *Journal of the American Oriental Society* 62 (1942): 151–56.

———. "Philosophical Materials of the Atharvaveda." In *Studies in Honor of Maurice Bloomfield.* New Haven: Yale University Press, 1920, pp. 119–35.

———. "Sources of the Filosophy [*sic*] of the Upaniṣads." *Journal of the American Oriental Society* 36 (1917): 197–204.

———. "The Upaniṣads: What Do They Seek and Why?" *Journal of the American Oriental Society* 19 (1929): 97–121.

Eliade, Mircea. *Yoga: Immortality and Freedom,* 2d ed. Trans. by Willard R. Trask. New York: Harcourt, Brace and World, 1959.

Eliot, Charles. *Hinduism and Buddhism: An Historical Sketch.* 3 vols. New York: Barnes and Noble, 1954.

Falk, Harry. "Vedisch *upaniṣad.*" *Zeitschrift der Deutschen Morgenländischen Gesellschaft* 136 (1986): 80–97.

Falk, Maryla. *Nāma-Rūpa and Dharma-Rūpa.* Calcutta: University of Calcutta, 1943.

Filliozat, Jean. "La Force organique et la force cosmique dans la philosophie médicale de l'Inde et dans le Véda." *Revue philosophique* 116 (1933): 410–29.

Gampert, W. *Die Sühnenzeremonien in der altindischen Rechtslitteratur.* Prag: Orientalisces Institut, 1939.

Gandhi, Mohandas. *In Search of the Supreme.* Comp. and ed. by V. B. Kher. Ahmedabad: Navajivan Publishing, 1961.

Ghosh, Manomohan. "Prātiśākhyas and Vedic Śākhās." *Indian Historical Quarterly* 11 (1935): 761–68.

Glasser, K. "Der indische Student." *Zeitschrift der Deutschen Morgenländischen Gesellschaft* 66 (1912): 1–37.

Goman, Thomas G., and Ronald S. Laura. "A Logical Treatment of Some Upaniṣadic Puzzles and Changing Conceptions of Sacrifice." *Numen* 19 (April 1972): 52–67.

Gonda, Jan. "Adhvara and Adhvaryu." *Vishveshvaranand Indological Journal* 3 (September 1965): 163–77.

———. "All, Universe and Totality in the Śatapatha Brāhmaṇa." *Journal of the Oriental Institute (Baroda)* 32 (September–December 1982): 1–17.

———. "Āyatana." *Adyar Library Bulletin* 23 (1969): 1–79.

———. "*Bandhu* in the Brāhmaṇas." *Adyar Library Bulletin* 29 (1965): 1–29.

———. "The Baudhāyana-Gṛhya-Paribhāṣā-Sūtra." In H. Härtel, ed., *Beiträge zur Indienforschuung: Ernest Waldschmidt zum 80. Geburtstag gewidmet.* Berlin: Museum für Indische Kunst, 1977, pp. 169–90.

———. *Change and Continuity in Indian Religion.* Disputations Rheno-Trajectinae, Vol. 9. The Hague: Mouton, 1965.

———. "The Creator and His Spirit." *Wiener Zeitschrift für die Kunde Südasiens* 27 (1983): 5–42.

———. "Etymologies in the Ancient Indian Brāhmaṇas." *Lingua* 5 (1955): 61–85.

———. *The Haviryajñāḥ Somāḥ: The Interrelations of the Vedic Solemn Sacrifices. Śāṅkhāyana Śrauta Sūtra 14, 1–13. Translation and Notes.* Amsterdam: North-Holland Publishing, 1982.

———, gen. ed. *A History of Indian Literature.* Wiesbaden: Otto Harrassowitz, 1975. Vol. 1, fasc. 1: *Vedic Literature (Saṃhitās and Brāhmaṇas),* by Jan Gonda.

———, gen. ed. *A History of Indian Literature.* Wiesbaden: Otto Harrassowitz, 1977. Vol. 1, fasc. 2: *The Ritual Sūtras,* by Jan Gonda.

———. *Hymns of the Ṛgveda Not Employed in the Solemn Ritual.* Amsterdam: North-Holland Publishing, 1978.

———. "In the Beginning." *Annals of the Bhandarkar Oriental Research Institute* 63 (1982): 43–62.

———. "The Indian Mantra." *Oriens* 16 (1963): 242–97.

———. *Loka. World and Heaven in the Veda.* Verhandelingen der Koninklijke Nederlandse Akademie van Wetenschappen, Afd. Letterkunde, Nieuwe

Reeks, Deel 73, no. 1. Amsterdam: N. V. Noord-Hollandsche Uitgevers Maatschappij, 1966.

———. *Notes on Brahman.* Utrecht: J. L. Beyers, 1950.

———. "The Popular Prajāpati." *History of Religions* 22 (November 1982): 129–49.

———. "Prajāpati and Prāyaścitta." *Journal of the Royal Asiatic Society* (1983): 32–54.

———. *Prajāpati and the Year.* Amsterdam: North Holland Publishing, 1984.

———. *Prajāpati's Rise to Higher Rank.* Leiden: E. J. Brill, 1986.

———. "Pratiṣṭhā." *Saṃjñāvyākaraṇa, Studia Indological Internationalia* 1 (1954): 1–37.

———. "The Redundant and the Deficient in Vedic Ritual." *Vishveshvaranand Indological Journal* 21 (June–December 1983): 1–34.

———. "Reflections on *Sarva-* in Vedic Texts." *Indian Linguistics* 16 (November 1955): 53–71.

———. *The Savayajñas (Kauśikasūtra 60–68).* Amsterdam: North-Holland Publishing, 1965.

———. "Upanayana." *Indologica Taurinensia* 7 (1979): 253–59.

———. "Vedic Gods and the Sacrifice." *Numen* 30 (July 1983): 1–34.

———. *Vedic Ritual: The Non-Solemn Rites.* Leiden: E. J. Brill, 1980.

Gopal, Ram. *India of the Vedic Kalpasūtras.* Delhi: National Publishing House, 1959.

———. "Influence of the Brāhmaṇas on the Gṛhyasūtras." *Vishveshvaranand Indological Journal* 1 (1963): 291–98.

———. "Manu's Indebtedness to Śānkhāyana." *Poona Orientalist* 27 (1962): 39–44.

Goswami, Krishna Gopal. "Philosophy of the Pañcayajñas." *Calcutta Review* 65 (1937): 203–10.

Goudriaan, T. "Vaikhānasa Daily Worship." *Indo-Iranian Journal* 12 (1970): 161–215.

Govinda, L. A. *Psycho-Cosmic Symbolism of the Buddhist Stūpa.* Emeryville, Calif.: Dharma Publishing, 1976.

Griswold, Hervey DeWitt. *Insights into Modern Hinduism.* New York: Henry Holt, 1934.

Gupta, S. K. "Ancient Schools of Vedic Interpretation." *Journal of the Ganganatha Jha Research Institute* 16 (November 1958–February 1959): 143–53.

Hacker, Paul. "Śraddhā." *Wiener Zeitschrift für die Kunde Süd-und Östasiens* 7 (1963): 151–89.

Hastings, J., ed. *Encyclopedia of Religion and Ethics.* New York: Charles Scribner's Sons, 1910. S.v. "Brahman," by Alfred Hillebrandt.

Hauer, J. W. *Der Vrātya: Untersuchenungen über die nichtbrahmanische Religion altindiens.* 2 vols. Stuttgart: W. Kohlhammer, 1927.

Haug, Martin, ed. and trans. *The Aitareya Brāhmaṇam of the Rigveda*. 2 vols. Bombay: Government Central Book Depot, 1863.

Hazra, R. C. *Studies in the Upapurāṇas*. Calcutta: Sanskrit College, 1963.

Heesterman, J. C. *The Ancient Indian Royal Consecration: The Rājasūya Described according to the Yajus Texts and Annoted* [*sic*]. Disputations Rheno-Trajectinae, Vol. 2. s'Gravenhage: Mouton, 1957.

———. "Die Autorität des Veda." In Gerhard Oberhammer, ed., *Offenbarung, geistige Realität des Menschen*. Vienna: Indologisches Institut der Universität Wien, 1974, pp. 29–40.

———. "Brahmin, Ritual and Renouncer." In *The Inner Conflict of Tradition: Essays in Indian Ritual, Kingship, and Society*. Chicago: University of Chicago Press, 1985, pp. 26–44.

———. "Householder and Wanderer." In T. N. Madan, ed., *Way of Life: King, Householder, Renouncer. Essays in Honor of Louis Dumont*. New Delhi: Vikas, 1981, pp. 251–71.

———. "Other Folks' Fire." In J. F. Staal, ed., *Agni: The Vedic Ritual of the Fire Altar*. 2 vols. Berkeley, Calif.: Asian Humanities Press, 1983, II: 76–94.

———. "Power and Authority in Indian Tradition." In R. J. Moore, ed., *Tradition and Politics in South Asia*. New Delhi: Vikas, 1979, pp. 60–85.

———. "Priesthood and the Brahmin." *Contributions to Indian Sociology* (new series) 5 (1971): 43–47.

———. "Reflexions on the Significance of Dakṣiṇās." *Indo-Iranian Journal* 3 (1959): 241–58.

———. "The Return of the Veda Scholar (*samāvartana*)." In J. C. Heesterman, ed., *Pratidānam: Indian, Iranian and Indo-European Studies Presented to F. B. J. Kuier on his Sixtieth Birthday*. The Hague: Mouton, 1968, pp. 436–47.

———. "The Ritualist's Problem." In S. D. Joshi, ed., *Amṛtadhārā. Professor R. N. Dandekar Felicitation Volume*. Delhi: Ajanta Books, 1984, pp. 167–79.

———. "Self-sacrifice in Vedic Ritual." In S. Shaked et al., eds., *Gilgul: Essays on Transformation, Revolution and Permanence in the History of Religions*. Leiden: E. J. Brill, 1987, pp. 91–106.

———. "Tradition in Modern India." *Bijdragen tot de Taal-, Land-, en Volkenkunde* 119 (1963): 237–53.

———. "Veda and Dharma." In Wendy Doniger O'Flaherty and J. D. M. Derrett, eds., *The Concept of Duty in South Asia*. Columbia, Mo.: South Asia Books, 1978, pp. 80–95.

———. "Veda and Society: Some Remarks apropos of the Film 'Altar of Fire.' " In Asko Parpola, ed., *Proceedings of the Nordic South Asia Conference, Helsinki, June 10–12, 1980*. Helsinki: Studia Orientalia, 1981.

———. "Vrātya and Sacrifice." *Indo-Iranian Journal* 6 (1962): 1–37.

Heimann, B. "The Supra-Personal Process of Sacrifice." *Rivista degli studi orientali* (Rome) 32 (1938): 731–39.

Henry, V. *La Magie dans l'Inde antique*. Paris: Dujarric, 1904.

Hillebrandt, Alfred. *Das altindische Neu- und Vollmondopfer in seiner einfachsten Form*. Jena: Gustav Fischer, 1879.

———. *Rituallitteratur. Vedische Opfer und Zauber*. Grundriss der Indo-Arischen Philologie und Altertumskunde, Vol. 3. Strassburg: Trübner, 1897.

———. *Vedic Mythology*. 2 vols. Trans. by S. R. Sarma. Delhi: Motilal Banarsidass, 1980.

Hiltebeitel, Alf. *The Ritual of Battle: Krishna in the Mahābhārata*. Ithaca, N.Y.: Cornell University Press, 1976,

Hopkins, Thomas. "The Social Teachings of the Bhāgavata Pūraṇa." In Milton Singer, ed., *Krishna: Myths, Rites, and Attitudes*. Chicago: University of Chicago Press, 1966, pp. 3–22.

Hubert, Henri, and Marcel Mauss. *Sacrifice: Its Nature and Function*. Trans. by W. D. Halls. Chicago: University of Chicago Press, 1964.

Joshi, J. R. "Prajāpati in Vedic Mythology and Ritual." *Annals of the Bhandarkar Oriental Research Institute* 53 (1972): 101–25.

Joshi, S. D. *Patañjali's Vyākaraṇamahābhāṣya*. Poona: University of Poona, 1968.

———. *Some Minor Divinities in Vedic Mythology and Ritual*. Pune: Deccan College Postgraduate and Research Institute, 1977.

Kaelber, Walter O. "The 'Dramatic' Element in Brāhmaṇic Initiation: Symbols of Death, Danger, and Difficult Passage." *History of Religions* 18 (August 1978): 54–76.

Kane, P. V. *History of Dharmaśāstra*, 2d ed. 5 vols. Poona: Bhandarkar Oriental Research Institute, 1968–75.

Karnik, H. R. "Morals in the Brāhmaṇas." *Journal of Bombay University* 27 (September 1958): 95–127.

Kashikar, C. G. "On the Bhāradvāja Gṛhyasūtra and Its Commentary." *Bulletin of the Deccan College Research Institute* 35 (1975): 65–75.

———. "The Idea of Ultimate Reality and Meaning according to the Kalpa Sūtras." *Ultimate Reality and Meaning* 2 (1979): 172–87.

———. "The Pitṛmedhasūtra of Bhāradvāja vis-à-vis Āpastamba and Satyaṣadha Hiraṇyakeśin." *Journal of Oriental Research* (Madras) 28 (1958–59): 1–10.

———. *A Survey of the Śrautasūtras*. Bombay: University of Bombay, 1968.

———. "The Vedic Sacrificial Rituals through the Ages." *Indian Antiquary* 1 (3d series), (April 1964): 77–89.

Kashikar, C. G., and Asko Parpola. "Śrauta Traditions in Recent Times." In Frits Staal, ed., *Agni: The Vedic Ritual of the Fire Altar*. 2 vols. Berkeley, Calif.: Asian Humanities Press, 1983. II: 199–251.

Keith, Arthur Berriedale. *The Religion and Philosophy of the Veda and Upaniṣads*. 2 vols. Harvard Oriental Series, Vols. 31 and 32. Cambridge, Mass.: Harvard University Press, 1925.

Kinsley, David R. *Hinduism: A Cultural Perspective*. Prentice-Hall Series in World Religions, ed. by Robert S. Ellwood, Jr. Englewood Cliffs, N.J.: Prentice-Hall, 1982.

Knipe, David M. *In the Image of Fire: Vedic Experiences of Heat*. Delhi: Motilal Banarsidass, 1975.

———. "One Fire, Three Fires, Five Fires: Vedic Symbols in Transition." *History of Religions* 12 (August 1972): 28–41.

———. "*Sapiṇḍakaraṇa*: The Hindu Rite of Entry into Heaven." In Frank E. Reynolds and Earle H. Waugh, eds., Religious Encounters with Death: Insights from the History and Anthropology of Religions. University Park: Pennsylvania State University Press, 1977, pp. 111–24.

Kramrisch, Stella. *The Hindu Temple*. 2 vols. Reprint Delhi: Motilal Banarsidass, 1976.

Krick, Hertha. *Das Rituel der Feuer (Agnyādheya)*. Österreichische Akademie der Wissenschaften. Philosophisch historische Klasse. Sitzungsberichte, bd. 399. Wien: Österreichischen Akademie der Wissenschaften, 1982.

Kuiper, F. B. J. *Ancient Indian Cosmogony*. New Delhi: Vikas Publishing House, 1983.

Laine, J. "The Notion of 'Scripture' in Modern Indian Thought." *Annals of the Bhandarkar Oriental Research Institute* 64 (1983): 165–79.

Lal, S. K. *Female Divinities in Hindu Mythology and Ritual*. Pune: University of Poona, 1980).

Lee, Orlan. "From Acts—to Non-Action—To Acts: The Dialectical Basis for Social Withdrawal or Commitment to This World in the Buddhist Reformation." *History of Religions* 6 (May 1967): 273–302.

Lester, Robert C. "Hinduism: Veda and Sacred Texts." In Frederick M. Denny and Rodney L. Taylor, eds., *The Holy Book in Comparative Perspective*. Columbia, S.C.: University of South Carolina Press, 1985, pp. 126–47.

Lévi, Sylvain. *Le Doctrine du sacrifice dans les Brāhmaṇas*. Bibliothèque de l'École des Hautes Études, Sciences religieuses, Vol. 11. Paris: Ernest Leroux, 1898.

Lincoln, Bruce. "Death and Resurrection in Indo-European Thought." *Journal of Indo-European Studies* 5 (Summer 1977): 247–64.

———. *Myth, Cosmos, and Society: Indo-European Themes of Creation and Destruction*. Cambridge, Mass.: Harvard University Press, 1986.

Lingat, Robert. *Classical Law of India*. Trans. by J. Duncan M. Derrett. Berkeley: University of California Press, 1973.

———. "Time and the Dharma." *Contributions to Indian Sociology* 6 (1962): 7–16.

Löbbecke, R. *Über das Verhältnis von Brāhmaṇas und Śrautasūtren*. Leipzig: Kreysing, 1908.

Lutgendorf, Philip. *The Life of a Text: Tulsidas's Rāmacāritamānasa in Performance*. Ph.D. dissertation. University of Chicago, 1986.

Macdonald, A. W. "A propos de Prajāpati." *Journal asiatique* 240 (1952): 323–38.

Macdonald, K. S. *The Brāhmaṇas of the Vedas*. Reprint Delhi: Bharatiya Book Corporation, 1979.

Macdonell, A. A. *A History of Sanskrit Literature*. New York: D. Appleton, 1900.

———. *The Vedic Mythology*. Grundiss der Indo-Arische Philologie und Alterthumskunde, Vol. 3. Strassburg: K. J. Trübner, 1894; reprint Varanasi: Indological Book House, 1963.

Malamoud, Charles. *Le Svādhyāya: Recitation personnelle du Veda*. Paris: Institut de Civilisation Indienne, 1977.

———. "Terminer le sacrifice: Remarques sur les honoraires rituels dans le brahmanisme." In Madeleine Biardeau and Charles Malamoud, *Le Sacrifice dans l'Inde ancienne*. Paris: Presses universitaires de France, 1976, pp. 155–204.

———. "La Théologie de la dette dans le brāhmanisme." *Puruṣārtha* 4 (1980): 39–62.

Marshall, P. J., ed. *The British Discovery of Hinduism in the Eighteenth Century*. Cambridge: Cambridge University Press, 1970.

Mayrhofer, Manfred. *Kurzgefasstes etymologisches Wörterbuches Altindischen. A Concise Etymological Sanskrit Dictionary*. 4 vols. Heidelberg: Carl Winter Universitäts-verlag, 1956–80.

Mayrhofer-Passler, E. "Haustieropfer bei dem Indoiraniern und den andern indo-germanischen Volkern." *Archiv Orientalni* 21 (1953): 182–205.

Minard, Armand. *Trois enigmas sur les cent chemins: Recherches sur le Śatapatha Brāhmaṇa*. 2 vols. Annales de l'Université de Lyon, troisime series, lettres, fascs. 17–18. Paris: Société d'édition les belles lettres, 1949.

Moghe, S. G. "The Evolution of the Mīmāṃsā Technical Term *atideśa*." *Annals of the Bhandarkar Oriental Research Institute* 58–59 (1977–78): 777–84.

Mookerji, Radha Kumud. *Ancient Indian Education (Brahmanical and Buddhist)*. London: Macmillan, 1947.

Müller, F. Max. *Chips from a German Workshop*. 2 vols. New York: Scribner, Armstrong, 1871.

———. *A History of Ancient Sanskrit Literature*, 2d ed. London: Williams and Norgate, 1859.

Murthy, U. R. Anantha. *Saṃskāra: A Rite for a Dead Man*. Trans. by A. K. Ramanujan. Delhi: Oxford University Press, 1978.

Mus, Paul. *Barabadur: Esquisse d'une histoire du Bouddhism fondée sur la critique archéologique des textes*. Paris and Hanoi: Paul Geuthner, 1935.

———. "Du Nouveau sur Ṛg Veda 10.90?" In Ernest Bender, ed., *Indological Studies in Honor of W. Norman Brown*. American Oriental Series, Vol. 47. New Haven, Conn.: American Oriental Society, 1962, pp. 165–85.

———. "Ou finit Puruṣa?" *Mélanges d'Indianisme à la mémoire de Louis Renou*. Paris: E. de Boccard, 1968, pp. 539–63.

———. "The Problematic of the Self, West and East and the Maṇḍala Pattern." In C. A. Moore, ed., *Philosophy and Culture, East and West*. Honolulu: University of Hawaii Press, 1960, pp. 594–610.

———. "La Stance de la plénitude." *Bulletin de l'École Francaise d'Extrême Orient* 44 (1947–50): 591–618.

Mylius, Klaus. "*Dakṣiṇā:* Eine Studie über den altindischen Priesterlohn." *Altorientalische Forschungen* 6 (1979): 141–79.

———. "Die Ideenwelt des Śatapatha Brāhmaṇa." *Wissenschaftliche Zeitschrift der Karl Marx Universität* 16 (1967): 47–55.

———. "Die Identifikationen im *Kauṣītaki-Brāhmaṇa*," *Altorientalische Forschungen* 5 (1977): 237–44.

———. "Die Identifikationen der Metren in der Literatur des Ṛgveda." *Wissenschaftliche Zeitschrift der Karl Marx Universität* 17 (1968): 267–73.

———. "Die vedischen Identifikationen am Beispiel des *Kauṣītaki-Brāhmaṇa*." *Klio* 58 (1976): 145–66.

Nagaswamy, R. "Vedic Scholars in the Ancient Tamil Country as Gleaned from the Sangam Classics and South Indian Inscriptions." *Vishveshvaranand Indological Journal* 3 (September 1965): 192–204.

Narahari, H. G. *Ātman in Pre-Upaniṣadic Vedic Literature*. Adyar: Adyar Library, 1944.

Narten, Johanna. "Ved. *āmayati* und *āmayāvin-*." *Studien zur Indologie und Iranistik* 5–6 (1980): 153–66.

Nehru, Jawaharlal. *The Discovery of India*. London: Meridian Books, 1960.

O'Flaherty, Wendy Doniger. *Asceticism and Eroticism in the Mythology of Śiva*. New York: Oxford University Press, 1973. Reissued as *Śiva: The Erotic Ascetic*, 1980.

———. *Dreams, Illusion and Other Realities*. Chicago: University of Chicago Press, 1983.

———. *The Origins of Evil in Hindu Mythology*. Berkeley: University of California Press, 1976.

———. "The Origins of Heresy in Hindu Mythology." *History of Religions* 10 (May 1971): 271–333.

———. *Other People's Myths*, New York: Macmillan, 1988.

———. *Tales of Sex and Violence: Folklore, Sacrifice, and Danger in the Jaiminīya Brāhmaṇa*. Chicago: University of Chicago Press, 1984.

———. With Daniel Gold, David Haberman, and David Shulman. *Textual Sources for the Study of Hinduism*. Manchester: Manchester University Press, 1989.

———. *Women, Androgynes, and Other Mythical Beasts*. Chicago: University of Chicago Press, 1980.

O'Flaherty, Wendy Doniger, and J. D. M. Derrett, eds. *The Concept of Duty in South Asia*. Columbia, Missouri: South Asia Books, 1978.

Oguibenine, B. L. *Structure d'un mythe védique: Le Mythe cosmogonique dans le Ṛg Veda.* The Hague: Mouton, 1973.

———. "*Bandhu* et *dakṣiṇā:* Deux termes védique illustrant le rapport entre le signifiant et le signifié." *Journal asiatique* 27 (1983): 263–75.

Oldenberg, Hermann. *Ancient India: Its Language and Religion,* ed. Calcutta: Punthi Pustak, 1963.

———. *Vorwissenschaftliche Wissenschaft: Die Weltanschauung der Brāhmaṇa-texte.* Göttingen: Vandenhoeck and Ruprecht, 1919.

Olivelle, Patrick. "A Definition of World Renunciation." *Wiener Zeitschrift für die Kunde Südasiens* 19 (1975): 75–83.

———. "Odes of Renunciation." *Wiener Zeitschrift für die Kunde Südasiens* 20 (1976): 91–100.

Organ, Troy Wilson. *The Hindu Quest for the Perfection of Man.* Athens, Ohio: Ohio University Press, 1970.

Pandey, Raj Bali. *Hindu Saṃskāras: Socio-Religious Study of the Hindu Sacraments,* 2d ed. Delhi: Motilal Banarsidass, 1969.

Parpola, Asko. "The Pre-vedic Indian Background of the Śrauta Rituals." In Frits Staal, ed., *Agni: The Vedic Altar of Fire.* Berkeley, Calif.: Asian Humanities Press, 1983, II: 41–75.

———. "On the Symbol Concept of the Vedic Ritualists." In H. Biezais, ed., *Religious Symbols and Their Functions.* Stockholm: Almquist and Wiksell, 1979, pp. 139–53.

Pathak, V. S. "Vedic Rituals in Early Medieval Period." *Annals of the Bhandarkar Oriental Research Institute* 40 (1959): 218–30.

Pillai, P. K. Narayana. *Non-Ṛgvedic Mantras in the Marriage Ceremonies.* Trivandrum: Travancore Devaswom Board, 1958.

Puhakka, Kaisa. "The Roots of Religious Tolerance in Hinduism and Buddhism." *Temenos* 12 (1976): 50–61.

Raghavan, V. *The Present Position of Vedic Recitation and Vedic Śākhās.* Kumbhakonam: Veda Dharma Paripalana Sabha, 1962.

Rai, Gangar Sagar. "Śākhās of the Atharvaveda." *Purāṇa* 14 (January 1972): 58–76.

———. "Śākhās of the Ṛgveda as Mentioned in the Purāṇas." *Purāṇa* 6 (January 1964): 97–112.

———. "Śākhās of the Sāmaveda in the Purāṇas." *Purāṇa* 8 (January 1966): 115–34.

———. "Śākhās of the Yajurveda in the Purāṇas." *Purāṇa* 7 (January–July 1965): 235–53.

———. "Vedic Śākhās." *Purāṇa* 15 (February 1973): 133–40.

Ramanujan, A. K. *Speaking of Śiva.* Baltimore: Penguin Books, 1973.

Ranade, H. G. "Some Darśapūrṇamāsa-Rites in the Śatapatha Brāhmaṇa and in the KātŚS." *Bulletin of the Deccan College Research Institute* 35 (March 1976): 121–26.

Rangacharya, V. "Śrī-Vaiṣṇavism in South India." In H. Bhattacharya, ed., *The*

Cultural Heritage of India, 2d ed. 2 vols. Calcutta: Ramakrishna Mission Institute of Culture, 1953, IV: 163–85.

Ravi Varma, L. A. "Rituals of Worship." In H. Bhattacharya, ed., *The Cultural Heritage of India,* 2d ed. 2 vols. Calcutta: Ramakrishna Mission Institute of Culture, 1953, IV: 445–63.

Reddiar, N. Subbu. *Religion and Philosophy of the Nālāyiram.* Tirupati: Sri Venkateswara University Press, 1977.

Renou, Louis. " 'Connexion' en védique, 'cause' en bouddhique." In *Dr. C. Kunhan Raja Presentation Volume.* Madras: Adyar Library, 1946, pp. 55–60.

———. "Les Connexions entre le rituel et la grammaire en sanskrit." *Journal asiatique* 233 (1941–42): 105–65.

———. "Les Débuts de la spéculation indienne." *Revue philosophique* 143 (1953): 334–41.

———. *The Destiny of the Veda in India.* Ed. and trans. by Dev Raj Chanana. Delhi: Motilal Banarsidass, 1965.

———. *Les Écoles védiques et la formation de Veda.* Cahiers de la Société Asiatique, Vol. 9. Paris: Imprimerie nationale, 1947.

———. *Études védiques et pāninéennes.* 17 vols. Paris: Publication de l'ICI, 1955–69.

———. "Un Hymne à énigmes du Ṛgveda (I.152)." *Journal de psychologie normale et pathologique* 46 (1949): 266–73.

———. *Hymnes spéculatifs de Veda.* Paris: Gallimard, 1956.

———. "La Maison védique." *Journal asiatique* 231 (1939): 481–504.

———. "On the Word *ātman.*" *Vāk* 2 (1952): 151–57.

———. "Le Passage des Brāhmaṇa aux Upaniṣad." *Journal of the American Oriental Society* 73 (1953): 138–44.

———. *Religions of Ancient India.* New York: Schocken Books, 1968.

———. "Sur le genre du sūtra dans la litterature sanskrite." *Journal asiatique* 251 (1963): 165–216.

———. "Sur la notion de brahman." *Journal asiatique* 237 (1949): 7–46.

———. *Vedic India.* Trans. by Philip Spratt. Delhi: Indological Book House, 1971.

———. "The Vedic Schools and the Epigraphy." In V. Bandhu, ed., *Siddha Bhāratī II.* Hoshiarpur: Vishveshvaranand Research Institute, 1950, pp. 214–21.

———. "Védique Nirṛti." *Indian Linguistics* 16 (November 1955): 11–15.

———. *Vocabulaire du rituel védique.* Paris: Librairie C. Klincksieck, 1954.

Renou, Louis, and Lilian Silburn. "Nirukta and Anirukta in Vedic." In J. N. Agrawal and B. D. Shastri, eds., *Sarūpa-Bhāratī or the Homage of Indology: The Dr. Lakshman Sarup Memorial Volume.* Hoshiarpur: Vishveshvaranand Institute Publications, 1954, pp. 68–79.

Rustagi, Urmila. *Darśapūrṇamāsa: A Comparative Ritualistic Study.* Delhi: Bharatiya Vidya Prakashan, 1981.

Sastri, V. A. R. "Arthavādas." In J. N. Agrawal and B. D. Shastri, eds., *Sarūpa-Bhāratī or the Homage of Indology: The Dr. Lakshman Sarup Memorial Volume.* Hoshiarpur: Vishveshvaranand Institute Publications, 1954, pp. 165–70.

Schayer, Stanislov. "Die Struktur der magischen Weltanschauung nach dem Atharva-Veda und den Brāhmaṇa-Texten." *Zeitschrift für Buddhismus* 6 (1925): 259–99.

———. "Über die Bedeutung des Wortes Upaniṣad." *Rocznik Orjentalistyczny* 3 (1925): 57–67.

Schwab, J. *Das altindische Thieropfer.* Erlangen: Andreas Deichert, 1886.

Sen, Chitrabhanu. *Dictionary of Vedic Rituals.* Delhi: Concept Publishing, 1978.

Sharma, Arvind. "Some Misunderstandings of the Hindu Approach to Religious Plurality." *Religion* 8 (Autumn 1978): 133–54.

Sharma, B. R. "Symbolism of Fire Altar in Vedas." *Annals of the Bhandarkar Oriental Research Institute* 33 (1952): 189–96.

Sharma, D. S. "The Nature and History of Hinduism." In Kenneth W. Morgan, ed., *The Religion of the Hindus.* New York: Ronald Press, 1953, pp. 3–47.

———. *The Renaissance of Hinduism.* Varanasi: Benares Hindu University, 1944.

Sharma, R. N. *Culture and Civilization as Revealed in the Śrautasūtras.* Delhi: Nag Publishers, 1977.

Shastri, Dakshina Ranjan. *Origin and Development of the Rituals of Ancestor Worship in India.* Calcutta: Bookland, 1963.

Shende, N. J. *Religion and Philosophy of the Atharva Veda.* Poona: Bhandarkar Oriental Research Institute, 1952.

Shivaganesha Murthy, R. S. *A Study of the Important Brāhmaṇas.* Mysore: Prasaranga, University of Mysore, 1974.

Silburn, Lilian. *Instant et cause: Le Discontinu dans le pensée philosophique de l'Inde.* Paris: Libraire philosophique J. Vrin, 1955.

Singer, Milton. "The Cultural Pattern of Indian Civilization: A Preliminary Report of a Methodological Field Study." *Far Eastern Quarterly* 15 (November 1955): 23–36.

Smith, Brian K. "Exorcising the Transcendent: Strategies for Defining Hinduism and Religion." *History of Religions* 27 (August 1987): 32–55.

———. "Gods and Men in Vedic Ritualism: Toward a Hierarchy of Resemblance." *History of Religions* 24 (May 1985): 291–307.

———. "Ideals and Realities in Indian Religion." *Religious Studies Review* 14 (January 1988): 1–9.

———. "Myth, Religion, and the Real World." *The World & I* (July 1987): 558–67.

———. "Ritual, Knowledge, and Being: Initiation and Veda Study in Ancient India." *Numen* 33 (1986): 65–89.

———. "Sacrifice and Being: Prajāpati's Cosmic Emission and Its Consequences." *Numen* 32 (1985): 71–87.

———. "The Unity of Ritual: The Place of the Domestic Sacrifice in Vedic Ritualism." *Indo-Iranian Journal* 28 (1985): 79–96.

———. "Vedic Fieldwork" *Religious Studies Review* 11 (April 1985): 136–45.

Smith, Brian K., and Wendy Doniger O'Flaherty. "Sacrifice and Substitution: Ritual Mystification and Mythical Demystification," *Numen* (1989, forthcoming).

Smith, Frederick Marcus. "The Āvasathya Fire in the Vedic Ritual." *Adyar Library Bulletin* 46 (1982): 73–92.

———. *The Vedic Sacrifice in Transition: A Translation and Study of the Trikāṇḍamaṇḍana of Bhāskara Miśra.* Ph.D. dissertation. University of Pennsylvania, 1984.

Spear, Percival. *India, Pakistan, and the West.* London: Oxford University Press, 1949.

Staal, J. F. (Frits). *Advaita and Neoplatonism: A Critical Study in Comparative Philosophy.* Madras: University of Madras, 1961.

———. *Agni: The Vedic Ritual of the Fire Altar.* 2 vols. Berkeley, Calif.: Asian Humanities Press, 1983.

———. "The Agnicayana Project." In Frits Staal, ed., *Agni: The Vedic Ritual of the Fire Altar.* 2 vols. Berkeley, Calif.: Asian Humanities Press, 1983, II: 456–75.

———. "The Concept of Scripture in the Indian Tradition." In Mark Juergensmeyer and N. Gerald Barrier, eds., *Sikh Studies: Comparative Perspectives on a Changing Tradition.* Berkeley Religious Studies Series. Berkeley, Calif.: Graduate Theological Union, 1979, pp. 121–24.

———. "The Meaninglessness of Ritual." *Numen* 26 (1979): 2–22.

———. "Ritual Syntax." In M. Nagotomi et al., eds., *Sanskrit and Indian Studies.* Dordrecht: D. Reidel, 1979, pp. 119–42.

———. *The Science of Ritual.* Poona: Bhandarkar Oriental Research Institute, 1982.

Tagore, Rabindranath. "Sacrifice." In *A Tagore Reader,* edited by Amiya Chakravarty. Boston: Beacon Press, 1966, pp. 125–48.

Tendulkar, D. G. *Mahātma: Life of Mohandas Karamchand Gandhi,* new ed. 8 vols. New Delhi: Publications Division, Ministry of Information and Broadcasting, Govt. of India, 1961–69.

Thite, G. U. *Medicine: Its Magico-Religious Aspects according to the Vedic and Later Literature.* Poona: Continental Prakashan, 1982.

———. *Sacrifice in the Brāhmaṇa-Texts.* Poona: University of Poona, 1975.

Tsuji, Naoshiro. *On the Relation between Brāhmaṇas and Śrautasūtras.* Tôyo Bunko Ronso series A, Vol. 33. Tokyo: Tôyo Bunko, 1952.

Van Buitenen, J. A. B. "A Brief History of the Literatures of South Asia." In Edward C. Dimock et al., eds., *Literatures of India: An Introduction.* Chicago: University of Chicago Press, 1974, pp. 14–20.

———. "Hindu Sacred Literature." *Encyclopedia Britannica,* 11th ed.

———. "Hinduism." *Encyclopedia Britannica,* 11th ed.

———. "On the Structure of the Sabhāparvan of the Mahābhārata." In J. Ensink and P. Gaeffke, eds., *India Maior: Congratulatory Volume Presented to J. Gonda.* Leiden: E. J. Brill, 1972, pp. 68–84.

———. *The Pravargya: An Ancient Indian Iconic Ritual Described and Annotated.* Poona: Deccan College, 1968.

Verpoorten, Jean-Marie. "Unité et distinction dans les spéculations rituelles védique." *Archiv für Begriffsgeschichte* 21 (1977): 59–85.

Vira, Raghu. "Śākhās of the Yajurveda." *Journal of Vedic Studies* 2 (April 1935): 61–77.

Vyas, R. T. "The Concept of Prajāpati in Vedic Literature." *Bhāratīya Vidyā* 38 (1978): 95–101.

Wasson, R. Gordon, and Wendy Doniger O'Flaherty. *Soma: Divine Mushroom of Immortality.* New York: Harcourt, Brace and World, 1968.

Weber, Albrecht. *The History of Indian Literature,* 6th ed. Trans. from 2d German ed. by J. Mann and T. Zachariae. Chowkhamba Sanskrit Series, Studies, Vol. 8. Varanasi: Chowkhamba Sanskrit Series Office, 1961.

———. *Über die Konigsweihe, den Rājasūya.* Berlin: Königlichen Akademie der Wissenschaften, 1893.

Willman-Grabowska, H. "Ekspiacja (prāyaścitti) w Brāhmaṇa (L'expiation [prāyaścitti] dans les Brāhmaṇas)." *Bulletin international de l'Académie Polonaise des Sciences et des Lettres* 7–10 (July–December 1935): 237–42.

Winternitz, Maurice. *A History of Indian Literature.* 3 vols. Trans. by S. Ketkar. New York: Russell and Russell, 1971.

———. "Notes on Śrāddhas and Ancestral Worship among the Indo-European Nations." *Wiener Zeitschrift für die Kunde morgenländische* 4 (1890): 199–212.

Witzel, Michael. "On Magical Thought in the Veda." Leiden: Universitaire Pers Leiden, 1979.

Young, Richard Fox. *Resistant Hinduism: Sanskrit Sources on Anti-Christian Apologetics in Early Nineteenth-Century India.* Vienna: Institut für Indologie der Universität Wien, 1981.

Younger, Paul. *Introduction to Indian Religious Thought.* Philadelphia: Westminster Press, 1972.

Zaehner, R. C. *Hinduism.* New York: Oxford University Press, 1966.

Zysk, Kenneth. *Religious Healing in the Veda.* Philadelphia: American Philosophical Society, 1986.

———. "Towards the Notion of Health in the Vedic Phase of Indian Medicine." *Zeitschrift der Deutschen Morganländischen Gesellschaft* 135 (1985): 312–18.

Secondary Sources (General)

Burkert, Walter. *Homo Necans: The Anthropology of Ancient Greek Sacrificial Ritual and Myth.* Trans. by Peter Bing. Berkeley: University of California Press, 1983.

Butchvarov, Panayot. *Resemblance and Identity: An Examination of the Problem of Universals*. Bloomington: Indiana University Press, 1966.

Capdeville, Gerard. "Substitution de victimes dans les sacrifices d'animaux a Rome." *Mélanges d'archéologie et d'histoire de l'École Francaise de Rome* 83 (1971): 283–323.

Church, Ralph W. *An Analysis of Resemblance*. London: George Allen and Unwin, 1952.

Denny, Frederick M., and Rodney L. Taylor, eds. *The Holy Book in Comparative Perspective*. Columbia: University of South Carolina Press, 1985.

Eliade, Mircea. *The Myth of the Eternal Return or, Cosmos and History*. Trans. by Willard Trask. Princeton, N.J.: Princeton University Press, 1954.

———. *Myth and Reality*. Trans. by Willard Trask. New York: Harper Colophon Books, 1963.

———. *The Sacred and the Profane*. Trans. by Willard R. Trask. New York: Harcourt, Brace and World, 1959.

Evans-Pritchard, E. E. "Lévy-Bruhl's Theory of Primitive Mentality." *Bulletin of the Faculty of Arts* (Alexandria) 2 (1934): 1–16.

———. *Nuer Religion*. Oxford: Oxford University Press, 1956.

———. *Witchcraft, Oracles and Magic among the Azande*. Oxford: Clarendon Press, 1937.

Firth, Raymond. "Twins, Birds and Vegetables: Problems of Identification in Primitive Religious Thought." *Man* (new series) 1 (1966): 1–17.

Foucault, Michel. *The Order of Things: An Archeology of the Human Sciences*. Trans. of *Les Mots et les choses*. New York: Vintage Books, 1973.

Freud, Sigmund. *The Future of an Illusion*. Ed. and trans. by James Strachey. New York: W. W. Norton, 1961.

———. "Obsessive Acts and Religious Practices." In *Character and Culture*. New York: Collier Books, 1963, pp. 17–26.

———. *Totem and Taboo*. Trans. by James Strachey. New York: W. W. Norton, 1950.

Geertz, Clifford. *Islam Observed: Religious Development in Morocco and Indonesia*. Chicago: University of Chicago Press, 1971.

———. "Religion as a Cultural System." In *The Interpretation of Cultures: Selected Essays by Clifford Geertz*. New York: Basic Books, 1973, pp. 87–125.

Girard, René. *Violence and the Sacred*. Trans. by P. Gregory. Baltimore: Johns Hopkins University Press, 1977.

Hamerton-Kelly, Robert G., ed. *Violent Origins: Walter Burkert, René Girard, and Jonathan Z. Smith on Ritual Killing and Cultural Formation*. Stanford, Calif.: Stanford University Press, 1987.

Hayley, Audrey. "Symbolic Equations: The Ox and the Cucumber." *Man* (new series) 3 (1968): 262–72.

Horton, Robin, and Ruth Finnegan., eds. *Modes of Thought: Essays on Thinking in Western and Non-Western Societies*. London: Faber and Faber, 1973.

Lévi-Strauss, Claude. *The Savage Mind.* Chicago: University of Chicago Press, 1966.

———. *Totemism.* Trans. by Rodney Needham. Boston: Beacon Press, 1963.

Lévy-Bruhl, Lucien. *How Natives Think.* Trans. by Lilian A. Clare. Princeton, N.J.: Princeton University Press, 1985.

Lovejoy, Arthur O. *The Great Chain of Being: A Study of the History of an Idea.* Cambridge, Mass.: Harvard University Press, 1936.

Mauss, Marcel. *A General Theory of Magic.* Trans. by Robert Brain. New York: W. W. Norton, 1972.

Montague, Ashley, ed. *The Concept of the Primitive.* New York: Free Press, 1968.

Moore, Sally F., Barbara G. and Meyerhoff, eds. *Secular Ritual.* Amsterdam: Van Gorcum, 1977.

Neusner, Jacob. "Alike and Not Alike: A Grid for Comparison and Differentiation." In Jacob Neusner, ed., *Take Judaism, for Example: Studies in the Comparison of Religions.* Chicago: University of Chicago Press, 1983, pp. 227–35.

———. "Judaism in the History of Religions." In James S. Helfer, ed., *On Method in the History of Religions.* Middleton, Conn.: Wesleyan University Press, 1968, pp. 31–45.

———, ed. *Take Judaism, for Example: Studies in the Comparison of Religions.* Chicago: University of Chicago Press, 1983.

O'Flaherty, Wendy Doniger, ed. *The Critical Study of Sacred Texts.* Berkeley Religious Studies Series. Berkeley, Calif.: Graduate Theological Union, 1979.

Penner, Hans, and Edward Yonan. "Is a Science of Religion Possible?" *Journal of Religion* 52 (1972): 107–33.

Proudfoot, Wayne. "Religion and Reduction." *Union Seminary Quarterly Review* 37 (Fall–Winter 1981–82): 13–25.

———. *Religious Experience.* Berkeley: University of California Press, 1986.

Puhvel, Jean. "Victimal Hierarchies in Indo-European Animal Sacrifice." *American Journal of Philology* 99 (1978): 354–62.

Otto, Rudolph. *The Idea of the Holy.* Trans. by John W. Harvey. New York: Oxford University Press, 1957.

Said, Edward. *Orientalism.* New York: Pantheon Books, 1978.

Sharpe, E. J. *Comparative Religion: A History.* London: Charles Scribner's Sons, 1975.

Skorupski, John. *Symbol and Theory: A Philosophical Study of Theories of Religion in Social Anthropology.* Cambridge: Cambridge University Press, 1976.

Smith, Jonathan Z. "Adde Parvum Parvo Magnus Acervus Erit." *History of Religions* 11 (August 1971): 67–90.

———. "The Bare Facts of Ritual." *History of Religions* 20 (Aug. and Nov., 1980): 112–27; reprinted in *Imagining Religion,* pp. 53–65.

———. "Fences and Neighbors: Some Contours of Early Judaism." In *Imagining Religion: From Babylon to Jonestown.* Chicago: University of Chicago Press, 1982, pp. 1–18.

———. "I Am a Parrot (Red)." *History of Religions* 11 (May 1972): 391–413.

———. *Imagining Religion: From Babylon to Jonestown.* Chicago: University of Chicago Press, 1982.

———. "No Need to Travel to the Indies: Judaism and the Study of Religion." In Jacob Neusner, ed., *Take Judaism, for Example: Studies in the Comparison of Religions.* Chicago: University of Chicago Press, 1983, pp. 215–26.

———. "Sacred Persistence: Toward a Redescription of Canon." In *Imagining Religion: From Babylon to Jonestown.* Chicago: University of Chicago Press, 1982, pp. 36–52.

Smith, Wilfred Cantwell. *The Meaning and End of Religion: A Revolutionary Approach to the Great Traditions.* San Francisco: Harper and Row, 1962.

Tambiah, S. J. "Form and Meaning of Magical Acts: A Point of View." In Robin Horton and Ruth Finnegan, eds., *Modes of Thought: Essays on Thinking in Western and Non-Western Societies.* London: Faber and Faber, 1973, pp. 199–229.

Van der Leeuw, Gerhard. *Religion in Essence and Manifestation.* 2 vols. Trans. by J. E. Turner. London: Allen and Unwin, 1938; reprint Gloucester, Mass.: Peter Smith, 1967.

Waardenburg, Jacques. *Classical Approaches to the Study of Religion.* 2 vols. The Hague: Mouton, 1973.

Weber, Max. *The Sociology of Religion.* Trans. by Ephraim Fischoff. Boston: Beacon Press, 1953.

Wilson, Bryan, ed. *Rationality.* Oxford: Basil Blackwell, 1977.

Index and Glossary